CW01597212

Me 262

VOLUME ONE

Me 262

VOLUME ONE

J. Richard Smith

and

Eddie J. Creek

With

Kenneth A. Merrick
Mike Norton
Stephen Ransom
Jürgen Rosenstock
Günter Sengfelder

Technical Drawings by
Arthur L Bentley and Günter Sengfelder

Colour Artwork
Tom Tullis

CLASSIC
PUBLICATIONS

J.Richard Smith is undisputedly one of the world's foremost authorities on the history of the Luftwaffe. His works include the landmark publication *Jet Planes of the Third Reich* as well as *Arado 234 Blitz, Luftwaffe Camouflage & Markings 1935-45* and numerous other leading aviation titles including several studies in the acclaimed *Close Up* series. He presently works in the business training sector with a national telecommunications company.

Eddie J.Creek, a qualified architect, has for many years worked in partnership with Richard Smith producing a wealth of the most historically accurate line drawings and colour artwork so far published on aviation in the Third Reich. As a historian and enthusiast, he has been actively collecting documents and photographs relative to the history of the Luftwaffe for over 30 years. He is co-author of *Jet Planes of the Third Reich, Arado 234 Blitz* and other highly regarded works.

First published in Great Britain in 1997 by Classic Publications, Quarry Ridge House, 7 Quarry Close, Burgess Hill, West Sussex RH15 0TJ, England.

Project Editor - Robert Forsyth

© 1997 Colour Illustrations - Thomas Tullis
© 1997 Line Drawings - Arthur Bentley
© 1997 Line Drawings - Günter Sengfelder

All rights reserved. No part of this book may be reproduced or transmitted in any form or by any means, electronic or mechanical including photocopying, recording, chemical, optical or otherwise without prior written permission from the publisher. All enquiries should be addressed to the publisher.

ISBN 0 9526867 2 4

Book and jacket design by Colin Woodman Graphic Design

Printed in Great Britain by Fotodirect, Enterprise Estate, CrowhurstRoad, Brighton, East Sussex, BN1 8AF

CONTENTS

AUTHORS' INTRODUCTION

FOREWORD by FRANZ STIGLER

CHAPTER ONE
"THE SKULL OF A GENIUS"
Page 8

CHAPTER TWO
"SOME THOUGHT MY IDEAS WERE PURE FANTASY"
Page 36

CHAPTER THREE
"A FEVER OF EXPECTATION"
Page 54

CHAPTER FOUR
"AN UNIMAGINABLE LEAD"
Page 84

CHAPTER FIVE
PROJECTED Me 262 DEVELOPMENTS
Page 122

CHAPTER SIX
"I'M NOT INTERESTED IN THIS AIRCRAFT AS A FIGHTER"
Page 140

CHAPTER SEVEN
"WE NEED THE Me 262 MORE THAN ANYTHING ELSE"
Page 168

APPENDIX ONE
CAMOUFLAGE AND MARKINGS
Page 198

APPENDIX TWO
Me 262 PROTOTYPE FLIGHTS
Page 208

APPENDIX THREE
GERMAN REACTION ENGINES DESIGNATION SYSTEM
Page 209

APPENDIX FOUR
MESSERSCHMITT PERSONALITIES AND COMPANY ORGANISATION
Page 210

GLOSSARY
INDEX

Authors' Introduction

It was the autumn of 1943. The spectre of the Allied invasion of North-West Europe loomed ever larger in the minds of the Nazi leadership. Hitler confided to General Rommel on 5 November 1943: "When the enemy invades in the West it will be the moment of decision in this war, and the moment must turn to our advantage. We must ruthlessly extract every ounce of effort from Germany."

Rommel in turn told *Oberst* Karl Hesse a local field commander based near Paris: "If we don't succeed in driving the enemy back into the sea by the fourth day at the latest, then the invasion will have succeeded."

It was against this background that Hitler saw a role for the Me 262 - a role which many considered ridiculous. He had anticipated that during the hours following the initial landings there would be considerable confusion among Allied troops seeking to establish a beach-head before the *Panzer* divisions could deliver their counter-attacks. How much more difficult things would be for the invaders if throughout that time they were under repeated bombing and strafing attack from German fighter-bombers. The problem was that, until the arrival of the Me 262, Germany did not possess an aircraft fast enough to evade the strong fighter umbrella that the Allies were bound to maintain over the invasion area.

At a conference on 20 December, Hitler delivered a confident speech to senior *Wehrmacht* officers in which he stated: "Every month that passes makes it more probable that we will get at least one *Gruppe* of jet aircraft. The most important thing is that they (the enemy) get some bombs on top of them just as they try to invade. That will force them to take cover, and in this way they will waste hour after hour! But after half a day our reserves will already be on their way. So if we can pin them down on the beaches for just six to eight hours, you can see what that will mean to us...."

What is perhaps not generally realised is that as early as 7 September 1943, and perhaps even March of that year, Hitler had foreseen such a role for the aircraft, as will be described in Chapter 6 of this book. But was his reasoning sound? The authors think it was. Many have said that the Me 262 possessed no accurate bombsight, and did not have the range to operate as a bomber. But for the role that Hitler envisaged, and its importance, did this matter? Where the authors think the Nazi leader went wrong was not to immediately order all future use of the aircraft as a fighter following the establishment of the Allied beach-head in June 1944. Then perhaps it could have at least slowed the American daylight bombing offensive against the German homeland, and particularly oil targets. It was probably the Allied bombing of the oil production plants that caused the final defeat of Nazi Germany in May 1945.

In this, and the volumes that follow, the authors have attempted to tell the story of the world's first operational jet aircraft from the early German work on turbojet engines to the final days in May 1945. They have been interested in this aircraft, its development, its politics and its operational use, since the mid-1960s when little was known about German wartime aviation. Only during the late 1970s, with the release of many documents from official archives, and the willingness of people directly involved to relate their experiences, did the details of the story become clear.

In this work the authors were fortunate to receive the help of many people, but they particularly wish to recognise the contribution of five individuals. First of all, Mike Norton, an acknowledged expert on wartime German aviation and personnel, contributed much to this volume, including a large portion of Chapter 2 which deals with turbojet engine development in Germany. Stephen Ransom, a contemporary project engineer, gave the authors the benefit of his considerable knowledge, both in historic and contemporary aviation. Stephen, who is at present working on a history of the Messerschmitt Me 163 rocket fighter in collaboration with a German colleague, was also able to correct our not very good German, and assist in many other areas. Jürgen Rosenstock, who served in the wartime *Luftwaffe* and who has his own fascinating story to tell, translated many of the German documents discovered by the authors. Günter Sengfelder, an expert in German aircraft landing gear gave us the results of his work on the Me 262 and let us use his excellent drawings. Finally, the authors wish to extend their special thanks to Kenneth A. Merrick, a specialist in *Luftwaffe* camouflage and markings who compiled Appendix 1 on the finish applied to the early Me 262s.

Apart from these five notable people, the authors would also like to thank Paul Bader, Nick Beale, Manfred Griehl, Arthur Bentley, Ken Bokelman, Steve Coates, Jim Crow, Horst Götz, Thomas H. Hitchcock, David Irving (via Robert Forsyth), Peter Kappus, Alfred Krüger, Richard Lutz, Peter Petrick, Alfred Price, Hans-Joachim Puffert, Willy Radinger, Fritz Schäfer, Walter Schick, Erich Sommer andWoldemar Voigt.

We also wish to record our thanks to Franz Stigler, a former Me 262 pilot, who has kindly written the most appropriate and enlightening foreword overleaf.

The following organisations also proved most helpful:- the Imperial War Museum, London, the Public Records Office, London, the National Air and Space Museum in Washington, D.C. and the Deutsches Museum, Munich.

And last, but not least, our good friend Robert Forsyth who not only contributed much from his own archive, but also edited the manuscript for us.

J. Richard Smith

Eddie J. Creek
1997

Foreword by
Franz Stigler
(formerly III./EJG 2 and Jagdverband 44)

I vividly remember the second half of the war as it was rushing headlong towards its conclusion. The nation's defences were gradually crumbling. A desperate mood had gripped the German people and its leadership - a mood of impending doom. Many felt that only some extraordinary action or miracle would save the nation. Bolstered by tantalising promises from the Reich's scientists and industry, a glimmer of hope arose within the bosom of the nation; a promise of fantastic weapons - weapons that would wreak havoc with the forces of the enemy. Terrible "vengeance" weapons. Although in their concept they were almost magical, the hard reality was that they actually existed. It was this fact that upheld the morale of the people. Now, in the eleventh hour, these efforts started to bear fruit in the form of such weapons as the V-1 flying bomb and V-2 rocket, as well as the incredible Messerschmitt Me 262 jet fighter.

I saw my first Me 262 in Lechfeld in October 1944. There I met a group of other experienced pilots who would undergo training in this new and revolutionary aircraft. By that time I had approximately 8,000 hours of flying experience in over 100 types of aircraft, including over 450 combat missions and 26 confirmed victories on the western front.

Despite the fact that during and after the war a number of attributes such as "sinister beauty" etc., were attached to this aeroplane, my first impression of the Me 262 was that of an "all business" machine built for speed. We needed such a machine to counter-balance the apparent superiority of Allied hardware and pilots who were decimating the ranks of new, inexperienced German pilots and relentlessly thinning out the numbers of the older, experienced ones.

Ground school was very short, lasting perhaps 3 to 4 hours. Next came taxiing practice with an instructor standing on the wing of the aircraft since the two-seater training version of the Me 262 was still under development leaving us pilots to learn first-hand, the handling characteristics of this machine.

After being thoroughly familiarised with the critical performance numbers to be observed during flight, we were let loose in the air. Sitting in the cockpit of the Me 262, my first impression was that of roominess which I never experienced flying the Bf 109. The next thing I noted was an ultra-long control stick, much longer than that of a 109. Then there were all the extra gauges and dials needed in a twin-engine aircraft.

A take-off in the Me 262 reminded me of a typical take-off of a gooney bird; it was long, slow and cumbersome until some wind was captured under its wings. In order to launch it into the air, flaps had to be engaged during the later stages of the ground roll and this would allow the machine to lift up. You actually had to fly it off the ground. Activation of the flaps during the ground roll had its hazards as the switches for the flaps and the landing gear retraction mechanism were positioned closely together. It was easy to retract the landing gear during the ground roll before flying speeds were reached, usually with disastrous consequences. Once the landing gear was retracted, a seemingly magical transformation took place. It became a graceful responsive machine, one which the competition could not match.

When manoeuvring in the mid-range performance envelope, I found the control stick forces quite light. However, when approaching the outer edges of the envelope, the forces became significantly higher, nearing 45 kg in order to keep it flying straight and level at its top speed. This explained the extra-long control stick.

The Me 262's manoeuvrability was excellent, but because of its speed, I quickly realised that it took a country mile to complete a turn. Landing was also a bit tricky. Once on finals with high approach speeds, you were committed to execute the landing, as the engines would not spool-up fast enough to allow for a go-around. The Me 262 was most vulnerable at that point and the enemy often took advantage of this weakness.

After three practice flights totalling approximately 2.5 hours, I became qualified to fly combat missions and in early 1945 I became a member of *Jagdverband* 44, the Me 262-equipped fighter unit known as "The Galland Circus". The function of this unit was to provide Germany with a glimmer of hope that the war, if it could not be won, could at least be negotiated and ended from a position of strength. Having flown the Bf 109 extensively, I considered the speed of the Me 262 a substantial life-insurance policy. Although it did not possess anything near the armour protection found in the Bf 109, its power made up for this handsomely. The Me 262 was a very stable firing platform once you had adjusted your reflexes to its speed. With the firepower concentrated in its nose and consisting of four 30 mm cannon, it was truly awesome. It could easily chew through a wing of a B-17 Flying Fortress in one burst. A rack of 55 mm R4M under-wing rockets added to this highly effective firepower. Over my next 16 combat missions, I claimed two victories and had no bullet holes in my machine.

Single engine performance was also relatively good. I discovered this on one mission when I managed to get a P-38 in my sights. I was just about to fire, when suddenly one of my engines exploded! Although, single engine performance was equivalent to that of a Bf 109 or Fw 190, I took no chances and returned to base. Even with one engine gone, once properly trimmed, I am happy to say that landing the Me 262 was uneventful in that configuration.

Looking back more than fifty years later, regrettably I realise that this aircraft was not used to its full potential at the time of its introduction. I feel that the Me 262 could have had a significant effect on the outcome of the war even at that late hour. Had it been introduced a year or so earlier, I am sure that the history of the war would have had a different ending. I hope that the pages in this highly detailed volume, and in those that follow, will serve to illustrate my belief.

CHAPTER ONE

"THE SKULL OF A GENIUS"

During the Second World War the name Messerschmitt became synonymous with the Bf 109 piston-engined fighter that equipped many of the *Luftwaffe's Jagdgruppen* throughout the conflict. It was ironic that Messerschmitt's name was better known to the average English schoolboy than that of Reginald Mitchell, the designer of the Supermarine Spitfire, which was the principal adversary of the German fighter during the Battle of Britain. Yet less than a decade before that epic air battle Messerschmitt's name was virtually unknown outside Germany. What lay behind Messerschmitt's rapid rise to international fame as an aircraft designer, and to Adolf Hitler declaring, on a number of occasions, that Messerschmitt possessed "the skull of a genius"?

Wilhelm Emil Messerschmitt was born on 26 June 1898, at Frankfurt-am-Main, the second child of Ferdinand and Anna Messerschmitt. In all, his parents had five children: three boys and two girls. Within the Messerschmitt family, he was known as 'Willy', and this diminutive became his accepted first name in both written and spoken form throughout his life. His father had originally trained as an engineer and had studied mechanics at the Zürich Polytechnic in Switzerland. In 1906 Ferdinand Messerschmitt moved his family to Bamberg, a beautiful old town in Bavaria, some 65 km (40 miles) north of Nuremburg, where he took over the management of his parent's wine merchant business in the Lange Strasse.

From an early age Willy proved to be a very intelligent child, with an interest in the natural sciences. In 1908 he entered the first class of the *Gymnasium* (Grammar School) in Bamberg. He first became interested in aviation at the age of eleven after reading in the newspapers of the crash of a Zeppelin airship at Echterdingen. During the summer of 1909, when the family were on holiday on Lake Constance, he first saw a Zeppelin at Friedrichshafen, and also managed a visit to the *Internationale Luftfahrt-Ausstellung* (International Aviation Exhibition) in Frankfurt in the same year. He was so excited by these events that he began to build his own rubber powered model aircraft.

In 1910 Messerschmitt made the acquaintance of Friedrich Harth, a 33-year-old architect who had pioneered gliding flight. Harth began building his first canard glider, the S 1, in 1910, but this failed to meet his expectations due to its poor flying controls. Messerschmitt, however, was

After Fritz Wendel had broken the World Speed Record in the Me 209 V1 on 26 April 1939, a reception was held to celebrate the event. At this reception were Willy Messerschmitt (left), Fritz Wendel (centre) and Hitler. With the specially modified DB 601 V10 engine, the aircraft had achieved a speed of 755.12 km/h (469.22 mph), a record that was to stand for over 30 years. Hitler declared on a number of occasions that Messerschmitt possessed the "skull of a genius."

Willy Messerschmitt running down the Ludwager Kulm in Bavaria with the S 1 glider, piloted by Friedrich Harth, in tow. The lightweight construction of the aircraft made single man towing a relatively simple proposition.

much impressed by Harth's work, but it was not until 1913 that he made his first gliding flight from the Ludwager Kulm, a hill 15 km (9 miles) north-east of Bamberg, in the S 1 which was launched by the primitive method of someone towing it into the air by running down a steep slope!

When Harth tested his fourth glider, Messerschmitt, who was then 15, helped him but they soon found that the area around Bamberg was not particularly suitable for gliders. Because of this, they decided to transfer their flying activities to the Heidelstein in the Rhön mountains during the summer of 1914. This was near to the Wasserkuppe where some Darmstadt students had already begun gliding experiments in 1911. Harth and Messerschmitt began construction of a wooden shed which they could use to continue their work, but the declaration of the First World War resulted in Harth being drafted into the German Army.

After he had left, Messerschmitt continued flight testing the S 4 glider that Harth had designed, but this was irreparably damaged by vandals during his absence. Undaunted, he then commenced construction work on Harth's next design, the S 5, and this was flown successfully in 1915 when Harth returned from the front. In 1916 the first jointly designed Harth-Messerschmitt glider, the S 6, was built. This was a high wing monoplane with an open fuselage of steel tube construction. It had a span of 12 metres (39 ft 4.5 ins) and control was achieved by means of a wing warping system. During a test flight made with a wind speed of 12 m/sec (40 ft/sec) the aircraft attained an altitude of about 8 to 10 metres (26 to 33 ft) and stayed in the air for 3.5 minutes, a remarkable feat for the time.

Because of his experience in aviation, Harth was transferred to the *Flieger-Ersatz-Abteilung* (Aircrew Reserve Battalion) at Schleissheim near Munich in 1917. In the same year, Messerschmitt also joined the German Army where he served for a short time with a *Minenwerfer-Einheit*, a mortar bomb unit. Then he too was transferred to Schleissheim, a town that has often been called the "Cradle of Bavarian Aviation". Following the armistice in November 1918, Harth began working for the Bayerische Flugzeugwerke (Bavarian Aircraft Company) a subsidiary of the famous Albatros company. At the same time Messerschmitt enrolled as a student at the Technical College in Munich.

Although the Treaty of Versailles severely curtailed aviation development in Germany,

Friedrich Harth at the controls of the S 6 glider which he designed jointly with Messerschmitt in 1916. The high wing monoplane had an open fuselage of steel tube construction with control achieved by a wing warping system. During a test flight, the aircraft attained an altitude of about 8 to 10 metres (26 to 33 ft) and stayed in the air for 3.5 minutes, a remarkable feat for the time.

Wilhelm Emil Messerschmitt

The Early Years

A photograph taken at the family home in Bamberg around 1911. Showing "Willy" Messerschmitt far right, with (*l to r*) younger brother Rudolf, mother Anna Maria, father Baptist Ferdinand, sisters Ello (*sitting*), Maja and elder brother Ferdinand.

Willy Messerschmitt, aged 15, made his first flight in one of Friedrich Harth's gliders from the Ludwager Kulm hill in 1913.

Messerschmitt (left) and a French prisoner of war, pose in front of the S 5 glider on the Heidelstein on 12 September 1915. The POW was employed to assist in the transporting and assembling of the aircraft.

Messerschmitt, aged 22, photographed when a student with the Technischen Hochschule (Technical College) in Munich.

glider flying continued unchecked. This freedom in unpowered flight led Oskar Ursinus, the editor of the famous magazine *Flugsport*, to call for all gliding enthusiasts to take part in a contest between 15 July and 15 September 1920 at the Wasserkuppe. Oddly, Harth and Messerschmitt did not rally to the call, preferring to work in secret at Heidelstein, some 8 km (5 miles) to the south east. During 1919 they completed work on their new S 7 glider in Munich and tested it later at Heidelstein. They then wrote an article for *Flugsport* describing their work which attracted much interest among the gliding fraternity.

Until 30 August 1921, the gliding duration record had been held by the American aviator Orville Wright who had made an uninterrupted eleven minute flight in 1910, but on that day the German pioneer, Wolfgang Klemperer, flying from the Wasserkuppe, improved the record by two minutes. This time it only stood for 5 days when Rudolf Martens completed a 15 minute flight on 4 September. Harth was convinced that his S 8 glider would stay in the air for over an hour. On 13 September in high wind conditions, he began an attempt on the record. Much to the delight of Messerschmitt, the S 8 easily broke the previous record, but, after staying in the air for 21 minutes, the glider suddenly plummeted into the ground from about 60 m (200 ft). In the resulting crash Harth broke his pelvis and received severe concussion from which he never completely recovered. Sadly, because no impartial observers were present, this potential world record was never ratified.

Although unsuccessful, the tailless S 9 glider was to prove the forerunner of things to come with its swept forward wings. These were designed to ensure that the aircraft's centre of lift coincided with its centre of gravity.

During Harth's six month stay in hospital Messerschmitt began work on the S 9, a tailless glider, and also developed a series of wing profiles. The S 9 proved unsuccessful and Harth had considerable reservations about some of Messerschmitt's improvements to his designs.

Shortly afterwards, the pair decided to move to the Wasserkuppe where they built a small wooden workshop that soon became the rallying point for many other gliding enthusiasts during periods of bad weather. These included Heinrich Hentzen, who was to break the world gliding duration and height records in 1922, Walter Georgii,[1] a world famous meteorologist and Walter Blume, a former fighter pilot and *Pour le Mérite* holder, who later became technical director of the Arado company.

Messerschmitt and Harth established a glider training school during 1922, the first pilot being Wolf Hirth who learned to fly on the new S 10. Hirth was later to become the most famous glider pilot in pre-Nazi Germany. Like most of their previous designs, the S 10 was a high wing monoplane with an open frame fuselage. By the start of the 1922 Rhön competition, the pair had managed to complete two S 10s but disaster struck when one of them crashed heavily shortly after take-off, damaging pilot Hirth's larynx which left him with a permanent speech impediment. Hirth was later to comment that, even at this time, Messerschmitt seemed little interested in the injuries sustained by the pilots, his main concern being to establish why a crash had happened.

The S 10 was followed by the S 11 which differed in having all the control wires contained within the wing. Harth made a few flights in this aircraft but, in 1923, after losing his job as an

Photo left: Three pioneers of German aviation following the First World War were, from left to right, Professor Walter Georgii, who later became director of the Deutsche Forschungsanstalt für Segelflug, Peter Riedel and Wolf Hirth. The three men joined by Heini Dittmar and Hanna Reitsch, organised a glider expedition to South America in 1934, using a Messerschmitt M 23b (W.Nr.559) registered D-2152, as towplane.

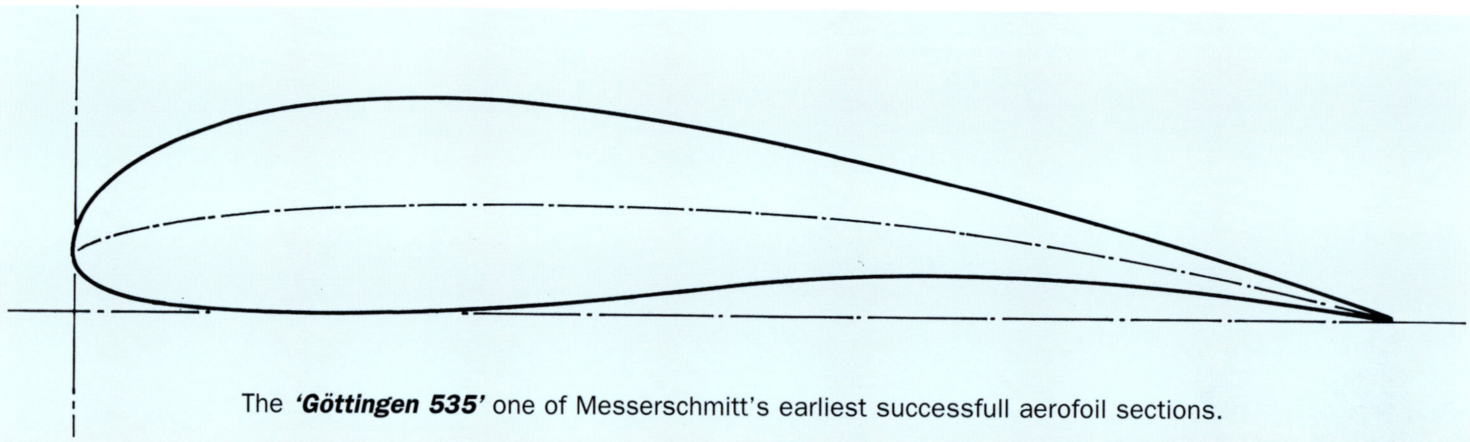

The ***'Göttingen 535'*** one of Messerschmitt's earliest successfull aerofoil sections.

architect because of his membership of the Nazi Party he became less and less interested in aviation. The two remained firm friends, although Harth considered that Messerschmitt was often too radical in his design ideas, particularly his favouring of lightweight constructional methods. In future years Messerschmitt was often to chide members of his design team that they were creating aeroplanes, not railroad locomotives! Nevertheless, Messerschmitt's predilection for such constructional methods and saving weight at all costs, sometimes bordered on recklessness; in fact, it was to have serious consequences in later years for both him and his company.

In 1923, Messerschmitt set up his own enterprise Flugzeugbau Messerschmitt at Bamberg, and completed construction of a new design, the S 14. This was his first design to have a covered fuselage and looked more like the gliders of today. Hirth test flew the glider, but injured his pelvis when it crashed from an altitude of 20 metres (60 ft). Despite the crash, the S 14 proved a financial success for Messerschmitt, who had by this time been awarded his engineering degree (*Diplom-Ingenieur*).

Wolf Hirth was to become one of the most famous glider pilots in Germany. He is shown here at the controls of an early glider at the Akaflieg Stuttgart. The glider is named after "Götz von Berlichingen", a 16th Century German knight who waged many wars and enjoyed many feuds. In 1505, at the siege of Landshut, his right hand was shot away and the iron replacement, which allowed him to continue fighting, earned him the nickname "Götz of the Iron Hand."

Around this time the young designer switched from the development of gliders to powered aircraft, but he had already designed one of the most successful aerofoils for gliders, the Göttingen 535. This was used on such famous designs as the *Consul* of 1923, the *Fafnir* of 1930, the *Windspiel*, *Rhön-Bussard* and *Rhönsperber* of 1924-33 and the DFS *Kranich* of 1935. This wing section had been developed from the Göttingen 534 designed by Harth. Messerschmitt's first powered aircraft was the S 15, a development of the S 14 with a 500 cc British Douglas motorcycle engine. The S 15 made one flight of 43 minutes, during which it attained an altitude of 600 m (2,000 ft).

For the 1924 Rhön contest, Oskar Ursinus decided to hold a special competition for powered gliders. Messerschmitt entered two new designs, the S 16a *Bubi* and the S 16b *Betti*, the former powered by a 14 hp Douglas Sprite engine, the latter by a 21 hp engine. Unfortunately for the young designer, both aircraft suffered accidents, the competition being won by Ernst Udet in his U 7 *Kolibri*. Udet had gained considerable fame as a fighter pilot in the First World War, ending that appalling conflict as the second highest scoring German ace with 62 victories. Ernst Udet was destined to become one of Messerschmitt's closest personal friends and had a considerable influence on the young aircraft designer's eventual success.

On 23 October 1922, Udet, together with Heinz Pohl, Erich Scheuermann and Hans Herrmann had formed their own aircraft company, *Udet Flugzeugbau*, with a capital of 100,000 *Reichsmarks*. The company, which was based in Munich, produced a number of aircraft designed by Hans Herrmann, perhaps the most famous of which was the U 12 *Flamingo* two-seat trainer. Although this was subsequently to prove very successful, it was too late to prevent the company getting into financial difficulties. By the spring of 1926, both Udet and Scheuermann had left and it was having to rely heavily on loans provided by the banking house of Merck, Fink and Company. On 30 July 1926, following negotiations with the *Reichsverkehrsministerium* (Ministry of Transport) and the Bavarian State Government, the company was dissolved and re-established as the Bayerische Flugzeugwerke AG (BFW or Bavarian Aircraft

The Messerschmitt S 14 was the first design to have a fuselage covered in wood. During the 1923 Rhön Glider Contest, the S 14 gained first prize for the best altitude attained, and proved a financial success for the fledgling company.

Factory). The new company (which should not be confused with the subsidiary of the old Albatros works) then took over the hangars of the defunct Rumpler Flugzeugwerke in Augsburg and began production of the U 12. Its management team was headed by Dr. Alexander Schruffer, with Heinz Pohl being replaced as commercial director on 13 August by Rakan Kokothaki. Following a disagreement, Hans Herrmann also left the company during the autumn, his place being taken by Karl Theiss.

Although Germany was denied an air force under the terms of the Treaty of Versailles, she obtained complete freedom in the sphere of

This aerial photograph of the Bayerische Flugzeugwerke AG factory at Augsburg was taken in 1927. Seven U12 Flamingos are lined up in front of the main hangar with a BFW 1 Sperber nearest the camera.

Otto Stromeyer (left), Chairman of the Board of Directors of Messerschmitt AG in 1931 and 1932, talking to his successor, Theo Croneiss, with Messerschmitt in the centre. The aircraft in the background is a BFW U 12 Flamingo.

civilian aviation with the signing of the Paris Air Agreement in May 1926. The earlier limitations, dating from 1922 (which had placed strict limits on the performance and payload of civilian aircraft), were withdrawn, and the country seized the opportunity to develop both civil and commercial aviation, with all its attendant flying clubs, airlines and training establishments for commercial aircrews. In this improved climate, Messerschmitt concentrated on the design of airliners and fast, light sporting aircraft, although under the cloak of civilian aviation the foundations of a future air force were being laid secretly by the military authorities.

Meanwhile, Messerschmitt had built his first aircraft designed from the beginning to be fitted with an engine, the M 17 *Ello* two-seat high wing monoplane. From then on until the introduction of the Air Ministry '8' series type number system, all new Messerschmitt designs received the prefix 'M'.[2] During 1925 another former First World War fighter pilot, Theo Croneiss, director of Sportflug GmbH, entered his M 17 in several contests and was able to achieve some very good results. Messerschmitt and Croneiss soon became firm friends and the latter was able to finance the establishment of the Messerschmitt Flugzeugbau GmbH at Bamberg. The success of the M 17, which the DVL (German Aeronautical Research Institute) described as "the best airframe design since 1917", led Croneiss to ask the fledgling company to produce a small airliner for his newly formed Nordbayerische Verkehrsflug. This aircraft, the M 18, could carry four passengers and cost less than 25,000 RM. It was to prove very successful, some 25 being built, a comparatively large number for that time.

The very success of the M 18 was to pose another problem for Messerschmitt. In order to go ahead with full scale production the company needed extended credit. During 1926 Messerschmitt and Croneiss approached the Bavarian government for a loan, but the difficulty was that the BFW were also requesting money from the same source. In order to solve the problem, the government suggested a compromise. BFW should give up all design work to concentrate on aircraft production, while Messerschmitt should be responsible for project development. After much argument, this plan was finally agreed on 8 September 1927 and Messerschmitt moved all his personnel and equipment to Augsburg.

The young designer's next two aircraft were the M 19 low wing lightplane and the M 20 airliner. The former was to win the *Sachsenflug* contest held by the DVL in 1927 when piloted by

Messerschmitt holding the propeller of the M 17 (W.Nr.25) registered D-779 which was powered by a 32 hp Bristol Cherub engine. This aircraft survives and is on show at the Deutches Museum in Munich.

The aircraft which first introduced the name of Messerschmitt to the German people was the M 18 eight seat airliner first built in 1925. This photo shows a Wright Whirlwind powered M 18d.

The M18 – Early Success

Taken at Nuremburg Fürth airport, this photo shows one of Nordbayerische Verkehrsflug's Messerschmitt M 18d airliners, D-1847, W.Nr.477, named "Düsseldorf". This aircraft was registered in May 1930 and powered by a 150 hp Walter Mars engine

Nordbayerische Verkehrsflug had a total of five M 18s in its fleet, four powered by Walter Mars engines, the other by a Wright Whirlwind. The aircraft, which had seating for the pilot and three passengers, was one of Messerschmitt's early successes.

The seventh production Messerschmitt M 18d which was powered by a 325 hp Wright Whirlwind engine and fitted with twin floats. The floats were attached to the fuselage by no less than 14 struts.

Theo Croneiss, flying a Messerschmitt M 19, D-1221, won the 1927 Sachsenflug - a flying contest organised by the Deutsche Luftfahrt e.V. This photo shows another of the competitors, an M 19 piloted by E. von Conta, D-1206, preparing for take-off.

Above: Willy Messerschmitt ducks under the nose of the second prototype Messerschmitt M 20, with Erich Scheuermann of the DVL to his left. In the cockpit is Theo Croneiss who made the first test flight in this aircraft on 3 August 1928.

Right: Powered by a 500 hp BMW VIa engine, the M 20 prototype made its first flight on 26 February 1928. During the course of this, fabric stripped from the trailing edge of the wing and the pilot, misjudging the seriousness of the situation bailed out at 75 m (250 feet). This reverse led to the cancellation of the two aircraft previously ordered by Lufthansa. The aircraft in the background is a BFW U 12b.

The tiny two-seat M 17 could easily be accommodated under the wing of the M 20 airliner. The Deutsche Versuchsanstalt für Luftfahrt (German Aviation Research Institute) described the M 17 as "the best airframe since 1917".

An Argus As 8 powered Messerschmitt M 23c (W.Nr.517) which was registered in July 1930. This particular aircraft took part in the 1930 Circuit of Europe race (with race number E9) but was destroyed in February 1931.

An early production Messerschmitt M 23, a two-seat sports aircraft which was powered by a 38 hp two-cylinder ABC Scorpion engine. Perhaps the greatest success achieved by the M 23 was the winning of the 1929 and 1930 Circuit of Europe races, the victorious aircraft being flown by Fritz Morzik (later to become commander of Luftwaffe air transport operations) on both occasions.

The Messerschmitt M 28 high-speed mailplane was powered by a 525 hp Pratt and Whitney Hornet nine-cylinder radial. Two aircraft are thought to have been built, but only one, D-2059 (W.Nr.527) has been positively identified. The aircraft was delivered to Lufthansa in 1932 and used on the airline's internal mail services until 1935.

Croneiss and the latter, while similar to the M 18, was larger and more powerful and could carry ten passengers. Unfortunately, the first prototype met with an accident on its first flight but after the successful tests of the second aircraft, the newly-formed German state airline, *Deutsche Lufthansa*, reinstated their order for two aircraft and added ten more. Although all seemed well for the future, the DLH M 20 contract was to have dramatic and far-reaching consequences for Messerschmitt and his fledgling company.

The M 21 and M 22 marked BFW's first venture into the field of military aircraft. They were designed on the orders of *Abteilung Wa Prüf 6F* (officially responsible for motor vehicle development and testing, but which included a small clandestine aviation section under *Hptm.* Kurt Student) of the *Heereswaffenamt* (Army Ordnance Office). The military authorities insisted that both these aircraft should be biplanes, although Messerschmitt, the advocate of the monoplane, felt this to be a retrograde step. The M21 was a two-seat trainer, similar to the U12 in appearance apart from its steel tube fuselage, improved control surfaces and a modified undercarriage. Only two prototypes were built as the M 21 offered no improvement over the U12. The curious twin-engined M 22, which received the code name *'Najaku'* (*Nachtjagd und Erkundungsflugzeug*), was a combined night fighter and reconnaissance aircraft, of which one prototype was built in 1929. For security reasons the M 22 was officially classed as a mailplane, but further development was abandoned after the prototype was lost during a test flight in 1930.

The M 23 was a two seat sporting aircraft designed to compete in the *Ostpreussenflug* (Circuit of East Prussia) competition of 1929. It was extremely successful, winning many races, and was the first Messerschmitt aircraft to be built in large numbers, about 70 being constructed.

The Messerschmitt M 24 was a larger development of the M 20 airliner with accommodation for eight passengers. This aircraft, which was later registered D-1767, was powered by a 310 hp Junkers L 5 engine.

Several versions were built with a variety of engines, and the type was to win international recognition. The M 24 was a development of the M 20, the M 25 was a project for a lightplane designed to the requirements of Udet, and the M 26 was a small passenger carrying airliner of which only one prototype was built. The M 27 was a further development of the M 23 with the fuselage constructed of steel tubing, and the M 28 was a fast mailplane of which possibly two were built for use by *Deutsche Lufthansa*.

During 1929, BFW drew up licence agreements with the Baltic states (Lithuania, Latvia and Estonia) and the Eastern Aircraft Corporation of Pawtucket, Rhode Island. The American company was to build the M 18 and M 26 airliners, but the Wall Street crash of 1929 meant that the agreement had to be cancelled after Messerschmitt had received a single payment of U.S. $189,000. The U.S. stock market crash created severe economic problems which rapidly reverberated around the globe, and by 1930 the situation in Germany was particularly bad, with soaring inflation and widescale unemployment affecting much of the population. Not only did the deteriorating German economic situation affect aircraft manufacturers such as Arado, BFW, Dornier, Heinkel and Junkers, but it also aided the growth of National Socialism (which until then had only manifested itself as a minor political party) and the rise of Hitler, who promised to redress the nation's economic difficulties.

By the end of 1930, BFW had losses in the region of 600,000 RM, and even a injection of 250,000 RM by the Stromeyer-Raulino family,[3] who had bought out the shares held in the company by the *Reichsverkehrsministerium* on 1 July 1928, failed to improve matters. Then, during the spring of 1931, two of *Deutsche Lufthansa's* M 20s crashed in unexplained circumstances, one near Dresden and the other near Breslau. In one of the crashes, the eight passengers, all *Reichswehr* officers, were killed and the accident received widespread adverse publicity in the German national press and was

The former Murrmann Brewery building at Bamberg where Messerschmitt built his first powered aircraft between 1923 and 1925. *Below*: The final assembly hall at Bayerische Flugzeugwerke's Augsburg plant photographed in 1930. The aircraft in the foreground, left, is the M 26 prototype, while at right, is a Messerschmitt M 19 with an M 18 in Swiss markings behind. In the background can be seen an M 20, D-1480.

Right: Dipl.-Ing. Robert Lusser was appointed by Messerschmitt to lead his newly formed Projektbüro on 1 November 1933. He moved to Heinkel in 1939 and Fieseler in 1941 and was later appointed Chairman of a special commission for rocket and ramjet propelled aircraft.

Responsibility for the design of the P.1065 (later Me 262) jet fighter project was placed in the hands of Dipl.-Ing. Woldemar Voigt's Probü (Project Office). Voigt joined BFW in 1933 and became head of the Project Office in 1939.

even discussed in the *Reichstag*. At that time, the managing director of *Deutsche Lufthansa* was Erhard Milch, a 39 year-old former artillery officer turned aviator, who had ended the First World War as commander of *Jagdgruppe* 6. Milch alleged that Willy Messerschmitt had not designed the M 20 with the necessary safety measures as a result of his tendency to save weight at all costs. Although Milch's allegations remained unproven, the latter promptly cancelled *Deutsche Lufthansa's* outstanding orders for the M 20 and demanded the repayment of all deposits the airline had paid to BFW. These demands could not be met by BFW, for manufacture of the remaining M 20s had advanced too far to accept cancellation. This was to prove the final blow in BFW's financial crisis, which was forced to register itself bankrupt on 1 June 1931. The Messerschmitt Flugzeugbau GmbH, which still retained a large degree of autonomy, was able to carry on, and eventually *Deutsche Lufthansa* was persuaded to honour its agreement to buy the M 20 and M 28. Understandably, the dispute created a climate of enmity between Messerschmitt and Milch that continued to the end of the Second World War and was to have no little impact on the development of the Me 262.

During the autumn of 1931, Messerschmitt was asked to develop a racing aircraft to take part in the Third International Circuit of Europe race to be held the following year. This resulted in the M 29, a two-seat low wing monoplane with an enclosed cabin and fixed, spatted undercarriage. Four of these aircraft and six Heinkel 64s made up the German team for the contest, but two M 29s crashed and the type was grounded. Investigations showed that the accidents were due to vibration causing disintegration of the tailplane.

The Messerschmitt M 29 high-speed monoplane which was built to compete in the Challenge de Tourisme International in 1932. After suffering two wing failures on successive days, the M 29 was banned from competing.

Messerschmitt's next five designs were either projects or one-off prototypes. The M 30 project was based on the M 26 but built of magnesium alloy. The M 31, of which one was built, was an attractive radial engined development of the M 27 and the M 32 was a futuristic project for a tailless amphibian to be powered by two Diesel engines. It was to have retractable caterpillar landing gear and an enclosed cabin. Only a mock-up of this and the tiny tailless M 33 were built. The latter was to be produced in kit form for home builders and was to be powered by a 15 hp DKW engine driving a propeller mounted just above the centre of the high wing via a gearing device. The M 34 was an extremely advanced long range aircraft to be powered by two Diesel engines. In this case only a model was completed.

On 1 November 1933, in order to strengthen his design team, Messerschmitt appointed *Dipl.-Ing.* Robert Lusser head of the newly formed *Projektbüro* (Project Office), which was responsible for aerodynamics and the design of new projects. An enthusiastic sports pilot, Lusser had worked previously for Klemm (1925-32) and Heinkel (1932-33) where he had been involved in the design of several successful sporting aircraft. Shortly afterwards he was joined by *Dipl.-Ing.* Woldemar Voigt, a 26 year old graduate, with whom he had worked at Klemm, and who was

appointed a group leader in the *Projektburo*. Voigt's abilities were recognised, and in early 1937, he became Lusser's personal assistant and deputy.

Unlike Messerschmitt, who specialised in ingenious structural design and construction, Lusser was an outstanding expert and teacher of project work which he considered an 'art'. The authors believe that he was one of the most outstanding, yet least known, German aircraft designers of his generation. He was responsible for directing the project work which resulted in the Bf 108, Bf 109, Bf 110 and for the preliminary P 1065 studies. After leaving Messerschmitt, he became Technical Director of Heinkel where he was involved with the He 280 jet fighter and early design studies for the He 219. He left Heinkel in the autumn of 1941 and joined Fieseler where he produced preliminary designs for a cheaply-built flying bomb. This was to materialize in June 1942 as the Fi 103 which is more commonly known as the V-1, approximately 33,000 of which were built during 1943-45. In December 1944 he became chairman of the Development Commission for Special Aircraft (a component of the Chief Development Commission for Aircraft within Speer's Armaments Ministry) which controlled the future development of all rocket and ramjet-propelled aircraft in Germany including supersonic research vehicles. After the war, Lusser had a distinguished career as a consultant

Top left: The deputy leader of the Nazi Party, Rudolf Hess, was a very keen aviator and in February 1935 won the Zugspitzflug flying the M 35.
Top right: Aerobatics champion and demonstration pilot for BFW, Willy Stör, at the controls of his Messerschmitt M 35 with its distinctive "sunburst" pattern in 1934.

A group of luminaries crowd around the cockpit of the He 280 V2 following its first jet flight. Standing is Dipl.-Ing. Carl Francke, with test pilot Paul Bader kneeling in front. Udet is sitting in the cockpit with Dipl.-Ing. Robert Lusser standing over and Dipl.-Ing. Hans Martin Antz of Department LC 7 (Airframe Development) of the Technical Office wearing a trilby hat.

to the U.S. Navy, returning to Messerschmitt in 1959 as Technical Director of *Entwicklungsring-Süd* for the development of the VJ 101 VTOL fighter.

BFW's next design was the M 35, a further development of the M 31 powered by a 150 hp Siemens Sh 14a radial engine. The first of fifteen M 35s was delivered during the summer of 1933, and achieved spectacular success in February 1935 when Rudolf Hess, deputy leader of the Nazi Party, won the *Zugspitzflug*, a race from Munich to Germany's highest mountain and back. Willy Stör was also to become German aerobatic champion in 1935 and 1936 flying an M 35, and later became head of production test flying at Augsburg. Even today, the M 35 is still regarded as one of the most successful aerobatic aircraft ever produced.

After an agreement was made with the majority of BFW's creditors late in 1932, an attempt was made to end the company's bankruptcy but this was temporarily frustrated by another aircraft designer, Ernst Heinkel. Heinkel was interested in taking over the company and its patents, and made a proposition to the city of Augsburg, offering to regulate the number of employees according to the wishes of the city. These attempts by Heinkel to interfere were frustrated and during a preliminary meeting held in December 1932, an agreement was made with all creditors, allowing BFW to recommence trading on 1 May 1933. At this time its total workforce amounted to 82 people.

Shortly after Hitler came to power in January 1933, a German Air Ministry (*Reichsluftfahrtministerium* or RLM) was established on 27 April. The new ministry was placed under the leadership of Hermann Göring with Erhard Milch, in the post of State Secretary, responsible for procurement. Almost immediately most German aircraft companies were awarded huge contracts and financial help for their expansion, but not BFW. Their sole order was a contract for the licence building of twelve He 45 C reconnaissance aircraft.

The lack of orders led Rakan Kokothaki to travel to Rumania in June 1933, where he gained an order from the I.C.A.R. factory for the design of a small airliner capable of carrying six passengers. This aircraft, the M 36, was a high wing monoplane powered by a 450 hp Gnôme-et-Rhône radial. I.C.A.R. bought the drawings for the aircraft outright, building a prototype in 1934 and delivering it to L.A.R.E.S., the Rumanian airline, which operated several internal services.

The fact that BFW had sought a foreign development contract incurred the wrath of *Obstlt.* Wilhelm Wimmer, then head of the RLM's Technical Office, who argued that German aircraft manufacturers should not be working for foreign countries at a time of such rapid expansion and re-armament. Messerschmitt countered by saying that since no German originated contracts had been forthcoming, he was forced to seek work abroad. As a direct result of this, the RLM gave BFW an order to design an aircraft to take part in the 4th *Challenge de Tourisme International* of 1934, and

Top: Hermann Göring
Above: Jewish by birth, Erhard Milch became the Chief Executive Officer of Deutsche Lufthansa in 1929. Responsible for cancelling that airline's order for the M 20 during the spring of 1931, he created a climate of ill feeling with Messerschmitt that was to last to the end of the war and had a considerable impact on the development of the Me 262.
Right: The head office of Messerschmitt A.G. in the southern outskirts of Augsburg-Haunstetten located on the Landsberg-Lech road.
Far right: Typical of the interior decor of the Nazi period, this photo shows Messerschmitt's conference room at Augsburg-Haunstetten.

Flugkapitän Fritz Wendel piloting Messerschmitt's personal Bf 108 communications aircraft registered D-IOIO with another Bf 108 in the background. The lady in the rear seat may be Frau Lilly Stromeyer, who married Messerschmitt in 1952. Below the cockpit of the aircraft can be seen the badge of the Messerschmitt company.

Below: On 17 November 1941, Generaloberst Ernst Udet, the head of the RLM's Technical Office, shot himself. The second highest scoring German fighter pilot of the First World War, he formed his own aircraft company in October, 1922, the Udet Flugzeugbau, in Munich, but financial difficulties led to it being dissolved and re-established as BFW. Udet is seen here watching a display of the He 280 V2 with Robert Lusser.

Bottom: The Me Bf 109 V1 was powered by an imported 695 hp Rolls Royce Kestrel engine and made its first flight in September 1935.

also allowed them to enter the competition for the design of a new fighter aircraft. Despite being permitted to enter the fighter competition, BFW was considered to be a rank outsider by the Technical Office. It was felt that Messerschmitt possessed no experience in the design of high-speed combat aircraft, and thus had little chance of winning against the more experienced Arado and Heinkel companies.

The sporting aircraft requirement was to result in three designs: the Kl 36 from Klemm, the Fi 97 from Fieseler and the M 37 from Messerschmitt. Following the decision by the RLM to allocate a uniform designation system to all German aircraft designs, the M 37 became the Bf 108 ('Bf' being an abbreviation of BFW) and was named *Taifun* (Typhoon). Due to its very advanced concept, the Bf 108 proved to be extremely successful in many pre-war air races, besides capturing several international flying-distance records for its class of machine. Furthermore, its layout set a new trend in touring and light aircraft design which was to last for the next three decades or more. In fact, post-war developments of the basic Bf 108 produced in France are still flying in the late 1990s and the aircraft has been used in popular films as a "stand-in" for the Bf 109 fighter to which it bore a superficial resemblance.

At some (as yet undetermined) point in early 1934, an event occurred that almost changed the entire course of Willy Messerschmitt's career and the future of BFW. The University of Danzig offered him the post of Professor of Aeronautics, acceptance of which would have released Messerschmitt from the many difficulties he had experienced in trying to establish himself as a leading member of the German aviation industry. Yet despite his undeniable successes in the field of transport and sporting aircraft design, Willy Messerschmitt felt he remained out of favour with the RLM who viewed his abilities with some suspicion. His initial impulse was to resign his position with BFW and accept the offer of the professorship which he personally found both attractive and flattering, since it implied that he was considered capable of heading a university department and instructing future generations of aeronautical engineers in aircraft design. In order to determine the extent of any prejudice the RLM's Technical Office might hold against him, Messerschmitt advised its head, *Obstlt*. Wimmer, of the offer and inquired if any importance was attached to his work in the future. Messerschmitt was promptly notified by Wimmer that no importance was attached to his person for the subsequent development of German aviation and that he would do well to accept the professorship at Danzig! Fortunately, however, Messerschmitt's friends (who included Rudolf Hess, the *Führer's* deputy) and supporters convinced him that he did have a future as an aircraft designer in Germany and, much to the annoyance of State Secretary Milch, he declined the offer of a professorship. Although, he was unaware of it at the time, Willy Messerschmitt's fortunes were about to improve for the better as work commenced on the fighter competition contract, which was to eventually result in the most famous and successful aircraft that ever bore his name, the Bf (later Me) 109.

Lusser's team in the *Projektbüro* began work on the new fighter (known as the *Verfolgungsjäger* - pursuit fighter) in March 1934, the intention being to power the aircraft with one of the new 20 litre class 12-cylinder liquid-cooled inverted-vee in-line engines under development by BMW (BMW 115 or 116) and Junkers (Jumo 210). Messerschmitt ensured that his *Projektbüro* employed the same latest techniques in structural and aerodynamic design that had been successfully embodied in the M 37. He felt that his company had nothing to lose by carrying the state-of-the-art to what was then considered the ultimate in aviation technology. The resulting fighter, which later received the RLM designation Bf 109, was very audacious in concept. It featured all-metal construction, a

monocoque fuselage, a cantilever wing with slotted flaps and automatic slots, a fully retractable main undercarriage and an enclosed cockpit with a hinged canopy. The fuselage was of the smallest possible cross-section, just large enough to house the Jumo 210 which had been selected by the Technical Office for mass-production in preference to the BMW engines.

In late April 1935, as the first prototype Bf 109 was being prepared for its initial taxiing trials, Ernst Udet visited Messerschmitt's Augsburg factory. Udet, who was still a civilian, was shown the new fighter in a private capacity.[4] He climbed into its cramped, enclosed cockpit and immediately took a dislike to the aircraft because his conservative views still demanded an open cockpit, a fixed undercarriage and a biplane configuration. Climbing out of the cockpit he said to Messerschmitt: "This machine will never make a fighter!", although he later changed his view to become one of the Bf 109's most ardent supporters.

The first prototype, the Bf 109 a (later to be redesignated Bf 109 V1) first flew on 28 May 1935. It was powered by an imported 695 hp Rolls Royce Kestrel engine because the intended Jumo 210 A was not yet available for installation. Apart from some problems with its narrow tracked and potentially weak main undercarriage, which made it difficult to handle on the ground, the Bf 109 proved to be an outstanding aircraft. Its flight performance more than compensated for its landing gear deficiencies. The evaluation of the competing fighter prototypes began at Rechlin in October 1935, the Bf 109 and He 112 quickly outclassing the Arado and Focke-Wulf contenders. The He 112 displayed cleaner lines than the Bf 109, but it was larger and appreciably

The third prototype Messerschmitt Bf 109, the V3, was the first aircraft to be fitted with an engine-mounted 20 mm MG FF cannon. Originally carrying the German civil registration D-IOQY and the W.Nr.760, the aircraft was later sent to Spain for operational evaluation by the Condor Legion late in 1936
Inset: The He 112 V4, D-IZMY, was the fourth prototype of the Heinkel fighter which competed with the Bf 109. This aircraft was intended to serve as forerunner of the A-series and was later fitted with an experimental rocket engine.

Above and right: During the spring of 1937 the first Bf 109 B-1s were delivered to Jagdgeschwader 132 Richthofen under Oberst Gerd von Massow. This was the first production model of a fighter with which, more than any other aircraft, the name of Messerschmitt is associated. These photos show 'Red 3" of 5./JG 132 with the famous 'script R' badge of the Geschwader beneath the cockpit.

This page and opposite bottom: Representative of a typical later operational Bf 109, these photos show a G-6/R2 in service in southern Italy with IV./JG 3 during the summer of 1943. This variant was fitted with two 21 cm WGr 21 mortar tubes under the wing, this weapon later being tested on the Me 262 by the Stabsstaffel of JG 7.

heavier due to its more complex structure. During evaluation trials it was found that the Bf 109, with a top speed of 467 km/h (290 mph), was 27 km/h (17 mph) faster than the favoured He 112, although the latter had a lower wing loading and better ground handling qualities. The aircraft were so similar in other respects that the Technical Office awarded contracts to both firms for ten prototypes for further testing. Eventually the Bf 109 was selected as the winner, largely because it was cheaper and easier to build than the He 112.

The first production model, the Bf 109 B-1, was the first monoplane fighter with a fully-enclosed cockpit and a retractable undercarriage to enter *Luftwaffe* service, deliveries to *Jagdgeschwader* 132 *Richthofen* commencing in the spring of 1937. This version first saw operational use in May 1937 with the 2.*Staffel* of *Jagdgruppe* 88 of the *Legion Condor* during the Spanish Civil War.

Six Bf 109 prototypes were also included in the German team which participated in the 4th International Flying Meeting held at Zürich-Dübendorf between 23 July and 1 August 1937, this being the first time that the aircraft had been shown to the public, apart from a brief appearance at the 1936 Olympic Games held in Berlin. The Bf 109 proved to be an outstanding success at Zürich and won four first prizes: the climb and dive competition (with the V13 flown by *Dipl.-Ing.* Carl Francke), the speed event around a 50 km (30 mile) closed circuit (with the V8 also piloted by Francke), the *Alpenflug* (with the V8 piloted by *Maj.* Seidemann) and the team *Alpenflug* (with the V8, V9 and B-2 piloted by *Hptm.* Restemeier, *Oblt.* Trautloft and *Oblt.* Schleif). At Zürich, the competing foreign teams were completely outclassed by the Bf 109's outstanding qualities, and its impact, along with that of the Do 17 bomber (which was also revealed for the first time at Zürich), came as something of an eye-opener to the British and French Air Forces. Eventually over 34,000 Bf 109s were produced by April 1945, the fighter serving in every theatre of war in which the *Luftwaffe* was involved. Post-war the Bf 109 was built in Czechoslovakia and Spain to bring the total production figure to about 35,000 machines - a world record for fighter aircraft.[5]

On 31 March 1936, the total capital of the company was increased to four million RM and gradually the factory switched from licence production of such types as the He 45, He 50, Ar 66 and Go 145 to the Bf 108 and Bf 109. The new emphasis placed on aviation development in Germany led the RLM to demand an expansion of the company's production facilities, but because Augsburg refused to let the company build a new facility within the city, construction of a new shadow factory was begun on a green-field site at Regensburg. Simultaneously, a personally owned company, Messerschmitt GmbH, was established.

Willy Messerschmitt's own standing was enhanced in 1937 when he received an honorary Professorship from Munich Technical College, where he had obtained his engineering degree some fourteen years earlier. On 1 April 1937, Professor Messerschmitt was appointed a member of the newly-formed *Deutsche Akademie der Luftfahrtforschung* (German Academy for Aviation Research). It was a high honour to belong to the Academy, and a clear indication that, after his many tribulations, Messerschmitt had been accepted by the aviation establishment in Germany.[6] The international prestige of BFW was increased on 11 November 1937, when the Bf 109 V13, powered by a specially-boosted Daimler-Benz 601 engine, achieved an average speed of 610.95 km/h (379.40 mph) over a 3 km (1.8 mile) course, and thus established a new World Speed Record for Landplanes - the first time this much coveted record had been won by Germany. Official recognition of Willy Messerschmitt's talents as an aircraft designer came on 6 September 1938, when, together with Ernst Heinkel, he was awarded jointly the *Nationalpreis für Kunst und Wissenschaft* (National Prize for Arts and Science) at an opera gala performance held in Nuremburg on the *Reichsparteitag* (Nazi Party Day).

Enormous expansion took place within the company during 1937. Hangars 1 and 2 were enlarged, a new purpose built administration and design department building was completed and the new hangars 3 and 4 were constructed. Within a year, the Regensburg factory had been completed, and production of the Bf 108 was handed over to this facility.

BFW's next important product, the Bf 110, was designed originally to meet a requirement issued by the *Technisches Amt* in 1934 for a *Kampfzerstörer* (literally "Battle Destroyer", but essentially a long-range fighter capable of undertaking the roles of bomber escort, ground-attack and armed reconnaissance). The specification, which called for a twin-engined, three-seat aircraft with a heavy armament of turret-mounted cannon and an internal bomb-bay, was issued to several companies, including Focke-Wulf, Henschel and the Bayerische Flugzeugwerke; the latter, it will be remembered, then possessed very little experience with combat aircraft and were only included on the suggestion of Ernst Udet. Willy Messerschmitt and Robert Lusser correctly concluded that the *Kampfzerstörer* concept was impractical in the form envisaged by the *Technisches Amt* and took an independent view by deciding to tacitly ignore many of the requirements of the specification, placing particular emphasis on a high performance, which was to be achieved by the use of the new Daimler-Benz DB 600A 950hp 12-cylinder in-line engines. Had it not been for this far-reaching decision, the resulting *Projekt* 1035 could well have conformed with the official requirement in most respects, to produce an entirely different aircraft from the Bf 110, and which, in all probability, would not have progressed beyond the prototype stage.

The first prototype, the Bf 110 V1, was powered by two Junkers Jumo 210 engines, due to the unavailability of the DB 600, and made its maiden flight on 12 May 1936. By that time, the

Technisches Amt had reconsidered the multi-facet roles envisaged for the *Kampfzerstörer* and came to the conclusion that they were unachievable. The revised requirement for a pure *Zerstörer* demanded a strategic fighter capable of clearing enemy airspace of hostile fighters ahead of the approaching German bomber formations by virtue of its high performance and extremely heavy firepower (by contemporary standards) which took the form of four 7.9mm machine guns and two 20mm cannon. The *Zerstörer* concept captured Göring's imagination and he subsequently boasted that the *Zerstörergruppen* were the elite units of the *Luftwaffe*, declaring "... If the (single-seat) fighters are the sword of the *Luftwaffe*, (then) the Me 110 *Zerstörer* is the point of that sword."

Meeting only token opposition, the *Zerstörergruppen* achieved easy victories in the Polish and French campaigns, but with the onset of operations against Great Britain in July 1940, Bf 110 losses mounted sharply at the hands of RAF Fighter Command. During August alone, 120 Bf 110s were lost on operations, thus dispelling the myth of the *Zestörer's* invincibility.

However, although the Bf 110's shortcomings as a *Zerstörer* were dramatically revealed during the Battle of Britain, it proved a very adaptable aircraft which was subsequently employed, amongst other roles, as a night-fighter. In this role, the Bf 110 excelled and proved to be extremely effective, becoming the mainstay of the *Nachtjagdverbände* until the spring of 1944, when it was replaced by the Ju 88G. In September 1944, it was decided to phase-out production of the Bf 110 due to its increasing obsolescence and by March 1945, when manufacture ceased, over 6,000 machines had been built, ranking it as the fifth most important German operational aircraft type in terms of numbers produced during the Second World War.

The early successes of aircraft such as the Bf 108, Bf 109 and Bf 110 led to BFW being renamed Messerschmitt AG on 11 July 1938, the abbreviation 'Me' then being used to identify all its subsequent products. Messerschmitt was now a world-class aviation company, having risen from relative obscurity in under five years - its success being largely due to the Bf 109 fighter.

During the spring of 1937, Messerschmitt put forward a design proposal to the RLM for an aircraft to make an attempt on the world airspeed record. Initially designated P 1059, the proposal was for the smallest and aerodynamically cleanest

The twin-engined Messerschmitt Bf 110 was to prove a failure in the role for which it was designed, that of a Zerstörer or bomber-destroyer. It was, however, to be built in large numbers, and provided the Luftwaffe's night-fighter force with a large part of its inventory until its gradual replacement by the Ju 88. This photo shows ground crews preparing a Bf 110 G-2 of 5./NJG 200 for operations on the Eastern front during April 1944.

Dr. Hermann Wurster, who was replaced as Messerschmitt's chief test pilot by Karl Baur, standing in front of the Me 209 V1. This aircraft should not be confused with the Me 209 V5 which was a DB 603 powered development of the Bf 109 G designed to replace that fighter. For many months, there was much dispute as to whether the Me 209 or the Me 262 should take preference for future fighter production.

possible airframe which could be designed around the Daimler-Benz DB 601 engine. After the proposals were accepted, a contract was awarded for the construction of three prototypes. As has been discussed, it was the Bf 109 which, more than any other aircraft, had made Messerschmitt a household name in Germany, and established the company as a world leader in fighter design. For this reason the designation Me 209 was allocated to the new design in the hope that it would continue the success of its predecessor. In fact, the Me 209 bore no similarity to the Bf 109 apart from being a cantilever low wing monoplane with a retractable undercarriage.

The first prototype, the Me 209 V1, (W.Nr.1185, registered D-INJR) was powered by a standard 1,100 hp DB 601 A engine, but employed surface evaporation cooling rather than conventional radiators. After its completion in June 1938, the aircraft underwent a series of ground runs to test the evaporation cooling, but these proved somewhat protracted. The prototype eventually made its first flight on 1 August 1938 piloted by *Dr.-Ing.* Hermann Wurster. His report on the aircraft was far from favourable, criticising both its handling characteristics and engine cooling system. Fritz Wendel, who later flew the early Me 262 prototypes, was to say of the machine "It was a brute ... it's flying characteristics made me shudder"; nevertheless these problems were considered acceptable if the machine could achieve its aim of breaking the world speed record.

The Me 209 V2 (W.Nr.1186, D-IWAH) flew for the first time on 8 February 1939, but its flying characteristics were little improved. During a test flight on 4 April with Wendel at the controls, the oil cooling system suddenly failed as the aircraft neared Augsburg-Haunstetten airfield, causing the engine to stop almost immediately. The undercarriage had already been lowered and the drag from this and the unfeathered propeller caused the machine to drop like a stone. Wendel managed to haul the aircraft up to miss the trees surrounding the airfield, but in the ensuing crash the prototype was destroyed, Wendel escaping with cuts and bruises.

Meanwhile, on 30 March 1939, the He 100 V8 had gained Germany the world airspeed record for the first time by attaining 746.606 km/h (463.92 mph). This prompted Messerschmitt to immediately re-engine the Me 209 V1 with the specially-boosted DB 601 ARJ (V10) engine which developed 1,550 hp for short periods and which had been intended for installation in the V3. With this aircraft, Wendel raised the record to 755.14 km/h (469.22 mph) on 26 April 1939. This record was to stand for over 30 years.

Two other prototypes of the Me 209 were completed, the V3 (W.Nr.1187, D-IVFP) and the V4 (W.Nr.1188, D-IRND). The latter aircraft was actually fitted with armament, being intended for use a fighter, but the weight of this, combined with the power of the standard DB 601 A engine and the introduction of conventional radiators, meant that the variant was *slower* than the contemporary Bf 109 E.

Still determined to produce a successor to the Bf 109, Messerschmitt began work on a new Me 209, based on the P 1091 project, during the spring of 1943. Bearing no relation to the earlier Me 209, this aircraft had a fuselage and the wing based on the Bf 109 G, but with an inwardly retracting undercarriage and much enlarged vertical tail surfaces. Intended to compete with the Ta 153 designed by Kurt Tank, the new fighter was to be powered by a 1,900 hp DB 603 G engine with an annular radiator, and carry various combinations of cannon and heavy machine-guns.

The prototype, the Me 209 V5, made its first flight on 3 November 1943, and was found to have an excellent performance. At this time, the DB 603 G engine was in very limited supply, so the Me 209 V6 was fitted with the 1,750 hp Jumo 213 E engine, but when it was found that this reduced the aircraft's performance so that it was slower than the Fw 190 D-9, which was then beginning to enter service, it was abandoned. Some further development of the aircraft was however, carried out for the role of high altitude fighter. Known as the Me 209 H, this variant was to be powered by the 2,000 hp DB 627 engine with conventional radiators and have a new wing centre section which increased span to 13.25 m (43 ft 5 ins). The abandonment of the DB 627 led to the prototype being fitted with a standard DB 603 G, and it is doubtful whether it ever flew.

Thus, despite Messerschmitt's attempts to promote the new fighter, often even at the expense of the much more advanced Me 262, the aircraft proved a failure.

In the autumn of 1938, Messerschmitt's *Projektbüro* began work on the P 1060, an ambitious project for a twin-engined multi-purpose aircraft, combining the primary roles of the *Zerstörer* and the dive bomber (*Sturzkampfflugzeug*) together with the secondary functions of reconnaissance and ground-attack. The P 1060 subsequently received the RLM designation Me 210 and was intended to start entering *Luftwaffe* service in mid-1941 with the aim of replacing both the Bf 110 and the Ju 87. The Me 210 was thus foreseen as a key aircraft in the *Luftwaffe Führungstab's* re-equipment plans for 1941-42, together with the He 177 heavy bomber and the Ju 88 medium bomber. Such was the *Technisches Amt's* absolute faith in Willy Messerschmitt's abilities as a designer to produce successful high-performance aircraft, no matter how difficult or demanding the official requirement might be. Up to that time, virtually all of his designs had proved moderately or outstandingly successful.

The first prototype of the Me 210 made its maiden flight on 5 September 1939, with *Dr.-Ing.* Hermann Wurster (then the company's Chief Test Pilot) at the controls. He reported the aircraft to be barely controllable, since it suffered from longitudinal and directional instability. After the first flight, Wurster told Messerschmitt that the rear fuselage needed to be lengthened in order to rectify the instability, to which Messerschmitt is reputed to have replied that such modification would mean scrapping some three million *Reichsmarks* worth of jigs and tools which had been built in readiness for series manufacture.

It is alleged that Messerschmitt had personally intervened in the design process to shorten the fuselage and made other questionable modifications to the Me 210 in order to reduce the aircraft's weight. This led to protests from Robert Lusser who objected to the modifications and to a deterioration in relations between himself and Professor Messerschmitt during the period in which the layout of the embryonic Me 210 was being finalised. Consequently, Lusser resigned his position and, as mentioned earlier, rejoined Heinkel, Messerschmitt's arch rival, in February 1939.

Following a series of prototype crashes in 1940, Ernst Udet, by now, the *Generalluftzeugmeister*, became increasingly concerned about continued development and, on 13 September 1940, Messerschmitt wrote to him with the reassurance: "*I can assure you that you need have no fears concerning the airframe...*".

Various modifications intended to counter the

A line up of factory-fresh Me 210s, still bearing factory codes, awaiting delivery to a unit. In a sarcastic reflection on the problems that the Me 210 caused the RLM, Göring spoke of a possible epitaph for himself: "He would have lived longer but for the Me 210".

aircraft's many problems were embodied on a new batch of test aircraft, but the Messerschmitt development team soon recognised that the modifications undertaken no more than alleviated the worst effects of the aircraft's vices. Flight testing at the *E-stelle* Rechlin by service test pilots resulted in their unanimous condemnation of the Me 210's appallingly bad handling characteristics. However, the numerous proposals which they put forward as possible solutions simply attempted to force changes to the airframe and were unacceptable to the *Generalluftzeugmeister's* office which relied on the implicit trust it had placed in Messerschmitt's abilities to solve any problems that might arise during the aircraft's development. As time passed, the problems associated with the Me 210 programme seemed to multiply rather than diminish and, under extreme pressure from the *Generalluftzeugmeister's* office, Messerschmitt had no option but to commence deliveries of the Me 210 to the *Luftwaffe* despite the machine's many apparent shortcomings. Udet found it necessary to write to Messerschmitt on 27 June 1941 specifically to express his growing concern about the Me 210 and other difficulties encountered with Messerschmitt aircraft.

By the end of 1941, the *Luftwaffe* pronounced the Me 210 A first production model as totally unsuitable for operational use but Udet's office remained reluctant to cancel the aircraft's production because there was no aircraft in prospect to replace it. Following Udet's suicide on 17 November 1941, matters were brought to a head when Milch assumed the post of *Generalluftzeugmeister*. In January 1942 he ordered a halt to Me 210 production in favour of the Bf 110 pending a solution to the Me 210's many unsolved problems. Meanwhile, testing of the Me 210 continued.

By February 1942, the imbalance between the purchase costs of new materials, half-finished Me 210 components and advance payments from the RLM amounted to 25 million *Reichsmarks*, while the Messerschmitt company's *monthly* overheads were running at 16 million *Reichsmarks*. After 17 machines had been lost in one week and faced with bankruptcy for a second time, Willy Messerschmitt finally admitted to Göring and Milch that the aircraft was not ready for service use. With a touch of sarcasm, Göring later proposed an epitaph for himself: *"He would have lived longer but for the Me 210."*

On 25 March 1943, Messerschmitt made a personal appeal over the Augsburg factory loudspeaker system exhorting the workforce to ignore rumours circulating about the uncertain future of the Me 210. At a *Generalluftzeugmeister's* conference on 14 April, Milch mentioned the possibility of removing the Professor from the Messerschmitt management executive before his "genius's skull" could do the *Luftwaffe* any further damage! He decided to dispatch *Generalstabsing.* Lucht, the *General-Chefingenieur der Luftwaffe*, to inspect the Messerschmitt factories. Lucht subsequently submitted a graphic report at the *Generalluftzeugmeister's* conference on 21 April: "I found Messerschmitt a broken man. He was physically at a very low ebb and crazy with emotion. He was crying like a baby."

Lucht recommended that Messerschmitt be removed from the management executive to which Milch readily agreed. Shortly afterwards, Milch secured Göring's approval that the Me 210 should be deleted from the existing GL production programme and on 25 April all work on the ill-fated Me 210 finally ceased.

Such was the eventual outcome of the Me 210 fiasco, which almost forced the Messerschmitt concern into bankruptcy and brought personal humiliation to Willy Messerschmitt who was compelled to resign as chairman of the management committee and as managing director of Messerschmitt A.G., the holding company. In future, his activities would be restricted to that of Technical Director and Head of Development; he would play no part in the day-to-day affairs of the company, Theo Croneiss becoming Chairman and Fritz Seiler filling the post of Managing Director.

The Me 210 A-012 (W.Nr.028) coded DI+NX, undergoing trials at Augsburg-Haunstetten airfield. Without doubt the most unsuccessful aircraft produced by Messerschmitt, it was to bring the company to near bankruptcy. The previous aircraft, the Me 210 A-011, DI+NW, was rebuilt as the prototype Me 410.

Hermann Wurster (in flying gear), Messerschmitt's Chief Test Pilot who made the first flight in the Me 210 warned the Professor of that aircraft's instability and lack of control. He is seen in this photo after attaining the World Speed Record for landplanes (610.95 km/h 379 mph) in the Bf 109 V13, coded D-IPKY and powered by DB 601 engine, on 11 November 1937. At far left, Fritz Wendel, while talking to Wurster are Kaden (another test pilot) and Robert Lusser (far right).

However, in the aftermath of the Me 210 disaster, an important event took place which almost passed unnoticed by the *Techisches Amt*. On 18 July 1942, the first successful flight of the Me 262 took place when the third Jumo 004-powered prototype was flown by Fritz Wendel. The Me 262, destined to become the second most famous and successful aircraft to bear Messerschmitt's name - which had become somewhat tarnished by the Me 210 affair - would, in the course of time, restore the company's reputation with the RLM and prove that it was still capable of producing first-class designs incorporating technical innovations of the most advanced kind. But before the story of the Me 262 can unfold, the reader will first need to become acquainted with the early history of German turbojet engine development, since it was the appreciation of this revolutionary method of propulsion which would, by mid-1944, make the Me 262 the most advanced fighter in production anywhere in the world.

---

1 *During the First World War, Walter Georgii had served as a meteorologist with Bogohl 3, known as the England Geschwader, which had bombed London and southern Britain in 1917-18 with Gotha bombers. He later became director of the Deutsche Forschungsanstalt für Segelflug (German Research Establishment for Gliding Flight).*

2 *Two alternative reasons for the introduction of the 'M' prefix have been suggested. One is that it was the initial of its new designer, the second that it denoted Motorflugzeug (powered aircraft), replacing the earlier 'S' prefix which denoted Segelflugzeug (glider).*

3 *A member of this family, Frau Lilly Stromeyer, later became Willy Messerschmitt's wife. They married in 1952.*

4 *On 1 June 1935, Udet joined the Luftwaffe with the rank of Oberst. He succeeded Wimmer as head of the RLM's Technical Office on 6 June 1936, although he was both temperamentally and intellectually unsuited for the role. Göring had reluctantly appointed Udet to the post at Hitler's insistence. His vastly increased responsibilities were far in excess of his capabilities as an administrator, and he was unable to cope with the stress and criticism resulting from his new task.*

5 *Only two other aircraft, both Russian, have exceeded the Bf 109's production record. Over 36,000 examples of the Ilyushin IL-2 ground-attack aircraft, probably the most famous Russian aeroplane of the Second World War, were built between February 1941 and August 1944. The all-time record, however, belongs to the little-known Polikarpov PO-2 trainer and general-purpose biplane, of which some 40,000 were produced between 1927-1945.*

6 *Membership of the DAL corresponded to being a Fellow of the Royal Aeronautical Society in Britain or a member of the National Academy of Sciences in the United States. From April 1939 to February 1944, Professor Messerschmitt served as Vice President of the Academy.*

CHAPTER TWO

"SOME THOUGHT MY IDEAS WERE PURE FANTASY"

As early as 1908, the French engineer, René Lorin,[1] had proposed a primitive form of jet propulsion for aircraft. However, it was not until the mid-1930s, aided by advances in technology and materials, that serious systematic research and development work on the problems associated with this method of propulsion commenced in several European countries. In 1929-30 theoretical work on gas turbine development was begun by Frank Whittle in Britain followed, in 1933, by Hans Joachim Pabst von Ohain in Germany and A.J. Lysholm in Sweden. Of these three pioneers only von Ohain was fortunate to gain early financial backing for his work. Six years later this backing was to culminate in the flight of the Heinkel He 178, the world's first turbojet-propelled aircraft, powered by an engine of his design.

During the autumn of 1933 von Ohain, then a 22 year old student of applied physics and aerodynamics at Göttingen University, began to consider the development of a turbojet engine. Two years later he was awarded a Doctorate for his thesis *'Ein Interferenz-Lichtrelais für weisses Licht'* ('An Interference Relay for White Light'). By that time he was already working on two other inventions: a method of producing sound on film and the turbojet. The patent for the former was bought by the Siemens company, leaving the young physicist to develop his turbojet, the German patent for which was granted on 9 November 1935.

At this time his engine comprised a two stage compressor (an axial fan stage followed by a centrifugal compressor), an annular combustion chamber and a radial turbine. The first model was built at von Ohain's expense by Max Hahn, an outstanding automotive engineer who worked for the Bartels and Becker company in Göttingen. Tests showed that there were considerable problems with the model, but there was enough promise to prompt further development. To quote von Ohain:

"These tests suggested to me that fundamental combustor investigations and systematic developments were necessary that would require time and money exceeding my private means. My Professor at Göttingen, Robert Pohl, came to my rescue. In a very cordial discussion, he declared that he was convinced of the great future potential of jet propulsion. He suggested that industrial support would be necessary, and said that he was willing to give me a letter of recommendation to any company of my choice. Intuitively, I thought the engine industry would be negative toward gas turbine development; and therefore I suggested the Heinkel corporation."

After meeting Dr. Ernst Heinkel in March

The He 280 V3 taxies past the camera after completing a test flight. Standing on the wing (wearing a hat) is Martin Antz with Hans von Ohain and Gotthold Peter (Heinkel test pilot – later killed flying the He 162 V1 prototype) to his right. The pilot of the aircraft on this and many flights of the He 280 was Fritz Schäfer.

1936 at his home in Warnemünde, two contracts were signed, one a royalty agreement, the other an employment contract. On 15 April 1936, von Ohain began working for Heinkel, taking Max Hahn with him. Shortly afterwards he was joined by *Dipl.-Ing.* Wilhelm Gundermann, a specialist in aircraft engineering and turbo-machinery, and by the summer he had between six and eight fitters and mechanics assigned to his workshop.

Von Ohain takes up the story again. "During 1936 we made only slow progress in the combustion chamber programme because the highest priority was placed upon the design and construction of the hydrogen powered demonstration engine, the HeS 1. This was completed and installed in a test rig around the end of February 1937. I am not certain about the exact date of the first run of this engine; it may have been in late February or early March. By April most of our test runs had been completed. We were delighted that the apparatus fully met our expectations. It reached the anticipated performance, it handled very well in acceleration and deceleration, but most of all the psychological effect was enormous. Heinkel and his engineers suddenly believed firmly in the feasibility of turbojet propulsion."

After the successful testing of the HeS 1, Heinkel pressed the team to accelerate the entire turbojet engine programme. At the same time he deliberately withheld details of these developments from the RLM's Technical Office. Heinkel was a shrewd businessman who foresaw the future possibilities of jet propulsion. He concluded that the RLM would disapprove of a private venture involving the development of such a radical powerplant by an airframe manufacturer. Therefore, to maintain his early lead in this field, he decided to keep von Ohain's work secret from officialdom and present a completed turbojet to the Technical Office as an accomplished fact.

Max Hahn with the first experimental turbojet designed by Dr. Hans von Ohain at Göttingen University in 1936. Although extremely rudimentary, this engine did prove the feasibility of the turbojet.

Development of a liquid-fuelled (in place of hydrogen) combustion chamber took about 18 months, about the same time as that of the turbine. Both were then incorporated into a new engine, the HeS 3b. Von Ohain: "Since the flight engine had to be completed in a very short time (early spring 1939), we had to freeze the design in about the early summer of 1938. At that time the combustor with atomized liquid fuel injection was

The first turbojet driven aircraft to fly anywhere in the world was the He 178 V1 which made its first flight on 27 August 1939 with Erich Warsitz at the controls. The aircraft was powered by the 500 kp (1,100 lbs) thrust HeS 3b engine designed by Hans von Ohain.

After the first flight of the He 178 V1 in August 1939, a party was held to celebrate the event. Left to right can be seen Erich Warsitz (the pilot), Ernst Heinkel and Dr. Hans von Ohain (the designer of the engine).

not working satisfactorily; therefore we used the system with internal fuel gasification for the first flight engines."

Early in 1938 detailed design of an aircraft to be powered by the HeS 3 engine began under the designation He 178. Two prototypes of this tiny shoulder wing monoplane were to be built. The first had a fixed undercarriage, the second a retractable unit and an enlarged wing. After considerable development, the HeS 3b, which then developed almost 500 kg (1,100 lbs) thrust was fitted to the He 178 V1. This aircraft, piloted by *Flugkapitän* Erich Warsitz, first flew on 27 August 1939 - the world's first turbojet powered flight. Further development of the Heinkel engine led to the HeS 8 (which later received the RLM designation 109-001) that was used to power the world's first jet fighter, the He 280.

Meanwhile, in early 1936, *Professor Dr.-Ing.* Herbert Wagner of the Junkers Flugzeugwerke AG had initiated a completely different avenue of gas turbine development. This was based on private studies which he had already undertaken for the design of a turboprop engine in 1934.

In May 1935, at the instigation of Dr. Heinrich Koppenberg, Junkers' General Manager, Professor Wagner, formerly of the *Institut für Luftfahrtwesen* (Institute for Aeronautical Affairs) and holder of the Chair of Aeronautical Sciences at the Technical College, Berlin-Charlottenburg, had been appointed to the new post of *Leiter der Sonderentwicklungen* (Head of Special Developments). Although only 35 years of age, Wagner was recognized then as one of the most brilliant and progressive aeronautical minds in Germany. The purpose of his appointment was "...to bring new life and new ideas into the somewhat inflexible field of aircraft construction".

In his new role Wagner was occupied with the problems of high-altitude flight and the development of pressurized cabins. During this work he became involved in a study for a large, long-range, high-altitude aircraft capable of trans-Atlantic flight. Wagner quickly reached the conclusion that no conventional aero-engine would be suitable to propel such an aeroplane, and his thoughts turned again to a turboprop unit. He considered that engine development under Professor Otto Mader at Junkers Motorenbau GmbH (this concern being separate, at that time, from the airframe company, Junkers Flugzeugwerke AG) was too slow and conservative to meet his requirements. His view was supported by Koppenberg, and Wagner obtained the latter's permission to begin his own research into new forms of aircraft propulsion.

In April 1936, Wagner formed a small research group under *Dipl.-Ing.* Max Adolf Müller,

The He 280 V3 touches down following a test flight. The prototype was powered by two HeS 8A (109-001) turbojets which developed 700 kg (1,540 lbs) thrust. The He 280 was the world's first turbojet driven fighter, but its conservative design and small dimensions led to its abandonment in favour of the Me 262.

The He 280 V3 with engine cowling removed showing the HeS 8 (109-001) engine. Unlike the Jumo 004 and BMW 003 fitted to the Me 262, the HeS 001 had a centrifugal compressor.

Wagner's former assistant at the *Institut für Luftfahrtwesen*. This was established at a Junkers' subsidiary the Magdeburger Werkzeugmaschinenfabrik (Magdeburg Machine Tool Factory), located some 56 km (35 miles) north-west of Dessau. The existence of Müller's group - which initially comprised only two other specialists, Wilhelm Peppler, an engineer and *Dipl.-Ing.* Rudolf Friedrich, an aerodynamicist - was kept secret from everyone except Koppenburg, who supplied the finance. Mader was not informed of Wagner's initiative even after the Junkers airframe and engine companies merged in July 1936 to form the Junkers Flugzeug-und Motorenwerke AG and Wagner became Head of Airframe Development.

Müller's initial studies were concentrated on a turboprop unit, while basic research work was undertaken on the problem of combustion chambers and heat-resistant materials. During these preliminary investigations, both experimental combustion chambers and axial flow compressors were built and tested. Two variations of the latter were tried, utilizing both single- and three-stage arrangements. These incorporated different profiles of reaction-type blading (in which the work load is shared equally between the rotor and stator blades of the compressor). By the summer of 1938 Müller had a staff of about thirty designers, engineers and draftsmen employed at Magdeburg, and their work was extended to cover turbojets, diesel-engine driven ducted-fans, and even stationary plant for power generation! Around this time Wagner approached the Technical Office for financial backing, but was told firmly that engine development was no task for airframe companies. In fact the RLM wanted to transfer Müller's work to the Junkers engine division.

In 1938 the construction of an experimental turbojet engine commenced under the designation RTO *(Rückstoss-Turbinen-Strahltriebwerk* - Reaction Turbojet Engine) that featured a twelve-stage axial-flow compressor, an annular combustion chamber and a two-stage turbine. This engine began bench testing in the autumn of 1938, but from the outset problems were encountered with combustion. Like von Ohain's early units, it could only operate on an external air supply. By the beginning of 1939 the RTO was run up to a speed of 6,500 rpm on the test stand by using a compressed air supply and burning propane gas as fuel. Despite this, it could not be persuaded to reach its full design speed of 12,900 rpm due to compressor and combustion difficulties. It also proved impossible to measure any precise thrust. The development of this turbojet continued into the spring of 1939, by

After leaving Junkers for Heinkel in June 1939, Max A. Müller's team designed a new and extremely advanced axial-flow turbojet. Known as the HeS 30 (RLM designation 109-006), the engine had a remarkably low weight and small diameter, and was potentially the best engine of its class developed in Germany during the war.

which time the construction of a turboprop unit and a wooden mock-up of the ducted fan engine had begun. To overcome difficulties with the RTO turbojet, Müller planned to lengthen and modify its combustion chamber, but bureaucracy was to prevent any further development work being undertaken at Magdeburg.

Official German interest in turbojet propulsion, and the establishment of a formal development programme, was largely due to the efforts of *Dipl.-Ing.* Helmut Schelp. Schelp was a 26 year old graduate who had studied in both Germany and at Stevens University at Hoboken in New Jersey, USA. Upon his return to Germany in 1936, he was selected to join a new advanced course in aeronautical engineering at the DVL in Berlin-Adlershof. This course, which included test pilot training, was designed to provide a nucleus of highly qualified personnel for positions of authority within the German aviation industry and the *Luftwaffe's* Engineer Corps.

Following the successful completion of his training, Schelp was given the title of *Flugbaumeister.*[2] After joining LC I, the *Forschungsabteilung* (Research Department) of the RLM's Technical Office in August 1937, he was given charge of pulse jet and ramjet research work. Schelp's main interest, however, lay with gas turbine powerplants. During his independent study period at the DVL, he had made a survey of all types of jet propulsion systems that might be suitable for high-speed flight. This led him to conclude that gas turbine units promised the best long term solution. Nearly half a century later Schelp recalled how his study was received at the DVL. "It caused a furor, but in the end my views prevailed and I was able to define and describe a family of jet engines, including turboprops and pure turbojets. Some distinguished engineers thought my ideas were pure fantasy, and my professors and examiners were very doubtful. At this time I was working on my own and knew nothing of Heinkel, Junkers or British work in this field."

Schelp was unable to arouse much interest in his ideas within the *Forschungsabteilung*, and eventually Dr. Adolf Baeumker, the head of the department, suggested that he should transfer to *Abteilung* LC 8 (responsible for aircraft engine development) where his theories might gain more support. In September 1938, Schelp transferred,

The Daimler-Benz DB 007 turbofan engine had a 17 stage axial-flow compressor, annular combustion chamber and single-stage turbine. It was designed to produce a thrust of 1,150 kp (2,530 lbs) with a weight of 1,335 kg (2,940 lbs). This photo shows the engine on its test rig.

with the status of *Hilfsreferent* (Assistant Technical Adviser), to LC 8[3] which was headed by *Flieger-Hauptstabsingenieur* Wolfram Eisenlohr who was initially sceptical of gas turbines. Schelp soon found an ally in *Dipl.-Ing.* Hans Mauch, the *Referent für Sondertriebwerke* (Technical Advisor for Special Powerplants) who, up to that time, had been interested primarily in rocket engines. Schelp explained the possibilities of gas turbine engines to Mauch, and was able to convince him that it was time to initiate the wider development of such powerplants.

Accordingly, in the autumn of 1938, they visited the four main aircraft engine manufacturers, Daimler-Benz, Junkers, BMW and Bramo (Brandenburgische Motorenwerke GmbH) but were only partly successful in arousing the interest of these companies to take up the development of gas turbine engines.

Due to his extremely conservative outlook, *Dipl.-Ing.* Fritz Nallinger, Daimler-Benz's Technical Director, flatly refused to participate in the proposed gas turbine development programme. By the end of 1939, however, he had reconsidered his position - on the grounds of competitive disadvantage - and later received a development contract for a turbofan engine.

Professor Mader of Junkers somewhat reluctantly accepted a study contract, but expressed the view that the arrival of the turbojet engine was still a very distant prospect. Mader's lack of enthusiasm was based on his belief that the evolution of jet engines would be an extremely long and expensive process. He felt that they would only divert resources from the further development of reciprocating engines, then the established medium of aircraft propulsion.

Helmuth Sachse, then BMW's Technical Director, was much more optimistic about the possibilities of the turbojet, mainly because his company's Munich plant had commenced

Towards the end of 1939, Daimler-Benz were forced to reconsider their opposition to the development of turbojet engines. Around this time Professor Karl Leist joined the company and later began work on the development of a turbofan engine which received the RLM designation 109-007 during 1941.

Due to his conservative outlook, Dipl.-Ing. Fritz Nallinger, Daimler-Benz's Technical Director, flatly refused to participate in the proposed gas turbine development programme, but finally reconsidered his position later in 1939.

Professor Otto Mader of the Junkers Motorenbau GmbH was considered by some, in particular Herbert Wagner, to be too limited in his views, preferring to continue with the development of reciprocating engines.

development work on turbo-superchargers for piston engines in 1937. He felt that the experience BMW had gained with high-temperature air-cooled turbines could be utilized in the design of a turbojet engine.

Bramo, the smallest of the major engine manufacturers, also accepted a contract, although this decision was undoubtedly influenced by their concern that *Gen.Lt.* Ernst Udet was threatening them with closure due to his need to rationalize the industry. He considered that Bramo was too small to compete successfully with BMW, its main rival. In these circumstances Bramo felt it prudent to accept a study contract, and thus avoid the possibility of incurring the Technical Office's displeasure.

A stimulus to the growing interest in jet-propulsion occurred on 23-24 August 1938, when a special session of the *Lilienthal Gesellschaft für Luftfahrtforschung* (Lilienthal Society for Aviation Research) was held in Munich. The theme of the session, which was attended by over 90 aviation specialists, was *'Flugwerk und Triebwerk'* (Airframes and Powerplants).[4] The programme included a lecture by Professor Karl Leist,[5] of the DVL's *Institut für Triebwerke*, entitled *'Gasturbinen als Haupttriebwerke für Flugzeuge'* (Gas Turbines as the Principal Powerplant for Aircraft). Among the advantages advanced by Professor Leist for gas turbine engines were:

Professor Georg Madelung, was married to Messerschmitt's youngest sister, Elisabeth, known as 'Ello' within the family. While head of the Aerodynamics Institute at Stuttgart Technical University, Madelung put forward the concept of a target-defence fighter which utilized: "... jet propulsion by means of extracting air for combustion and additional supercharged air masses from the atmosphere." He later became director of the Luftfahrtforschungs-anstalt Graf Zeppelin (Count Zeppelin Aviation Research Institute) at Stuttgart-Ruit.

- The lack of any reciprocating components and a very high rate of revolution, resulting in a low unit weight.
- Use of cheap home-produced fuels.
- No variation of loads, high tensile stress limited to a few easily replaceable parts, thus resulting in a long useful life with fewer causes for breakdowns and increased reliability.
- Reduced risk of fire.
- Small dimensions.
- Reduced frontal resistance.
- Easy starting.

Commenting on the research undertaken by the *Institut* since 1936, Professor Leist stated: "The DVL investigated various *Sondertriebwerke* (Special Powerplants) of different modes of operation. Two of these, whose main method of propulsion was by means of propellers, were driven by gas turbines. Air is supercharged by the slipstream and pressed into the combustion chamber by a turbo-compressor, which in turn accelerates the turbine. The turbine drives the compressor as well as the propeller. The propulsion is increased to a degree by the gases exhausting from the turbine wheel."

Professor Leist's remarks indicated that he, and his fellow research workers, possessed a sound appreciation of the theory and advantages of gas turbine engines, but that there was a definite preference for turbo-prop power plants, probably on account of the aircraft speeds then in prospect. As a result, the turbojet engine was only briefly discussed during this meeting, and in very little detail. However, a possible application for the engine was submitted by Professor Georg Madelung,[6] head of the Aerodynamics Institute of Stuttgart Technical University. The Professor put forward the concept of a target-defence fighter which utilized: "... jet propulsion by means of extracting air for combustion and additional supercharged air masses from the atmosphere."

One of the principal early objections against the axial flow turbojet, namely that compressors of suitable efficiency did not exist, was largely overcome by the important research work undertaken by *Dipl.-Ing.* Walter Encke, leader of the *Institut für Strömungsmaschinen* (Institute for Aerodynamic Machinery), a component of the AVA in Göttingen. By 1938 Encke had succeeded in obtaining axial compressor efficiencies averaging 80% under test, over a wide range of loads. This was achieved by the careful

On 2 November 1943, Göring and Milch watched a test flight of the Me 262 V6 at Lechfeld. From left to right are an unknown Luftwaffe officer, Fritz Wendel, Göring, Messerschmitt and Anselm Franz.

application of aerodynamic principles. The compressor blades were designed as aerofoils and were arranged in cascades, that is in several stages, one behind another, to force the air at each stage up to the required pressure. The speed of the airflow through the compressor assembly was controlled by a row of stationary or stator blades placed in front of each moving (rotor) row. In Encke's compressor the pressure rise took place largely in the moving blades; about 70 to 80% of the work being done by the rotors, the remainder by the stator blading. Encke's compressor featured impulse-type blading in contrast to the reaction-type blading used by Müller, where the work of compression was shared between the stator and rotor blades. Encke subsequently designed the compressors used in the first BMW and Junkers turbojets developed under RLM contracts.

The axial compressor, as opposed to the simpler centrifugal type (used by both von Ohain and Whittle), came to dominate German gas turbine design. It was selected from the outset by Schelp for power units built under official contracts, because it offered a smaller frontal area and less drag. Despite its greater complexity and expense, the axial-flow configuration ultimately gained universal acceptance, and today most medium-sized and large turbojets, turbofan and turboprop engines employ compressors of this type. (The use of the centrifugal-flow compressor is now largely confined to small gas-turbine engines used for powering trainers, target aircraft, helicopters and light civil aircraft.).

In April 1939 the Technical Office put pressure on Junkers to transfer its interest in gas turbines to its engine division at Dessau. Professor Wagner reluctantly agreed to hand over the work at Magdeburg to the engine division, and Müller was forced to negotiate with Professor Mader, the division's head. Following a visit to Magdeburg, Mader made it known that he was willing to take on the development of only one type of engine. Müller disliked Mader's plans, as this meant giving up complete control of his work. While the disgruntled Müller continued to have discussions with Mader he made secret approaches to Ernst Heinkel, who promptly offered him and his entire group employment at Rostock with increased salaries!

Finally, in May 1939, Müller and most of his staff resigned, but the Junkers management then invoked German labour laws to delay the move by a month. In mid-June 1939, after much acrimony, Müller and twelve members of his group joined Heinkel. Here they continued the development of an entirely new, and extremely advanced, axial-flow turbojet. The preliminary design of this engine, which was named HeS 30 (RLM designation 109-006), had been initiated at Magdeburg. Müller promised Heinkel that he would have the HeS 30, which featured a remarkably low weight and small diameter, running within a year of his arrival at Rostock. In fact development problems meant that it did not run under its own power until April 1942, and at the end of that year Schelp very short-sightedly cancelled the development contract due to his distrust of the engine's reaction-type compressor blading.

During 1936 *Dipl.-Ing.* Anselm Franz, a 36-year old graduate of Graz Technical College in Austria, had joined *Junkers Motorenwerke* as head of the department responsible for piston engine supercharger and reaction development. In August 1938, Mader appointed Franz to undertake a general survey of all gas turbine possibilities, the company accepting a Technical Office study contract a month later. Following detailed weight estimates of free-piston engines arranged as gas producers, Franz concluded that there would be great difficulty in getting the required performance from such systems within any reasonable weight limits. He felt that only a simple turbojet would be light enough for aircraft use. With Müller's departure to Heinkel, Franz visited Magdeburg in July 1939 to survey and report on the results achieved up to that time. He formed the opinion that none of the engines being developed by Müller was worth pursuing, which angered Hans Mauch of LC 3 since he refused to believe that all Müller's work was worthless and should be discarded without further investigation.

Franz later recalled that: "In 1939 the RLM wanted us to take over Wagner's engine, but I refused and during the autumn of that year we received a government contract for our own T 1, later to become known as the Jumo 004 A. This can claim to be the world's first successful axial flow turbojet, a configuration that became the standard for jet engine design. The Jumo 004 was also the first jet engine in volume production and combat service." In Franz's view, Wagner was: "... a very aggressive person, attempting to go, as Mader saw it, beyond what was then possible. He was a brilliant man, but he did not have a feel for the realities." In retrospect, it is obvious that Wagner had allowed Müller to spread his very limited manpower over too many divergent projects. It would have been better if he had concentrated on a particular type of engine and placed all available resources behind its development.[7]

In July 1939, Junkers received an official development contract for a new axial-flow turbojet. The requirement was for 600 kp (1,320 lbs) thrust at 900 km/h (559 mph) at sea level, or about 700 kp (1,540 lbs) static. Mader placed Franz in charge of this development, which possessed no novel or questionable features. It was designed to be brought into production and operation as quickly as possible, and was developed from the outset to burn diesel oil. Franz recalls: "To reduce the risk and ensure success, I decided not to try for the maximum that seemed achievable, but set a rather conservative goal. I believe this approach was one of the main reasons why this completely new type of engine could be developed and put into production in such a short time."

At that time, the Junkers engine division was under great pressure from the Technical Office to develop and improve its range of piston engines, such as the Jumo 211 and Jumo 222. Professor Mader gave Franz a free hand with the new turbojet project, with the proviso that no engineers could be transferred from piston engine work. Franz therefore started work with only three key staff from his piston engine supercharger department, and gradually built up, mainly with newly-qualified young engineers fresh from university, an independent organisation for the development of turbojet engines. Only a few of Müller's staff stayed on to take jobs in the new group under Franz, the most notable of these being Dr. Heinrich Adenstadt, whom Schelp considered one of the best metallurgists in Germany. The new group grew to around 30 engineers and designers in 1940, and by 1944 about 500 personnel were working under Franz's direction. Fortunately there was never any shortage of finance, which was always plentiful. This enabled quite elaborate experimental and test facilities to be built at Dessau. These included a material's laboratory, test stands for compressor, combustion chamber and complete engine testing and, by 1942, a high-altitude engine test cell. In 1939, however, such specialized test facilities simply did not exist, and initial construction work on the turbojet project was undertaken in the experimental piston engine workshops of the Otto Mader Werke in Dessau.

The design of the Junkers engine began in October 1939 under the leadership of Fritz Böttger, with Franz in overall control. To obtain data for the first design, it was decided to build a small-scale engine to allow independent testing of components without excessive expenditure of resources. The compressor was designed to absorb about 400 shaft horsepower at a rotational speed over 30,000 rpm, so as to allow use of the test facilities then available. The model unit was completed in late 1939 but its small scale resulted in inadequate combustion and the engine suffered from vibration. Independent tests were then made with the compressor alone, but this was wrecked by blade failures during one test at high speeds. With the failure of this model, it was decided that studies should be concentrated on a full-size engine, and work on this, the Jumo T 1 (004 A), began in December 1939.

In selecting the essential features of the engine it was decided to use an eight-stage axial compressor, the blading of which was based on data provided by *Dipl.-Ing.* Encke of the AVA. While Franz was familiar with centrifugal compressors from his supercharger work, he chose an axial system because of its smaller diameter and his conviction that a straight-through airflow would prove more efficient. Although Franz felt that an annular combustion chamber would be superior, he selected six individual can-type combustors. This was mainly because they appeared to present fewer development problems, since one can-type chamber could be more easily tested and modified. For the design of the single-stage turbine wheel, which at first had solid blades, Franz relied on Professor Kraft of AEG in Berlin, this concern having previous experience in the manufacture of steam turbines. From the outset, the jet exhaust pipe of the turbojet was designed for the later incorporation of after-burning. The engine was equipped with a variable-area exhaust nozzle, mounted in the tailpipe, which could be adjusted to various operating conditions by means of a servo-motor controlled from the throttle lever.

The design of the Jumo T 1 was completed in the spring of 1940, and the prototype made its initial test run on 11 October 1940, without an exhaust nozzle. In December of that year the engine was run at its full design speed of 9,000 rpm, and by the end of January 1941 a thrust of 430 kp (950 lbs) was reached. Considerable problems were then encountered with stator blade vibration in the compressor which resulted in the prototype engine being almost destroyed through blade failure. Some six months of very laborious work were required before a partial remedy to the vibration problem was found by substituting steel blades for the original light alloy stator blades. During this period, several more prototype engines were brought near to completion, and on 6 August 1941, the design thrust of 600 kp (1,320 lbs) required by the development contract was achieved. In December of that year a ten hour test run was completed and a thrust of 1,000 kp (2,200 lbs) attained with the fifth prototype Jumo T 1 (004 A). This was achieved by operating at an unacceptably high temperature for a short period. The first flight of the T 1 in a Bf 110 test bed took place on 15 March 1942. Based on these promising results, the Technical Office issued a contract for 80 Jumo T 1 engines in the late summer of 1942. These engines, rated at 840 kp (1,850 lbs) thrust, were used for further engine development and airframe application testing in the first prototypes of the Me 262 and the Ar 234.

The Jumo T 1 (004 A) was designed and built as an experimental engine. No limitations were placed on weight or manufacturing considerations, or the use of strategic materials so that a running unit could be built in the shortest

As far as is known, the only surviving Jumo 004 A-0 engine, the A-022, is on display at the Luftfahrt Museum at Hannover-Laatzen. The cowlings have been partly removed to show the engine's interior detail.

Messerschmitt P 65/P 1065/Me 262 Turbojet Development

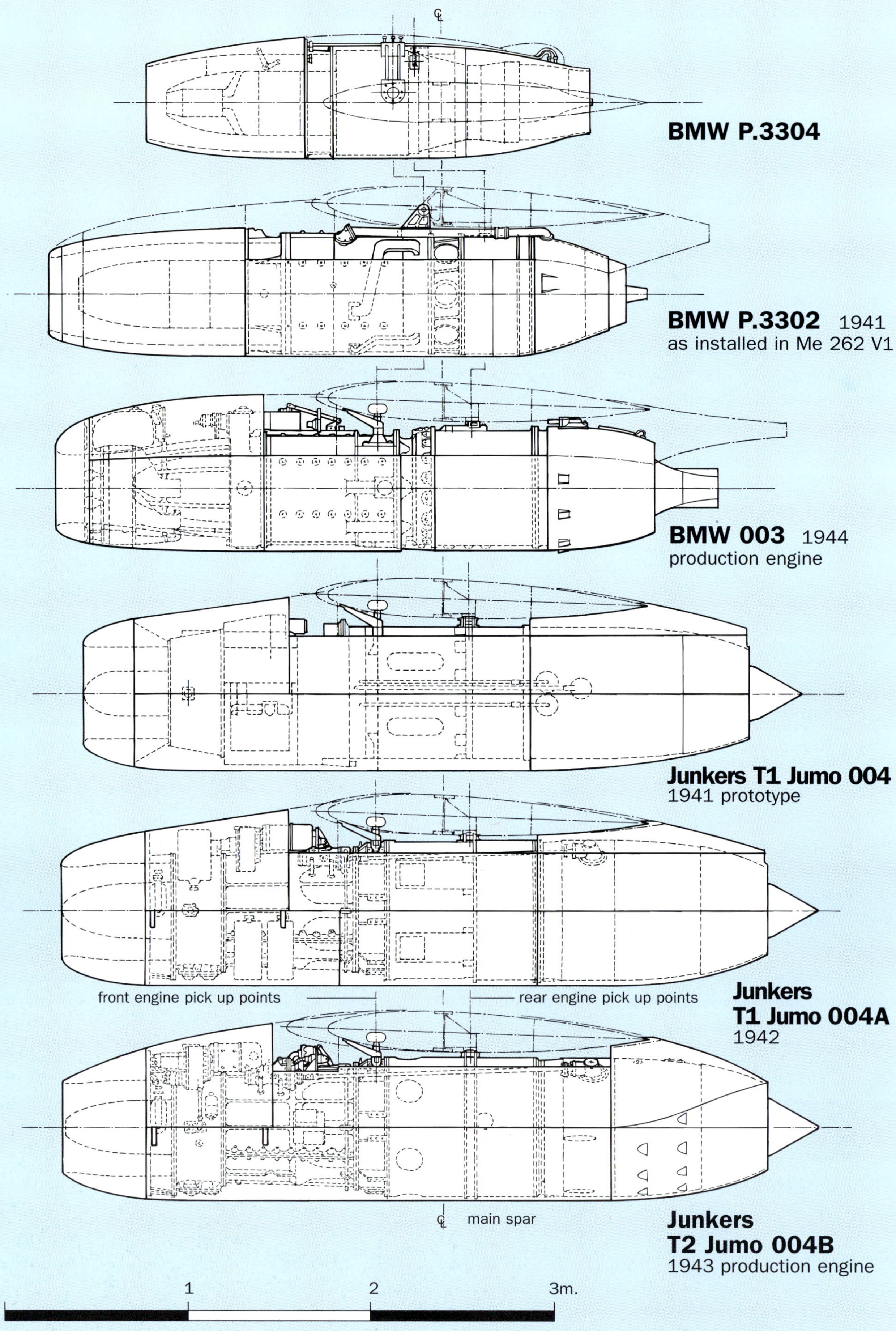

possible time. As a result it weighed 830 kp (1,830 lbs) - a power to weight ratio of roughly one to one. This was too heavy for normal aircraft installation. It also used many scarce heat-resistant metals such as nickel, cobalt and molybdenum in all 'hot' engine parts. The Jumo T 1 was thermodynamically and aerodynamically identical to the intended mass production variant (the Jumo T 2 or 004 B), and served to provide invaluable experience with the problems involved in the design and development of a practical turbojet. Franz accepted that once the Jumo T 1 had proved that the turbojet principle was sound, his team would have to redesign it as a production engine using materials that were more readily available. This resulted in the Jumo 004 B which is described in Chapter 4.

In 1940, Franz obtained his Doctorate from Berlin Technical College with a thesis on his basic research work on exhaust jet propulsion. The Jumo 004, developed under his direction, was to become the most successful German turbojet, powering both the Me 262 and Ar 234 B. Backed by between 25,000 and 30,000 hours of bench testing, over 6,000 engines were built by the time of the German collapse in May 1945.

BMW accepted an official study contract for jet propulsion in 1938, the work being placed under the control of Dr. Kurt Löhner, the company's Head of Research. It was decided that valuable experience would be gained by the construction and testing of a turbojet engine by utilizing, where possible, the knowledge BMW had already gained with exhaust-driven turbo-superchargers for piston-engines. Under Löhner's direction, the BMW Munich team produced a proposal for a turbojet with a two-stage centrifugal-flow compressor, an annular combustion chamber and a single-stage axial-flow turbine, the latter employing hollow air-cooled blades enabling it to operate at temperatures up to 900° C (1650° F). While the detailed design of this engine (which is believed to have received the project designation P.3301) was being undertaken, experiments proceeded with the turbine wheel, with which difficulties were soon encountered. By the outbreak of war, however, the impetus was for less experimental and more development work, so it was agreed with the Technical Office that Löhner's centrifugal-flow turbojet should be cancelled, in order to concentrate on the development and production of urgently-needed piston-engines such as the BMW 801.

At first, *Dipl.-Ing.* Bruno Bruckmann, Bramo's Technical Director, and *Dr.-Ing.* Hermann Oestrich, his Head of Development, were reluctant to embark on the design of a turbojet engine.[8] Instead they examined the possibilities of using a piston engine to power a ducted fan. Within the classification system for jet engines, as devised by Helmut Schelp, this type of unit was known as a *ML-Triebwerk (Motor-Luftstrahl-triebwerk)*. To test the feasibility of such a powerplant, a specially modified Fw 44 J two-seat biplane trainer was fitted with a 160 hp Bramo 325 seven-cylinder radial engine. This drove a four-bladed axial fan housed within a short annular duct, the entry to which was partly enclosed by a streamlined hub. The Fw 44 J testbed was flown in October 1938, with encouraging results, by Hanna Reitsch, the well-known woman test pilot, and this prompted Bramo to proceed with a much larger and more ambitious ML-unit. Wind tunnel tests with this unit, employing a 1,500 hp Bramo 329 fourteen-cylinder radial engine to drive a large variable-pitch ducted fan, with provision for afterburning in the airstream aft of the fan to increase thrust, were conducted at the AVA in Göttingen, but proved very disappointing. The tests gave results far below the calculated performance, this being partly due to low fan efficiency and inadequate engine rotational speeds, and by early 1939, it was decided to concentrate all future work on the design of a pure turbojet. This decision was no doubt influenced by the Technical Office placing a development contract, at the beginning of 1939, for a turbojet engine with a static thrust of 600 kp (1,320 lbs) and a diameter of 600 mm (23.6 in).

Dr.-Ing. Hermann Oestrich, Head of Development at Bramo.

To establish the best line of development, *Dipl.-Ing.* Hermann Hagen, Oestrich's assistant and Head of Basic Design, examined the characteristics and parameters of centrifugal- and axial-flow compressors, and came to the conclusion that a *counter-rotating* axial-flow design was the optimum unit. This appeared both lighter and smaller for a given thrust than any other type of turbojet. Bramo would have preferred to develop this type of engine immediately, but because of their lack of gas turbine experience, they decided to proceed first with the design of a simple straight axial-flow turbojet. During the spring of 1939 Oestrich's team laid down the basic design of a turbojet engine featuring a six-

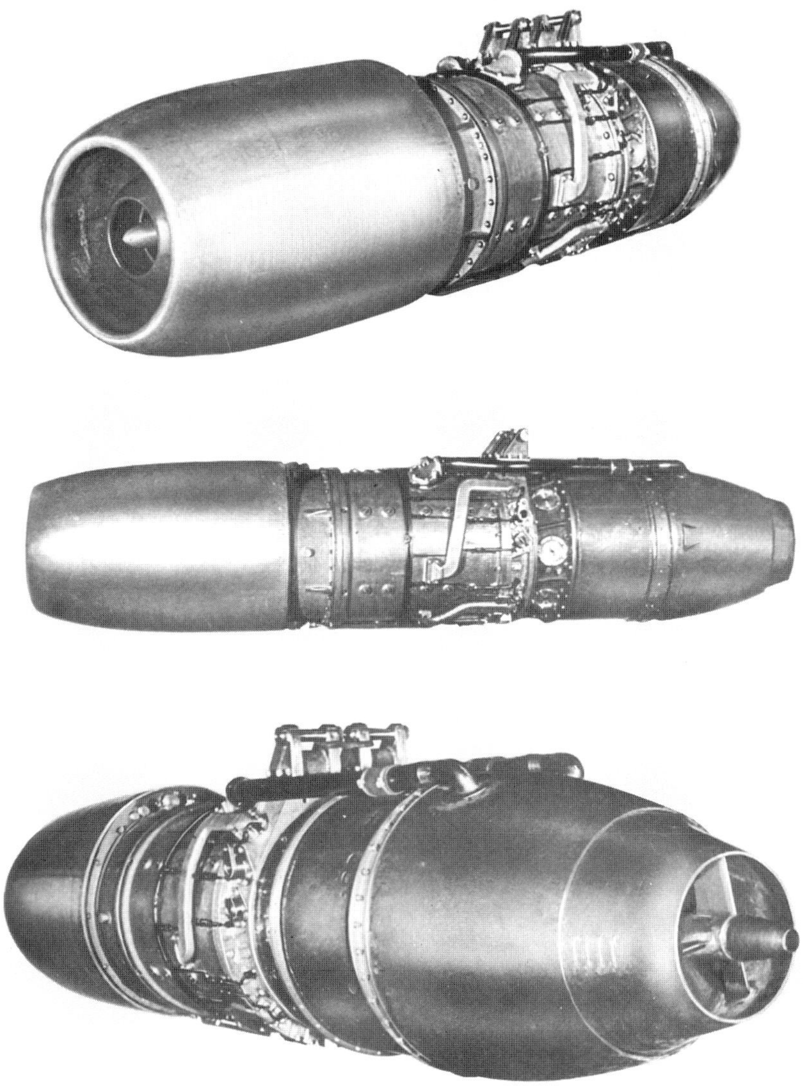

A very early BMW P.3302 engine. A pair of these engines were fitted to the Me 262 V1 on 25 March 1942, but just after leaving the ground both suffered compressor blade failures which forced a major redesign.

stage axial-flow compressor driven by a single-stage turbine. The compressor gave a pressure ratio of only 2.77 to 1 at 9,000 rpm. An annular combustion chamber operating at the very low temperature of 600° C (1,110° F) was originally planned, but this was later raised to the much higher figure of 900° C (1,650° F) by using the air-cooled turbine, with hollow blades, developed by BMW. Like the competing Jumo T1, the turbojet was designed to produce 600 kp (1,320 lbs) thrust at 900 km/h (560 mph) or about 700 kg (1,540 lbs) static thrust at sea level.

Bruno Bruckmann's efforts to merge with BMW, so as to avoid total closure, were successful, and collaboration began at a technical level in late 1938. The two companies were then amalgamated, under BMW stewardship, in July 1939, Bramo then being known as BMW Flugmotorenwerke Brandenburg GmbH.

Following the amalgamation, the Bramo turbojet was given the project designation P.3302. With the agreement of the Technical Office, this engine was initially considered as a research unit to assist in the development of the more complicated axial-flow turbojet with a counter-rotating compressor, the P.3304. To help with the design of the P.3304 assistance was sought from *Ing.* Helmut Weinrich, an independent engineering consultant from Chemnitz. Weinrich had unsuccessfully submitted plans to the Technical Office in 1936 for a turboprop engine employing a counter-rotating compressor *and* turbine. The P.3304, which was also known as the *Weinrich Gerät*, featured a four-stage counter-rotating axial-flow compressor, an annular combustion chamber and a three-stage turbine. With a diameter of only 610 mm (24 inches) and a length of 2.44 m (8 feet), the P.3304 was the smallest known gas-turbine engine worked on in Germany during the war years. It had an estimated thrust of 600 kp (1,320 lbs) at sea level. By 1940, about twenty designers and engineers were working at Spandau on the P.3304, which received the official designation 109-002. Individual stages of the counter-rotating compressor were built and tested, but as BMW gained experience it was realized that the technical difficulties in developing even a simple axial-flow turbojet were very considerable. By mid-1942 the 109-002 was abandoned, without a prototype engine being completed, in order that all resources could be concentrated on the P.3302.

In 1939 there were about 40 engineers and designers available for jet engine work at the Berlin-Spandau plant. Initially, construction and experimental work had to be conducted in the same workshops used for piston-engine development, but by 1942 (when piston-engine work ceased at Spandau) there were about 200 designers and technical personnel available, plus about 700 people in the workshops. By 1945 these figures had increased to approximately 550 and 1,000 respectively, largely by transferring BMW personnel from piston-engine work.

Experiments with the turbine wheel for the P.3302 led BMW to conclude that a combustion chamber temperature of 900° C was too high, and this was lowered to 750° C (1,380° F) before work commenced on the construction of ten experimental engines. The prototype experimental engine, the P.3302 V1, first ran in December 1940, but the result was very disappointing.[9] Only 150 kp (330 lbs) thrust was obtained at 8,000 rpm on the test stand, and it was evident that every major component of the engine was beset with problems. The main problems were as follows:

(1) Insufficient airflow for a combustion temperature of 750° C, as the original design allowed for a working temperature of 900° C.
(2) Poor turbine efficiency, since the lowering of the combustion temperature had reduced the velocity of the gas efflux, which, in turn, lowered the power to the compressor and its air delivery.
(3) The efficiency of the combustion chamber was only 60 to 70 per cent, resulting in much fuel leaving the chamber unburnt.
(4) Uneven temperature distribution within the combustion chamber, with as much as 370° C difference between the hottest and coldest parts. This caused distortion of the chamber's inner liner and the turbine inlet nozzle, leading to friction in the engine bearings.

To eliminate these faults, a complete redesign of the engine was undertaken, this work commencing in the spring of 1941. For this work, the P.3302 V2-V10 engines were used to develop new components, while outside assistance was sought from specialist organizations. Brown-Boveri, Brückner-Kanis and M.A.N.[10] assisted with the development of the new turbine, while Henschel and the *Technische Akademie der Luftwaffe* at Gatow provided help with the new combustion system. By the summer of 1941, the P.3302 had been persuaded to give about 450 kp (990 lbs) thrust on the test stand. This was achieved mainly by means of an improved fuel injector system, although the increase in performance was still far from satisfactory. Flight trials with a prototype unit began from Berlin-Schönefeld airfield, the turbojet being mounted beneath the fuselage of a Bf 110 twin-engined fighter. Difficulties were still experienced with the turbine wheel, and blade failures occurred at speeds as low as 8,000 rpm due to welding fatigue and heat-induced brittleness.

In late November 1941 two of the P.3302 V2-V10 engines were delivered to Messerschmitt for installation in the Me 262 V1 airframe. By this time improvements to the P.3302 had raised its static thrust to around 500 kp (1,100 lbs). On 25 March 1942, an unsuccessful test flight took place with the Me 262 V1, as related in Chapter 4. This disappointing test flight, and the persistent problems encountered with the development of the P.3302, at least temporarily eliminated the BMW turbojet as a potential power plant for the Me 262. By this time, the rival Jumo 004 was beginning to show promise, and it was adopted as the standard engine for the aircraft.

During the spring of 1942, construction commenced on six further experimental engines, designated P.3302 V11-V16, which incorporated the redesign work initiated the previous year. These featured a new seven-stage axial compressor of BMW design with NACA[11] blading and a 30 per cent greater airflow, which increased the pressure ratio to 3.1 to 1. A turbine wheel of greatly improved efficiency was also introduced, and overall diameter was increased to 690 mm (26.9 inches). Test stand running of the P.3302 V11 began in the autumn of 1942, and resulted in a thrust of about 550 kp (1,210 lbs). No attempt was made to fly an aircraft under the power of these improved engines, and flights with the P.3302 V11-V16 series were confined to the Bf 110 flying test bed. During the course of these tests a new air intake cowling of improved aerodynamic shape was introduced, and the first trials with a variable-area exhaust nozzle began. Further test stand running with the V11-V16 series eventually increased the thrust to 600 kp (1,320 lbs), as required by the Technical Office development contract, but revealed a number of deficiencies. These included blade fractures due to vibration in the first-stage rotor blades of the compressor and turbine blade failures of lesser frequency, while serious difficulties remained with the combustion chamber efficiency and temperature distribution.

By the end of 1942, however, solutions had been found, or were within sight, for the most serious difficulties, and a new engine was under design. This final major redesign of the BMW engine, which had by then received the official designation 109-003, resulted in it being fitted to a few Me 262s, as will be described in a later volume of this work.

Meanwhile, towards the end of 1939, Hans Mauch had left *Abteilung LC 3* to be succeeded by Dr. Ernst Beck as the *Referent für Sondertriebwerke*. Dr. Beck, a civilian employee of the RLM, proved to be an uninspiring administrator, and as a result Helmut Schelp's authority was much increased in negotiations with the aero-engine manufacturers. Schelp later rose to become leader of the Technical Office

Gruppe GL/C-E3/VII responsible for the policies covering jet engine development, and by the end of the war he had attained the rank of *Flieger-Stabsingenieur*.

By the outbreak of war, in September 1939, Hitler's Germany alone - of all the major powers - had embarked on an official development programme for aircraft gas-turbine engines, together with a corresponding programme to study their application to airframes suitable for military purposes.[12] It seemed a promising start, but it was not a monopoly Germany was to maintain or exploit to any decisive advantage during the Second World War. The failure to exploit fully this major technological advance was largely due to high-level vacillation and indecision, and is exemplified by the Messerschmitt Me 262, the story of which will unfold in the following chapters.

Photo right: Although the HeS 8a turbojet had been flown in the He 280 V2 during March and April 1941, it was still extremely temperamental. Therefore, it was decided to mount a prototype engine beneath an He 111 bomber for flight tests.

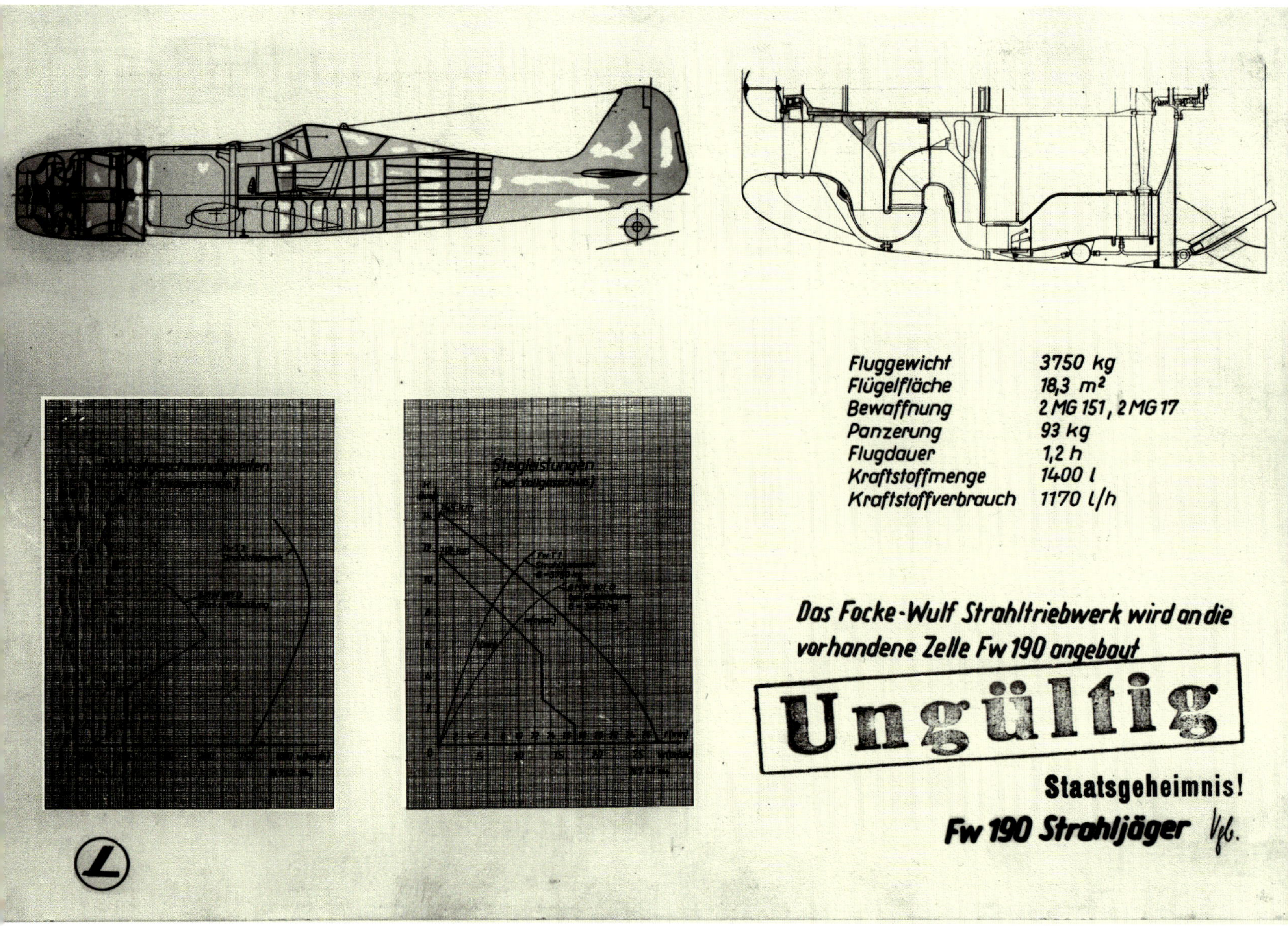

Similar to Messerschmitt's nebulous proposal for a jet-powered Bf 109 TL, a similar proposal was drawn up by Focke-Wulf in July 1942 to incorprate a turbojet engine onto the Fw 190. This official Focke-Wulf drawing shows the design proposal and also indicates that the idea was - "Ungültig" - scrapped.

1 *Lorin is best remembered as the inventor of the ramjet engine. His first proposals for ramjet propulsion were made in 1913, although the speed of contemporary aircraft were far too low for the practical realisation of this power plant. Up to recent times the ramjet was termed the 'Lorin duct' in several European countries, including Germany.*

2 *"Flugbaumeister" is a qualification allowing an engineer to practice in aircraft construction in a senior position. It can be translated literally as "Master in Aircraft Engineering". The Flugbaumeister who were trained at the DVL were also qualified test pilots, and frequently flew assessment flights in prototype aircraft.*

3 *On 1 February 1939, the Abteilungen of the Technisches Amt were reorganised and renumbered, LC 8 becoming LC 3. Another reorganisation took place at the end of 1941, and LC 3 was redesignated GL/C-E3.*

4 *The Lilienthal Gesellschaft was named after Otto Lilienthal, the famous German gliding pioneer, who was killed in 1896 while flying one of his machines. The Society promoted the advancement of aviation research, and its membership included a wide cross-section of the German aviation industry, serving and retired officers from the armed forces, academics from universities and research institutes, and civilian aviation. It is believed that Professor Messerschmitt and Woldemar Voigt (who were both members of the Society) attended the meeting, but this has yet to be confirmed.*

5 *In 1939, Professor Leist joined Daimler-Benz for the purpose of developing turbo-superchargers for high-altitude piston-engines, and to investigate the possibilities of a piston-engine driven ducted-fan power-plant based on the DB 604. He was later to direct the development of the Daimler-Benz 109-007 turbofan engine.*

6 *Professor Madelung was a brother-in-law of Willy Messerschmitt through his marriage to the latter's youngest sister, Elisabeth, known as 'Ello' within the family. Professor Madelung later became director of the Luftfahrtforschungsanstalt Graf Zeppelin (Count Zeppelin Aviation Research Institute) at Stuttgart-Ruit, which was primarily concerned with research into bomb ballistics, stabilising parachutes for bombs and torpedoes, acoustic proximity fuzes and underwater detonation phenomena.*

7 *Late in 1939 Wagner left Junkers and in January 1940 he joined the Henschel Flugzeugwerke at Berlin-Schönefeld as head of a new department formed for the development of guided missiles. His work at Henschel culminated in the Hs 293/294/295 series of air-to-surface missiles, the Hs 298 air-to-air missile and the Hs 117 Schmetterling (Butterfly) anti-aircraft missile, although only the Hs 293 saw operational use during the war.*

8 *In 1928, Dr.-Ing. Oestrich had joined the staff of the Motorenabteilung of the DVL in Berlin-Adlershof, where he was employed in research work on aircraft engines. In 1931 he became interested in jet propulsion, and a summary of his studies were published in a paper entitled "The Prospects of Jet Propulsion for Aircraft with Particular Consideration of an Exhaust Jet Drive" which appeared in the DVL Year Book. In 1935 Oestrich joined Siemens und Halske Flugmotorenwerke (renamed Bramo in 1936) in Berlin-Spandau, being responsible for piston and high-altitude engine development. Thus, by 1938, when Bramo accepted a Technical Office study contract, Oestrich was well aware of the problems involved in developing a turbojet, and this may explain Bramo's initial reluctance to develop an engine of this type.*

9 *The early chronology of the P 3302 (BMW 003) is less well documented than the Jumo 004, and there are discrepancies with some important dates (e.g.: some sources quote August 1940 as the date when the P 3302 V1 was first test run.) The dates quoted by the authors are based on an account of BMW turbojet engine development written by Dr. Oestrich in 1950, which is considered to be the most reliable source.*

10 *M.A.N. = Maschinenfabrik Augsburg-Nürnberg AG, a company engaged in the development of gas turbines for stationary power generation.*

11 *NACA (now NASA - National Aeronautics and Space Administration) = National Advisory Committee on Aeronautics; set up by the U.S. government in the 1920s to devise and set standards for the developing avation industry. Prominent in aerodynamics - airfoil sections, low drag cowlings, streamlined shapes, propellers, (thermodynamics) radiator ductings etc.*

12 *The British Air Ministry did not give large-scale backing to Whittle's turbojet development work until June 1940.*

The earliest known free-hand sketch prepared by Willy Messerschmitt dated 17 October 1939 showing his preliminary ideas for the P 1065 in which he favoured an oval shaped fuselage section with mid wing configuration, tricycle undercarriage and horizontal tail position half way up the fin.

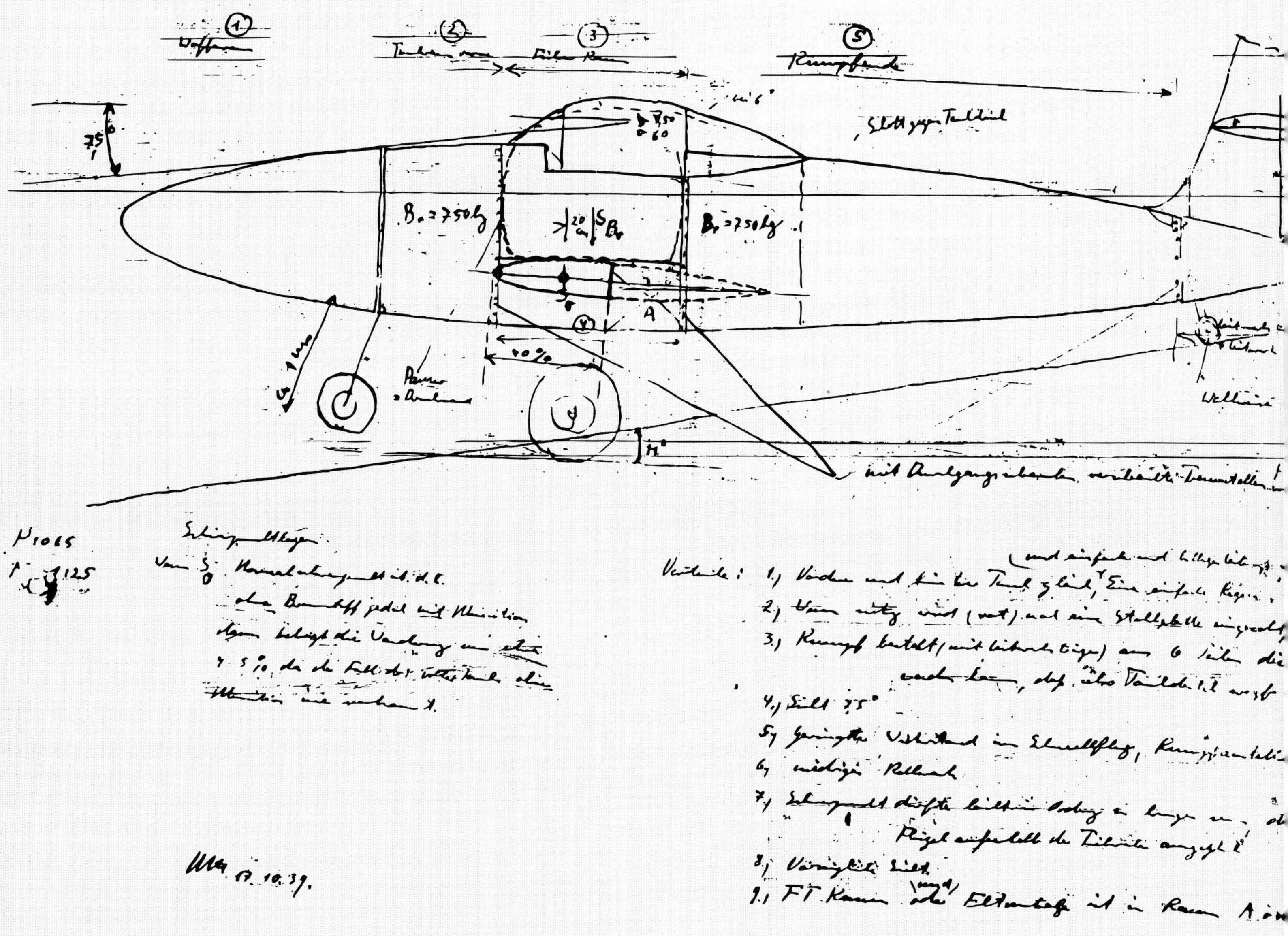

CHAPTER THREE

"A FEVER OF EXPECTATION"

In the autumn of 1938, while Mauch and Schelp were trying to arouse the interest of the aero-engine manufacturers in an official turbojet programme, a corresponding programme for high-speed airframes was being formulated by *Dipl.-Ing.* Hans Martin Antz of Department LC 7 (Airframe Development) of the Technical Office. Antz soon formed a close working relationship with Schelp, who supplied the basic data for jet engines, and, as far as possible, the two development programmes were integrated. Antz was then 29 years old and his academic background bore many similarities to that of Schelp. After obtaining his *Diplom-Ingenieur* degree at Darmstadt Technical University, he had received an International Exchange Fellowship in 1933 to study at the Massachusetts Institute of Technology in the USA. Here he completed a course in engineering and later took up research work on aircraft engines. Antz returned to Germany during the latter part of 1935, and during the following year, he enrolled in the *Flugbaumeister* course at the DVL where the emphasis was on speed and the possibility of increasing aircraft performance by means of improved aerodynamics. After completing his *Flugbaumeister* training, he worked at the *E-Stelle* Rechlin as an experimental engineer and test pilot. In the late summer of 1938 he transferred to LC 7 where he was employed as a *Referent* in *Gruppe III*, which was responsible for fighter aircraft development.

In October 1938, following discussions with Antz, Professor Messerschmitt authorised Robert Lusser, his *Projektbüro* head, to undertake feasibility studies for a single-seat fighter with turbojet propulsion. By the end of December 1938 Messerschmitt had received an official study contract from the Technical Office. Their requirements were outlined on 4 January 1939, in a specification entitled '*Vorläufige technische Richtlinien für schnelle Jagdflugzeuge mit Strahltriebwerk*' (*'Preliminary Technical Criteria for a High-Speed Fighter Aircraft with a Jet Engine'*), issued by LC 7/III. The specification described, in very broad terms, the anticipated requirements for the proposed aircraft. Two versions were proposed, one for the role of high-speed pursuit, the second for target defence. The only difference was that the latter carried less ammunition and had a shorter range.

The essential aspects of the specification were as follows:

Operational Deployment:
(For operations against aerial targets.)
a) High-speed fighter
b) Interceptor fighter *(Heimatschützer)*

Number and type of power plant:
One turbojet engine (make unspecified)

Crew:
One

Armament:
a) *As high speed fighter*
2 x MG 17 machine-guns with 1,000 rpg.
1 x MG 151/20 cannon with 500 rounds.
b) *As interceptor*
2 x MG 17 machine-guns with 500 rpg.
1 x MG 151/20 cannon with 250 rounds.

Installation of weapons:
Possibly in the fuselage, or close to the fuselage

Radio equipment:
FuG VII (radio transmitter/receiver)

Maximum speed:
900 km/h (559 mph)

Landing speed:
Possibly not over 120 km/h (75 mph)

Flight duration:
a) *As high-speed fighter*
1 hour at maximum performance
b) *As interceptor*
30 mins at maximum performance

Airframe:
Complete metal construction throughout. Simple and cheapest construction is required. The construction expense for series aircraft is not to be greater than 3,000 hours.

Dipl.-Ing. Hans Martin Antz of the Airframe Development Department of the RLM's Technisches Amt (centre) photographed with Heinkel's Karl Schwärzler (right) prior to a test flight of the He 280 V2. Gen.-Ing. Gottfried Reidenbach, head of airframe development at the Technisches Amt, stands to the far left.

By early 1939 there were over 8,000 people working for Messerschmitt at Augsburg-Haunstetten, approximately 175 of which were design engineers, split between two departments. Following Lusser's departure in February, Voigt became head of the *Projektbüro* (or *Probü* for short), while detail design was the responsibility of the *Konstruktionsbüro* (or *Kobü*) under *Ing.* Walter Rethel. Voigt's first task had been to work on the Bf 108 and then he became project engineer for the Bf 162 twin-engined high-speed bomber and the Bf 163 liaison aircraft (not to be confused with the Me 163 rocket fighter). In 1939, after working on the design of the Me 210, he suggested to the Technical Office, the fitting of bomb racks to the Bf 109 and Bf 110 for the fighter-bomber *(Jabo)* role.

During the First World War, Rethel had been chief designer for the Kondor Flugzeugwerke and after the end of hostilities he worked for Fokker in the Netherlands where his most notable design was the F.VII airliner that was further developed into the famous trimotor, built under licence by Ford in the USA. In 1926 he returned to Germany where he worked for the fledgling Arado company, being responsible for most of the company's early designs for training and fighter aircraft. The last type on which he worked for Arado was the Ar 80 monoplane fighter, which initially was to have a fixed undercarriage. This aircraft was designed to compete against the Bf 109, but its fixed undercarriage placed it at a serious disadvantage. It was the intention of Walter Blume, Arado's Technical Director to develop a retractable undercarriage for the Ar 80, the design of which was entrusted to Rethel. Unfortunately, he was unable to perfect the operation of this complex undercarriage, which led to friction between himself and Blume. As a result, Rethel left Arado and joined Messerschmitt as head of the *Konstruktionbüro* (Design Office) in March 1938.

Overall responsibility for the design of the jet fighter project was placed in the hands of Woldemar Voigt's *Probü* (Project Office) whose staff included Hans Hornung, Wolfgang Degel, Rudolf Seitz, and Karl Althoff. Aerodynamic expertise was contributed by Riclef Schomerus, Walter Eisenmann, Hans Joachim Puffert and Ludwig Bölkow, the last joining the Aerodynamics and Flight Mechanics section of the Project Office in March 1939, developing the necessary high speed wing profiles.

After receiving brief details of the turbojet engines, Voigt's team began design work on the project. It received the company designation P 1065, but was referred to in most Messerschmitt documents as the P 65. (For the sake of clarity, the authors have used the designation P 1065 when referring to the project). The team's brief was extremely nebulous. All they had to work from was an approximation of the engine's size and weight. From this they attempted to produce an aircraft that would have an endurance of 30 minutes and a speed of 850 km/h (528 mph).

Voigt remembered: "Since both the engine weight formula and manufacturing considerations seemed to favour smaller engines, we suggested to the RLM that the proposed fighter should have two turbojets of about 315 kg (690 lbs) thrust each. We had not, at this stage, sketched out any firm design proposals and we had seriously underestimated the drag divergence Mach number[1] and, in consequence, the speed for which the projected aeroplane was to be designed. Furthermore, owing to our limited experience with the production of combat aircraft at that time, we failed to make allowance for the inevitable weight escalation - new powerplants almost invariably exceed their estimated weight and consume more fuel than anticipated compounded by afterthoughts by the customer that result in demands for more effective and heavier armament and additional equipment."

Perhaps the greatest problem facing the Messerschmitt design team was the lack of information on high speed aerodynamics. At this time Germany possessed only one small high speed wind tunnel at Göttingen, and the results they obtained were treated with considerable caution by the company's project office. Therefore the design of the P 1065 presented the team with a great challenge. Ludwig Bölkow remembers: "We felt that we were participating in a new aviation age. This was the motivation that formed an enthusiastic team living with new problems by day and night. There was a fever of expectation, an eager expectation of the results."

The straight-winged version of the Me 262 free-fall model which was tested by the DFS at Ainring in the period November 1943-March 1944. Here it is seen being unpacked from a storage and transit crate. It was used in comparison with a similar model fitted with swept wings. The tail of the aircraft in the background, right, is that of a disassembled glider.

The straight-winged version of the Me 262 free-fall model which was tested by the DFS at Ainring in the period November 1943-March 1944. It was used in comparison with a similar model fitted with swept wings and had a carefully polished fuselage, but the wings appear to be of more rudimentary construction, because their design was still being finalised.

The first concrete proposal for the fighter evolved from a series of quite different design studies. After the RLM had increased the thrust requirements for the turbojets, Voigt's team began to consider a single engine layout for the new fighter. The earliest proposal to mount the engine inside the fuselage with an intake in the extreme nose and efflux in the tail was quickly abandoned in favour of a twin-boom arrangement similar to that later adopted by the Focke-Wulf *Flitzer* in Germany and the de Havilland Vampire in Britain. This in turn was replaced by a pod and boom layout which, at the expense of a fairly long intake duct, reduced the fuselage cross section and total wetted areas to a minimum. Though this seemed to offer the best possible solution it began to be realised that a single-engine would not offer the performance for which the team were aiming. Therefore, somewhat reluctantly, it was abandoned only to be employed some five years later in the company's P 1101 swept-wing fighter.

Voigt: "The first twin-engined configuration examined was basically a straightforward low-wing aeroplane with the engine nacelles mounted centrally in the wings. The main undercarriage units retracted into the wing fuselage intersection, one main leg being arranged to retract into a well forward of the single main spar and the other into a well aft of the spar. From the viewpoint of drag, this arrangement seemed optimum, but it was unacceptable to us structurally for the attachment points had of necessity to be situated unreasonably far aft for a tailwheel aircraft and we could find no satisfactory method of handling the wing and fuselage forces and moments in the areas cut up by the retracted wheels."

Following these preliminary studies, work on the P 1065 began on 1 April 1939. The first proposal, which was submitted to the RLM on 7 June 1939, had a wing virtually identical in planform to that of the early Bf 109 and Bf 110 with an area of 18 m^2 (194 sq ft). It was to be powered by two BMW TL (*Turbinen-Luftstrahltriebwerk* or turbojets) and specification figures included a span of 9.4 m (30 ft 10 ins), a length of 9.3 m (30 ft 5.25 ins), a height of 2.8 m (9 ft 2.25 ins) and a maximum speed of 840 km/h (522 mph) at 100% thrust. After examining the proposal, the RLM gave permission for construction of a mock-up of the P 1065.

By September 1939 three different armament combinations were being suggested for the P 1065 project. The first proposed the installation of four 7.9 mm MG 17 machine-guns and two 20 mm MG 151 cannon, the second two MG 17s and three MG 151s and the third two 30 mm 30/7 or 30/8 cannon and two MG 151 or four MG 17. In all cases a *Revi* C 12C gunsight was to be provided with a standard FuG VII radio transceiver.

At the same time as these first armament proposals were made, it was also planned to increase the project's wing area to 22 m^2 (237 sq ft) by the fitting of a parallel section to each tip. As can be seen from the following calculated performance figures (dated 29 September 1939), the larger wing gave the project a much improved take-off and landing performance at the expense of maximum speed:

P 1065 - 22 m^2 WING	P 1065 - 18 m^2 WING
Landing speed (landing weight)	
130 km/h (81 mph)	150 km/h (93 mph)
Landing speed (max.weight.)	
154 km/h (96 mph)	177 km/h (110 mph)
Landing weight with ammunition, fuel for 10 mins at 60% performance	
3196 kg (7,050 lbs)	3110 kg (6,860 lbs)
Maximum all-up weight	
4321 kg (9,530 lbs)	4325 kg (9,350 lbs)
Max speed at 3000 m (10,000 ft) with 100% thrust	
840 km/h (522 mph)	915 km/h (569 mph)
Max speed at 3000 m (10,000 ft) with 130% thrust	
950 km/h (590 mph)	975 km/h (606 mph)
Take-off run to 20 m (66 ft) altitude, 100% thrust	
800 m (2,600 ft)	950 m (3,100 ft)
Take-off run to 20 m (66 ft) altitude, 130% thrust	
700 m (2,300 ft)	800 m (2,600 ft)

Two armament combinations were now being preferred, *Bewaffnung I* with three 20 mm MG 151 cannon and *Bewaffnung II* with one 30 mm 30/7 cannon and two 7.9 mm MG 17 machine-guns. Three fuselage fuel tanks were to be provided each protected by 16 mm armour. A pressurized cabin and the experimental FuG 18 radio set were also suggested. In addition to these two proposals, a very lightly armed *Interzeptor* project was suggested but this was soon discarded.

The earliest drawing for the P 1065 so far discovered is a hand sketch, dated 17 October 1939, and originated from Messerschmitt's own hand. This shows that the Professor favoured an oval section fuselage *(ovale Rumpfform)*, mid wing, tricycle undercarriage and horizontal tail positioned halfway up the fin. Because of the complexity of undercarriage stowage described earlier by Voigt, another study was produced by the Project Office with a triangular section fuselage *(dreieckige Rumpfform)* and a low-mounted wing which would slightly increase the wing area from 22 m^2 to 22.4 m^2 (241 sq ft). This in turn would allow the mainwheels to be stowed flat in the base of the fuselage centre section. This design was that preferred by the project team, in particular by Degel, Althoff and Seitz. The advantages of these two layouts were compared in some detail in a report dated 15 December 1939.

The conclusions (with comments by a contemporary project engineer) were as follows:

ADVANTAGES OF THE MID-WING CONFIGURATION

1) **Low thrust moment.** *This relates to the vertical relationship of the centre of gravity of the complete aircraft and the engines' thrust axes. If both coincide then there is no change in the pitching moment about the centre of gravity when thrust is applied. If the thrust axis is below the centre of gravity then the nose of the aircraft will pitch up when thrust is applied and vice versa.*
2) **Reduced total height (undercarriage).** *This advantage derives from the relationship of the fuselage to the ground when the undercarriage is extended. Depending on where the engines are located, however, the main undercarriage length will be longer (more weight) for a mid-wing design than for a low-wing configuration. The closer the fuselage to the ground, the easier it is for the pilot to reach into the cockpit.*

ADVANTAGES OF THE LOW WING CONFIGURATION

1) **Highest possible location of horizontal tail surfaces in relation to the wing (downwash, temperature).** *This advantage relates to engine exhaust effects on the horizontal tail (temperature) and the placement of the tailplane away from the wake/downwash/airflow behind the wing, i.e. the tailplane was located in a position free of turbulence. At the time the Me 262 was conceived this high tailplane position was acceptable because the aircraft was designed to fly at less than high subsonic speeds. In the 1950s, when aircraft started to fly above the speed of sound, it was discovered that the high tailplane position could lead to longitudinal instability of the aircraft at supersonic speeds. This was the main reason why the tailplanes were later located below the level of the wing (e.g., the British Lightning) or had a large amount of anhedral (e.g., the American Phantom).*
2) **Smallest possible overall dimensions (length).** *The advantage derives from being able to position the fuselage over the top of the wing. At that time the spars of a mid-wing design would have been attached to full fuselage bulkheads located at the positions of the spars, thus perhaps increasing fuselage length unnecessarily. This disadvantage could have been overcome by attaching the spars to ring frames, but this might have added weight and caused production problems. There*

Messerschmitt P 65 with 2 x BMW P.3304 turbojets fitted below wings (14 July 1940)

Messerschmitt P 65 with 2 x BMW P.3304 turbojet fitted above wings (14 July 1940)

was a preference at that time to build single piece wings to simplify production (increased production rates) and to simplify their attachment and replacement in the event of damage.

3) **Tanks of similar capacity.** *Here the advantage derives from the fact that the low wing does not interfere with the internal layout of the fuselage. Messerschmitt, however, proposed fitting tanks of equal capacity forward and aft of the cockpit so that there would be no or little movement of the centre-of-gravity as the fuel was used.*

4) **Improved view (downwards, sideways across the engines).** *There is an advantage if the engines are located below the pilot's line of sight when he is looking sideways out of the cockpit. Early project drawings show the engines alongside and ahead of the pilot. In this position, they would have blocked the pilot's forward field of view, a disadvantage in combat.*

5) **Energy absorption during belly landings.** *Here the wings and not the fuselage would have absorbed the impact on landing. At that time the engines were located within the wing. Later, the engines were located below the wing, in which case they would have taken the brunt of the crash landing. This would have lead to rupture of the wing and possibly have resulted in the aircraft catching fire, even though the wings did not contain fuel.*

6) **Lower critical speed of the airflow over the upper surface of the wing (effectiveness of the wing fillets at the wing/fuselage junction)** *This advantage relates to the onset of compressibility effects at high subsonic speeds. The introduction of the wing leading edge fillet (initially very small) reduced the interference at the wing/fuselage junction, i.e. smoothed the airflow. It is not known if Messerschmitt at that time appreciated the fact that an increase in chord length effectively reduces the thickness/chord ratio which in turn delays the onset of compressibility. This effect is similar to increasing the sweep of the wing.*

7) **Less interference between the fuselage and engine nacelles.** *This advantage relates to interference drag.*

8) **Reduced temperature effects on the fuselage.** *Concerns effects of heat from engine efflux.*

9) **Nearly horizontal fuselage axis.** *This advantage applies only if the aircraft is fitted with a tricycle undercarriage but this was not fitted to early prototypes.*

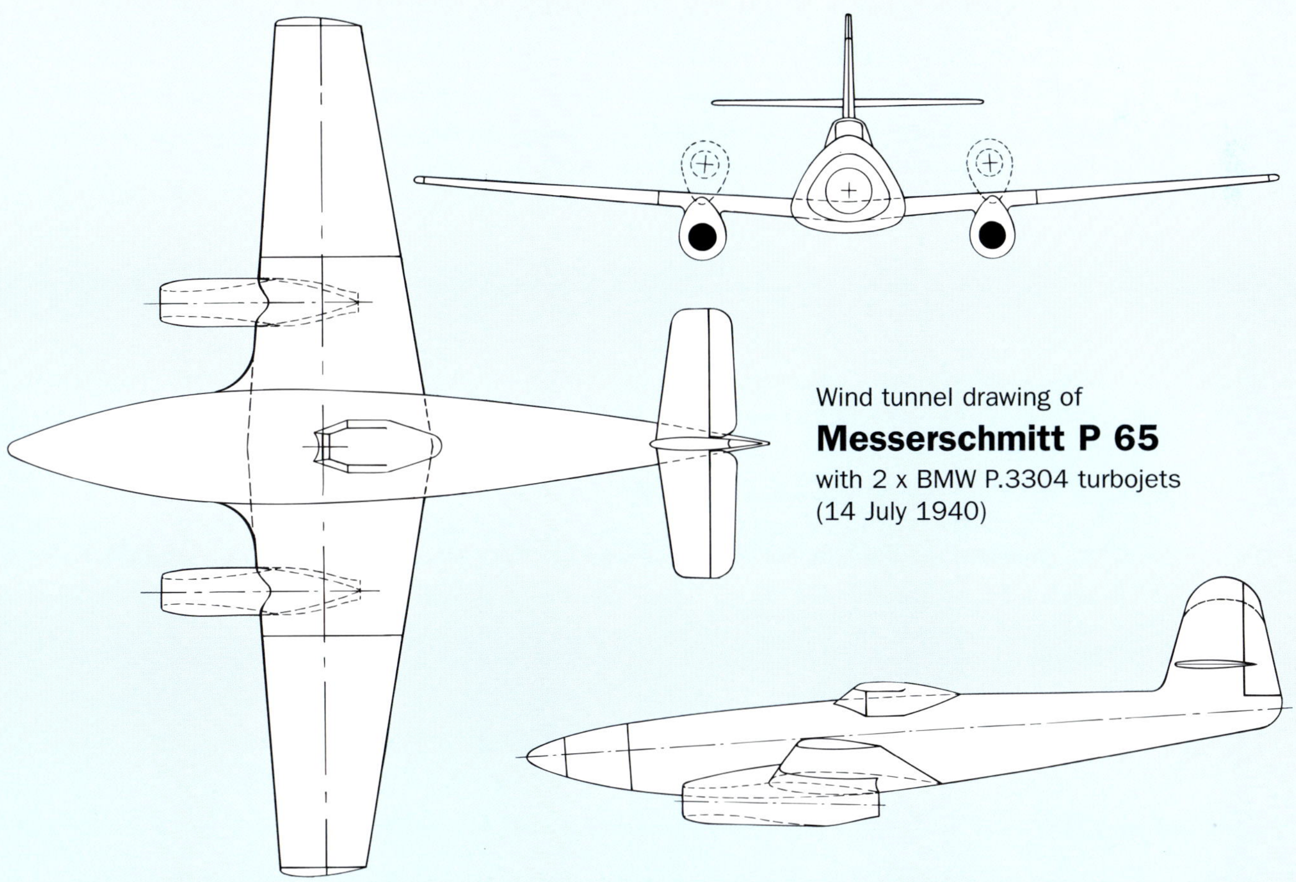

Wind tunnel drawing of
Messerschmitt P 65
with 2 x BMW P.3304 turbojets
(14 July 1940)

As Voigt remembered: "We had now reached the point of deciding which configuration would form the basis of our submission to the RLM. The choice was now between our mid-wing study and our low-wing concept which we now tended to favour. From some aspects the choice was a difficult one: the mid-wing concept with its smaller oval cross section fuselage offered a smaller wetted area, but its complex swivel-wheel undercarriage offended our religious belief that an acceptable design must be simple and cheap to manufacture and maintain. Thus, we submitted our proposal based on the low wing concept."

The wing itself was still similar in planform to the Bf 109 E but by February 1940 Bölkow's theoretical calculations had produced the Wxy-E 4 series of wing profiles which were later tested successfully in the AVA wind tunnel at Göttingen. In fact these were never fitted to the Me 262, but later became an important feature of the design of the post-war North American F-86 Sabre. Two engine layouts were proposed initially; either two BMW P.3302 engines slung beneath the wings or two of the slimmer BMW P.3304s mounted centrally but, by November 1939, a third engine had also entered the picture when details of Anselm Franz's Junkers T 1 (Jumo 004 A) became available.

On 19 December 1939, a mock-up of the P 1065 was inspected by representatives of LC 2/III, with a mock-up of the proposed cabin layout being examined a month later. By early February 1940 a description of the layout proposed for the first prototype was issued. Two BMW P.3302 engines were to be mounted below the wings, the leading edges of the outer sections of which were now to be swept back some 18 degrees. This was done originally to solve problems that higher engine weight estimates and an increase in diameter of the turbojets from 600 to 690 mm (23.5 to 27 inches) were causing with the aircraft's centre of gravity. Subsequent investigation was to show that this sweep-back decreased compressibility effects and therefore substantially improved the aircraft's limiting Mach number.

On 1 March 1940, it was proposed that 20 prototypes of the P 1065 would be completed, all powered by BMW P.3302 engines. Fifteen days later, Messerschmitt issued its first *Projektübergabe* (project description) on the P 1065. Some pages in this 22 page report are dated as early as 9 November 1939, with others at least five months later. This causes problems for the historian in attempting to fix how the design was advancing at a particular date. What is known is that by March 1940, it had a straight wing with an area of 18.1 m^2 (195 sq ft) and a span of 10.4 m (34 ft 1 3/4 ins). Even at this stage an alternative wing with the swept outer panels was being considered. The prototype was to be powered by two BMW P.3302 engines slung beneath the wings (although the Junkers T 1 unit was being considered as an alternative). For series production machines, the much smaller centrally-mounted P.3304 was still favoured. At this stage all these engines were designed to produce 600 kg (1,320 lbs) thrust at sea level. Two fuel tanks were to be mounted in the centre of the fuselage protected by 16 mm armour plate, and armament was crystalising around three 20 mm MG 151 cannon in the nose. In addition an ejection seat and dive brakes were to be provided, as were leading edge slots.

The leading edge slots for thin wings were patented by Ludwig Bölkow. Similar to Handley Page slots, they were free enough to be operated by one finger when on the ground and would open automatically when the pilot was pulling the aeroplane hard in a manoeuvre or flying it slowly. Their action was to allow high energy air to flow through them and over the upper surface of the wing, providing the pilot with extra lift. In practice they were exceedingly gentle and benign in operation and worked very smoothly.

The early project report was soon replaced on 12 April by a second and much more detailed report known as *Projektübergabe II*. This detailed two different wing areas intended for the aircraft: 18.1 m^2 (span 10.4 m) and 20 m^2 (span 12.35 m). Like the earlier report, the project was to be powered by two BMW P.3302 engines under the wings, the series production aircraft by two centrally mounted P.3304s though this engine was already suffering development problems. The P 1065 was also to be fitted with an ejection seat, a pressurized cabin and a braking parachute. A tailwheel undercarriage was to be provided, the mainwheels measuring 770 x 270 mm (30.3 x 10.6 inches), the tailwheel 380 x 150 mm (15 x 6 inches). Armament was standardised as three MG 151 cannon in the nose, possibly supplemented by two MG 17 machine-guns. It was also planned to install air brakes above the wings, a feature that was never fitted to any aircraft but one which would have proved extremely valuable to combat pilots. Radio equipment was standardised as the FuG VII

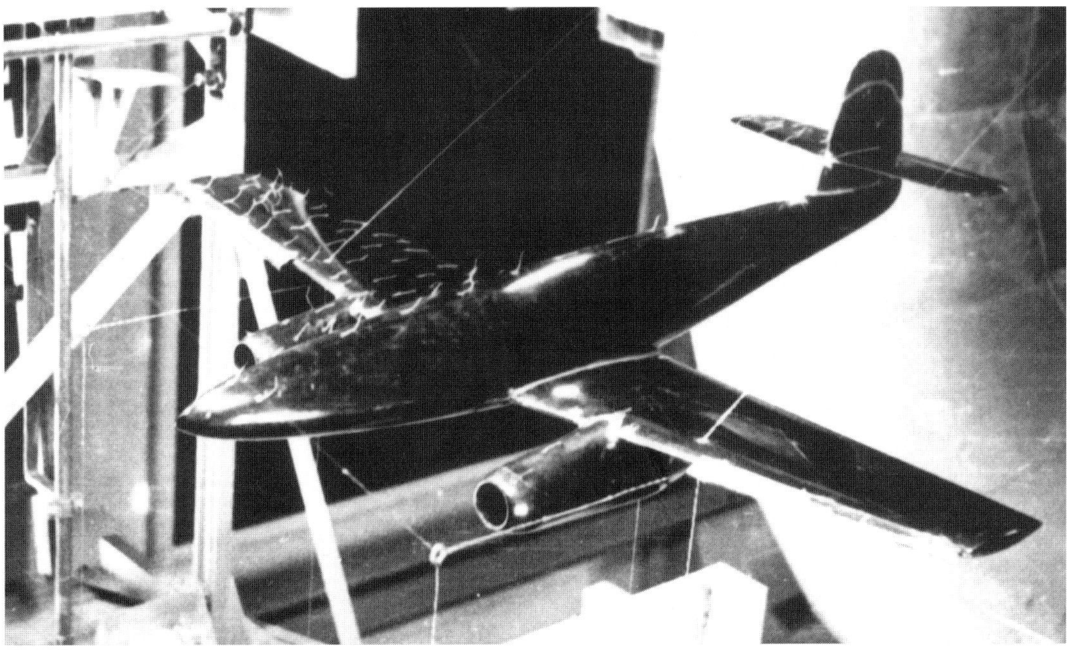

Wind tunnel tests being carried out with the early Messerschmitt P 1065 design with straight wing and underslung BMW P.3302 engines. At this stage, as can be seen in these photographs, the wing was very similar in planform to that of the Bf 109 E.

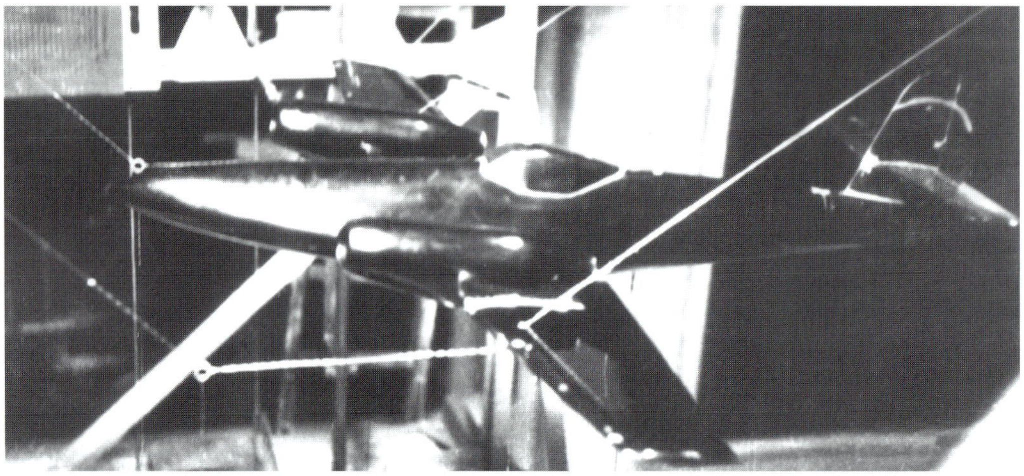

As an alternative to the underslung turbojets, Messerschmitt proposed mounting them above the wing as can be seen in these wind tunnel models.

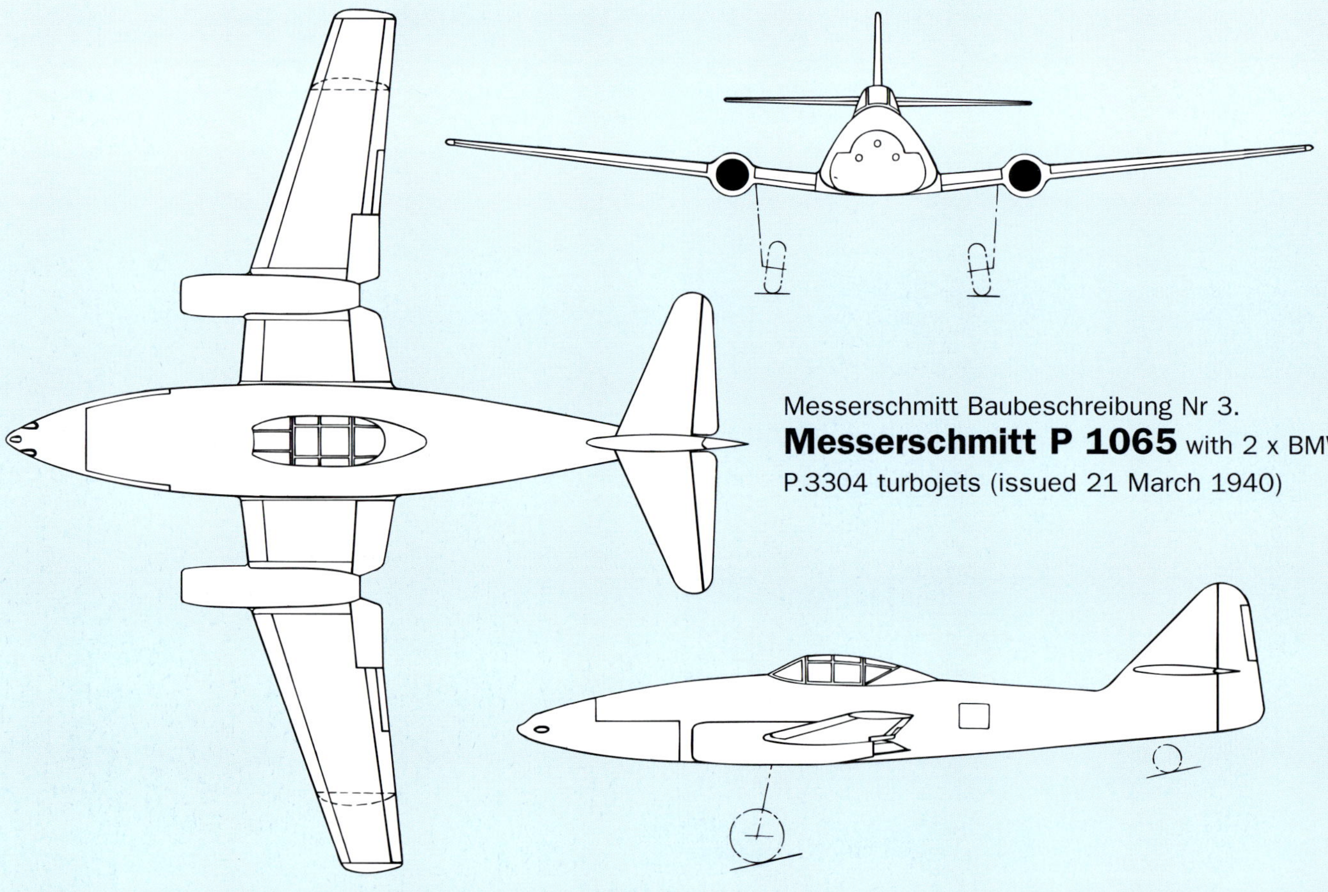

Messerschmitt Baubeschreibung Nr 3.
Messerschmitt P 1065 with 2 x BMW P.3304 turbojets (issued 21 March 1940)

The overwing engine layout designed for the Messerschmitt P 1065 was tested in the wind tunnel at the AVA – Aerodynamische Versuchsanstalt – Aerodynamic Test Establishment at Göttingen. These photos show the crude streamlining applied to the test model.

Above: A wind tunnel model of the Messerschmitt P 1065 project with the centrally-mounted BMW P.3304 engines. These engines, of remarkably slim dimensions, were finally abandoned during the middle of 1942.

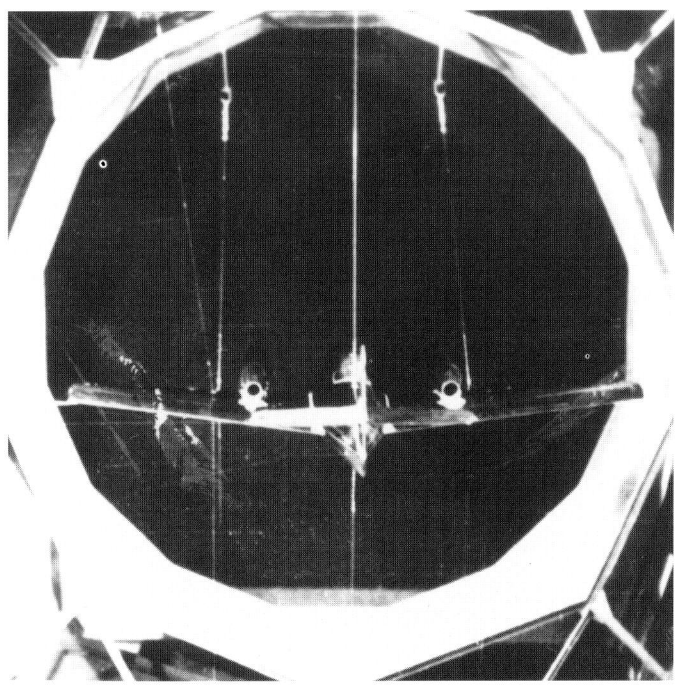

Messerschmitt P 1065 first project with "Bf 109 wing"

The first firm P 1065 proposal was submitted to the RLM on 7 June 1939 had a wing virtually identical in planform to that of the early Bf 109. It was to be powered by two BMW turbojets, preferably of the P.3304 (109-002) type developed by Bramo, mounted centrally in the wings.

Messerschmitt P 1065 second project with swept-back wing

By February 1940, the design of the P 1065 had been modified to have the outer sections of its wings swept back some 18 degrees. Originally this was done to solve problems that heavier engine weight estimates were causing with the positioning of the aircraft's centre of gravity. The BMW P.3304 turbojets were still proposed at this time.

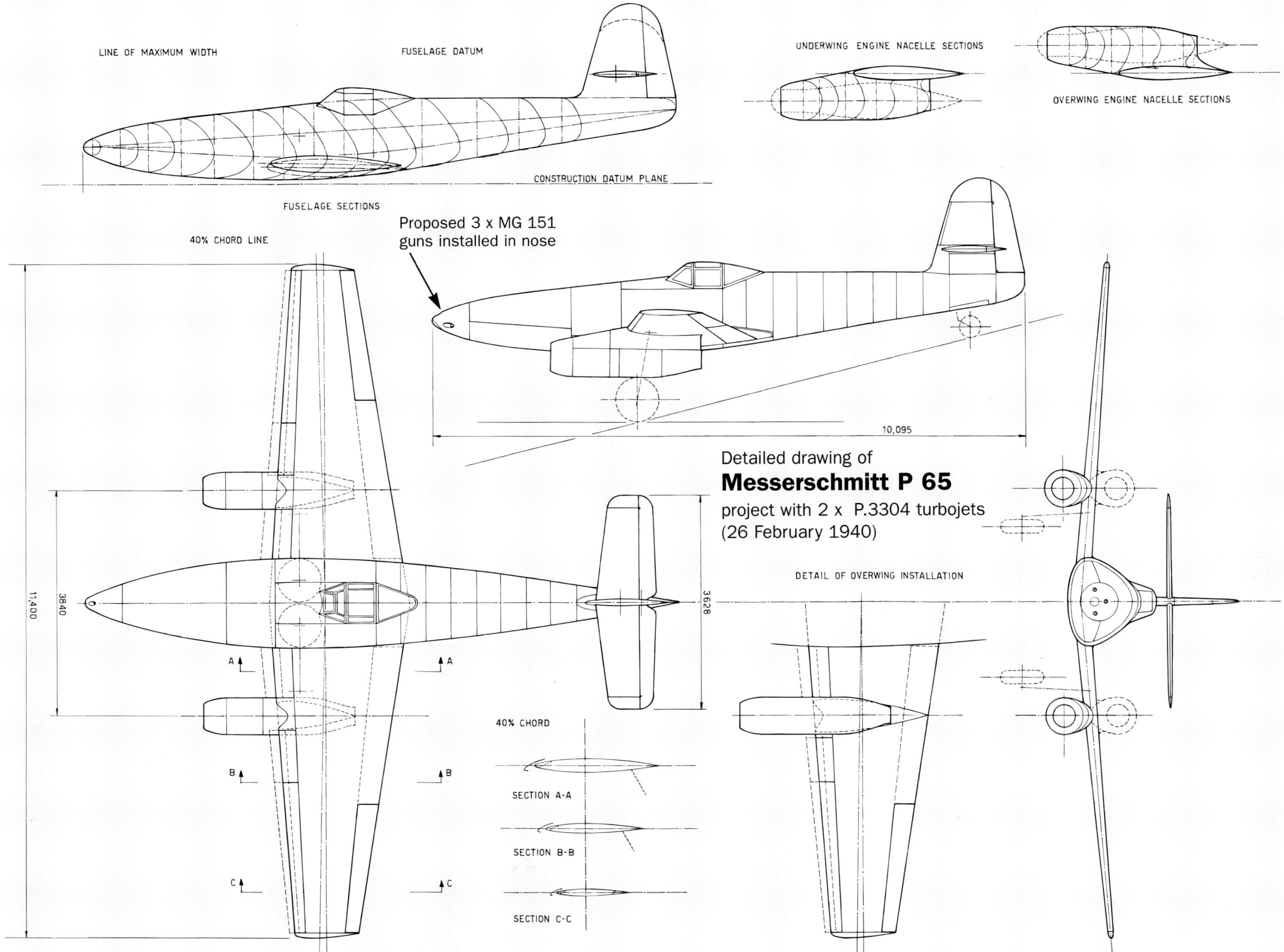

Detailed drawing of
Messerschmitt P 65
project with 2 x P.3304 turbojets
(26 February 1940)

transmitter/receiver and FuG 25 IFF. Dimensions, estimated weights and maximum speeds for the alternative wings were as follows:

Wing area		
	18 m^2	20 m^2
	194 sq ft	215 sq ft
Wing span		
	10.4 m	12.35 m
	34 ft 1.5 ins	40 ft 6.25 ins
Length		
	10.6 m	10.6 m
	34 ft 9.25 ins	34 ft 9.25 ins
Height (minus undercarriage)		
	2.8 m	2.8 m
	9 ft 2.25 ins	9 ft 2.25 ins
Empty weight		
	2,872 kg	3,030 kg
	6,330 lbs	6,673 lbs
Loaded weight		
	4,442 kg	4,510 kg
	9,790 lbs	9,936 lbs
Maximum speed		
	793 km/h	744 km/h
	493 mph	462 mph

This second proposal was submitted to the RLM on 15 May 1940.

The major problem besetting Voigt's team at this time was that the thrust of the BMW turbojets had yet to be confirmed by Oestrich, and the P.3304, as we have seen, was suffering major development problems. To help with the testing of these engines, Messerschmitt put forward a proposal to make available two Bf 110s for use as engine test beds.[2] By the spring of 1940, the design of the Jumo 004 A had been completed by Franz's team and this gave the Messerschmitt designers another option.

Problems with the engines led Messerschmitt to produce a third *Projektübergabe*. This, like the earlier report had pages dated between 30 May 1940 and 4 April 1941. In order to get the prototype P 1065 flying as soon as possible, it was proposed to fit it with a single 700 hp Jumo 210 G piston engine in the nose, using a similar installation to that of the Bf 109 D. As soon as they became available, two BMW P.3302 engines were to be mounted under the wings (in July 1940 the AVA at Göttingen carried out tests with both under and *over* wing engine installations). The forward fuel tank would be used to supply the piston engine, the rear fuel tank, the two turbojets. The estimated empty and loaded weights were 3,720 kg (8,200 lbs) and 4,665 kg (10,280 lbs).

It was fortunate that Messerschmitt proposed conducting initial flying tests with a piston engine in the nose of the P 1065 because problems continued to be experienced with the development of all three turbojet types. As these problems continued to manifest themselves, Messerschmitt put forward another proposal on 10 January 1941, to power the first prototype with two Walter R II 211 (RLM designation 109-509) rocket engines. A maximum speed of 690 km/h (429 mph) was anticipated, but powered endurance was only seven minutes. By this time, the construction of five P 1065 prototypes was proposed, as follows:

- **P 1065 V1** with one Jumo 210 G piston engine and two 750 kg (1,650 lbs) thrust Walter rocket engines.
- **P 1065 V2** with one Jumo 210 G and two 600 kg (1,320 lbs) thrust BMW P.3302 (or Jumo TL) turbojets.
- **P 1065 V3** with TL (turbojets) only.
- **P 1065 V4** with TL (turbojets) only.
- **P 1065 V5** with *Pfeilflügel* (swept-back wing).

After wind tunnel testing at Göttingen had shown that sweeping the wing back 18 degrees improved the aircraft's limiting Mach number, a proposal was outlined, on 4 April 1941, to develop a 35 degree swept back wing under the designation *Pfeilflügel I*. This was to have an area of 20 m^2 (215 sq ft) and a span of 10 m (32 ft 9.5 ins). Wind tunnel tests with the wing were made by the AVA in June 1941 and led, eventually, to the Me 262 HG II project described in a later volume of this work.

Wind tunnel model of the P 1065 in its final design configuration of April 1943 showing the slender, centrally-positioned BMW P.3302 engines. The outer-wing panels show a swept-back design later used in the early Me 262 prototypes.

Evolution of Wing Design

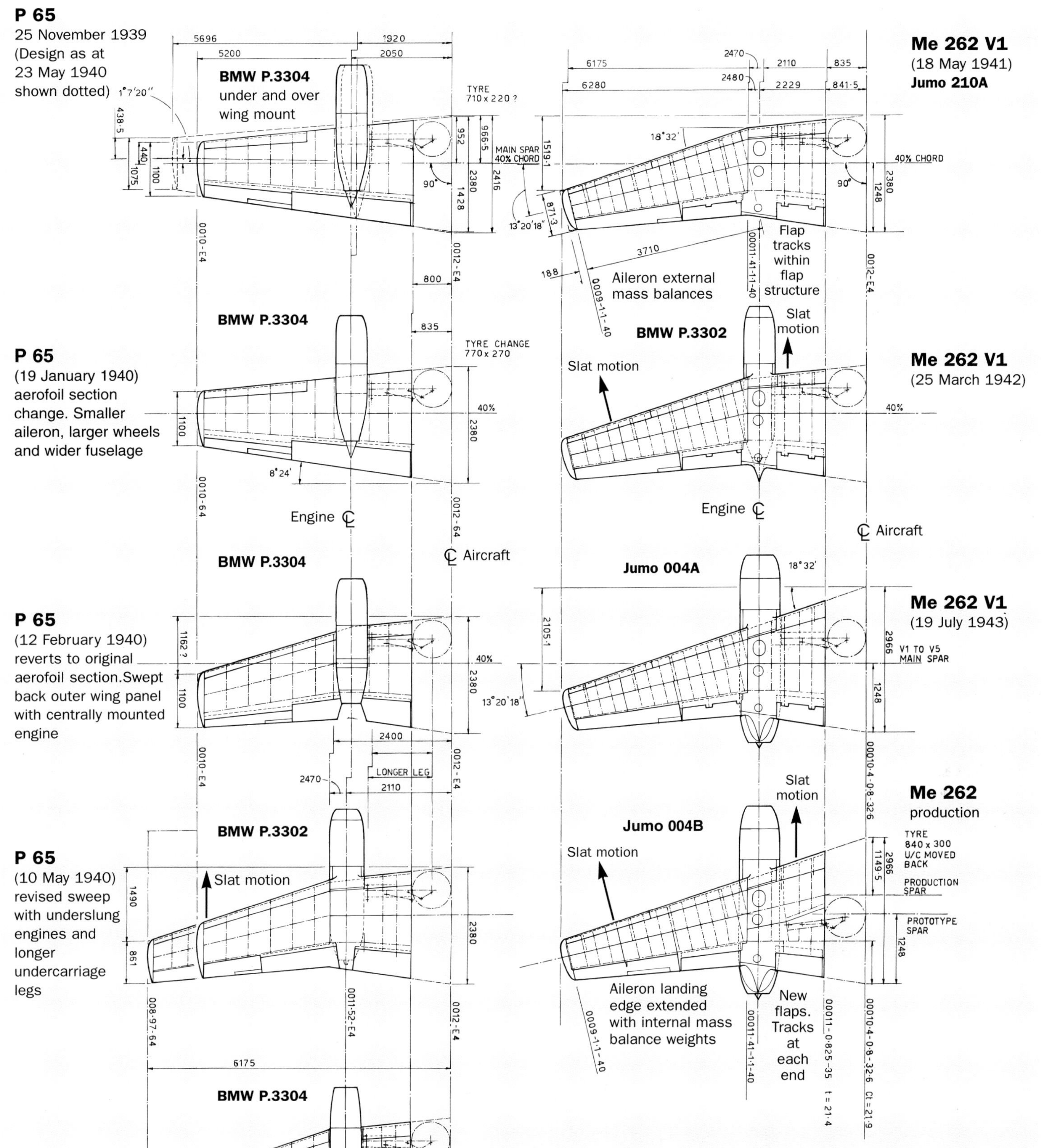

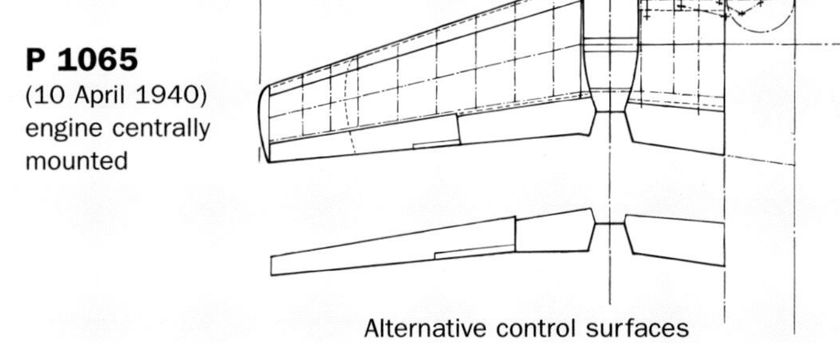

The dates shown on these drawings were taken from official documents which in some cases contradict the exact evolution of the wing designs. The spread of dates on these designs suggest that some may have been re-issues of pages taken from other reports. The wing layouts have been arranged in the order of evolutionary development as taken from several key datum dimensions which show the logical progression of the design.
These are:- (a) increase wing span to cater for weight increase. (b) change of tyre sizes - forcing wider fuselage which also indicates progressive weight increase. (c) increase in undercarriage leg length - to give ground clearance for the ever increasing engine sizes. (d) location of engine datums resulting from changes to the undercarriage.

Note:- The actual production aircraft had twice as many wing ribs which were configured at right angles to the main spar and not in line of flight as compared with the Projects. This is indicative of the increasing weight problems but also served to increase the wing stiffness needed for high speed flight. Aligning the ribs in this way provided more favourable slat track geometry which resulted in much more efficient increase in the operation of the wing slats on the outer wing sections.

Messerschmitt P 1065
Internal layout (21 March 1940)

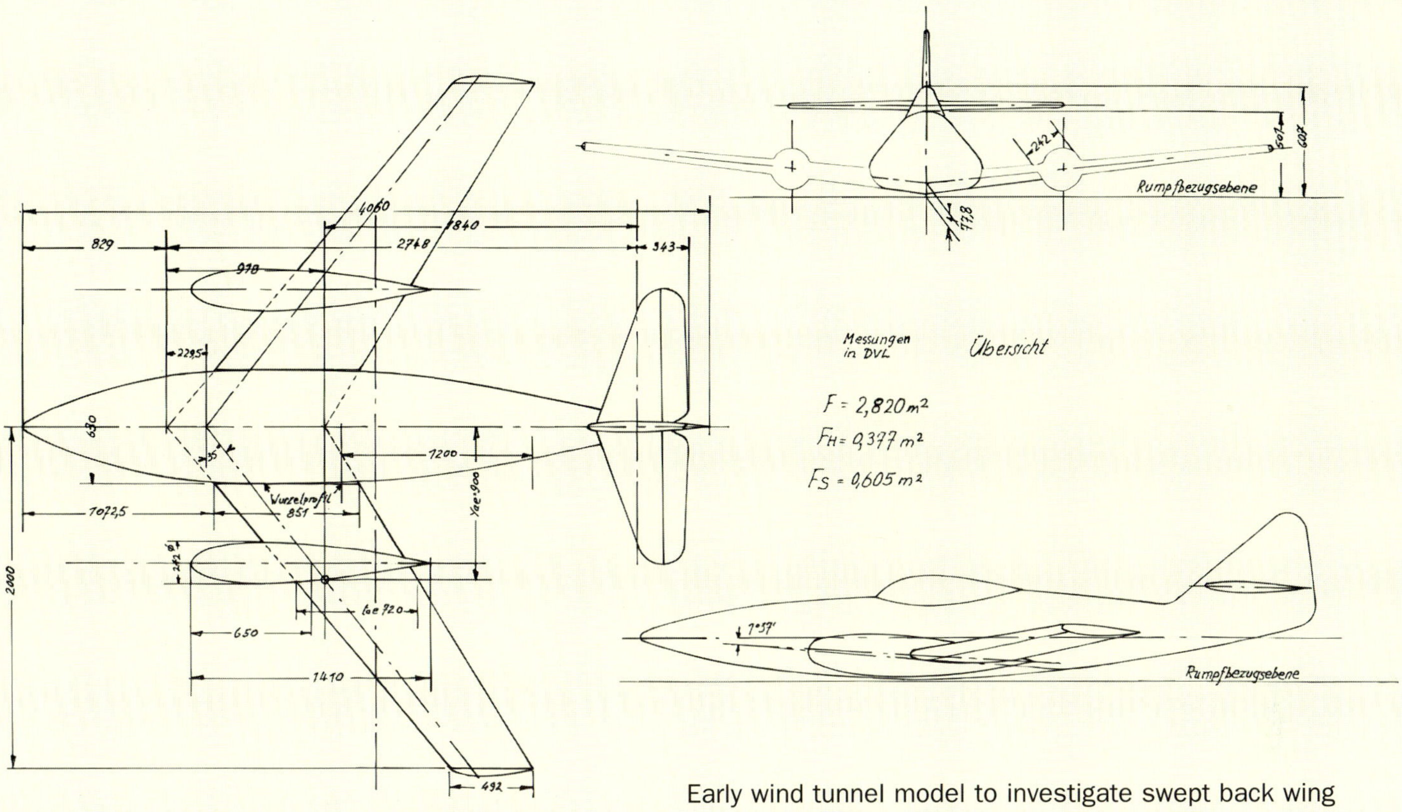

Early wind tunnel model to investigate swept back wing (Document dated 1940)

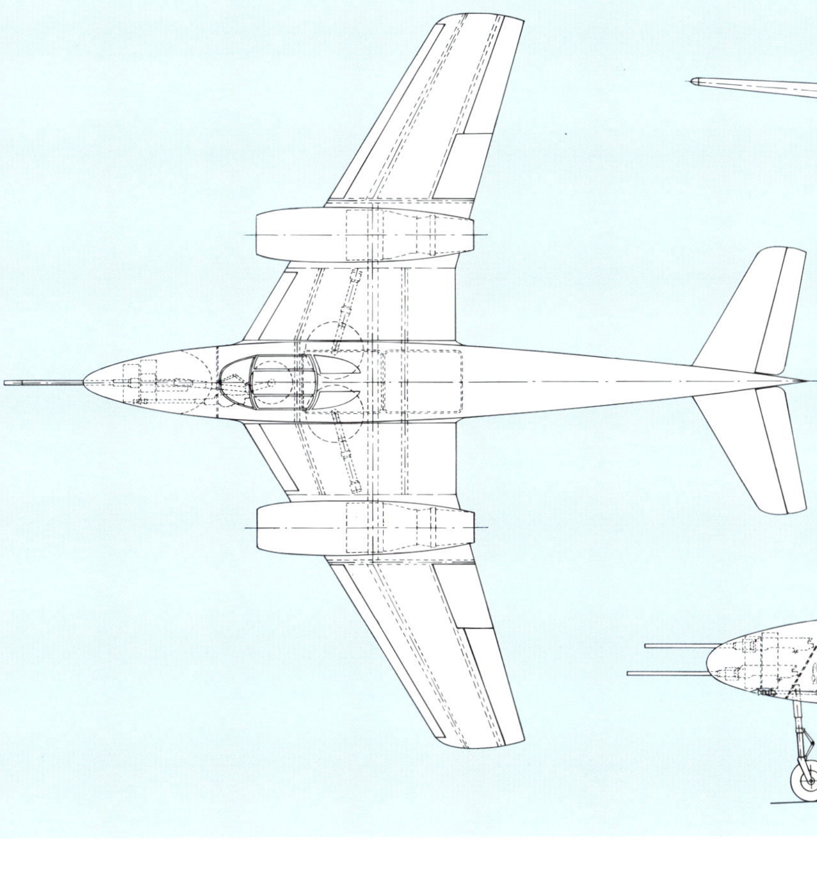

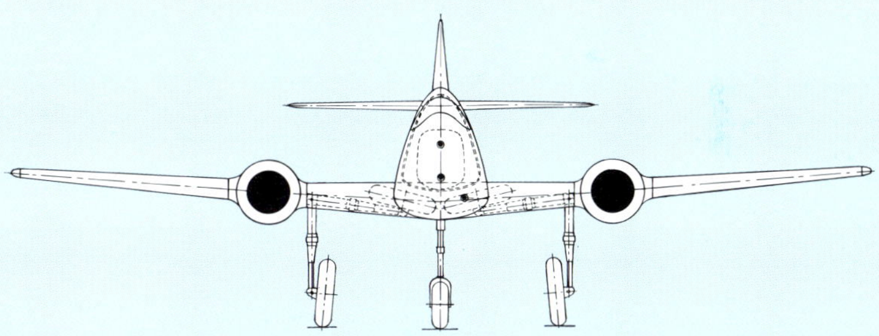

Messerschmitt P 1070 (P 70)

This was a smaller parallel running project design as an alternative to the P 65. The original drawing is dated simply 1940. The design featured a tricycle undercarriage with a wing span of 8.3 m and length of 7.2 m. Max. speed 1,100 km/h. The engines proposed were 2 x BMW P.3304 turbojets. Armament 2 x MG 151s and 1 x MG 17 mounted in the nose.

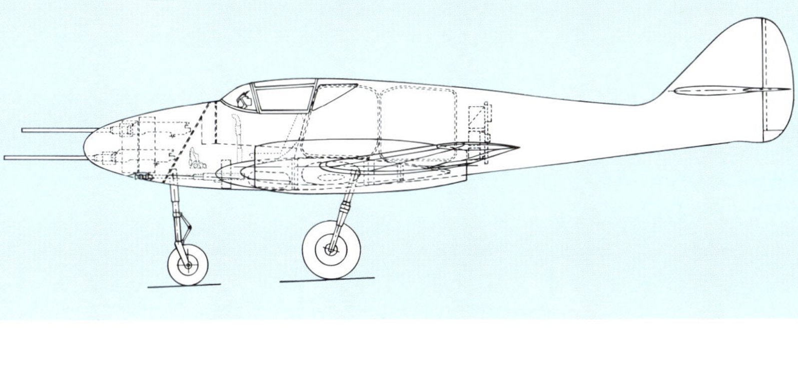

Heinkel test pilot Fritz Schäfer standing on the wing of the He 280 V2 with Robert Lusser second from the right. The He 280 was the world's first turbojet driven fighter, making its maiden flight on 30 March 1941 with Schäfer at the controls.

Construction of the first P 1065 prototype took place between February and March 1941, the project receiving the official RLM designation Me 262 on 8 April. Just previously, on 30 March, Heinkel's jet fighter, the He 280 had made its first flight powered by two 720 kg (1,590 lbs) thrust HeS 8A turbojets.

At 19.35 on the evening of 18 April, the Me 262 V1 flew for the first time from Augsburg. It was piloted by the Messerschmitt test pilot, *Flugkapitän* Fritz Wendel. At this stage the aircraft (W.Nr.262 000 0001, carrying the radio call sign PC+UA) was powered by a single 700 hp Jumo 210 G piston engine (W.Nr.42013) in the nose. Subsequent tests were to show that the prototype, fitted with this engine, could attain a maximum speed of 420 km/h (261 mph) in level flight and 540 km/h (335 mph) in a dive from 7,000 m (23,000 ft).

Ludwig Bölkow remembers the excellent co-operation between the test pilots and the designers at that time: "Flight test reports were at the disposal of the development engineers a few hours after each flight. In important tests we often awaited the return of the pilots in the flight test centre. Immediately after landing the pilots informed us of the results of measurements and of their general impressions during flight. We could ask them questions and discuss problems with them. Relevant results that required changes were discussed with Professor Messerschmitt himself - often on the same day - and the measures to be taken were ordered immediately."

On 25 July 1941, the Technical Office issued order LC 2/T.St. Nr. 6303/41 (III) which called for the construction of five V-series and twenty pre-production (0-series) Me 262s. The first

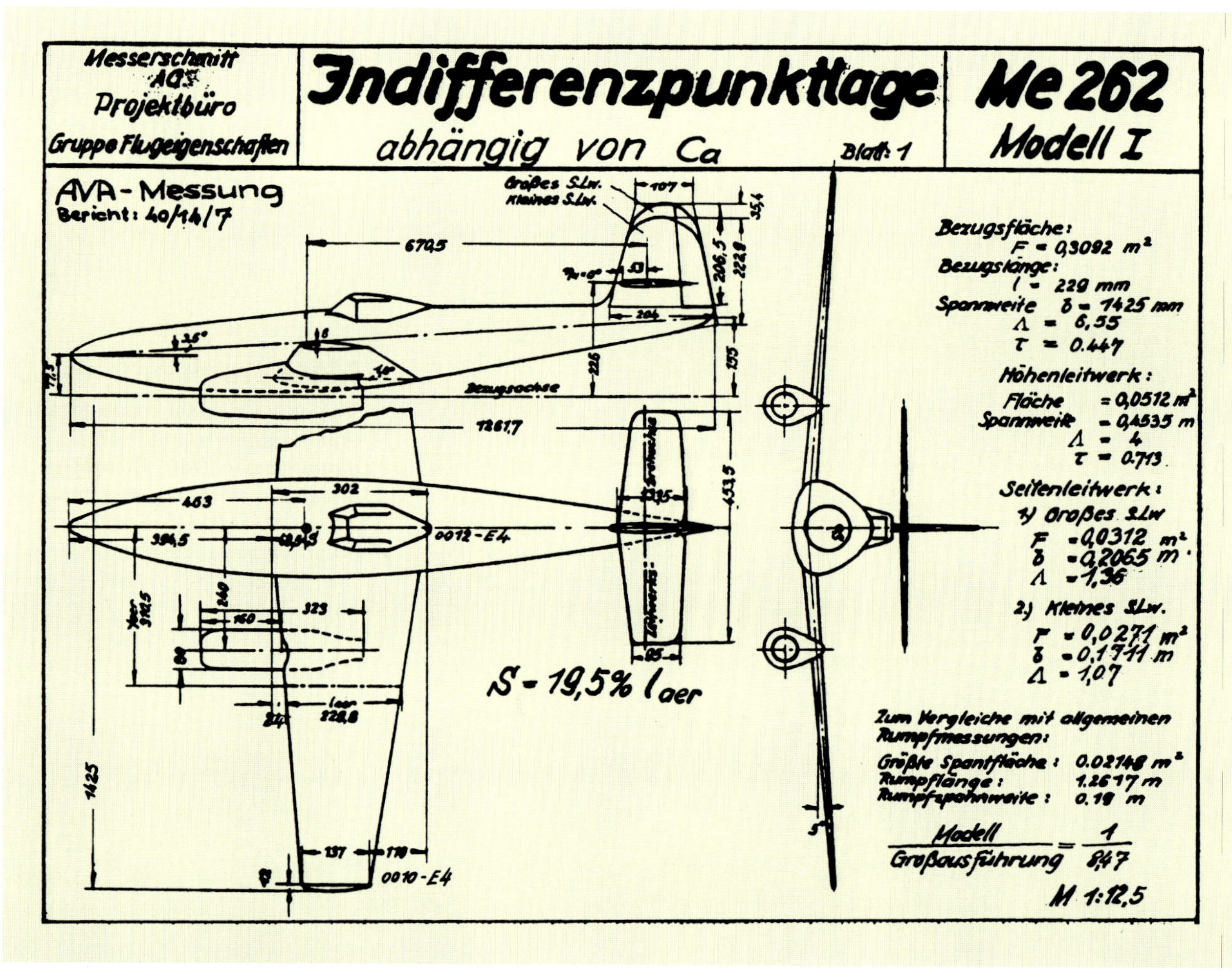

A Messerschmitt Projektbüro drawing dated 6 March 1940 of a proposed wind tunnel model of the P 1065 showing the dimensions and technical data. This is one of the earliest known occasions that the designation "Me 262" appears on a Messerschmitt document even though the project design is P 65 and the RLM had still not applied "Me 262" officially at this time. The English translation of "Indifferenzpunktlage" means "Neutral Point Position Dependent on Lift Coefficient". This document was prepared by AVA wind tunnel engineers E. Hildenbrand and A. Scherer.

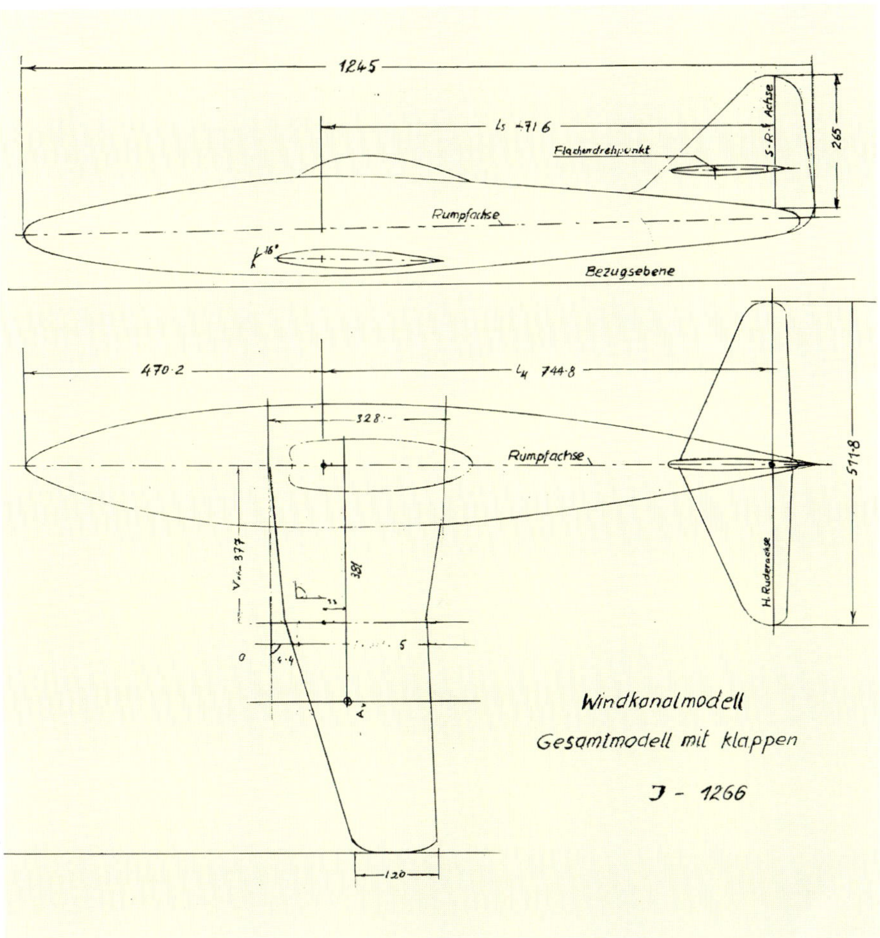

Wind tunnel tests at the AVA at Göttingen were to show that the 18 degree swept back outer wing panels much improved the P 1065's limiting Mach number.

Messerschmitt P 1065 final project with swept wing of increased area

By April 1940 two wings of different areas had been proposed for the P 1065 project. The latter, and that eventually preferred, had a span of 12.35 m (40 ft 6in) instead of 10.4 m (34 ft 1½ in). At this stage two BMW P.3302 turbojets were to be mounted under the wings with series production aircraft (as shown in this drawing) having two centrally mounted P.3304s.

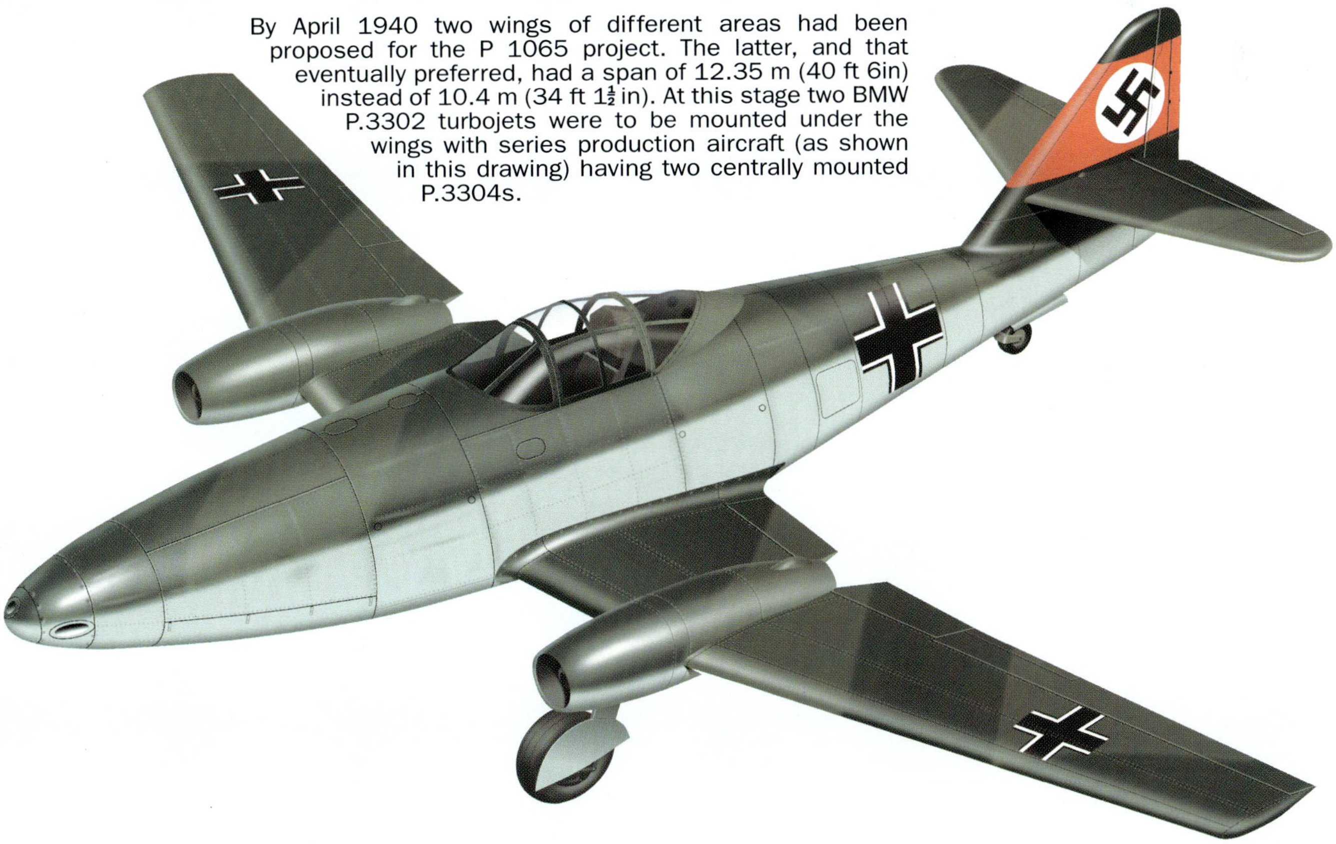

A typical Jumo 210 G installation as fitted to a Bf 109 D fighter. This arrangement was very similar to that fitted to the Me 262 V1.

Left: The Me 262 V1, PC+UA which was fitted with a Jumo 210 G piston engine in the nose. To save time the installation was adapted from that of a Bf 109 D single-engined fighter.
Below: Photographs of the early Me 262 prototypes are, unfortunately, rare. This shows, at left, the V1 with the Jumo 210 G piston engine, carrying the four letter code PC+UA.

Close-up of the oil cooler fitted to the Jumo 210 G (W.Nr.42103) piston engine installation used by the Me 262 V1.

To enable the airframe of the Me 262 to be flight tested, the V1 was fitted with a Jumo 210 G engine in the nose. This photo shows the large radiator which was mounted below the engine.

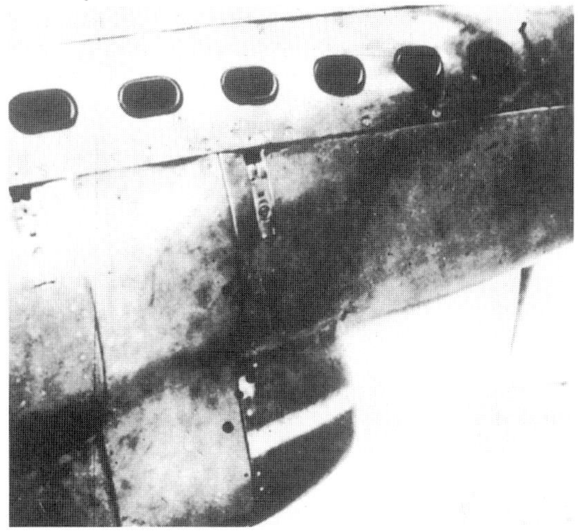

This close-up shows the Jumo 210 G installation fitted to the Me 262 V1. Copied from that of the Bf 109 D, the 700 hp engine enabled the prototype to attain a maximum speed of 420 km/h (261 mph) in level flight and 540 km/h (335 mph) in a dive from 7,000 m (23,000 ft).

Canopy of the Me 262 V1.

Messerschmitt Me 262 V1 PC+UA W.Nr. 262 000 0001

Below: Several functional tests were carried out with a compressed air ejector seat in both the Me 262 V1 and Me 210 V14. The photo shows the three air containers which were pressurized to 120 atü (atmospheres) to provide the power for the seat. *Right*: This photo shows the ejector seat mechanism experimentally fitted to the Me 262 V1.

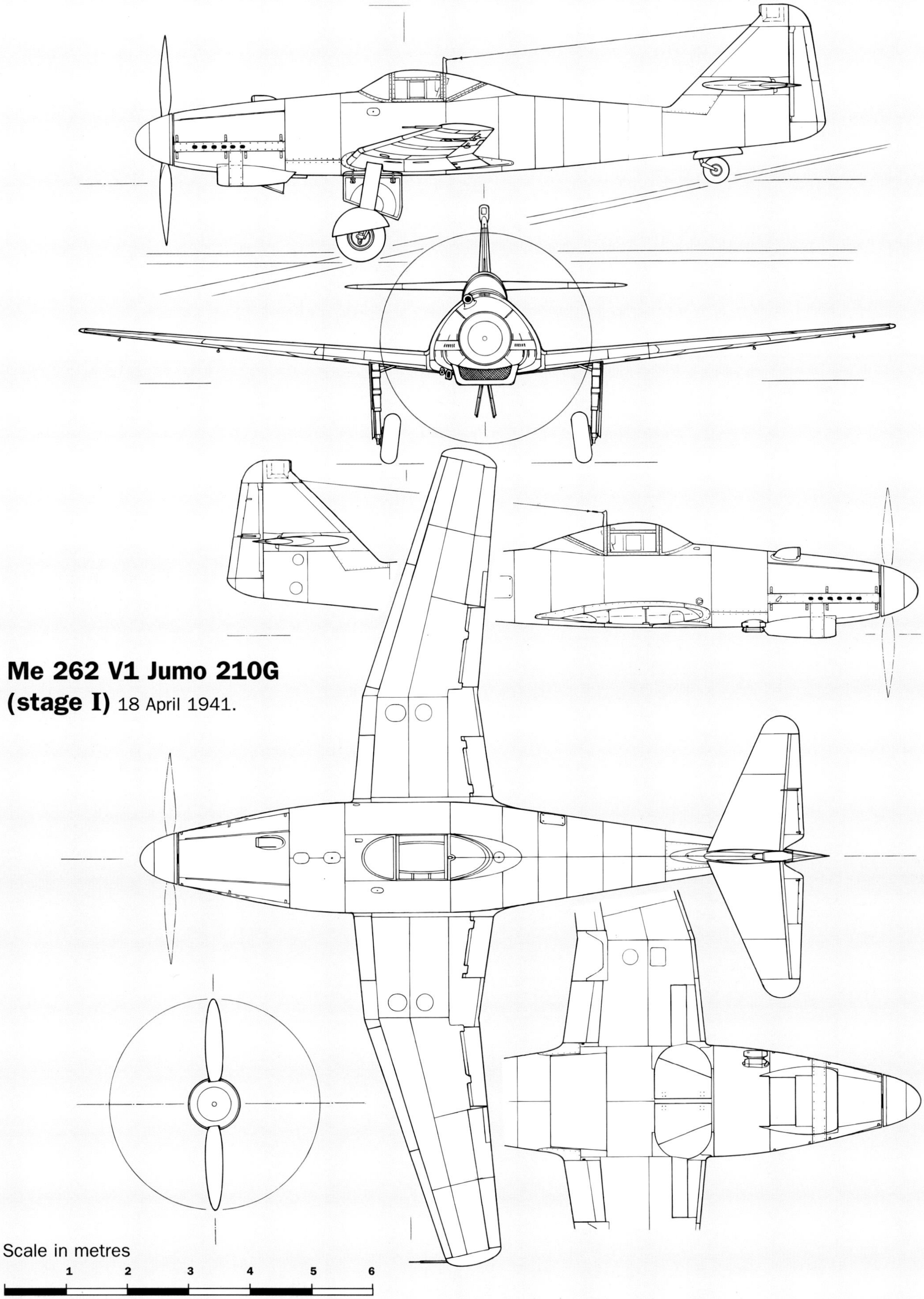

Me 262 V1 Jumo 210G (stage I) 18 April 1941.

Me 262 V1 PC + UA W.Nr. 262 000 0001 in its original form with Jumo 210G piston engine

This machine first flew on 18 April 1941 with Fritz Wendel at the controls. It made 47 flights with the Jumo 210 engine totalling 20 hours 20 minutes. The aircraft was fitted with the rudder taken from the V2 and had a small camera mounted on top of the fin. The aircraft is in overall natural metal finish with black green (70) spinner and propeller and radio call sign PC+UA in black.

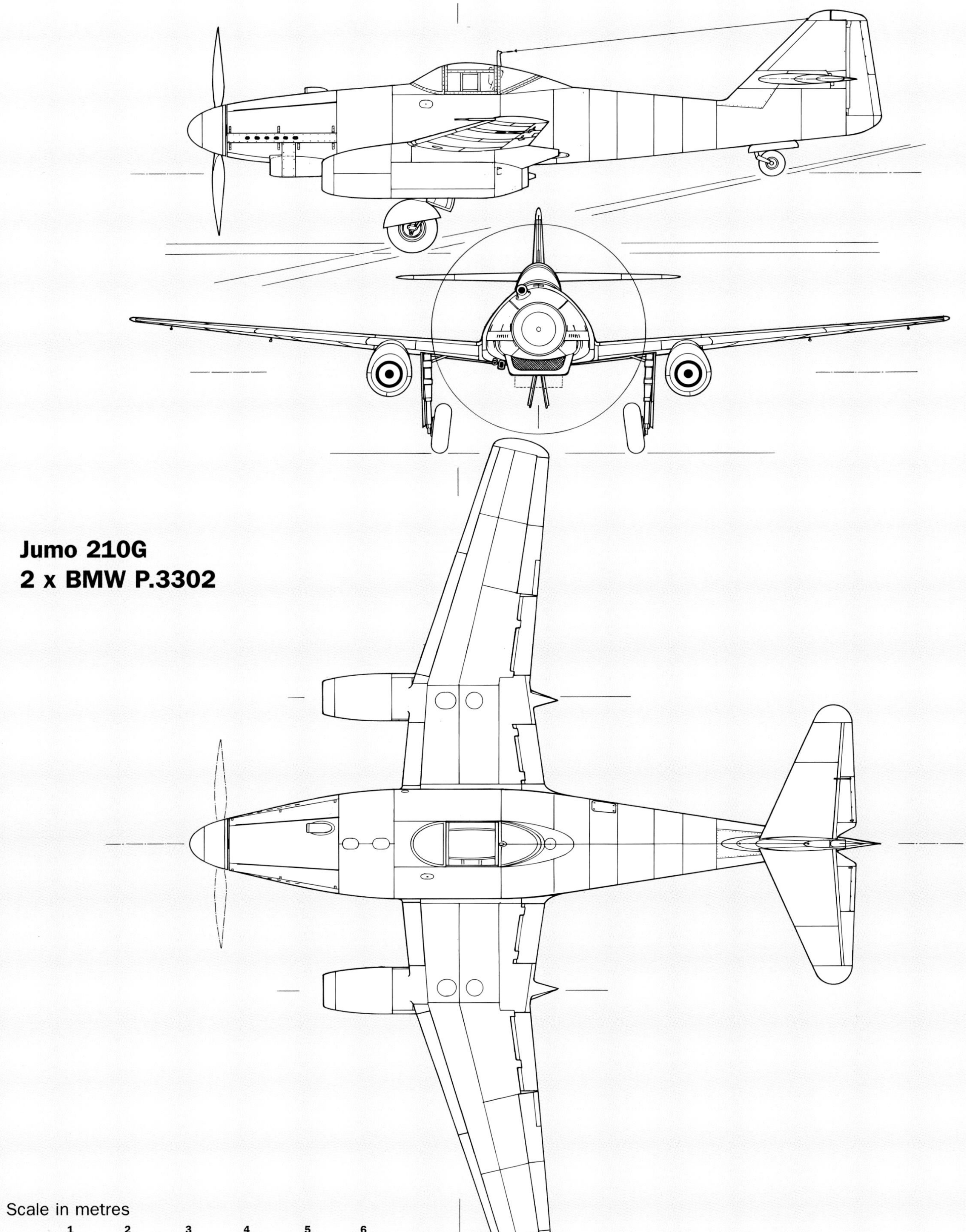

Jumo 210G
2 x BMW P.3302

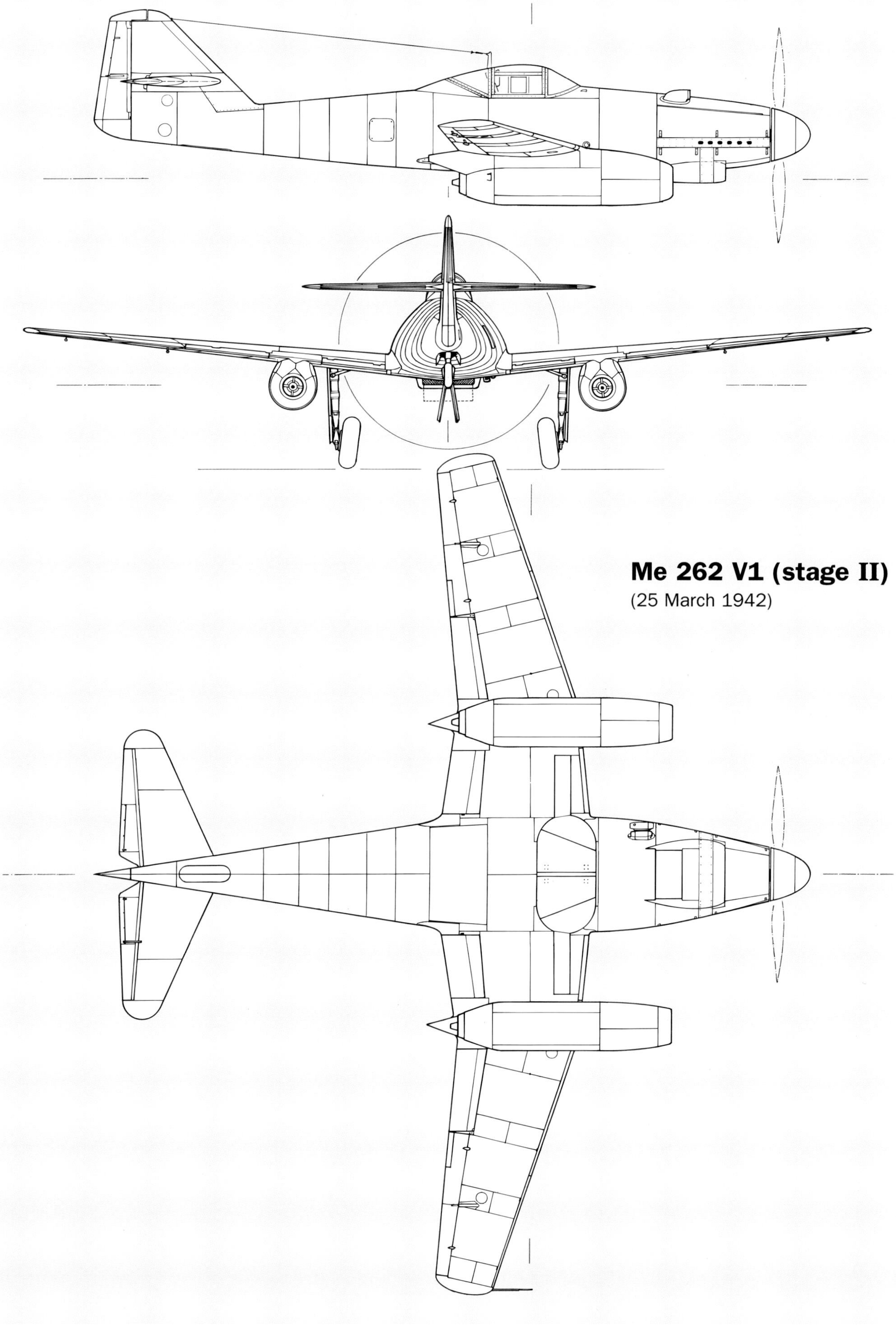

Me 262 V1 (stage II)
(25 March 1942)

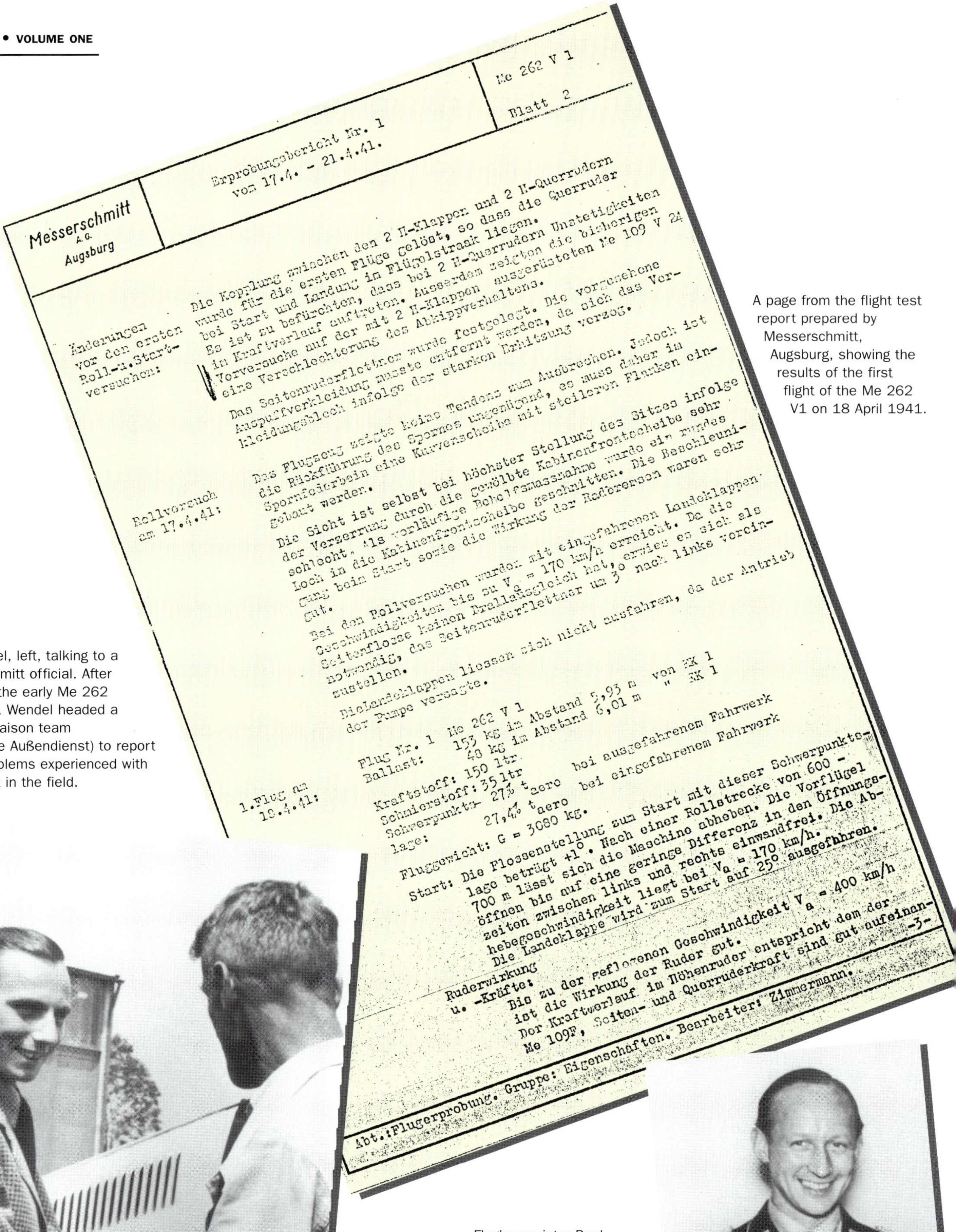

Messerschmitt A.G. Augsburg

Erprobungsbericht Nr. 1
vom 17.4. – 21.4.41.

Me 262 V 1

Blatt 2

Änderungen vor den ersten Roll-u.Startversuchen:

Die Kopplung zwischen den 2 H-Klappen und 2 H-Querrudern wurde für die ersten Flüge gelöst, so dass die Querruder bei Start und Landung im Flügelstraak liegen. Es ist zu befürchten, dass bei 2 H-Querrudern Unstetigkeiten im Kraftverlauf auftreten. Ausserdem zeigten die bisherigen Vorversuche auf der mit 2 H-Klappen ausgerüsteten Me 109 V 24 eine Verschlechterung des Abkippverhaltens.

Das Seitenruderflettner wurde festgelegt. Die vorgesehene Auspuffverkleidung musste entfernt werden, da sich das Verkleidungsblech infolge der starken Erhitzung verzog.

Rollversuch am 17.4.41:

Das Flugzeug zeigte keine Tendenz zum Ausbrechen. Jedoch ist die Rückführung des Spornes ungenügend, es muss daher im Spornfederbein eine Kurvenscheibe mit steileren Flanken eingebaut werden.

Die Sicht ist selbst bei höchster Stellung des Sitzes infolge der Verzerrung durch die gewölbte Kabinenfrontscheibe sehr schlecht. Als vorläufige Behelfsmassnahme wurde ein rundes Loch in die Kabinenfrontscheibe geschnitten. Die Beschleunigung beim Start sowie die Wirkung der Radbremsen waren sehr gut.

Bei den Rollversuchen wurden mit eingefahrenen Landeklappen Geschwindigkeiten bis zu V_a = 170 km/h erreicht. Da die Seitenflosse keinen Drallausgleich hat, erwies es sich notwendig, das Seitenruderflettner um 3° nach links voreinzustellen.

Die Landeklappen liessen sich nicht ausfahren, da der Antrieb der Pumpe versagte.

1.Flug am 18.4.41:

Flug Nr. 1 Me 262 V 1
Ballast: 153 kg im Abstand 5,93 m von SK 1
40 kg im Abstand 6,01 m " SK 1
Kraftstoff: 150 ltr
Schmierstoff: 35 ltr
Schwerpunktslage: 27% t_{aero} bei ausgefahrenem Fahrwerk
27,4% t_{aero} bei eingefahrenem Fahrwerk
Fluggewicht: G = 3080 kg.

Start: Die Flossenstellung zum Start mit dieser Schwerpunktslage beträgt +1°. Nach einer Rollstrecke von 600 – 700 m lässt sich die Maschine abheben. Die Vorflügel öffnen bis auf eine geringe Differenz in den Öffnungszeiten zwischen links und rechts einwandfrei. Die Abhebegeschwindigkeit liegt bei V_a = 170 km/h. Die Landeklappe wird zum Start auf 25° ausgefahren.

Ruderwirkung u. -Kräfte: Bis zu der geflogenen Geschwindigkeit V_a = 400 km/h ist die Wirkung der Ruder gut. Der Kraftverlauf im Höhenruder entspricht dem der Me 109F, Seiten- und Querruderkraft sind gut aufeinan- -3-

Abt.: Flugerprobung. Gruppe: Eigenschaften. Bearbeiter: Zimmermann.

A page from the flight test report prepared by Messerschmitt, Augsburg, showing the results of the first flight of the Me 262 V1 on 18 April 1941.

Fritz Wendel, left, talking to a Messerschmitt official. After test flying the early Me 262 prototypes, Wendel headed a technical liaison team (Technische Außendienst) to report on the problems experienced with the aircraft in the field.

Flugbaumeister Paul Bader from the Rechlin Experimental Station who had flown both the unpowered He 280 V1 and the He 280 V2 with jet engines, also tested the Me 262 V1 which was fitted with a Jumo 210 G piston engine in the nose.

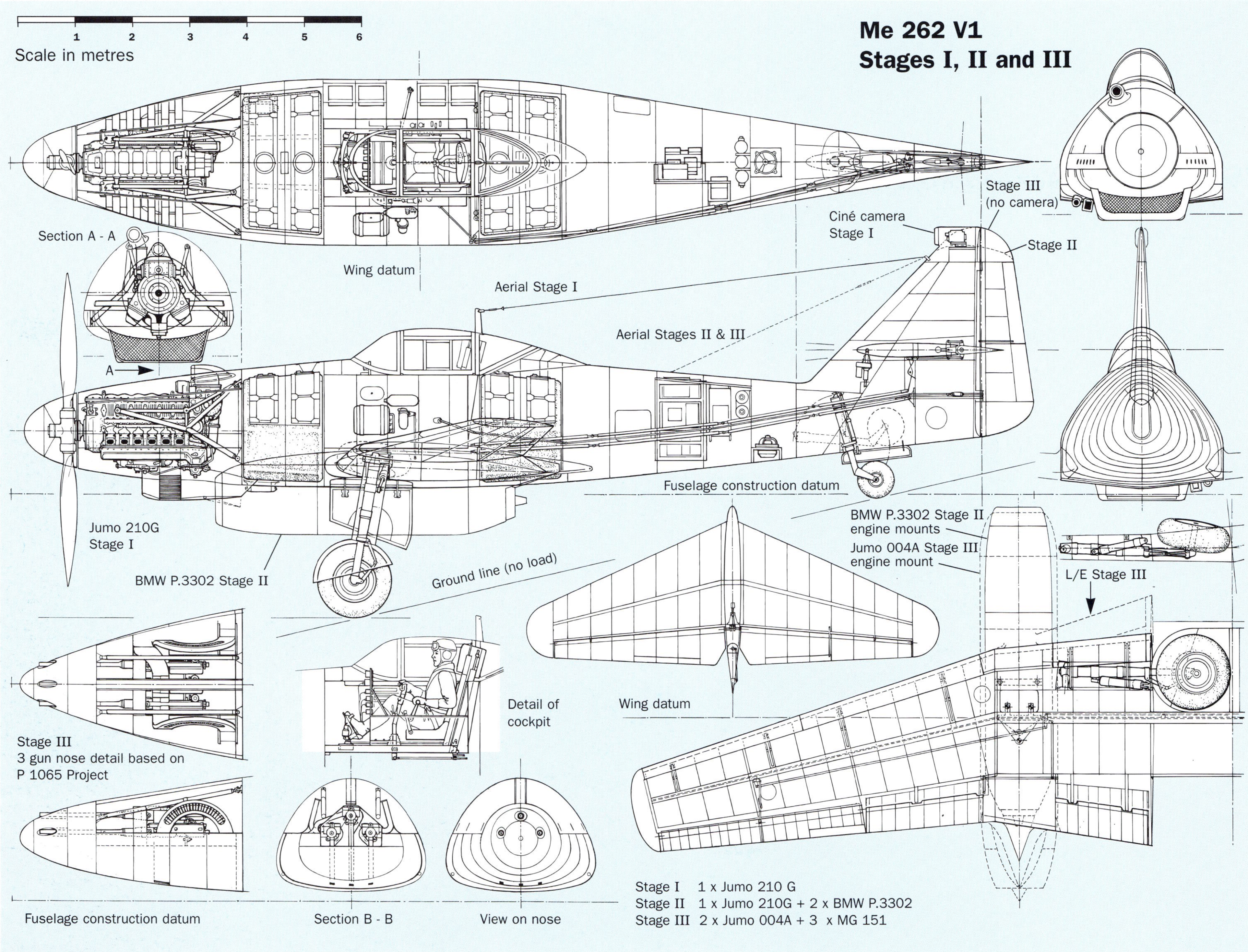
Me 262 V1
Stages I, II and III
1 2 3 4 5 6
Scale in metres
Section A - A
A
Wing datum
Aerial Stage I
Aerial Stages II & III
Ciné camera
Stage I
Stage III
(no camera)
Stage II
Fuselage construction datum
Jumo 210G
Stage I
BMW P.3302 Stage II
Ground line (no load)
BMW P.3302 Stage II
engine mounts
Jumo 004A Stage III
engine mount
L/E Stage III
Detail of
cockpit
Wing datum
Stage III
3 gun nose detail based on
P 1065 Project
Fuselage construction datum
Section B - B
View on nose
Stage I 1 x Jumo 210 G
Stage II 1 x Jumo 210G + 2 x BMW P.3302
Stage III 2 x Jumo 004A + 3 x MG 151

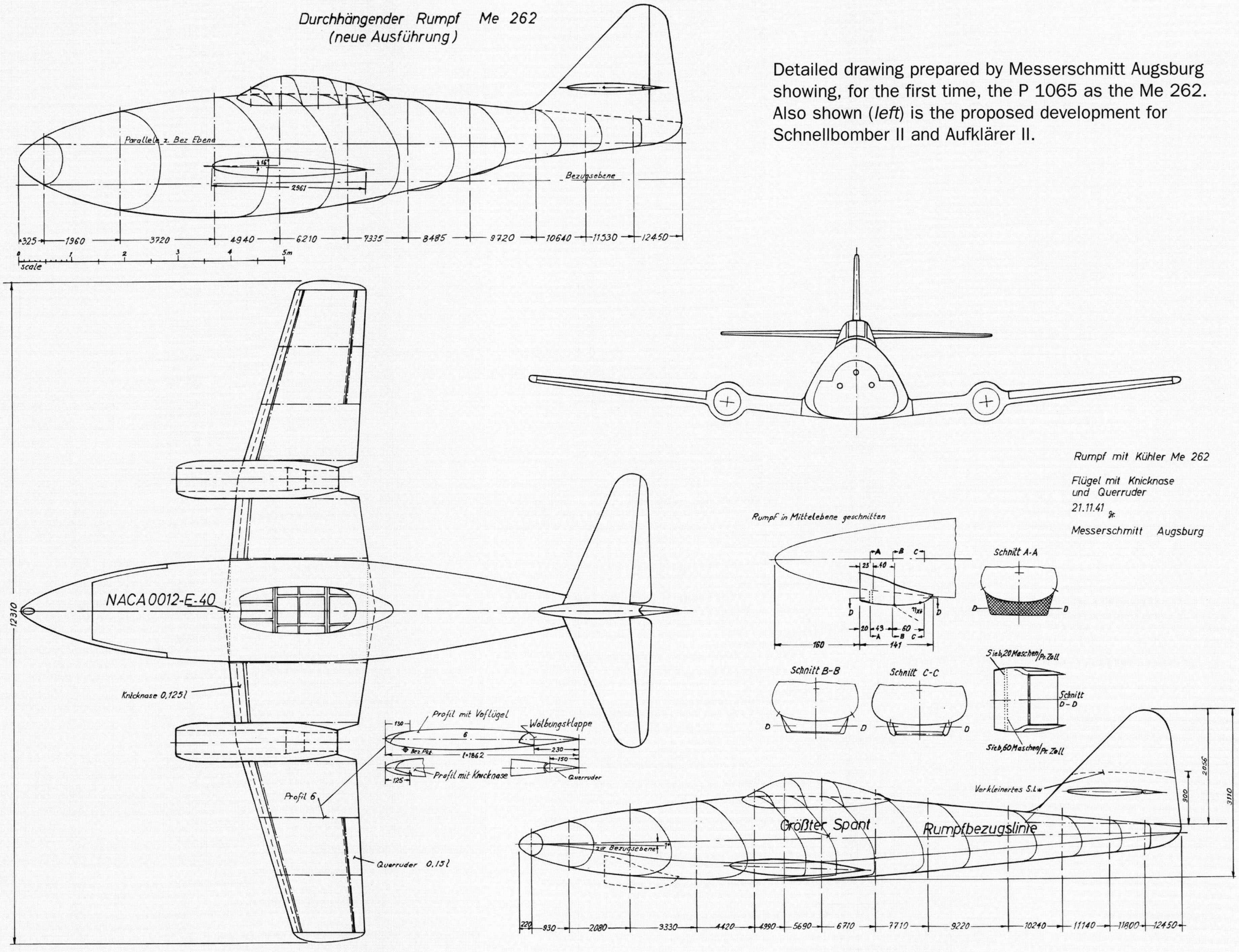

Detailed drawing prepared by Messerschmitt Augsburg showing, for the first time, the P 1065 as the Me 262. Also shown (*left*) is the proposed development for Schnellbomber II and Aufklärer II.

prototype was flown by Heinrich Beauvais and Paul Bader, both fighter aircraft specialists from the *Erprobungsstelle* (Test Centre) at Rechlin, on 4 August. Three days later Udet (in his role as *Generalluftzeugmeister* - responsible for aircraft production) and Milch visited Messerschmitt at Augsburg and were shown an Me 262 prototype with wooden mock-up engines.

Although the Jumo 004 was beginning to show more promise and BMW expected that prototype P.3302 (109-003) turbojets should be ready for testing by December 1941, Messerschmitt were still considering alternative engines for the Me 262. Apart from the Walter rocket engines described earlier, Voigt's team proposed, on 23 September, that 150 kg (330 lbs) thrust Argus As 014 or 500 kg (1,100 lbs) thrust As 044 impulse duct engines should be used to power the second prototype Me 262. These simple, but extremely fuel-consuming, jet engines were intended originally to provide auxiliary thrust for *Luftwaffe* bomber aircraft, either for shortening the take-off run or for boosting combat performance. This idea was dropped when the pulsejet progressed to flight tests, as it was found that the vibrations induced by its intermittent operation made it impractical, and even dangerous, to apply the engine to normal service aircraft. The Argus pulsejet was later used as an expendable power unit for the Fi 103 (V-1) flying bomb. The following weights were anticipated for a fully equipped Me 262 with weapons and ammunition:

without engines	2,590 kg (5,710 lbs)
with 6 Argus As 014, empty tanks	2,890 kg (6,370 lbs)
with 6 Argus As 014, full tanks	3,770 kg (8,310 lbs)
with 8 Argus As 014, empty tanks	2,990 kg (6,590 lbs)
with 8 Argus As 014, full tanks	3,870 kg (8,530 lbs)
with 2 Argus As 044	max speed - 680 km/h (422 mph)
with 4 Argus As 044	max speed - 960 km/h (590 mph)

By 16 October, the three alternative engine proposals, six or eight As 014s, two Walter 509 rockets or two As 044s received the interim designations Me 262 W1, W2 and W3 respectively.

Meanwhile, on 26 September 1941, the RLM had requested the development of a short range reconnaissance or *Aufklärer* version of the Me 262, Messerschmitt submitting a preliminary proposal on 21 October. The project was to be powered by two Jumo T 2 (004 B) engines each with an estimated thrust of 765 kg (1,690 lbs), be unarmed and carry two Rb 50/30 cameras. An estimated maximum speed of 758 km/h (471 mph) was anticipated at sea level with a flying weight of 5,770 kg (12,720 lbs) and a landing weight of 3,500 kg (7,730 lbs). The RLM inspected a mock-up of the Me 262 *Aufklärer* on 5 February 1942, but were not entirely satisfied with its layout. They proposed that a second mock-up be built, fitted with FuG 16Z or EZ 6 radio equipment and Rb 75/30 cameras. The possible conversion of twenty aircraft was suggested.

An experimental Argus As 014 impulse duct was tested on a Bf 110 twin-engined fighter. This type of engine was intended originally to provide auxiliary thrust for bomber aircraft, either for shortening the take-off run or for boosting combat performance, but was at one time proposed to power the early prototype Me 262s.

By now Junkers were promising to have their first engines ready for production in 1942/43, an experimental Jumo T 1 (004 A) having made its first test flight beneath a Bf 110 on 15 March 1942, a speed of 7,000 rpm being achieved for 15 minutes. Messerschmitt felt that a nine month delay had been introduced into the conversion of the Bf 110 for testing the Jumo 004 by the RLM's decision to offer the project to Weserflug.

1 *The speed at which drag begins to increase significantly. It is not known if Voigt knew anything about "drag divergence Mach number" in early 1939. This phenomena was probably given this name at a later date.*

2 *In July 1940 Abteilung LC 2 of the Technical Office suggested modifying the Jumo 210 G powered Bf 110 V8 (W.Nr.913 - D-AIJO) and two Bf 110 B-0s (W.Nr's 918 and 941), as test-beds for the P.3302. The plan was to suspend the turbojet beneath the centre of the fuselage. It is not known if all three aircraft were converted, but the V8 was definitely tested with the turbojet late in 1941, Fritz Wendel flying the aircraft on 8 January 1942.*

PE

CHAPTER FOUR

"AN UNIMAGINABLE LEAD"

Between September and December 1941 the Me 262 V1 was fitted with a pair of BMW P.3302 V2/V10 prototype series engines but the Jumo 210 piston engine was retained as a safety measure. On 25 March 1942, the aircraft attempted to take off from Augsburg on the power of all three engines (its 48th flight), but just after leaving the ground both turbojets suffered compressor blade failures. This forced Fritz Wendel to land the heavily laden prototype on the power of the piston engine alone. This setback led the RLM to reduce its order for Me 262 production to five prototypes on 29 May 1942. A decision regarding the remaining 15 aircraft was to be made only after the completion of flight tests. The Me 262 V3 was to be tested at Leipheim, and the V4 and V5 were to be fitted with Junkers engines. If the decision was made to go ahead with the remaining 15 pre-production aircraft then these were to be completed at Leipheim.

Fortunately, the less ambitious Jumo 004 was showing much more promise than its BMW counterpart which had to undergo a major

Below: This interesting photo shows the wing of the Me 309 V4 in the foreground, the Me 209 V5 (which Messerschmitt often tried to promote in favour of the Me 262) to the left and the BMW 003-engined Me 262 V1 in the background. The upper photo is an enlargement showing the only known picture of the Me 262 V1, which, after completing 47 flights with the Jumo 210 piston engine totalling 20 hrs 20 mins, was fitted with two prototype BMW 003 turbojets. Its only flight, on 25 March 1942, ended with both turbojets failing.
Opposite page: Professor Willy Messerschmitt confers with his test pilot Fritz Wendel in front of a works hangar.

On this page and opposite: A sequence of four photos showing the long, shark-like nose section of the Me 262 V3. These photos were taken at Leipheim on the morning of 18 July 1942 just prior to the machine's first turbojet-driven flight.

redesign. On 1 June 1942, the first two flight cleared A-0 engines (W.Nr.003 and 005) were delivered to Messerschmitt and fitted to the Me 262 V3 (W.Nr.0003, call sign PC+UC).

Early in the morning of 18 July Fritz Wendel undertook a series of high speed taxiing trials with the prototype, but at the calculated unstick speed he found it impossible to lift the tailwheel off the ground. After some discussion, it was realised that the airframe was masking the elevators, rendering them ineffective. It was therefore suggested that Wendel apply the brakes briefly to jerk the tail off the ground, a white line being painted across the runway to suggest the appropriate moment for this manoeuvre. Using this technique Wendel lifted the prototype off the runway at Leipheim at twenty minutes to nine, completing a 12 minute trouble free test, the first pure turbojet driven flight by the aircraft. This was followed by another 13 minute flight just after midday, the aircraft attaining a speed of 550 km/h (342 mph).

Early tests with the Me 262 were to prove the airframe excellent, the only modification being to increase the wing root chord by continuing the leading edge sweep back of the outer panels across the centre section. This eliminated a tendency for the airflow to break away early from the wing centre section. This change was introduced on the V3 after its first two flights and added to all subsequent aircraft.

Four further test flights were made by Wendel with the Me 262 V3 before *Dipl.-Ing.* Heinrich Beauvais, chief assessor for fighter aircraft at the *Erprobungsstelle* at Rechlin, arrived at Leipheim on 11 August to fly the aircraft. Wendel informed him of the method to be adopted to raise the tail of the aircraft and stood at the 800 m (2,600 ft) mark on the runway to help show the point at which the brakes should be applied. Unfortunately, Beauvais failed to attain the necessary speed and after three abortive attempts to raise the tail the aircraft ploughed through into a cornfield, the starboard wing hitting a manure heap, slewing it round and ripping off both undercarriage and engines and causing serious damage.

Despite this setback, the Me 262 had proved promising enough for the RLM to decide, at a meeting held the next day, to proceed with the construction of five more prototypes and ten pre-production 0-series aircraft. The minutes of the meeting *(Amtsprotokoll Nr.6)* proposed the following roles for the prototypes: The Me 262 V1 with central engine was to test ailerons, dive brakes and Argus impulse duct engines. The V2 was to be converted to Jumo turbojets and to be completed by the end of September 1942. The badly damaged V3 was to be rebuilt and the V4 and V5 completed in January and March 1943 respectively. Construction of the V6 was to begin in May 1943, with four additional prototypes completed at monthly intervals. These aircraft were to be used to test ejection seats. As far as is known only one Me 262 was actually fitted with an

ejection seat, a compressed air device of Heinkel design being tested by the V1 in early February 1942. Only ground tests were undertaken, the rear fuselage and tail being covered by a protective roof.

The ten Me 262 0-series, otherwise known as the V11 to V20, were to test the following features:

1. Tricycle undercarriage
2. Pressurized cabin
3. FuG 16 ZY radio transmitter/receiver and FuG 25a IFF equiupment
4. Three 20 mm MG 151 cannon in the nose or one 30 mm MK 108 and two MG 151, also a conversion pack *(Rüstsatze)* for two 13 mm MG 131 machine-guns in the wings.
5. Armour protection
6. Dive brakes
7. Wing span of 12.00 m (39 ft 4.5 ins)

At least one part of the programme proposed by the RLM actually proceeded on time when the Me 262 V2 made its first and second flights on 1 October 1942, piloted by Wendel. Next day the aircraft was flown again by Wendel and then by Beauvais. These flights were made from the much longer *Luftwaffe* runway at Lechfeld the use of which, it was hoped, would prevent any repetition of the crash suffered by the V3. The second prototype was essentially similar to the V3, powered by two Jumo 004 A-0 engines (W.Nr.009 and 010). The success of this flight led the RLM to demand that their order be expanded from 15 to 30 pre-production aircraft, all to be fitted with tricycle undercarriages. These were to be completed by the end of 1943, but lack of production capacity led Messerschmitt to reject the demand, stating that only the ten V-series could be built during this period.

In the past, it has been alleged that Milch and his senior advisers in the Technical Office failed to recognise the potential of jet-propelled aircraft sufficently early, and neglected to give the

Messerschmitt Me 262 V3
PC+UC W.Nr. 262 000 0003

Before the first flight of the Me 262 V3 in the early morning of 18 July 1942, a Messerschmitt ciné photographer filmed the aircraft from all angles. These stills, extracted from the film, show many details of the aircraft and its camouflage and markings.

After the first two flights, the wing root chord was increased by continuing the leading edge sweep back of the outer panels across the centre section. This eliminated a tendency for the airflow to break away early from the wing centre section. This change was added to all subsequent aircraft. The first four prototype aircraft had tailwheel undercarriages which necessitated the pilot briefly applying the brakes to bring the tail up when attempting to take-off. If this was not done the airframe would continue to mask the elevators, rendering them ineffective. Using this technique on the maiden flight of the V3, Fritz Wendel lifted the prototype off the runway at Leipheim at 08.40 hrs, completing a 12 minute trouble free test.

Mechanics work on the Jumo 004 A-0 (T 1) engines fitted to the Me 262 V3. Work on the A-series engine began in December 1939, the prototype making its initial test run on 11 October 1940. In December of that year the engine was run at its full design speed of 9,000 rpm, and by the end of January 1941 a thrust of 430 kg (950 lbs) was reached. Several problems then manifested themselves and it was not until 6 August 1941 that the design thrust of 600 kg (1,320 lbs) was achieved. The first flight of the T 1 in a Bf 110 test bed took place on 15 March 1942, the first pure jet flights being made in the Me 262 V3.

This sequence of photos also shows a mechanic opening the sideways hinging canopy of the aircraft and climbing into the cockpit. Although it was difficult to escape through this type of canopy in an emergency, the production aircraft had the facility to jettison the centre and rear sections which made baling-out a much easier proposition.

Messerschmitt test pilot, Flugkapitän Fritz Wendel, leans against the rear fuselage of the Me 262 V3 prior to an early test flight.

Ground crew prepare the Me 262 V3 for flying. The aircraft has dark grey (74) and medium grey (75) mottled uppersurfaces with pale blue grey (76) beneath. The upper part of the nose has a patch of dark green (70) applied.

Two people who were to have a considerable influence on the early development of the Me 262 were Fritz Wendel, who flew the early prototypes, and Hans Martin Antz who promoted jet fighter aircraft development in Germany. The two men are seen here in discussion just before Wendel embarked on his flight in the Me 262 V3.

Another sequence of stills from the cine film of the Me 262 V3 show the aircraft taxiing to its take-off point. Fritz Wendel made a total of six test flights before Dipl.-Ing. Heinrich Beauvais arrived from Rechlin on 11 August to fly the aircraft. Unfortunately, Beauvais failed to attain the necessary speed and after three abortive attempts to raise the tail, the aircraft ploughed into a cornfield and was severely damaged.

Mechanics and airfield personnel watch as Fritz Wendel taxies out in the Me 262 V3 towards a rain dampened runway at Leipheim, almost lost in a cloud of jet efflux, 18 July 1942.

necessary support and priority for their development and production. This allegation is dispelled by a top secret order issued by Milch on 10 December 1942 in his dual role of State Secretary for Aviation and *Generalluftzeugmeister*, to the relevant departments of the RLM, concerning the establishment of the *Vulkan* Development and Supply Programme. The order stated:

"*The absolute demand for qualitative superiority of Luftwaffe equipment, over that of enemy countries, has led me to order the creation of an urgent development and production programme under the code word* Vulkan.

Tasks proceeding under this code-word have absolute overriding priority within the Luftwaffe.

The programme encompasses jet-propelled aircraft and guided missiles, including associated equipment and the ground organisation necessary to support these activities.

A request has been made to the Reichsminster for Armaments and Munitions to extend the legal force of the code-word Vulkan *throughout the entire armaments field. Development of some of the following equipment is already taking place under priority 'DE'.*[1] *Through the code-word* Vulkan *priority will also apply to the procurement of this equipment, for which extensive preparations will have to be made as before.*"

In part, the *Vulkan* programme encompassed the following types:

Bottom of pages 96-101: Cinè stills depicting Fritz Wendel taking off in the Me 262 V3 at Leipheim in the early morning of 18 July 1942 on its maiden flight. Wendel had to apply the brakes at a precise speed and moment, in order to jerk the tail off the ground to assist take-off. To facilitate this, a white line was painted across the runway.

Aircraft:
Me 163, Me 262, He 280, Me 328, Ar 234.
Jet engines:
Jumo 004, BMW 003, BMW 018, HeS 011, DB 007, As 014

By December 1942, the course of the war had begun to turn against Germany, so Milch may have forseen the *Vulkan* programme as a means of countering the growing quantative superiority of the Allied powers.

This order is conclusive proof that Milch accorded the highest priority to the Me 262 and other jet-propelled aircraft at a relatively early stage in their development, despite post-war assertions by Professor Messerschmitt and others that the RLM vacillated on this issue. The principal obstacle to the early realisation of the *Vulkan* programme were the many technical difficulties still besetting the development of turbojets and other types of reaction engines, which prevented their quantity production until 1944. Until an acceptable level of reliability had been attained for the BMW 003 and Junkers 004 turbojets, these engines were only suitable for installation in experimental aircraft, and could not be considered for operational use.

In early December 1942 the first of a further series of problems began to affect the development of the Me 262. On the 8th, the Messerschmitt company wrote to *Obstlt.* Georg Pasewaldt, the Chief of Development in the Technical Office (GL/C-E), stating that before large scale production could begin, the Me 262 would have to be redesigned since it was already three years old! Also its armament and other equipment would have to be brought up to the current standards. Then, on the 9th, Messerschmitt pilots Fritz Wendel and Karl Baur, after carrying out trials with the V2, submitted a report stressing the unsuitability of the tailwheel undercarriage for operational use. A third problem manifested itself on 16 December when, at a GL/C-E conference, it was asked why only ten Me 262 V-series were to be built in 1943. Junkers had promised delivery of 900 Jumo 004s during the same year, although this promise proved unduly optimistic. The result was that highest priority was allocated to the project, Messerschmitt being asked to state extra staff requirements before 21 December.

Messerschmitt duly informed the RLM of their requirements by telex, also submitting a tentative time schedule for initial production of the Me 262. Simultaneously they warned that as only makeshift manufacturing jigs were available, there could be problems. It was also suggested that manufacture of sub-assemblies should be

Heinrich Beauvais (right) talking to Otto Behrens in the cockpit of a Bf 108. Beauvais, who evaluated interceptor fighters for the experimental station at Rechlin, was the second pilot to fly the Me 262 V3. Behrens was later appointed as the Typenbegleiter 8-262 ("Development Co-ordinator Me 262")

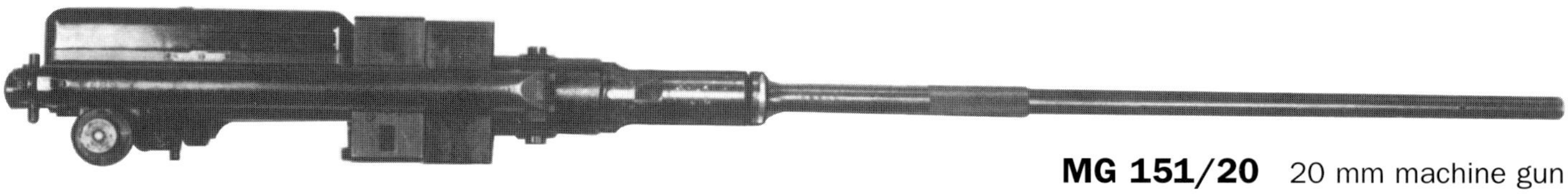

MG 151/20 20 mm machine gun

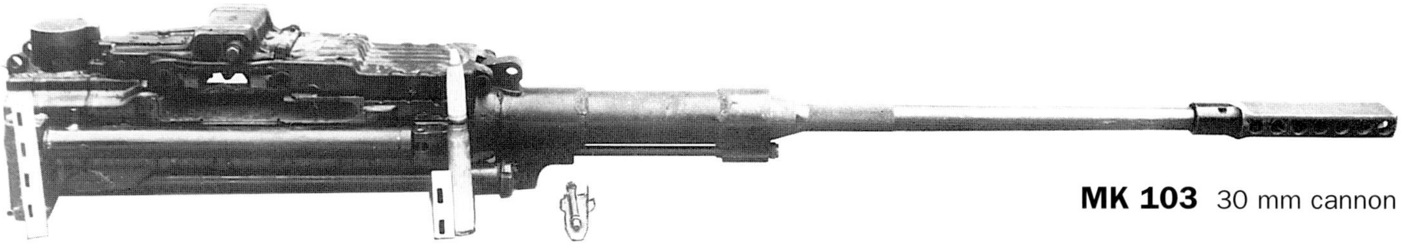

MK 103 30 mm cannon

spread over several companies. On 22 January 1943, the Me 262 received the highest development priority (class DE) for the first time.

Possible problems with the production of the Me 262 airframe led Messerschmitt to propose (at an RLM conference also held on 22 January) the development of a jet propelled version of the Bf 109 to be known as the Bf 109 TL. This rather nebulous project was to have the fuselage of the Bf 109's shipboard derivative, the Me 155 and the wing and undercarriage of the Me 309. Two Jumo 004 turbojets were to be slung under the wings and the only entirely new components were to be the nose, housing two 20 mm MG 151 and one 30 mm MK 103 cannon, and the tail assembly. The project was dropped when it was found that so many modifications would be needed that little if any time advantage would be gained over producing the Me 262.

Meanwhile, a series of conflicting plans were being put forward for production of the Me 262. On 4 February 1943, *Oberst* Wolfgang Vorwald,[2] (Chief of the RLM's Technical Office) proposed at a GL/C-*Chef* conference, that 40 to 50 aircraft per month until early 1945 would be sufficient. This could then be increased to 100 aircraft per month. Messerschmitt suggested that 50 Me 262s could be built at Augsburg, together with the Me 410, on the condition that Gablingen airfield was made available for flight tests.

At a second conference, held two weeks later, *Obstlt.* Pasewaldt[3] made mention of a proposal to concentrate development of all jet aircraft at one company (Siebel). No decision whether the Me 262 or He 280 was to be selected had yet been made. The Messerschmitt company pointed out that high performance aircraft such as the Me 262 could not be built by Siebel as planned by the RLM, but only under the personal leadership of Professor Messerschmitt. As an alternative they suggested that Siebel should take over production of the Me 410. This proposal was accepted by the RLM a week later, the Me 262 receiving a similar development priority to that allocated to the production of U-boats.

In March 1943, the first successful bench test was carried out on the prototype of the improved Jumo 004 B-series engine. The new sub-type introduced a modified compressor and improved air intake and was some 100 kg (220 lbs) lighter

than the A-series. In the same month, on the 2nd, conversion of the Me 262 V1 to Jumo 004 engines began.

The minutes of the ninth of a series of meetings on the progress of the Me 262 held at Messerschmitt on 4 March *(Protokoll Nr.9)*, indicated that, following a request from the *General der Jagdflieger*, considerable thought was being given to increasing the Me 262's armament. It was planned to replace the three 20 mm MG 151/20 cannon with either six 30 mm MK 108s or four MK 108 and two MG 151/20s. Should the MK 108s not be available in time, an armament of three MG 151/20 and four 13 mm MG 131 machine-guns was suggested. Other proposals involved the use of the longer range 30 mm MK 103 cannon in various combinations with other weapons. Armour protection was to be increased, airbrakes fitted, FuG 16 Ze and FuG 25 A radio to be carried and an ejection seat installed. It was also hoped to change to the 1,000 to 1,200 kg thrust Jumo 004 C engines. Of the first seven V-series aircraft, two were to be fitted with nosewheels.

MK 108
30 mm cannon.

Between October 1942 and March 1943 the only Me 262 prototype available for flight tests was the V2, but on 20 March it was joined by the rebuilt V3. Just before this, on 16 March, the He 280 V2, which had been re-engined with Jumo 004 A-0 engines (W.Nr.011 and 012) for comparison tests with the Me 262, made its first flight. Heinkel test pilot, Fritz Schäfer, later reported: "The problem with these engines was that they were too big for the He 280, the clearance between them and the ground being only a matter of centimeters. This was just about acceptable for an experimental aircraft, but certainly not for production. I did, however, manage to reach 800 km/h (497 mph) in horizontal flight with the aircraft, but, at that speed, it began to swing around its vertical axis, forcing me to abandon any further advance of the throttles." Only eleven days after Schäfer's flight the RLM cancelled its order for 300 of the proposed production model, the He 280 B, and the Heinkel fighter was reduced to the role of flying test bed.

After the Me 309 had been abandoned on 30 January 1943, the Messerschmitt company began tooling up for the production of the piston-engined Me 209 during the spring of 1943. This was a much modified version of the Bf 109 G powered by a DB 603 engine not to be confused with the earlier record-breaking Me 209 V1. In a document, issued over a year later on 31 March 1944, Messerschmitt complained that Me 262 development had been hampered by the RLM not having determined or announced the degree of priority for the type. He felt that development of the Me 209 had a higher priority than that of the Me 262. This, he maintained, had resulted in a temporary reduction of Me 262 design work in favour of the Me 209. An interesting insight on

this is given in the following table of drawing board staff employed on the Me 209 and Me 262 during 1943:

		Me 209	Me 262
January	1.	-	5
	15.	-	14
February	1.	1	20
	15.	12	14
March	1.	26	40
	15.	34	41
April	1.	38	25
	15.	71	3
May	1.	83	4
	15.	57	27
June	1.	56	48
	15.	37	60
July	1.	14	115
	15.	13	100
August	1.	14	66
	15.	9	28
September	1.	19	41
	15.	13	44
October	1.	15	40
	15.	14	26
November	1.	17	31
	15.	12	37
December	1.	14	62
	15.	6	65

Despite Messerschmitt's attempt to absolve his company from the delays in getting the Me 262 into production, there is much evidence to suggest that he was largely responsible. As we have seen, the aircraft had been allocated a high development priority as early as January 1943, but the company continued to drag its heels.

At this time the following weight and performance estimates were being quoted for the Me 262 production series:

Equipped weight	3820 kg	8,420 lb
Crew	100 kg	220 lb
Ammunition	220 kg	490 lb
Fuel	330 kg	2,930 lb
All-up weight	5470 kg	12,060 lb

Maximum speed
805 km/h (500 mph) at sea level
880 km/h (547 mph) at 6 km (19,700 ft)
875 km/h (544 mph) at 9 km (29,500 ft)

Climbing speed
22.0 m/s (72 ft/s) at sea level, 100% thrust
12.0 m/s (39 ft/s) at 6 km, 100% thrust
6.2 m/s (20 ft/s) at 9 km, 100% thrust

Time to climb
to 6 km (19,700 ft) with 100% thrust, 5.9 min
to 9 km (29,500 ft) with 100% thrust, 11.5 min

Service ceiling
12.2 km (40,000 ft)

Range
(with 1,800 ltrs or 396 Imp gals of fuel)
235 km (146 mls) with 100% thrust at sea level
460 km (286 mls) with 100% thrust at 6 km
540 km (336 mls) with 100% thrust at 9 km

Duration
17.5 min with 100% thrust at sea level
36.0 min with 100% thrust at 6 km (19,700 ft)
47.5 min with 100% thrust at 9 km (29,500 ft)

On 17 April 1943, at the instigation of the Messerschmitt company, *Hptm.* Wolfgang Späte, a 72-victory *Ritterkreuzträger* and former *Staffelkapitän* of 5./JG 54 now heading the experimental Me 163 rocket fighter unit, *Erprobungskommando 16*, flew the Me 262 V2, the first service pilot to do so. Two days later he submitted a report on the aircraft to *Generalmajor* Adolf ('Dolfo') Galland, the *General der Jagdflieger* (commanding General of the *Luftwaffe* fighter force).

"*Flight characteristics are such that an experienced fighter pilot would be able to handle the aircraft. In particular, the increase in air speed when compared to the fastest conventional fighter deserves attention.*

Maximum speed at ground level measured so far is 780 km/h (485 mph). This is not expected to decrease markedly when armament and radio equipment have been fitted, the more so since jet engines of increased power will be available for production aircraft. Characteristically, jet engines will not only maintain this speed at altitude, but increase it. The climbing speed of the Me 262 surpasses that of the Bf 109 G by 5 to 6 m/sec (16 to 20 ft/sec) at a much better speed (420 km/h or 261 mph). The superior horizontal and climbing speeds will enable the aircraft to operate successfully against numerically superior enemy fighters. The extremely heavy armament (six 30 mm guns) permits attacks on bombers at high approach speeds with destructive results despite the short time the aircraft is in the firing position. As a fighter-bomber, and carrying bombs, the aircraft would still be faster than any enemy fighter."

"As to flying characteristics, some handling problems will still have to be solved. These should not prevent the aircraft's operational employment, since they will either have been corrected on production aircraft, or are unimportant."

"Due to the tailwheel undercarriage, the view from the cockpit during take-off is bad. The nose wheel, planned from the V6 onward, will solve the problem."

"The underslung engines cause an upward momentum along the lateral axis. Use of the servo-tab to counteract this momentum causes the aircraft to become nose heavy as speed increases. Proper use of the servo tab overcomes this problem. This minor disadvantage would be acceptable if control forces at sudden speed increases (diving) can be mastered without retrimming the aircraft. Flight tests are still outstanding."

Professor Messerschmitt greeting Fritz Wendel after he had broken the World Speed record in the Me 209 V1 registered D-INJR. With the specially modified DB 601 V10 engine, the aircraft achieved a speed of 755.12 km/h (469.22 mph), a record which stood for over 30 years.

"The curved canopy sides distort downward view during landing, making it difficult to judge height. Flat panels will solve the problem."

"Aileron forces and efficiency are similar to the Bf 109, they are acceptable at high speeds. The turning circle is rather large. This should not be a disadvantage, since jet engines demand entirely new combat tactics. (Jet thrust increases at high speeds, making the aircraft unsuitable for dog fighting). Rudder forces and effectiveness are sufficient and acceptable."

The Me 262 V3, landing after its first flight on 18 July 1942 from Leipheim airfield. As the aircraft touched down, surplus fuel, which had collected in the cowling of the port engine, caught fire - a not unusual occurrence during early flights. The fire was quickly extinguished and the aircraft little damaged. As can be seen, a large number of Me 321 transport gliders, which were built at Leipheim, were parked around the airfield. These machines were designed to carry both troops and armoured vehicles during "Operation Sea Lion" - the proposed invasion of the British Isles.

Messerschmitt Me 262 V3

Completion of first flight 18 July 1942

Dipl.-Ing. Hans Martin Antz of Department LC 7 (Airframe Development) of the Technical Office talks to Fritz Wendel after the first flight of the Me 262 V3. It was Antz, who in October 1938 proposed the development of a jet fighter by Messerschmitt. To left is Dipl.-Ing. Gerhard Caroli.

Fritz Wendel clambers on to the wing of the Me 262 V3 just after completing the first flight of the Me 262 V3 with Jumo 004 jet engines on 18 July 1942.

"Landing is simple, as with the Bf 109. However, the approach angle is much flatter and speed reduces much slower than with propeller aircraft."

"The aircraft deserves the highest attention; its development should receive the greatest possible support. High speeds can be obtained by jet propulsion. The Me 262 is only a first step..."

Despite this enthusiastic report, Späte's testing of the aircraft had been curtailed on 18 April when the Me 262 V2 crashed on its 48th flight killing test pilot *Ofw.* Wilhelm Ostertag. After attaining an altitude of 500 m (1,600 ft), the aircraft suddenly went into a steep dive and crashed. From the radio transcript it was established that one engine had flamed out before the accident. Wendel reported that the adjustable tail cone in the rear of the turbojet had detached itself and blocked the exhaust orifice, causing it to flame out. This made the aircraft skid sideways, rendering the tailplane ineffective and forcing it into a steep dive from which it never recovered. An official Messerschmitt investigation was, however, to conclude that the crash was due to the failure of the electrically operated trimming tabs. Ostertag's place was taken by Gerd Lindner who was to become the most experienced Me 262 test pilot.

On 15 May 1943, the Me 262 V4 joined the flight test programme, this prototype being similar to the rebuilt V3. By this time, *Generalfeldmarschall* Milch realised that he would soon have to select the next generation of single-seat fighters to enter

Hptm. Wolfgang Späte, a 72-victory fighter Experte who, at the instigation of the Messerschmitt company, flew the Me 262 V2 on 17 April 1943. His enthusiastic report led Adolf Galland to fly the V4 in May, the General enthusiastically reporting to Göring that: "... it flew as though angels were pushing".

This photo is thought to show the Me 262 V3 after it was rebuilt following the accident on 11 August 1942 when it was badly damaged. The aircraft returned to flight testing on 20 March 1943 and could be distinguished by the painting of its Versuchs (experimental) number on the fin.

Me 262 V2 PC + UB W.Nr. 262 000 0002 with two early Jumo 004 A-0 engines

The aircraft first flew 1 October 1942. It was completely destroyed in a crash on its 48th flight on 18 April 1943 killing *Ofw.* Wilhelm Ostertag. At this time the aircraft had completed a total of 18 hours 17 minutes flying. The aircraft had the standard fighter camouflage for the period of overall pale blue grey (76), with dark grey (74) and medium grey (75) having been applied over the top on the upper surfaces and mottling of dark green (71) and RLM grey (02) on the fuselage sides.

Me 262 V3 PC + UC   W.Nr. 262 000 0003 with two early Jumo 004 A-0 engines

At 08.40 on 18 July 1942, Fritz Wendel lifted the Me 262 V3 off the runway at Leipheim, completing a 12 minute trouble free flight. This was the first flight made by the Me 262 without piston-engine assistance. After six successful flights, using two prototype Jumo 004 engines, the aircraft crashed and was badly damaged on 11 August 1942. It was rebuilt to resume flight testing on 20 March 1943. Its last recorded flight (the 149th) was on 11 September 1944 after having amassed 54 hours flying time. On 12 September it was finally written off after an Allied air attack on Lechfeld. At the time of its first flight the V3 carried the standard fighter camouflage for the period of overall pale blue grey (76) with dark grey (74) and medium grey (75) having been applied over the top on the upper surfaces, with mottling of RLM grey (02) on the fuselage sides. The upper part of the nose was finished in black green (70) giving the appearance of a false spinner.

Right: For some time the Me 262 V2 stood idle before it could be fitted with engines. This photo shows it in this state with the wing of the Me 309 V1 in the foreground. It is interesting to note that at this time the aircraft has dark green uppersurfaces, but by the time it flew, this was replaced by mottled greys.

Below:This rare photo shows the Me 309 V1, seen here still without armament, which was first flown by Karl Baur on 18 July 1942. The Me 309 programme was later scrapped when all development was switched to the Me 262. The Me 262 V2 can clearly be seen in the background and although camouflaged is still awaiting engines.

Messerschmitt Me 262 V2 PC+UB W.Nr. 262 000 0002

Seen here with Jumo T1 engines, W.Nr. 03 on the port and V13 on the starboard, the Me 262 V2 made its first and second flights on 1 October 1942, piloted by Fritz Wendel. These flights were made from the much longer runway at Lechfeld the use of which, it was hoped, would prevent any repetition of the accident to the V3.

Messerschmitt's works photographer, Herr Lüttgau, (right) stands on the wing of the Me 262 V2 accompanied by Messerschmitt technicians.

This close-up of the cockpit area of the Me 262 V2 shows the early type canopy and retaining stay (the V3 differed in having a cable rather than the stay). Between October 1942 and March 1943 this prototype was the only one available for flight testing.
It was fitted with two Jumo 004 A (T1) engines.

Messerschmitt test pilot Ofw. Wilhelm Ostertag (third from left) discusses an item of equipment with (directly to his left), Ing. Jung and (to his right), Dr. Schmidt, of the Junkers engine flight test department. The aircraft in the background
is the Me 262 V2 which crashed on 18 April 1943, killing Ostertag. Investigation of the accident showed that the adjustable tail cone in the rear of the turbojet had detached itself and blocked the exhaust orifice, causing the aircraft to skid sideways, rendering the tailplane ineffective and forcing it into a steep dive from which it never recovered.

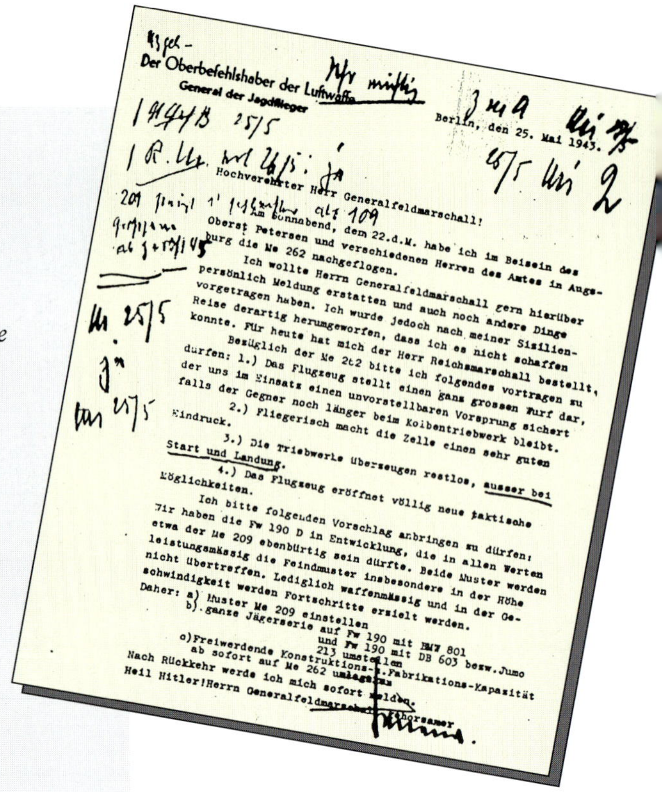

Der Oberbefehlshaber der Luftwaffe
General der Jagdflieger

Berlin, den 25. Mai 1943.

Hochverehrter Herr Generalfeldmarschall!

Am Sonnabend, dem 22.d.M. habe ich im Beisein des Oberst Petersen und verschiedenen Herren des Amtes in Augsburg die Me 262 nachgeflogen.

Ich wollte Herrn Generalfeldmarschall gern hierüber persönlich Meldung erstatten und auch noch andere Dinge vorgetragen haben. Ich wurde jedoch nach meiner Sizilien-Reise derartig herumgeworfen, dass ich es nicht schaffen konnte. Für heute hat mich der Herr Reichsmarschall bestellt.

Bezüglich der Me 262 bitte ich folgendes vortragen zu dürfen: 1.) Das Flugzeug stellt einen ganz grossen Wurf dar, der uns im Einsatz einen unvorstellbaren Vorsprung sichert falls der Gegner noch länger beim Kolbentriebwerk bleibt.

2.) Fliegerisch macht die Zelle einen sehr guten Eindruck.

3.) Die Triebwerke überzeugen restlos, ausser bei Start und Landung.

4.) Das Flugzeug eröffnet völlig neue taktische Möglichkeiten.

Ich bitte folgenden Vorschlag anbringen zu dürfen: Wir haben die Fw 190 D in Entwicklung, die in allen Werten etwa der Me 209 ebenbürtig sein dürfte. Beide Muster werden leistungsmässig die Feindmuster insbesondere in der Höhe nicht übertreffen. Lediglich waffenmässig und in der Geschwindigkeit werden Fortschritte erzielt werden.

Daher: a) Muster Me 209 einstellen
b) ganze Jägerserie auf Fw 190 mit BMW 801 und Fw 190 mit DB 603 bzw. Jumo 213 umstellen
c) Freiwerdende Konstruktions- u. Fabrikations-Kapazität ab sofort auf Me 262 umlegen.

Nach Rückkehr werde ich mich sofort melden.

Heil Hitler! Herrn Generalfeldmarschall gehorsamer

Der Oberbefelshaber der Luftwaffe — *Berlin, 25 May 1943.*

General der Jagdflieger

Most esteemed Herr Generalfeldmarschall!

On Saturday, the 22nd of the month, I tested the Me 262 at Augsburg in the presence of Oberst Petersen and other persons from the Technical Office.
I would have preferred to report personally to the Generalfeldmarschall and also elaborate on other matters, however I was so occupied after my visit to Sicily that there was simply no time. The Reichsmarschall has ordered me to report today.
Concerning the Me 262, I beg to state the following:
1.) The aircraft represents an enormous leap forward, it would give us an unimaginable lead over the enemy if he adheres to the piston engine.
2.) In-flight handling (of the airframe) is impressive.
3.) The powerplants are fully convincing, except during take-off and landing.
4.) The aircraft offers entirely new tactical prospects.

I beg to submit the following proposal : The Fw 190 D is under development, its performance should match the Me 209's in all respects. The performance of the two types, however, will not be superior to the enemy's models, particularly at altitude. The only progress seems to be in armament and (higher) speeds.
Conclusion : a) Me 209 to be discontinued.
b) Total fighter production to switch from the Fw 190 with BMW 801 to the Fw 190 with DB 603 and Jumo 213 respectively.
c) The construction and industrial capacities thus released to be concentrated on the Me 262, with immediate effect.
I shall report immediately on my return.

Heil Hitler! Herr Generalfeldmarschall your most obedient servant.

(signed) Galland

Generalfeldmarschall Erhard Milch faced a dilemma over the deployment of the Me 262.

Luftwaffe service in 1944-45, and this presented him with a dilemma: to order the Me 209 (which his advisors told him would probably be inferior to the Fw 190 D) into production as the *Luftwaffe's* next piston-engined fighter, or to make the transition directly to the still-untried and revolutionary jet-propelled Me 262. To reach a decision, Milch asked Adolf Galland, whose judgement he trusted unreservedly, to test fly one of the Me 262 prototypes and to report on its performance.

Early in the morning of 22 May, Galland arrived at Lechfeld to test the Me 262. Apart from Professor Messerschmitt, *Oberst* Edgar Petersen, commander of the Test Centres, and his fighter specialist, *Hptm.* Otto Behrens, were also present. Both surviving prototypes, the V3 and V4, were ready for flight, but when Galland attempted to start the engines of the V3, one of them caught fire, and he had to make a hurried exit while the fire was quickly extinguished. He then switched to the V4 and made a successful flight, even performing a mock interception of the experimental Me 264 V1 four-engined bomber as it came in to land. He found the new form of propulsion more than impressive, later conveying his enthusiasm in a report to Milch dated 25 May 1943.

Later that day Galland reported in person to Göring who was staying at his medieval castle at Veldenstein, near Nuremburg. Galland described his first flight in the Me 262 to the *Reichsmarschall* in glowing terms, stating that: "It flies as if there is an angel pushing." He then showed Göring the report he had sent to Milch and shortly afterwards, probably as part of a pre-arranged plan, a telephone call came through from Milch in Berlin. Milch spoke to Göring and said: "I want your permission to drop the Me 209 and turn out every Me 262 we can, as a matter of urgency." Göring appeared uneasy at the prospect of having to make such a decision, and glanced at Galland (who was listening to the telephone conversation on an extension) for re-assurance, saying: "Well?" Galland nodded to the *Reichsmarschall* who then gave his approval to Milch with a terse "Agreed!" The future of the Me 262 seemed assured and that evening Milch must have experienced a certain degree of self-satisfaction as he recorded these momentous

Undercarriage Details
P 1065 AND Me 262 V1-V4

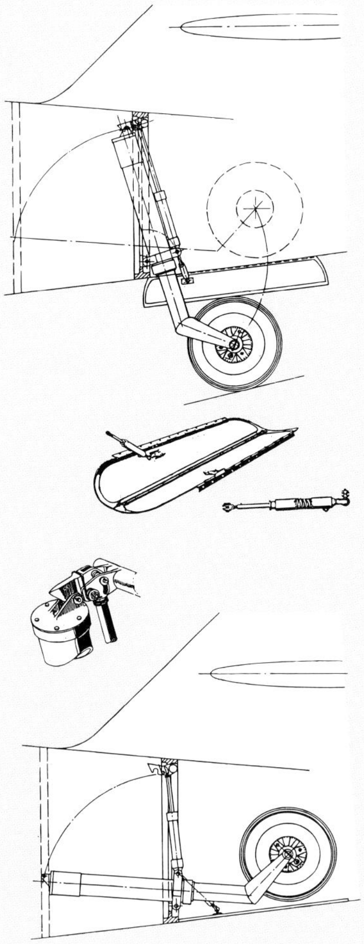

Tail wheel and undercarriage doors as used on the Me 210/410

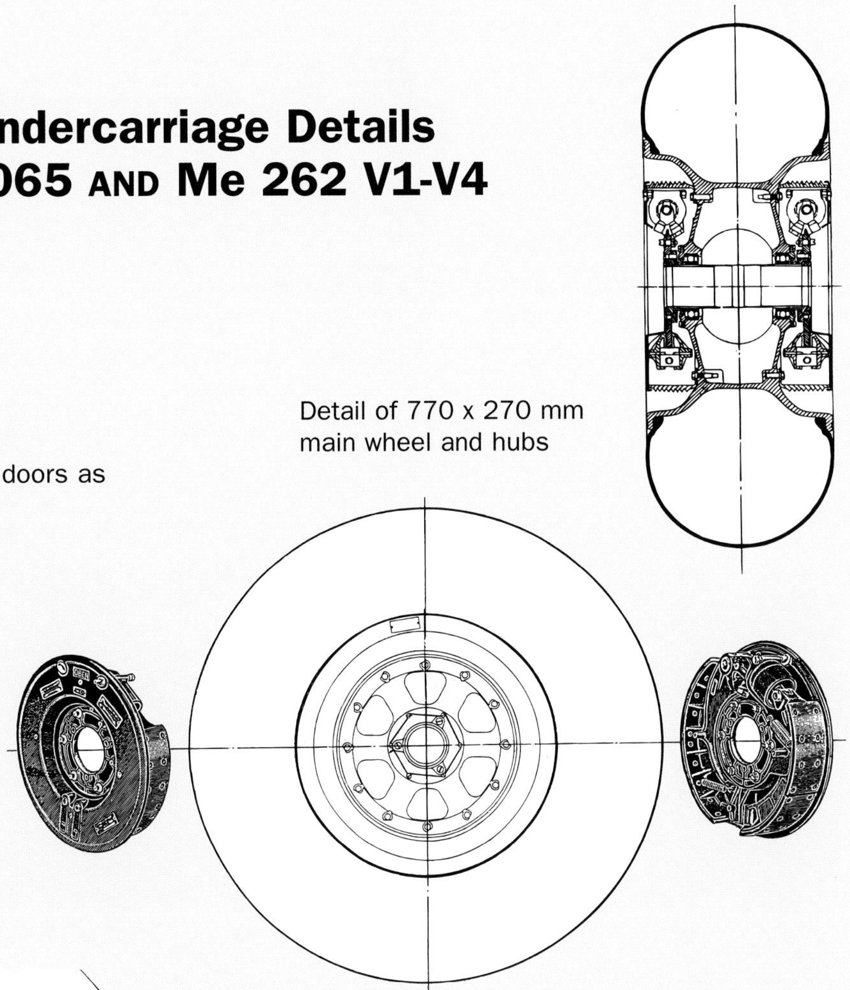

Detail of 770 x 270 mm main wheel and hubs

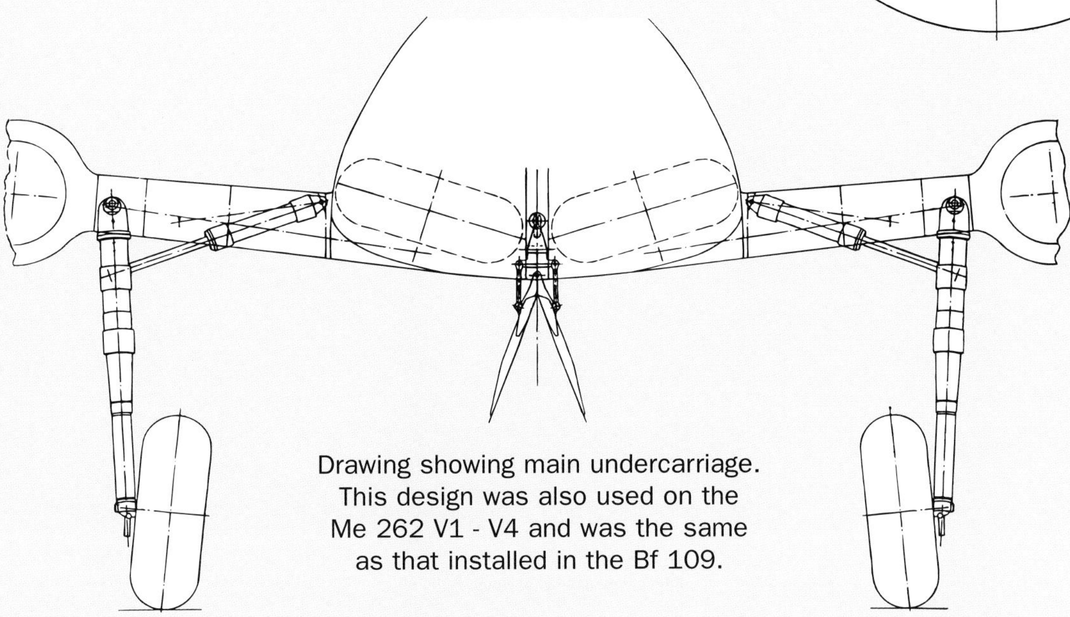

Drawing showing main undercarriage. This design was also used on the Me 262 V1 - V4 and was the same as that installed in the Bf 109.

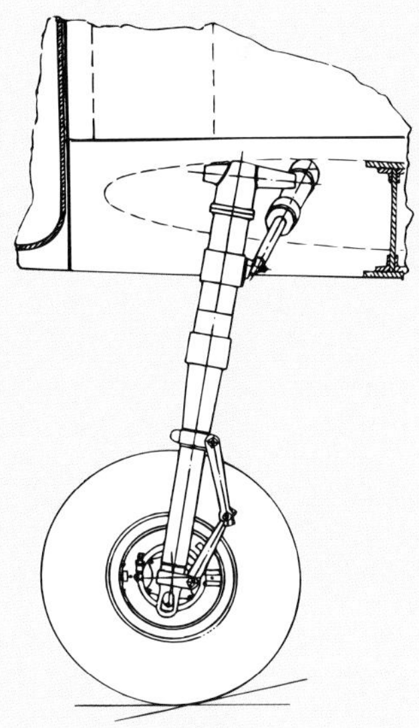

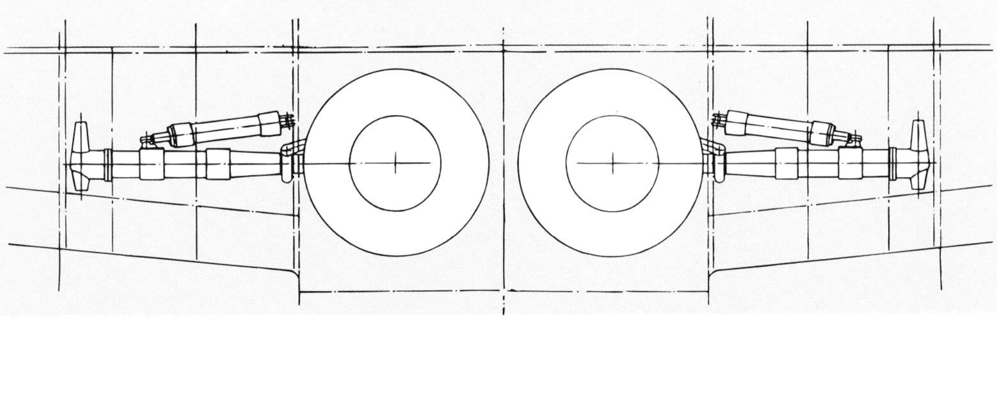

Drawing of P 1065 shown

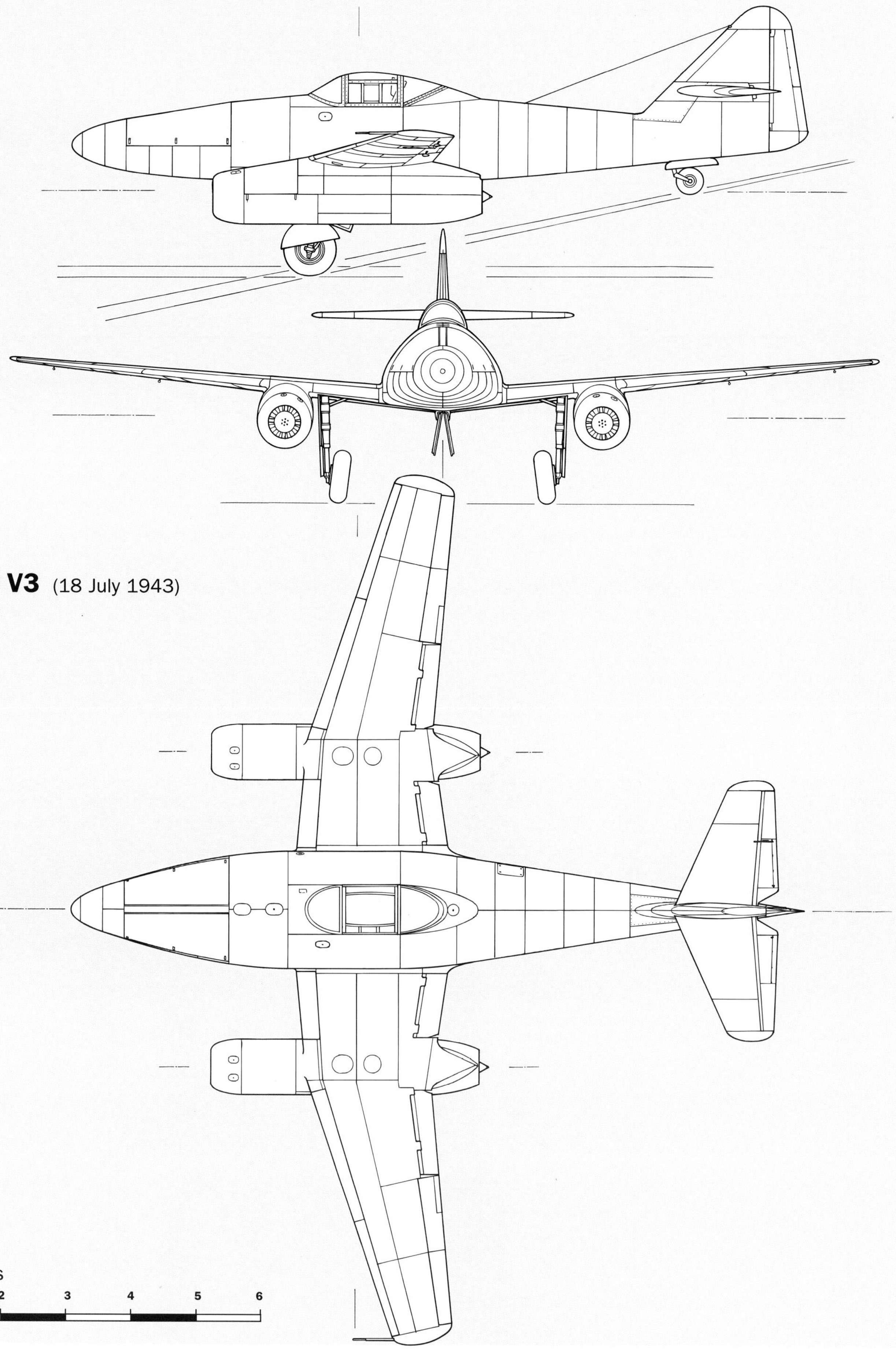

Me 262 V3 (18 July 1943)

Scale in metres

1 2 3 4 5 6

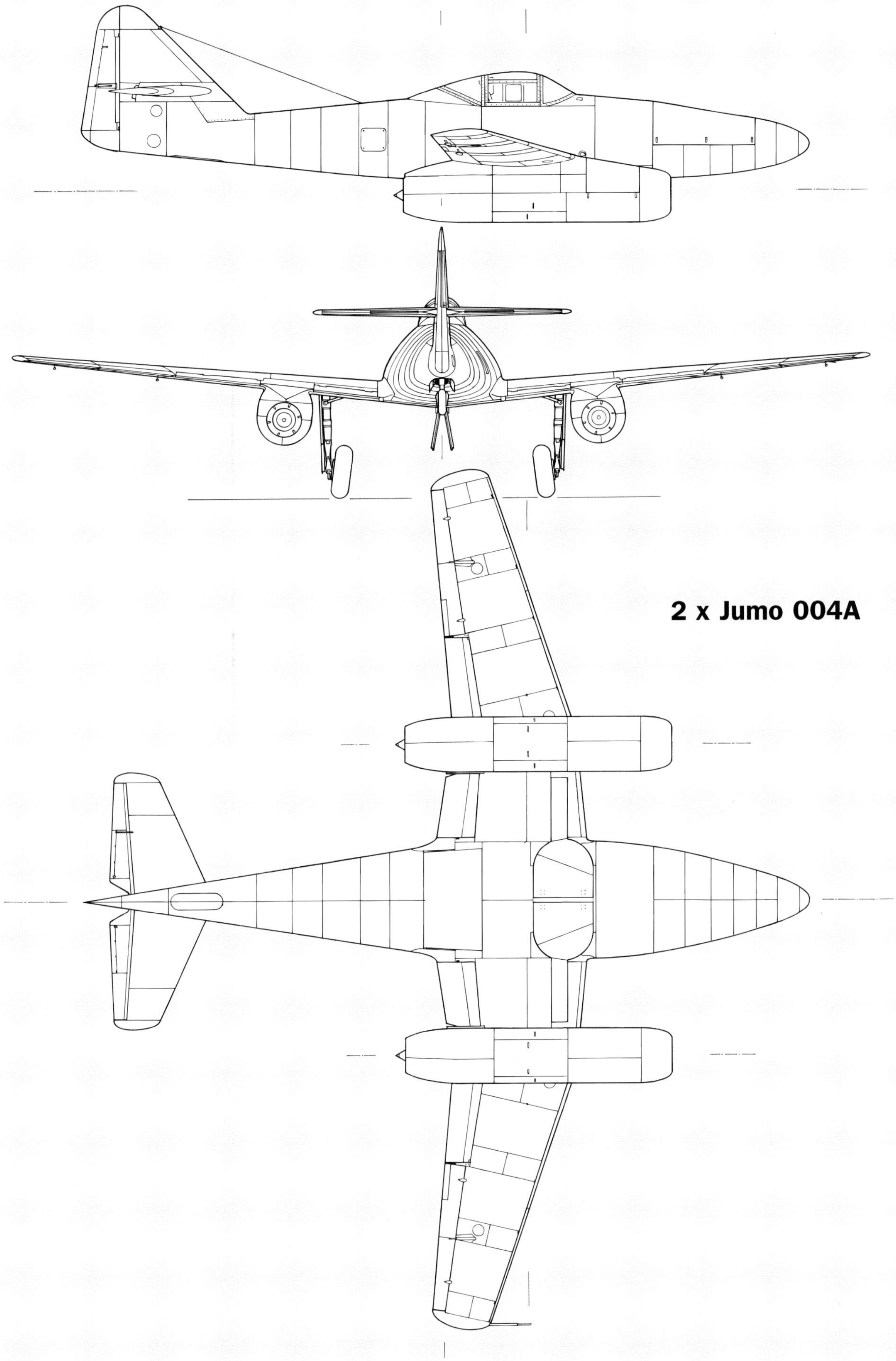

2 x Jumo 004A

Me 262 V5 PC + UE W.Nr. 262 000 0005 with two Jumo 004 A-0 engines

The aircraft first flew on 6 June 1943 and was the first aircraft fitted with a fixed, tricycle undercarriage. It crashed on its 74th flight on 4 August 1943 having completed 6 hours 17 minutes flying. Repaired to fly again in January 1944 and delivered to *Erprobungskommando 262* where it was flown by *Hptm.* Thierfelder. The aircraft was destroyed on 1 February 1944. The V5 also introduced the newly modified forward engine cowlings similar to those designed for the Jumo 004 B engines. This was also the first Me 262 to be tested with Rheinmetall-Borsig R 109-502 RATO boosters. The tail surfaces had counter balance horns fitted above the elevators. The aircraft had a similar paint finish to the Me 262 V4.

events with a succinct entry in his pocket diary: "Afternoon, telephoned Göring: Drop the Me 209, put the Me 262 in its place."

Nevertheless, it would appear that Milch had anticipated gaining Göring's approval, for at a GL (Director General of Air Force Equipment) conference held on the morning of 25 May, Milch had ordered that preference should be given to an early start of Me 262 production, that one hundred aircraft should be manufactured in 1943, and that *Oberst* Edgar Petersen, Head of the *Erprobungsstellen* (Test Centres), should be appointed Me 262 *Kommissar*.

Milch's order was reflected in the Me 262 *Protokoll Nr.11*, dated 28 May, which recorded that 100 aircraft were to be built powered by Jumo 004 B-1 or B-2 engines. These were to carry an armament of three 20 mm MG 151/20 cannon with 320 rpg, although these were to be replaced later by six 30 mm MK 108s. Armour protection was to be provided for the pilot, and FuG 16 ZY with ZVG 2 and FuG 25a radio fitted. At this stage it was decided to abandon the idea of equipping the aircraft with air brakes or an ejection seat. Consideration was given to increasing the size of the mainwheels from 770 x 270mm to 840 x 300mm, and the nosewheel to 650 x 150 mm. The minutes also recorded that the *E-Stelle* (Test Centre) at Tarnewitz would carry out tests with the *Revi* 16 B against a captured Hawker Typhoon on 15 June, this gunsight being intended for the Me 262.

Apart from Messerschmitt personnel such as the Professor himself, Rakan Kokothaki, Dr. Carl

Ofw. Wilhelm Ostertag (right) discussing a piece of equipment with Hans Martin Antz (centre). Ostertag was killed on 18 April 1943 when the Me 262 V2 crashed on its 48th flight.

Oberst Edgar Petersen, (left), Head of the Luftwaffe Test Centre organisation, was appointed by Milch to be "Kommissar" of the Me 262. Petersen is seen here at Lechfeld talking to Adolf Galland.

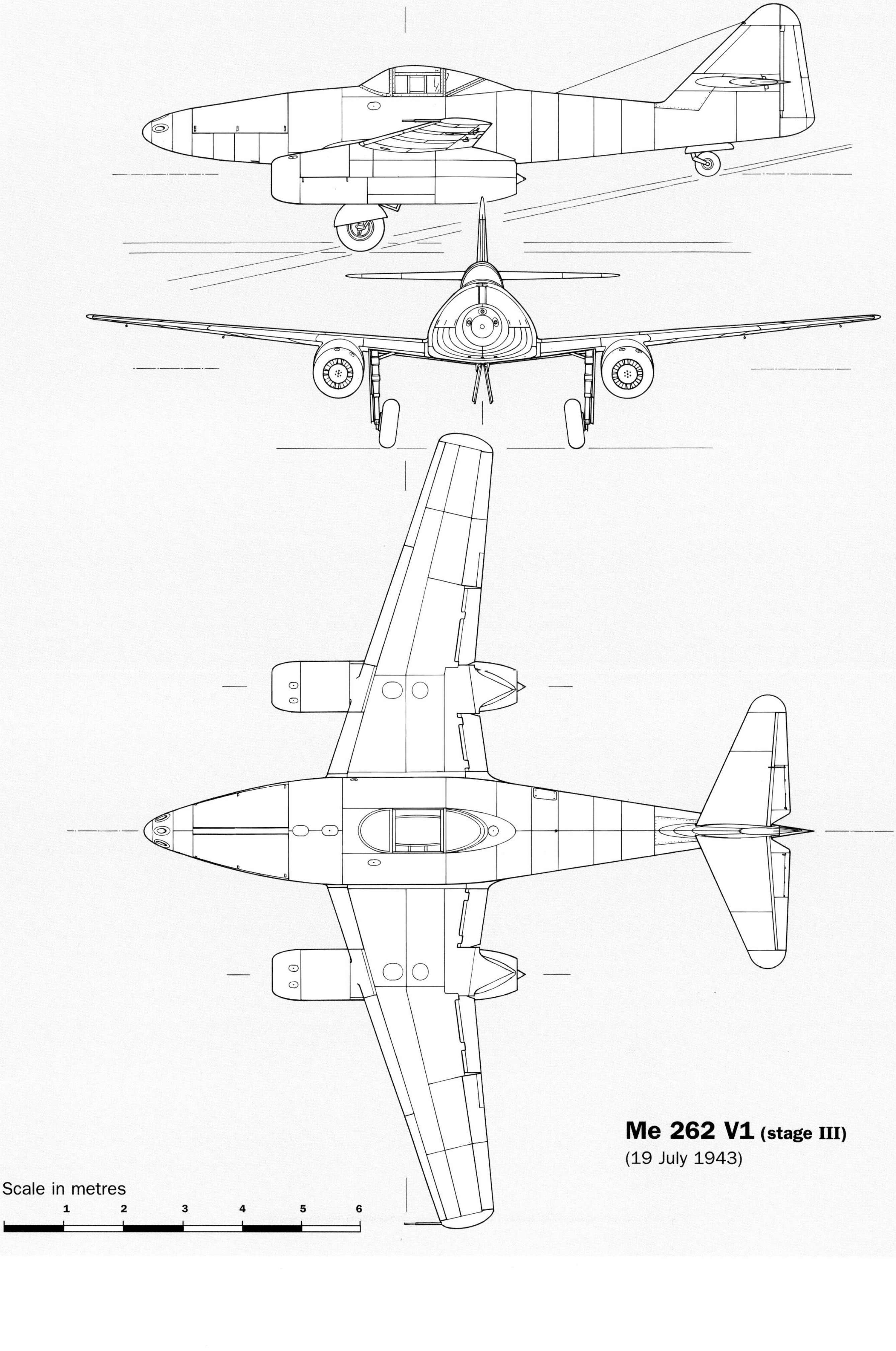

Me 262 V1 (stage III)
(19 July 1943)

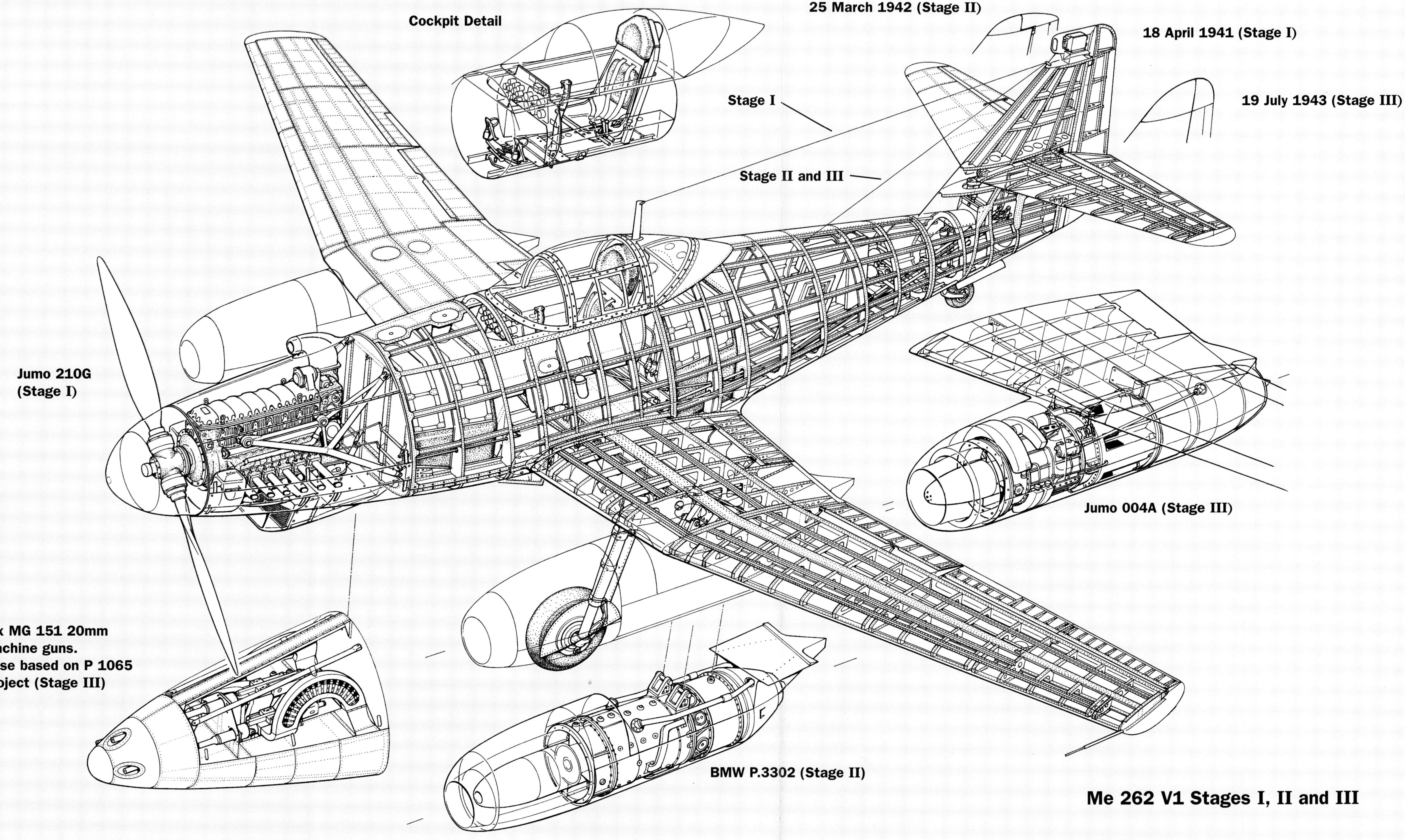

Me 262 V1 Stages I, II and III

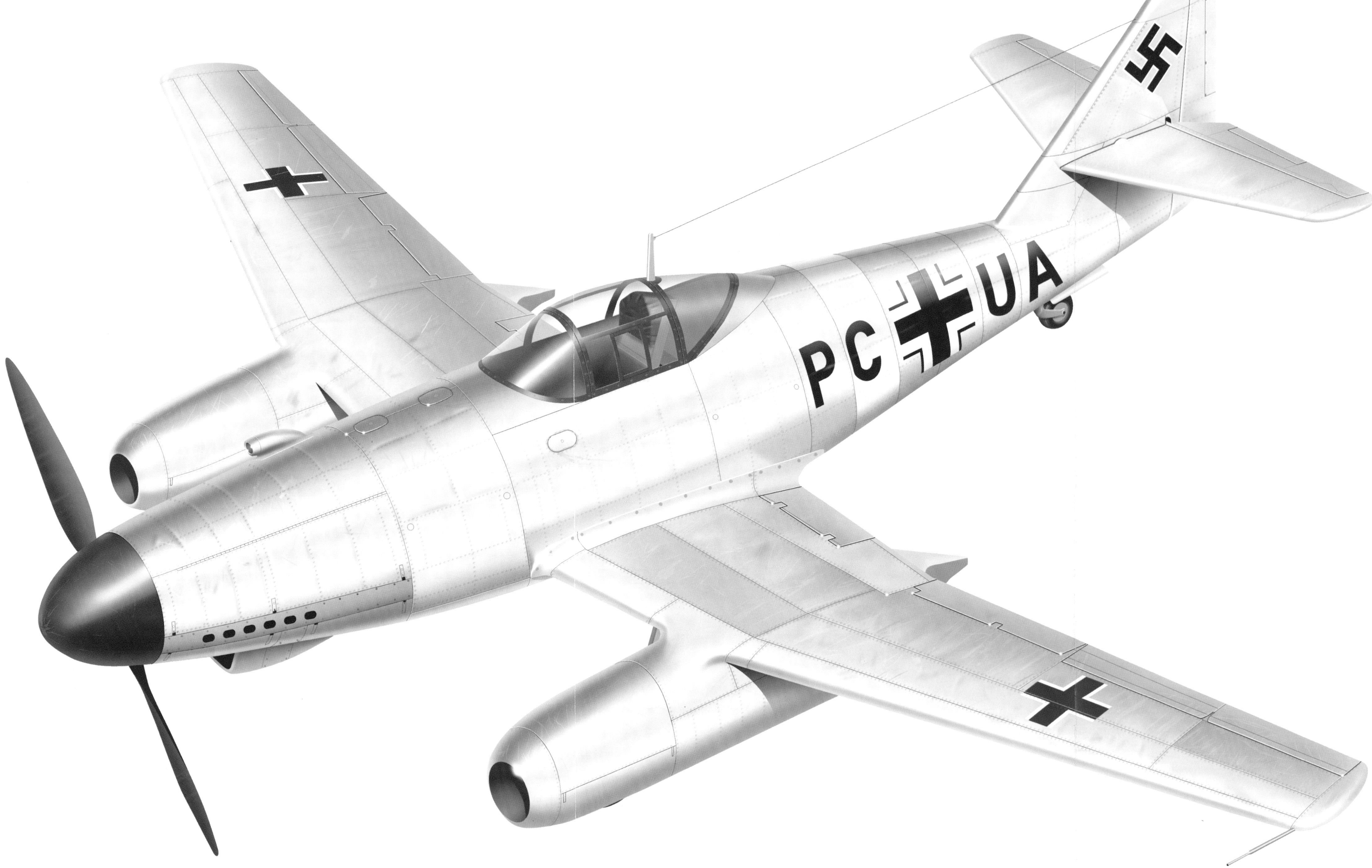

Me 262 V1   PC + UA   W.Nr. 262 000 0001 in its later form with Jumo 210G piston engine and two early BMW P.3302 (003) turbojets

Towards the end of 1941 the Me 262 V1 was fitted with two of the prototype series turbojet engines, the BMW P.3302 V2 & V10, although the Jumo 210 piston engine was also retained. The first attempted flight with these engines on 25 March 1942 failed due to both turbojets suffering compressor blade failures. This led the RLM to temporarily reduce its order for Me 262 production to five prototypes. The V1 was eventually rebuilt with two Jumo 004 A-0 engines with provision for cabin pressurisation and three MG 151 cannon. The first flight in this form took place on 19 July 1943 but the aircaft crashed and was damaged on its 95th flight on 7 June 1944 with a total flying time of 33 hours 11 minutes and probably never flew again.

Faber du Fauer, Gerhard Caroli, Woldemar Voigt, Wolfgang Degel and Josef Helmschrott, other persons present at this meeting were *Hptm.* Wolfgang Späte of *Erprobungskommando 16* who had recently given his enthusiastic report on the aircraft, *Hptm.* Otto Behrens and *Fliegerstabsing.* Heinz Pfister of the Kdo.d.E,[4] *Fliegerstabsing.* Heinrich Beauvais of *E-Stelle* Rechlin, *Oblt.* Werner Thierfelder who was to lead the first operational Me 262 test unit and several officials from the Technical Office.

A further impetus was given to the programme on the same day when *Obersting.* Dietrich Schwenke, head of the Technical Office's *Auslandsluftrüstung* (Foreign Air Equipment Department), responsible for assessing enemy aviation equipment and development, announced that a RAF prisoner of war had reported seeing a jet aircraft flying "very fast" at Farnborough. This was obviously the Gloster E.28/39 which had made its first flight at Cranwell on 15 May 1941.

Finally, on 31 May 1943, Göring agreed to the temporary suspension of the Me 209 in favour of the Me 262. On 17 June, Messerschmitt submitted the following plan to the RLM for production of the Me 262. This plan, approved on the 22nd, provided for the following deliveries:

January 1944	1
February	8
March	21
April	40
May	60

– and a further 60 per month until November 1944 when mass production was scheduled to begin. Although this was the plan, Milch was still extremely suspicious of Messerschmitt's intentions as can be seen from a planning conference transcript dated 17 June:

Milch: *"This is complete nonsense. Who prepared the file?"*

***Obersting.* Alpers:** (Chief of GL/C-B2 - Aircraft Procurement) *"The file originates from Messerschmitt. It was compiled by Herr Bley and signed by Herr Kokothaki as company manager. The stipulations are arranged as follows..."*

Milch: *"We won't need that now. We have decided what is justified and what we can manage to do now."*

Alpers: *"It has not yet been checked."*

Milch: *"Obviously this is what we shall have to do. Once we have everything, everybody will be ordered here including Messerschmitt, Bley and Kokothaki. I shall speak to them."*

Vorwald: *"The main thing is the order for the material. This we shall have to do as a special effort (or emergency)."*

Milch: *"I hope everything needed has been ordered?"*

Alpers: *"Can't say yet."*

Milch: *"After this meeting you must telephone to ask whether all items required by Messerschmitt have been ordered and if some material has not yet been ordered. I shall want a report on this. Once the gentlemen have left here, demand all purchasing details (from them). I am quite convinced that Messerschmitt has not yet ordered one single item despite the fact that, four weeks ago, they were informed that the Me 262 is to be manufactured. They have wasted four weeks, and we are now supposed to make up for this by a* DE-Auftrag *(top priority order)... Vorwald, I don't trust these people."*

Following this discussion, *Protokoll Nr. 15* of 21 June reported that 100 Me 262s were to be built by the end of 1943 on the orders of Milch. Details were given of the DE-order *Wehrmachtsnummer (49.)* under which 50 Me 262s were to be built. Labour for the Me 262 programme was to be obtained by abandoning the Me 209. Messerschmitt also asked about the possibility of

As a measure of his support for the Me 262, in May 1943, Milch (far right) sought Göring's (centre) permission to "... drop the Me 209 and turn out every Me 262 we can as a matter of urgency." Seen here, Göring and Milch greet Walter Blume, director of Arado. Bruno Loerzer looks on.

Left: During his first flight in the Me 262 V4 on 22 May 1943, Adolf Galland performed a mock interception of the experimental Me 264 V1 four-engined bomber as it came in to land. This aircraft - known as the "Amerikabomber" - was designed to be capable of bombing New York.

Right: "It flew as though angels were pushing." Generalmajor Adolf Galland (left) pictured after making his flight in the Me 262 on 22 May 1943 with (in the centre with spectacles) Flugkapitän Karl Baur and (right) Fritz Wendel.
Below: Flugkapitän Fritz Wendel (left) talking to Galland after the latter's first flight in the Me 262 V4 on 22 May 1943 with Horst Geyer from Galland's personal staff in the centre. The open canopy of the V4 can be seen in the background, far right.

Right: A group of Messerschmitt engineers talking with Galland and other Luftwaffe officers after his successful flight in the Me 262 V4. Directly to the right of Galland (in uniform with his hands clasped behind his back) can be seen Heinrich Beauvais of the experimental station at Rechlin, while to the extreme right is Karl Baur. To Galland's left is Heinrich Hentzen. Also visible in the light suit between two Luftwaffe officers is Gerhard Caroli. The aircraft in the background is the Me 262 V4, one of the few known photos of this prototype.

Me 262 V4 PC + UD W.Nr. 262 000 0004 with two early Jumo 004 A-0 engines

The aircraft first flew 15 May 1943. It crashed and badly was damaged on its 51st flight on 25 July 1943 at Schkeuditz due to very hot weather conditions causing the engines to overheat. It completed 17 hours 18 minutes flying time. The aircraft carried similar camouflage to the Me 262 V2. The extreme tip of the fuselage nose was white.

Gerd Lindner carried out several high altitude tests in the Me 262 V5 for which he was fitted with a specially-designed suit to enable him to be comfortable up to an altitude of 12,000 m (39,000 ft). From left to right in these photos are Meister Moritz Asam, leader of the Versuchsbau, Wöckner, Lindner, and Gerhard Caroli who headed Messerschmitt's flight test department. The tail of the aircraft in the background is of the V5, the first prototype to be fitted with a tricycle undercarriage.

using Gablingen and Lechfeld airfields for testing the Me 262. Lechfeld was at that time being used by *Erprobungsstaffel 410* for testing the Me 410. Me 262 production was to be incorporated into Programme 223/1, and the possible involvement of the Augsburg, Regensburg, Wiener Neustadt and Erla factories was suggested.

Meanwhile, a small boost was given to the aircraft's development when the Me 262 V5 made its first flight on 6 June 1943. This was the first prototype to be fitted with a tricycle undercarriage, the nosegear based on that of the experimental Me 309 piston-engined fighter. The undercarriage of the Me 262 V5 was not designed to retract, but the innovation did considerably improve the aircraft's take-off performance. It also provided the pilot with a much improved forward view, prevented the problem from stones and debris being thrown in the air by the jet efflux, and rendered unnecessary the need to apply the brakes in order to bring the elevators into the airstream.

Ing. Tilch (left) helps to extricate Gerd Lindner from the pressure suit designed to operate at altitudes of up to 12,000 m (39,000 ft). To the left of Tilch is Wöckner with Caroli in the centre. Also present at this event were Dipl.-Ing. Wolfgang Degel of Messerschmitt's design team and Stabs.Ing Otto Cuno from the Rechlin experimental station.

Concerned about the many technical difficulties which had frequently bedevilled the development of new aircraft scheduled to enter into *Luftwaffe* service, Hitler invited representatives of the German aviation industry, including Dr Ernst Heinkel, Professor Dornier and Professor Kurt Tank of Focke-Wulf to a private meeting at his *Berghof* residence on the Obersalzburg, near Berchtesgaden. This took place on 27 June 1943, without Göring's knowledge, and was attended by Professor Messerschmitt and six other leading aircraft designers, each of whom the *Führer* interviewed individually.[5] When Hitler questioned Messerschmitt about the Me 262, the Professor used the opportunity to criticise Erhard Milch who one month earlier had cancelled the Me 209. The over-sensitive Professor had taken the Me 209's cancellation as a personal slight, and was now seeking vindication of his injured pride. Messerschmitt warned Hitler against mass-producing the Me 262, since the jet fighter's fuel consumption would be much higher than the piston-engined Me 209. As a result, Messerschmitt secured a *Führer* Order reversing Milch's decision of 25 May. However, Messerschmitt did not tell Hitler that the Me 262's jet engines used low-grade fuel, which was far more plentiful than the high-octane aviation spirit required for piston engines. Professor Messerschmitt's machinations, which were yet another episode in the long-running feud with Milch, were to help to delay production of the Me 262 for several months.

The Me 262 V5 seen here before rocket-assisted take-off units were fitted. The success of the tricycle undercarriage led to a fully retractable type being fitted to all subsequent Me 262s beginning with the V6.

1 *A 'DE order' was the highest priorty production status that could be accorded to an order within the German armaments industry.*

2 *Vorwald was promoted to Generalmajor on 1 March 1943.*

3 *In November 1943, Oberstleutnant Siegfried Knemeyer succeeded Pasewaldt as the Chief of Development in the Technical Office (GL/C-Entwicklungs Chef).*

4 *Kdo.d.E = Kommando der Erprobungsstellen or Tests Centres Headquarters.*

5 *The designers and manufacturers who attended this meeting were Dr. Heinkel, Prof. Dornier, Dipl.-Ing. Blume (Arado), Prof. Hertel (Junkers), Prof. Tank (Focke-Wulf) and Dr. Vogt (Blohm und Voss).*

CHAPTER FIVE

PROJECTED Me 262 DEVELOPMENTS

Perhaps prompted by Hitler's enquiries, Messerschmitt began studying a series of further developments of the basic Me 262 design with improved range and load carrying capacity. The results of the studies, which were conducted during July and August 1943 were issued in a comprehensive Projektbaubeschreibung (Detailed Project Description) and published on 11 September 1943. This report included, for comparison purposes, the standard fighter (Jäger) and then went on to describe a new fighter-bomber (Jabo) variant, three fast bombers, (Schnellbomber I, Ia and II), three reconnaissance aircraft, (Aufklärer I, Ia and II), three interceptors, (Interzeptor I, II and III) and a trainer (Schulflugzeug).

Me 262 A-1 *Jäger*

At this time the standard Me 262 fighter was powered by two 900 kg (1,980 lb) Jumo 004 B engines and carried an armament of four 30 mm MK 108 cannon in the nose of the fuselage. The standard fuel load was two 900 ltr (198 Imp gal) tanks, one forward and one aft of the cockpit, with a further 250 ltr (55 Imp gal) tank forward of the mainwheel wells beneath the pilot's feet.

All the projects described in this chapter had the same overall dimensions:

Wing span	12.65 m	41 ft 6 in
Length	10.60 m	34 ft 9.25 in
Height	2.80 m	9 ft 2.25 in
Wing area	21.7 m^2	233.58 sq ft

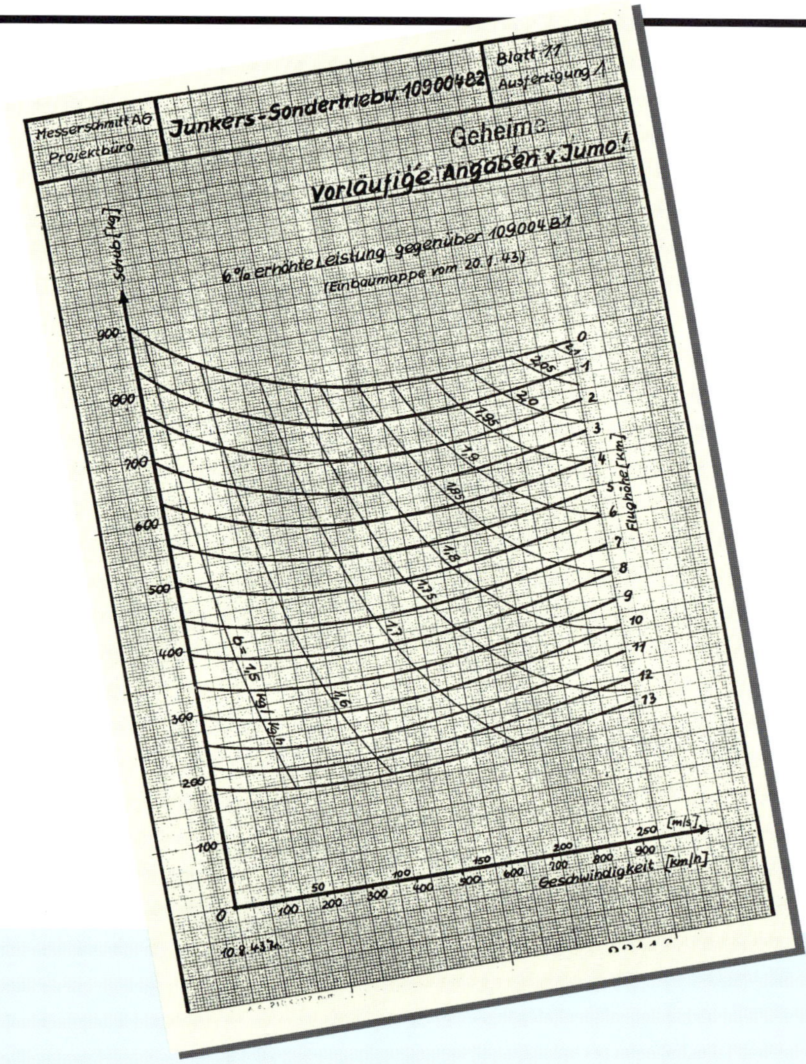

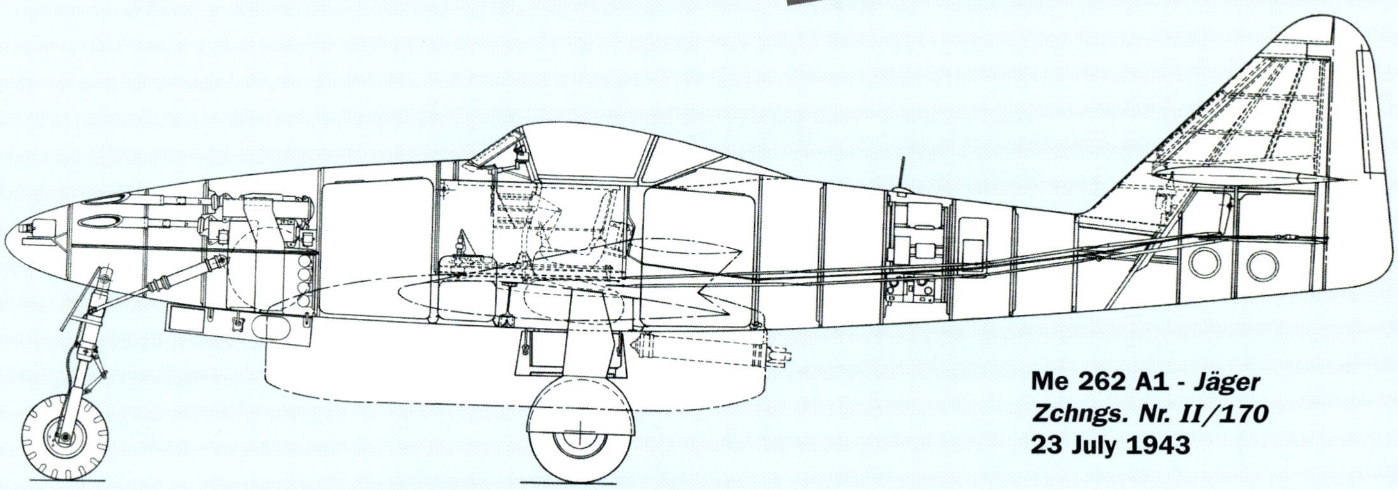

Me 262 A1 - *Jäger*
Zchngs. Nr. II/170
23 July 1943

Me 262 A-2 *JÄGER* AND *JABO*

As originally proposed, this variant differed from the A-1 in having an additional pair of MK 108 cannon in the nose and a new 750 ltr (165 Imp gal) fuel tank in the rear fuselage. When the Me 262 A-2 actually left the assembly line, the variant had its armament *reduced* to two MK 108 cannon. It also had the then standard two 900 ltr (198 Imp gal), one 170 ltr (37 Imp gal) and one 600 ltr (132 Imp gal) fuel tanks. The A-2 could carry one 500 kg (1,100 lb) or two 250 kg (550 lb) bombs.

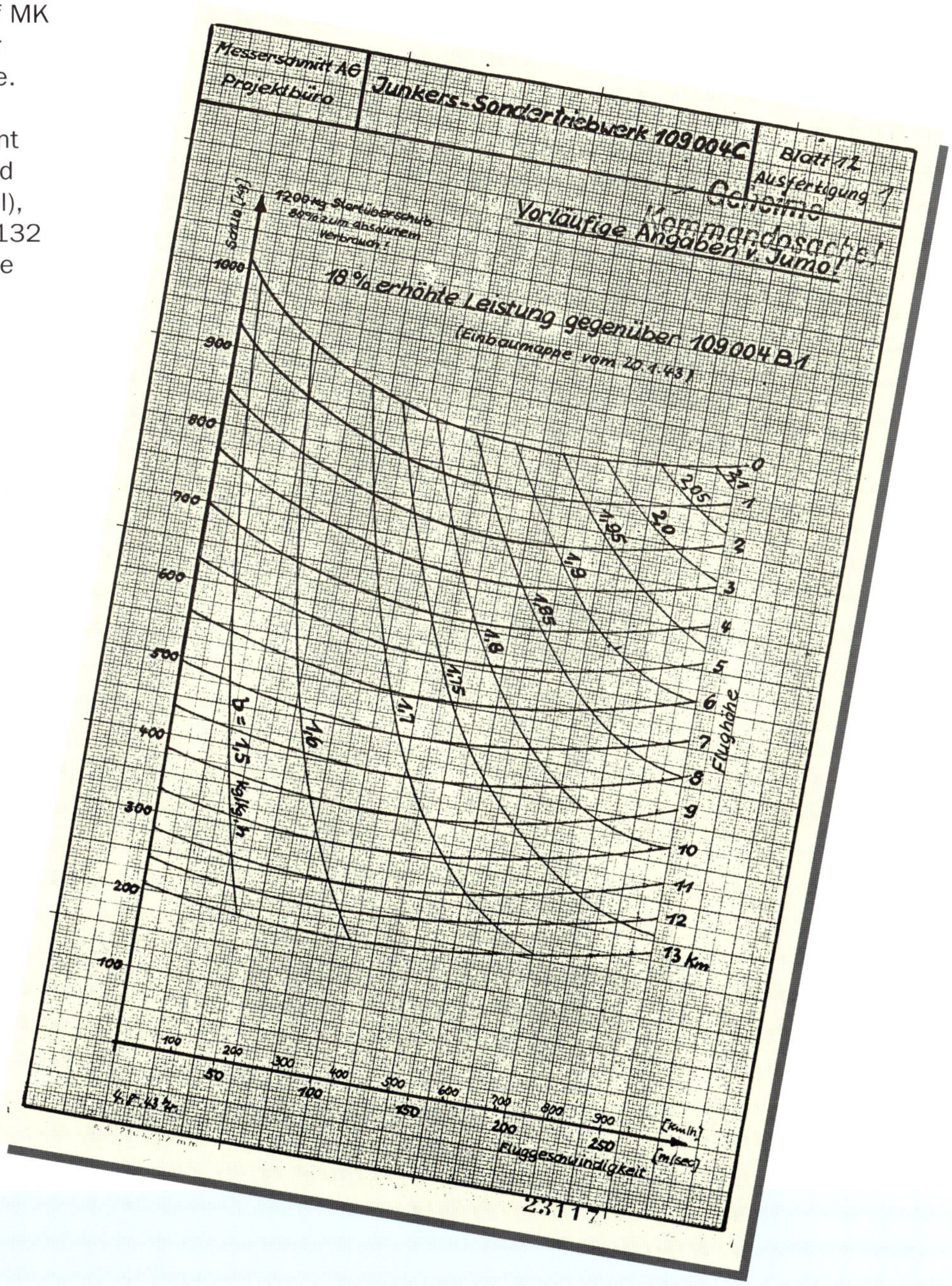

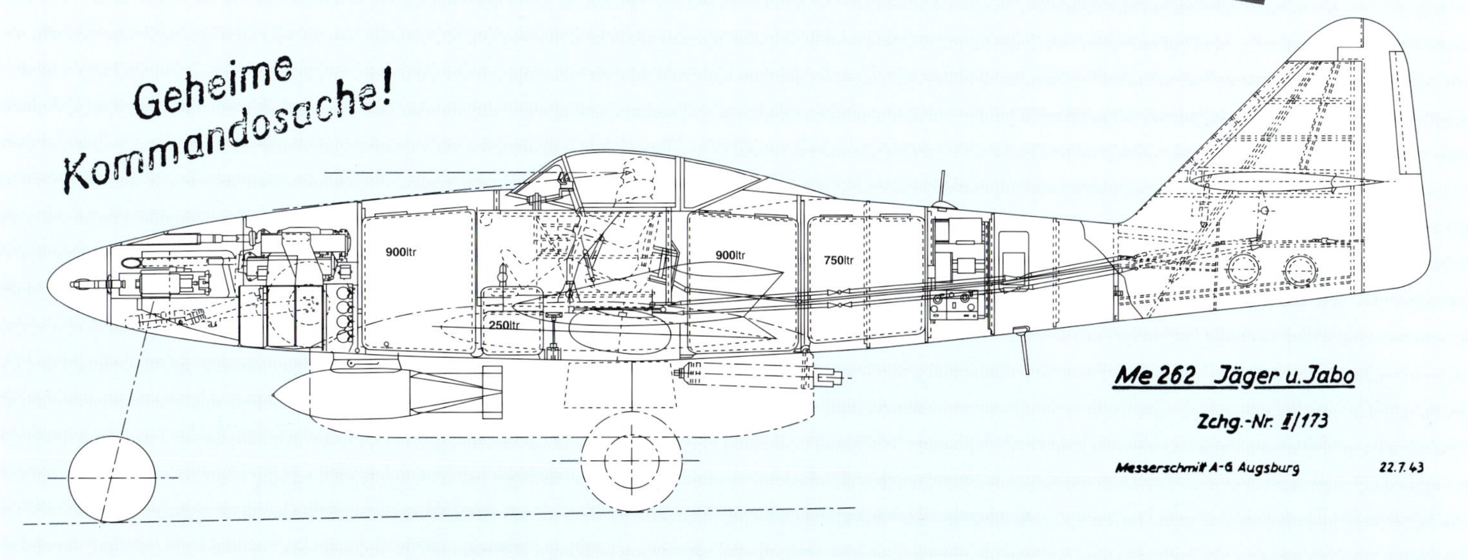

Me 262 *Schnellbomber* I

Similar in shape to the standard Me 262 A-1 *Jäger*, this design was fitted with a modified nose housing an additional 1,000 ltr (220 Imp gal) fuel tank. A further 1,000 ltr tank was to be mounted in the rear of the fuselage, the radio equipment being relegated further toward the tail. To compensate for the increased weight of the new tanks, the aircraft was to be powered by two 1,000 kg (2,200 lb) thrust Jumo 004 C engines and have rocket assisted take-off units. A pair of additional jettisonable mainwheels with a diameter of 770 x 270 mm (30.3 x 10.6 inches) were also to be fitted. No defensive armament was to be carried but the following alternative bomb loads were proposed:

- One 1,000 kg bomb
  (SE 1000, PC 1000 RS or SB 1000)
- Two 500 kg bombs
  (SE 500, SC 500, SD 500 or Flam C 500)
- Two 250 kg bombs
  (SE 250, SD 250 or Stabo 250)
- One 700 kg BT 700 torpedo bomb.

All-up weight	8,330 kg	18,360 lb
Landing weight	4,740 kg	10,450 lb
Max. speed at: sea level	755 km/h	469 mph
6 km (19,700 ft)	785 km/h	488 mph
9 km (29,500 ft)	742 km/h	461 mph
Rate of climb: sea level	14.0 m/sec	45.9 ft/sec
6 km (19,700 ft)	6.0 m/sec	19.7 ft/sec
9 km (29,500 ft)	1.3 m/sec	4.3 ft/sec
Endurance at: sea level	0.81 hrs	
6 km (19,700 ft)	1.60 hrs	
9 km (29,500 ft)	2.16 hrs	
Service ceiling	9,450 m	31,000 ft
Normal range at: sea level	650 km	404 miles
6 km (19,700 ft)	1,180 km	733 miles
9 km (29,500 ft)	1,560 km	969 miles
Landing speed	173 km/h	107 mph

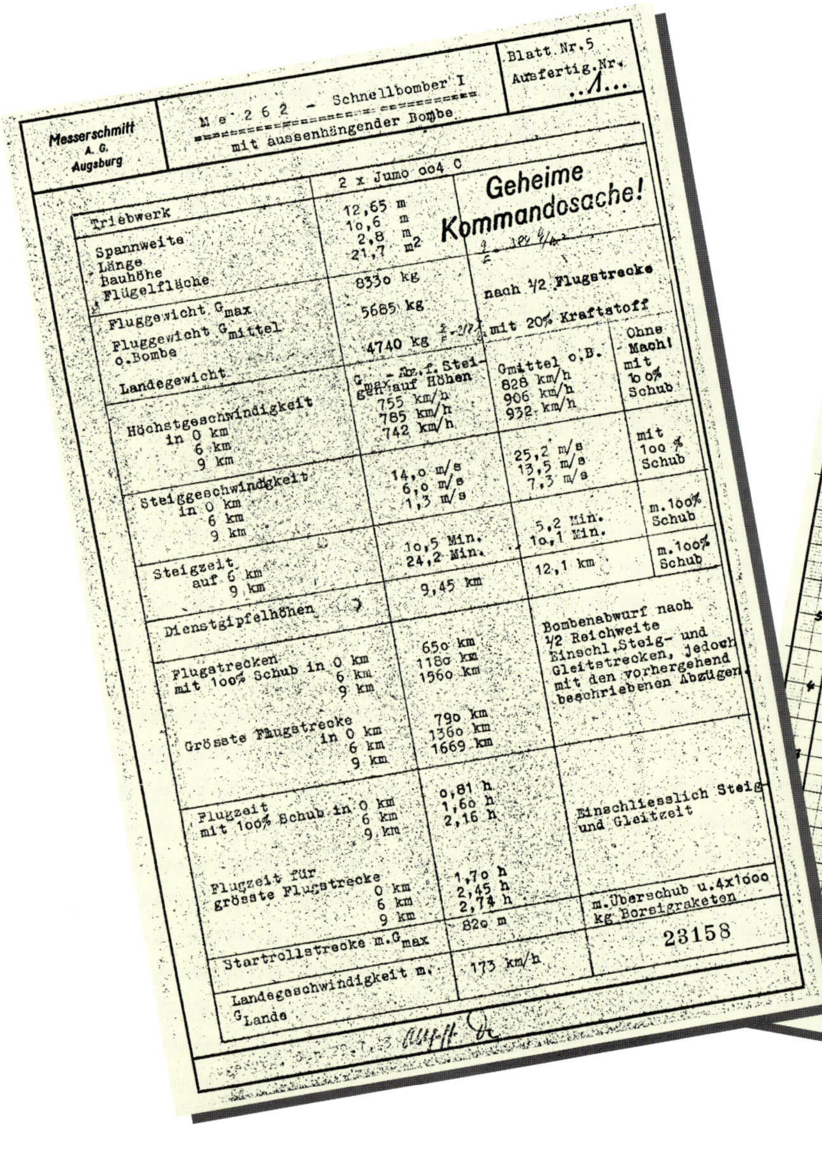

Messerschmitt A.G. Augsburg — Me 262 – Schnellbomber I mit aussenhängender Bombe — Blatt Nr. 5, Ausfertig. Nr. 1

Geheime Kommandosache!

	2 x Jumo 004 C		
Triebwerk			
Spannweite, Länge, Bauhöhe, Flügelfläche	12,65 m, 10,6 m, 2,8 m, 21,7 m²		
Fluggewicht G_{max}	8330 kg	nach 1/2 Flugstrecke	
Fluggewicht G_{mittel} o. Bombe	5685 kg	mit 20% Kraftstoff	
Landegewicht	4740 kg		
Höchstgeschwindigkeit in 0 km, 6 km, 9 km	G_{max} – Abz. f. Steigen auf Höhen: 755 km/h, 785 km/h, 742 km/h	G_{mittel} o. B.: 828 km/h, 906 km/h, 932 km/h	Ohne Mach! mit 100% Schub
Steiggeschwindigkeit in 0 km, 6 km, 9 km	14,0 m/s, 6,0 m/s, 1,3 m/s	25,2 m/s, 13,5 m/s, 7,3 m/s	mit 100% Schub
Steigzeit auf 6 km, 9 km	10,5 Min., 24,2 Min.	5,2 Min., 10,1 Min.	m. 100% Schub
Dienstgipfelhöhen	9,45 km	12,1 km	m. 100% Schub
Flugstrecken mit 100% Schub in 0 km, 6 km, 9 km	650 km, 1180 km, 1560 km	Bombenabwurf nach 1/2 Reichweite Einschl. Steig- und Gleitstrecken, jedoch mit den vorhergehend beschriebenen Abzügen.	
Grösste Flugstrecke in 0 km, 6 km, 9 km	790 km, 1360 km, 1669 km		
Flugzeit mit 100% Schub in 0 km, 6 km, 9 km	0,81 h, 1,60 h, 2,16 h	Einschliesslich Steig- und Gleitzeit	
Flugzeit für grösste Flugstrecke 0 km, 6 km, 9 km	1,70 h, 2,45 h, 2,74 h	m. Überschub u. 4x1000 kg Borsigraketen	
Startrollstrecke m. G_{max}	820 m	23158	
Landegeschwindigkeit m. G_{Lande}	173 km/h		

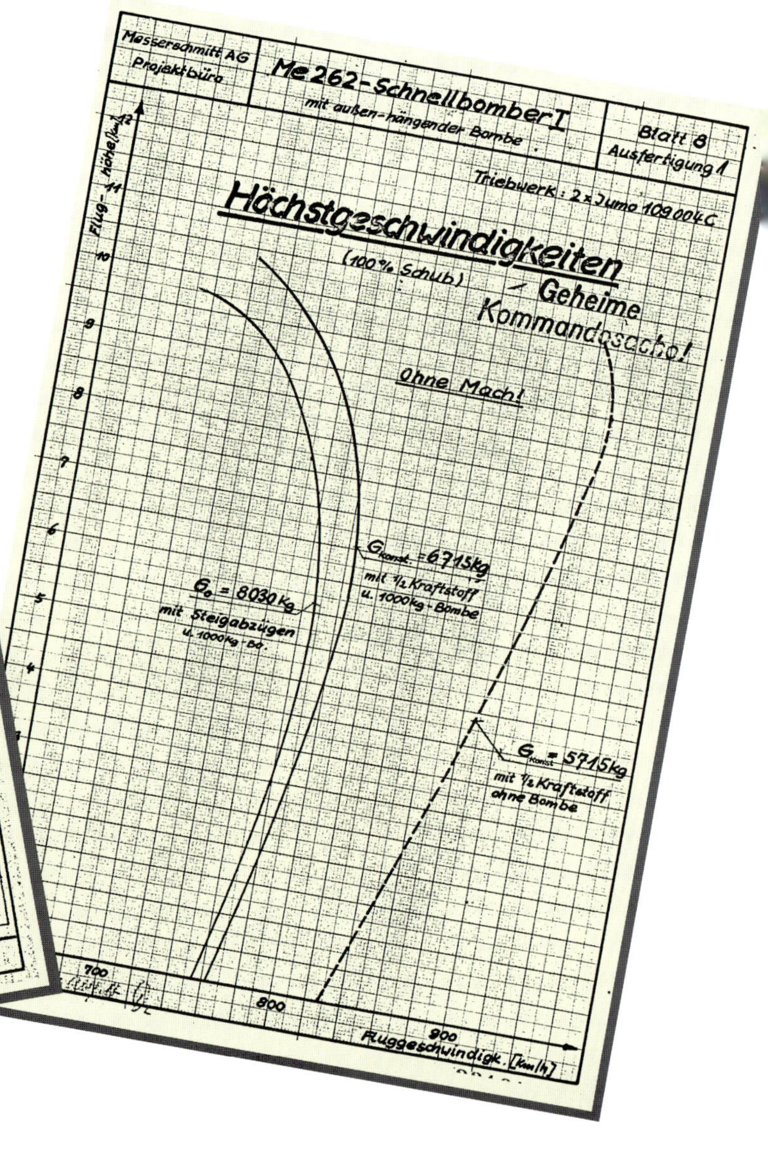

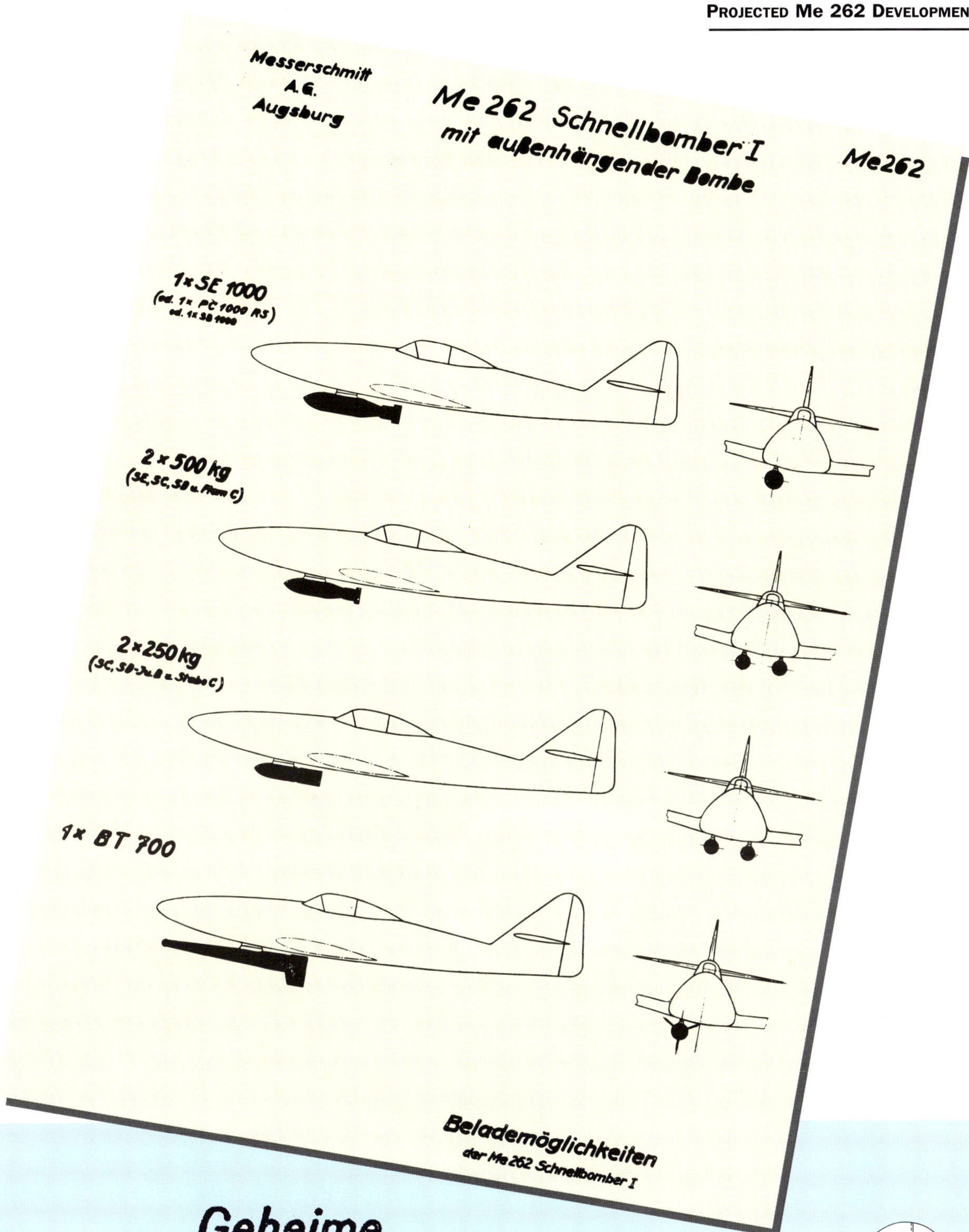
Messerschmitt
A.G.
Augsburg
Me 262 Schnellbomber I
mit außenhängender Bombe
Me262
1×SE 1000
2×500 kg
2×250 kg
1× BT 700
Belademöglichkeiten
der Me 262 Schnellbomber I

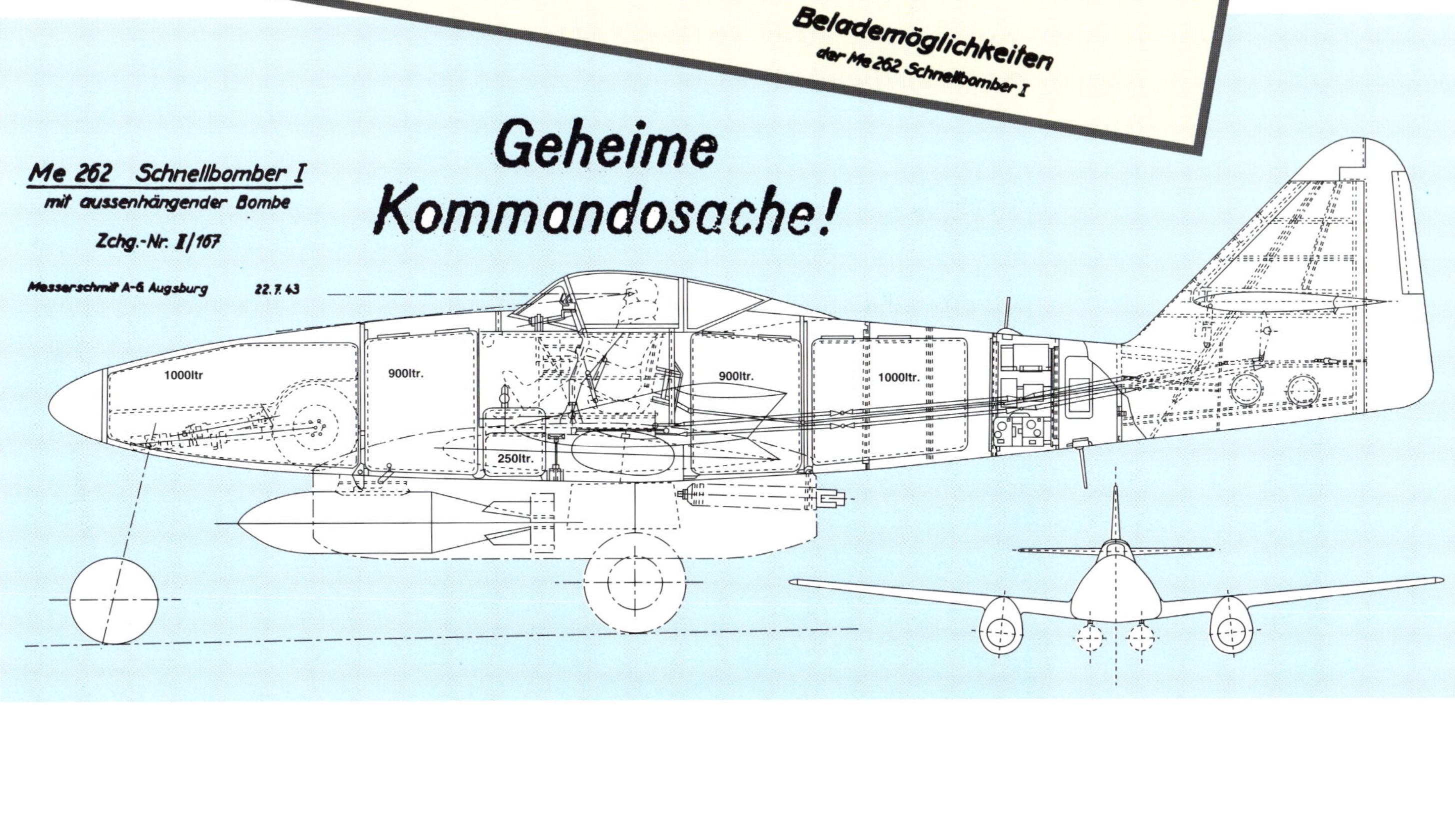
Geheime
Kommandosache!
Me 262 Schnellbomber I
mit aussenhängender Bombe
Messerschmitt A-G Augsburg
22.7.43
1000ltr
900ltr.
900ltr.
1000ltr.
250ltr.

Me 262 *Schnellbomber* Ia

In this design the pilot's cockpit and radio equipment was to be moved forward to the nose of the aircraft, and three additional fuel tanks provided. The two in the centre fuselage were to carry 700 and 500 ltrs (155 and 110 Imp gals) of fuel, with that in the rear containing an extra 1,000 ltrs. Like the *Schnellbomber* I, the design was to be powered by Jumo 004 C engines and have additional mainwheels with strengthened undercarriage legs. A similar bomb load to the *Schnellbomber* I was to be carried, but two MK 108s could be mounted in the nose. No estimated performance figures were given in the report, but the adjacent weights were quoted.

All-up weight	8,500 kg	18,740 lb
All-up weight with four 1000 kg thrust assisted take-off rockets	8,905 kg	19,630 lb
Landing weight	4,000 kg	8,820 lb

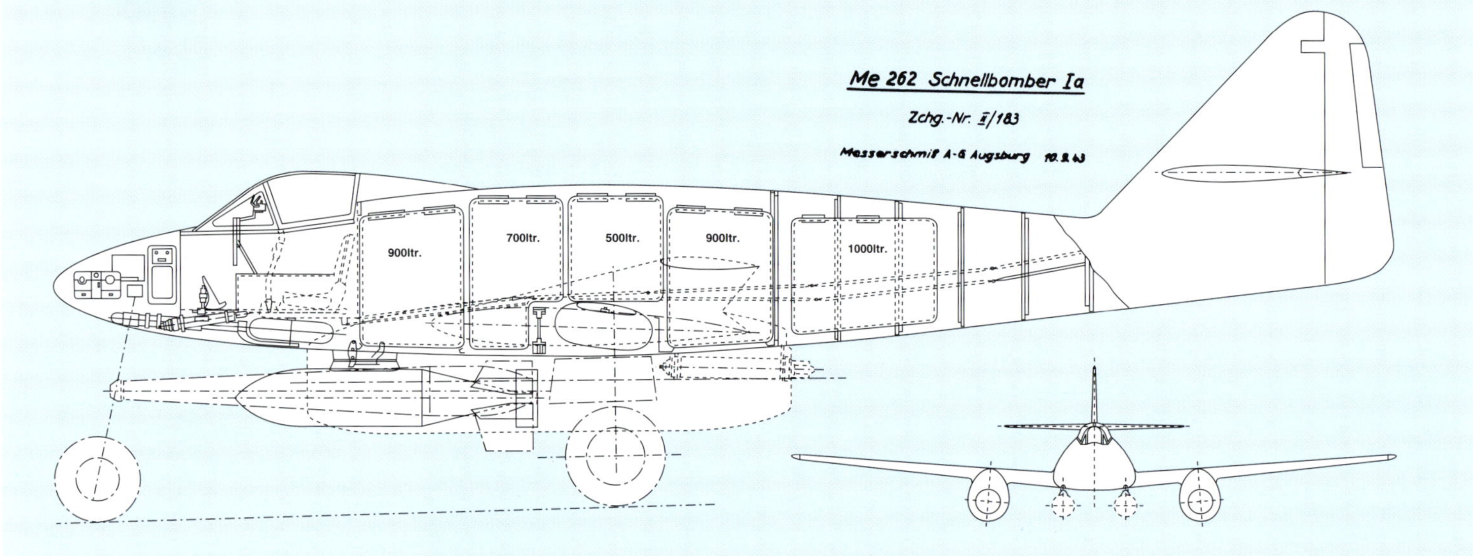

Me 262 *SCHNELLBOMBER* II

The *Schnellbomber* II had a new and much deeper fuselage and enlarged vertical tail surfaces giving it a somewhat pregnant look. In this design, fuel supply was increased by a 450 and 650 ltr (100 and 145 Imp gal) tank in the nose and a 1,300 ltr (285 Imp gal) tank behind the cockpit. Again the variant was to be powered by Jumo 004 C engines and have strengthened undercarriage legs and additional mainwheels. The bomb load was similar to that of the previous two designs but this was housed internally in the lower part of the forward fuselage.

All-up weight	9,070 kg	20,000 lb
Landing weight	6,255 kg	13,790 lb
Max. speed at: sea level	826 km/h	513 mph
6 km (19,700 ft)	882 km/h	548 mph
9 km (29,500 ft)	826 km/h	513 mph
Rate of climb: sea level	15.0 m/sec	45.2 ft/sec
6 km (19,700 ft)	6.6 m/sec	21.7 ft/sec
9 km (29,500 ft)	1.8 m/sec	5.9 ft/sec
Endurance at: sea level	0.91 hrs	
6 km (19,700 ft)	1.70 hrs	
9 km (29,500 ft)	2.31 hrs	
Service ceiling	9,700 m	31,800 ft
Normal range at: sea level	760 km	472 miles
6 km (19,700 ft)	1,370 km	851 miles
9 km (29,500 ft)	1,790 km	1,110 miles
Landing speed	182 km/h	113 mph

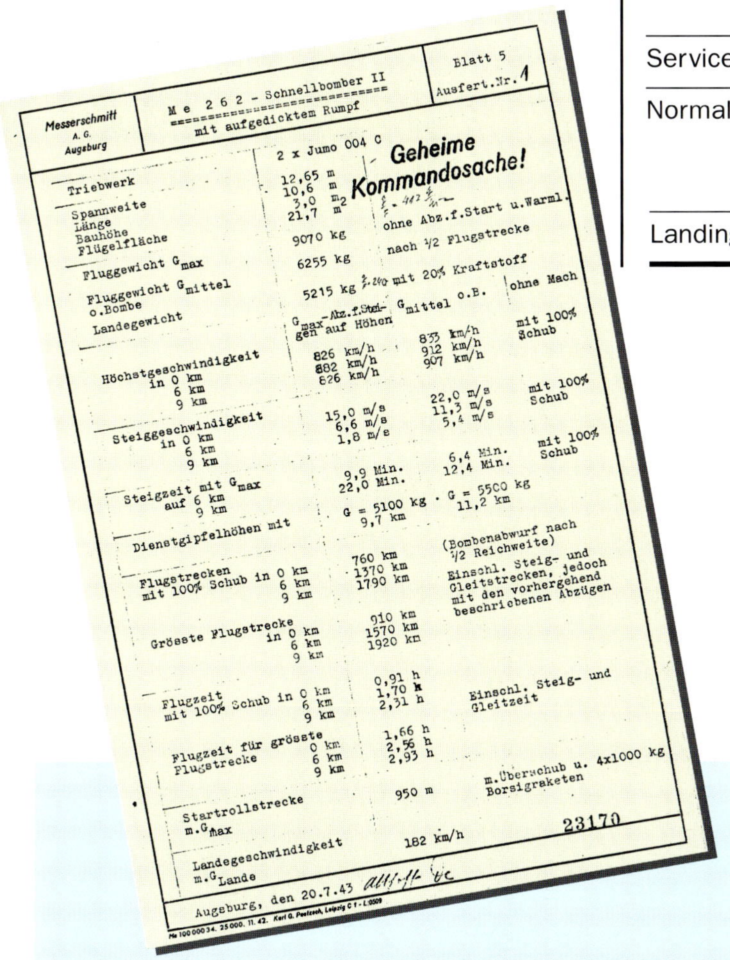
Messerschmitt A. G. Augsburg | Me 262 - Schnellbomber II mit aufgedicktem Rumpf | Blatt 5 Ausfert.Nr. 1

Geheime Kommandosache!

Triebwerk	2 x Jumo 004 C		
Spannweite Länge Bauhöhe Flügelfläche	12,65 m 10,6 m 3,0 m 21,7 m²		
Fluggewicht G_{max}	9070 kg	ohne Abz.f.Start u.Warml.	
Fluggewicht G_{mittel} o.Bombe	6255 kg	nach 1/2 Flugstrecke	
Landegewicht	5215 kg	mit 20% Kraftstoff	
	G_{max}-Abz.f.Steigen auf Höhen	G_{mittel} o.B.	ohne Mach
Höchstgeschwindigkeit in 0 km 6 km 9 km	826 km/h 882 km/h 826 km/h	833 km/h 912 km/h 907 km/h	mit 100% Schub
Steiggeschwindigkeit in 0 km 6 km 9 km	15,0 m/s 6,6 m/s 1,8 m/s	22,0 m/s 11,3 m/s 5,4 m/s	mit 100% Schub
Steigzeit mit G_{max} auf 6 km 9 km	9,9 Min. 22,0 Min.	6,4 Min. 12,4 Min.	mit 100% Schub
Dienstgipfelhöhen mit	G = 5100 kg 9,7 km	G = 5500 kg 11,2 km	
Flugstrecken mit 100% Schub in 0 km 6 km 9 km	760 km 1370 km 1790 km	(Bombenabwurf nach 1/2 Reichweite) Einschl. Steig- und Gleitstrecken, jedoch mit den vorhergehend beschriebenen Abzügen	
Grösste Flugstrecke in 0 km 6 km 9 km	910 km 1570 km 1920 km		
Flugzeit mit 100% Schub in 0 km 6 km 9 km	0,91 h 1,70 h 2,31 h	Einschl. Steig- und Gleitzeit	
Flugzeit für grösste Flugstrecke 0 km 6 km 9 km	1,66 h 2,56 h 2,93 h		
Startrollstrecke m.G_{max}	950 m	m.Überschub u. 4x1000 kg Borsigraketen	
Landegeschwindigkeit m.G_{Lande}	182 km/h		23170

Augsburg, den 20.7.43

Me 100 000 34. 25 000. 11. 42. Karl G. Peetzsch, Leipzig C 1 - L 0509

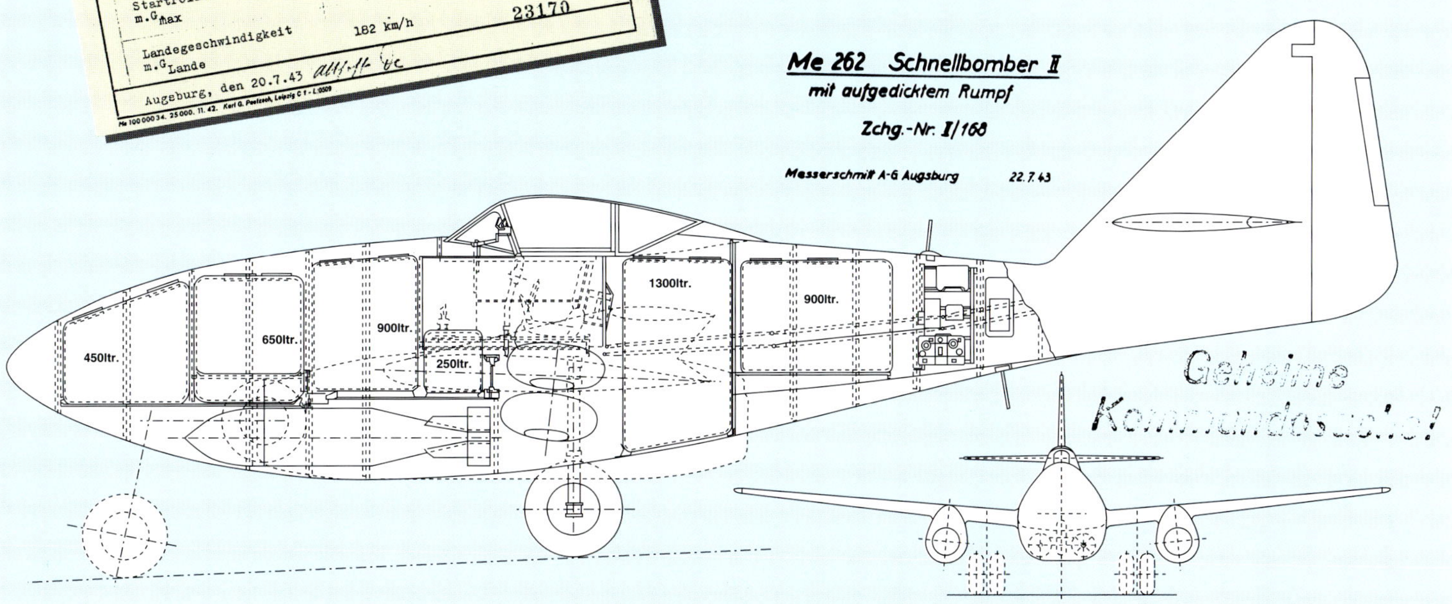

Me 262 *Aufklärer* I

The Me 262 *Aufklärer* I was similar in shape to the Me 262 *Jäger* but was to be fitted with a new 500 ltr (110 Imp gal) fuel tank in the extreme nose. Either one Rb 75/30 and one Rb 20/30 or two Rb 75/30 cameras could be mounted behind the new fuel tank, with a glazed panel to cover the lenses. The 250 ltr tank beneath the pilot's feet was removed and replaced by one of 750 ltr (165 Imp gal) capacity in the rear fuselage. The project was to be powered by two Jumo 004 C engines but no armament was to be carried.

All-up weight	6,600 kg	14,550 lb
Landing weight	4,520 kg	9,960 lb
Max. speed at: sea level	848 km/h	527 mph
6 km (19,700 ft)	922 km/h	573 mph
9 km (29,500 ft)	950 km/h	590 mph
Rate of climb: sea level	27.6 m/sec	90.6 ft/sec
6 km (19,700 ft)1	1.9 m/sec	39.0 ft/sec
9 km (29,500 ft)	6.5 m/sec	23.3 ft/sec
Endurance at: sea level	0.65 hrs	
6 km (19,700 ft)	1.30 hrs	
9 km (29,500 ft)	1.74 hrs	
Service ceiling	11,750 m	38,500 ft
Normal range at: sea level	540 km	336 miles
6 km (19,700 ft)	1,020 km	634 miles
9 km (29,500 ft)	1,380 km	858 miles
Landing speed	170 km/h	106 mph

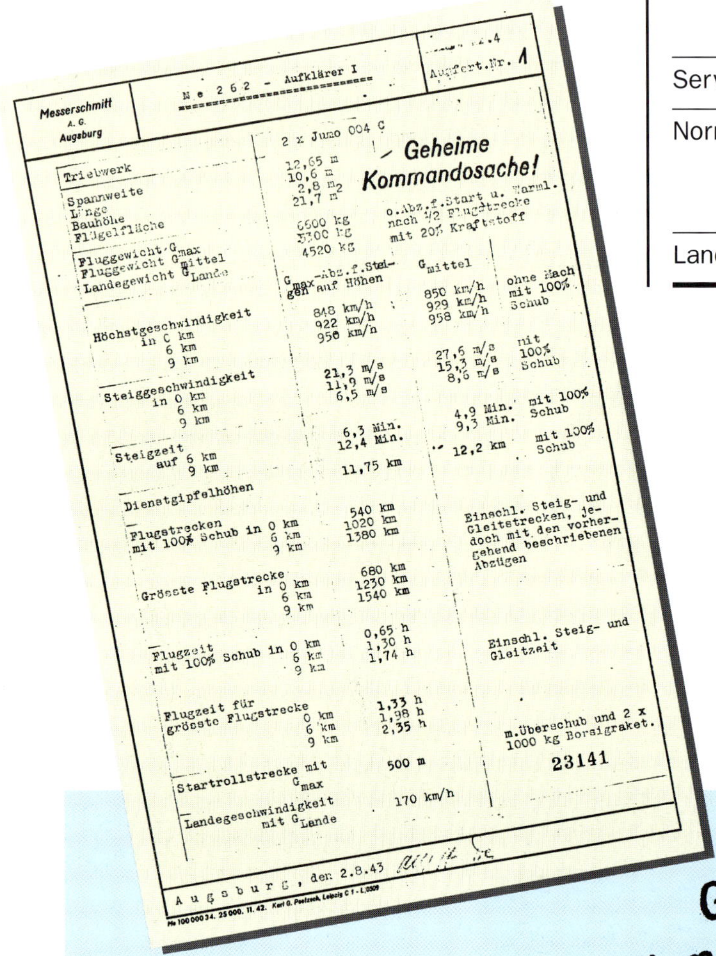
Messerschmitt A. G. Augsburg
Me 262 - Aufklärer I
Ausfert.Nr. 1
Geheime Kommandosache!
Triebwerk — 2 x Jumo 004 C
Spannweite — 12,65 m
Länge — 10,6 m
Bauhöhe — 2,8 m
Flügelfläche — 21,7 m2
Fluggewicht G_{max} — 6600 kg
Fluggewicht G_{mittel} — 5300 kg — o.Abz.f.Start u. Warml. nach 1/2 Flugstrecke mit 20% Kraftstoff
Landegewicht G_{Lande} — 4520 kg
G_{max}-Abz.f.Steigen auf Höhen — G_{mittel}
Höchstgeschwindigkeit in 0 km, 6 km, 9 km — 848 km/h, 922 km/h, 950 km/h — 850 km/h, 929 km/h, 958 km/h — ohne Mach mit 100% Schub
Steiggeschwindigkeit in 0 km, 6 km, 9 km — 21,3 m/s, 11,9 m/s, 6,5 m/s — 27,6 m/s, 15,3 m/s, 8,6 m/s — mit 100% Schub
Steigzeit auf 6 km, 9 km — 6,3 Min., 12,4 Min. — 4,9 Min., 9,3 Min. — mit 100% Schub
Dienstgipfelhöhen — 11,75 km — 12,2 km — mit 100% Schub
Flugstrecken mit 100% Schub in 0 km, 6 km, 9 km — 540 km, 1020 km, 1380 km — Einschl. Steig- und Gleitstrecken, jedoch mit den vorhergehend beschriebenen Abzügen
Grösste Flugstrecke in 0 km, 6 km, 9 km — 680 km, 1230 km, 1540 km
Flugzeit mit 100% Schub in 0 km, 6 km, 9 km — 0,65 h, 1,30 h, 1,74 h — Einschl. Steig- und Gleitzeit
Flugzeit für grösste Flugstrecke 0 km, 6 km, 9 km — 1,33 h, 1,98 h, 2,35 h
Startrollstrecke mit G_{max} — 500 m — m.Überschub und 2 x 1000 kg Borsigraket.
Landegeschwindigkeit mit G_{Lande} — 170 km/h
23141
Augsburg, den 2.8.43
Me 100 000 34. 25 000. 11. 42. Karl G. Poetzsch, Leipzig C 1 - L 0509

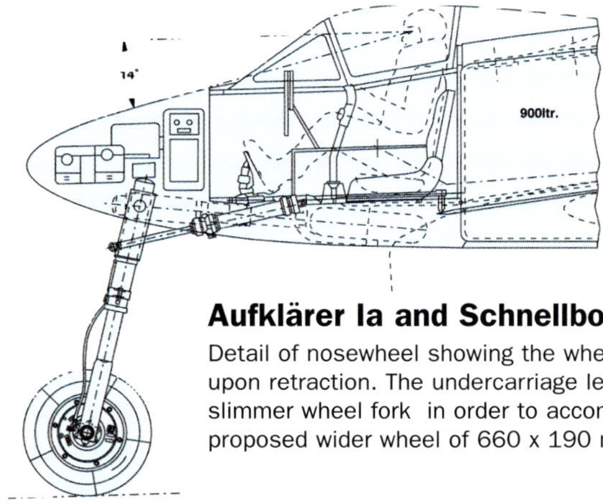

Aufklärer Ia and Schnellbomber Ia

Detail of nosewheel showing the wheel rotated at 90° upon retraction. The undercarriage leg is fitted with a slimmer wheel fork in order to accommodate the proposed wider wheel of 660 x 190 mm.

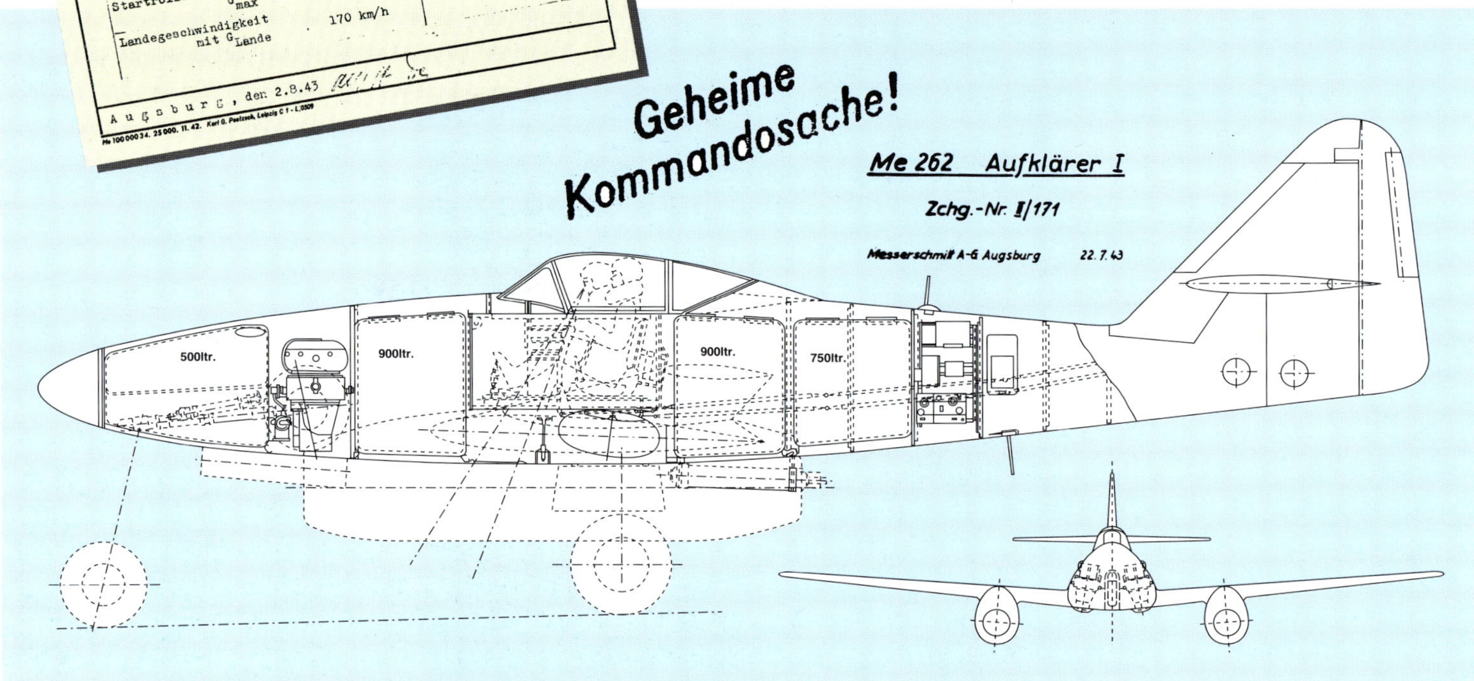

Me 262 *Aufklärer* Ia

Similar in appearance to the *Schnellbomber* Ia, the project had the cockpit moved forward and two additional 700 and 500 ltr (155 and 110 Imp gal) fuel tanks mounted in the centre of the fuselage. Two Rb 75/30 cameras would have been carried in the rear fuselage with provision for two MK 108 cannon in the nose. Although the design was to be powered by Jumo 004 C engines, standard mainwheels were to be fitted. Only the adjacent weights were quoted in the report, but the performance was similar to that of the *Aufklärer* I.

All-up weight	6,550 kg	14,440 lb
All-up weight with four 1000 kg thrust assisted take-off rockets	6,710 kg	14,790 lb
Landing weight	3,900 kg	8,600 lb

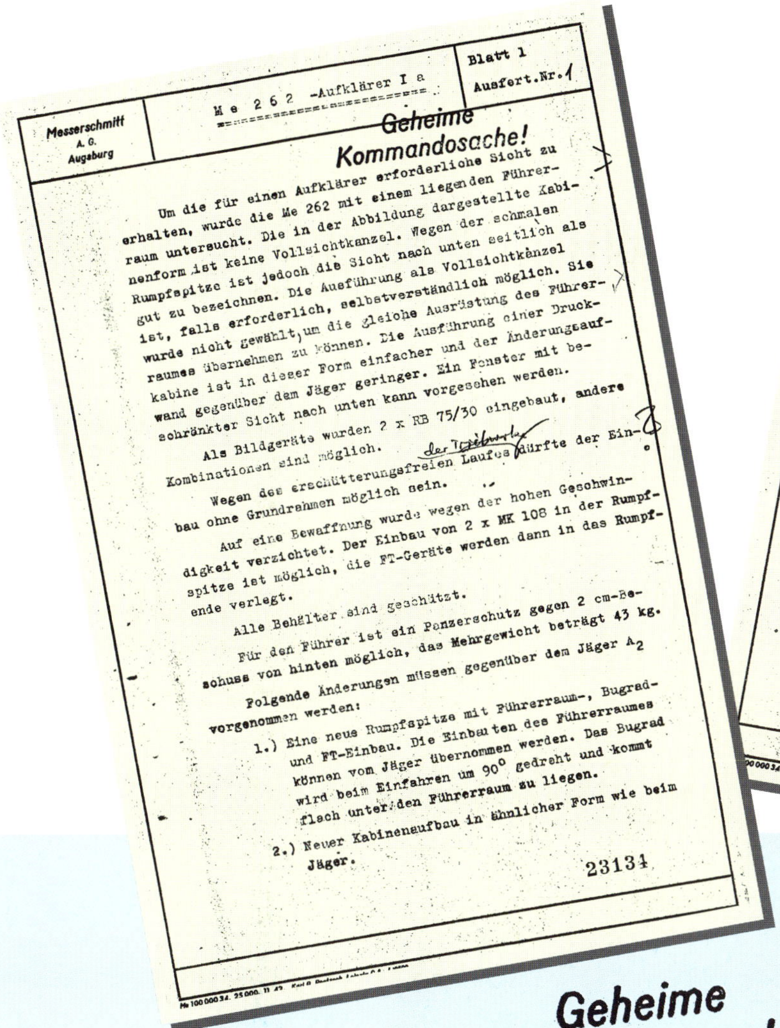

Messerschmitt A. G. Augsburg

Me 262 -Aufklärer I a

Blatt 1

Ausfert.Nr. 1

Geheime Kommandosache!

Um die für einen Aufklärer erforderliche Sicht zu erhalten, wurde die Me 262 mit einem liegenden Führerraum untersucht. Die in der Abbildung dargestellte Kabinenform ist keine Vollsichtkanzel. Wegen der schmalen Rumpfspitze ist jedoch die Sicht nach unten seitlich als gut zu bezeichnen. Die Ausführung als Vollsichtkanzel ist, falls erforderlich, selbstverständlich möglich. Sie wurde nicht gewählt, um die gleiche Ausrüstung des Führerraumes übernehmen zu können. Die Ausführung einer Druckkabine ist in dieser Form einfacher und der Änderungsaufwand gegenüber dem Jäger geringer. Ein Fenster mit beschränkter Sicht nach unten kann vorgesehen werden.

Als Bildgeräte wurden 2 x RB 75/30 eingebaut, andere Kombinationen sind möglich.

Wegen des erschütterungsfreien Laufes der Triebwerke dürfte der Einbau ohne Grundrahmen möglich sein.

Auf eine Bewaffnung wurde wegen der hohen Geschwindigkeit verzichtet. Der Einbau von 2 x MK 108 in der Rumpfspitze ist möglich, die FT-Geräte werden dann in das Rumpfende verlegt.

Alle Behälter sind geschützt.

Für den Führer ist ein Panzerschutz gegen 2 cm-Beschuss von hinten möglich, das Mehrgewicht beträgt 43 kg.

Folgende Änderungen müssen gegenüber dem Jäger A_2 vorgenommen werden:

1.) Eine neue Rumpfspitze mit Führerraum-, Bugrad- und FT-Einbau. Die Einbauten des Führerraumes können vom Jäger übernommen werden. Das Bugrad wird beim Einfahren um 90° gedreht und kommt flach unter den Führerraum zu liegen.

2.) Neuer Kabinenaufbau in ähnlicher Form wie beim Jäger.

23134

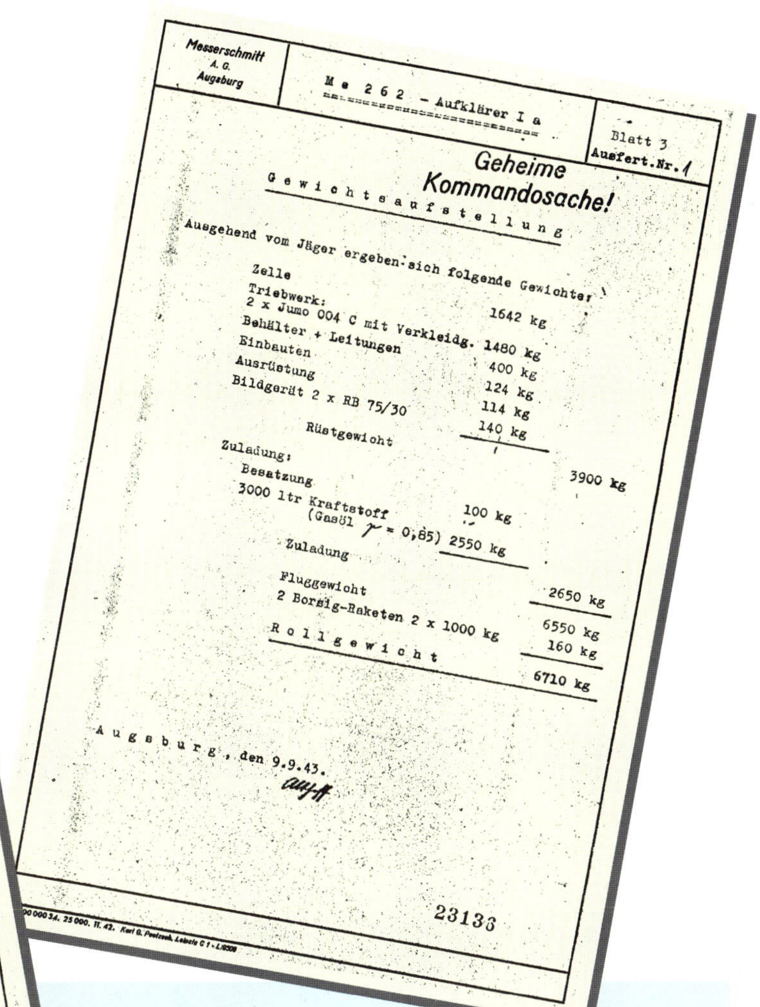

Messerschmitt A. G. Augsburg

Me 262 - Aufklärer I a

Blatt 3

Ausfert.Nr. 1

Geheime Kommandosache!

Gewichtsaufstellung

Ausgehend vom Jäger ergeben sich folgende Gewichte:

Zelle		
Triebwerk:	1642 kg	
2 x Jumo 004 C mit Verkleidg.	1480 kg	
Behälter + Leitungen	400 kg	
Einbauten	124 kg	
Ausrüstung	114 kg	
Bildgerät 2 x RB 75/30	140 kg	
Rüstgewicht		3900 kg
Zuladung:		
Besatzung	100 kg	
3000 ltr Kraftstoff (Gasöl γ = 0,85)	2550 kg	
Zuladung		2650 kg
Fluggewicht		6550 kg
2 Borsig-Raketen 2 x 1000 kg		160 kg
Rollgewicht		6710 kg

Augsburg, den 9.9.43.

23133

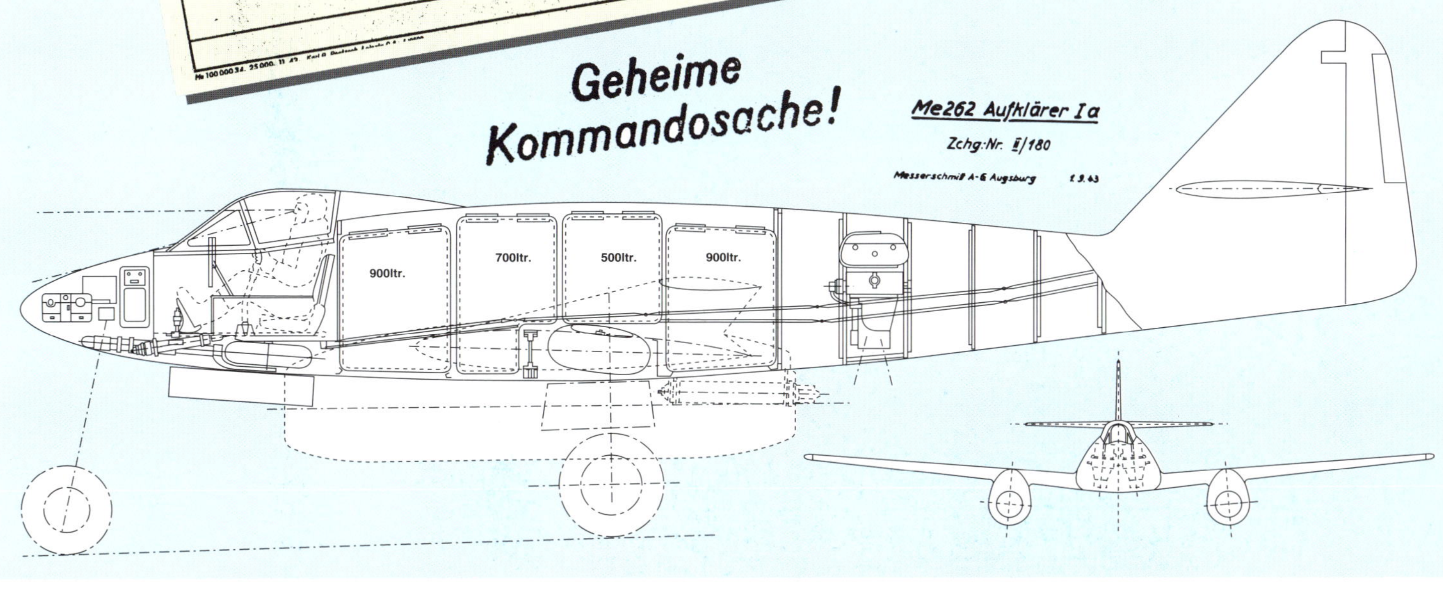

Me 262 *Aufklärer* II

The *Aufklärer* II was similar in appearance to the parallel fast bomber project, with a bulged fuselage housing additional fuel capacity and enlarged vertical tail surfaces. The project was to have the 650 ltr (145 Imp gal) tank in the nose and the 1,300 ltr (285 Imp gal) tank behind the cockpit with an additional 1,450 ltrs (320 Imp gal) in the lower part of the forward fuselage. The variant was to have Jumo 004 C engines, strengthened undercarriage legs and an additional pair of mainwheels which were jettisoned on take-off. A Rb 20/30 and two Rb 75/30 cameras were to be mounted in the extreme nose and like all the reconnaissance and fast bomber projects, no defensive armament was carried. At one stage the project was to have a second crew member, but this plan was later dropped.

All-up weight		9,050 kg	19,950 lb
Landing weight		5,530 kg	12,190 lb
Max. speed at:	sea level	826 km/h	513 mph
	6 km (19,700 ft)	882 km/h	548 mph
	9 km (29,500 ft)	826 km/h	513 mph
Rate of climb:	sea level	15.0 m/sec	49.2 ft/sec
	6 km (19,700 ft)	6.7 m/sec	22.0 ft/sec
	9 km (29,500 ft)	2.0 m/sec	6.6 ft/sec

Me 262 Aufklärer II
2 x Jumo 004C turbojets (26 May 1943)

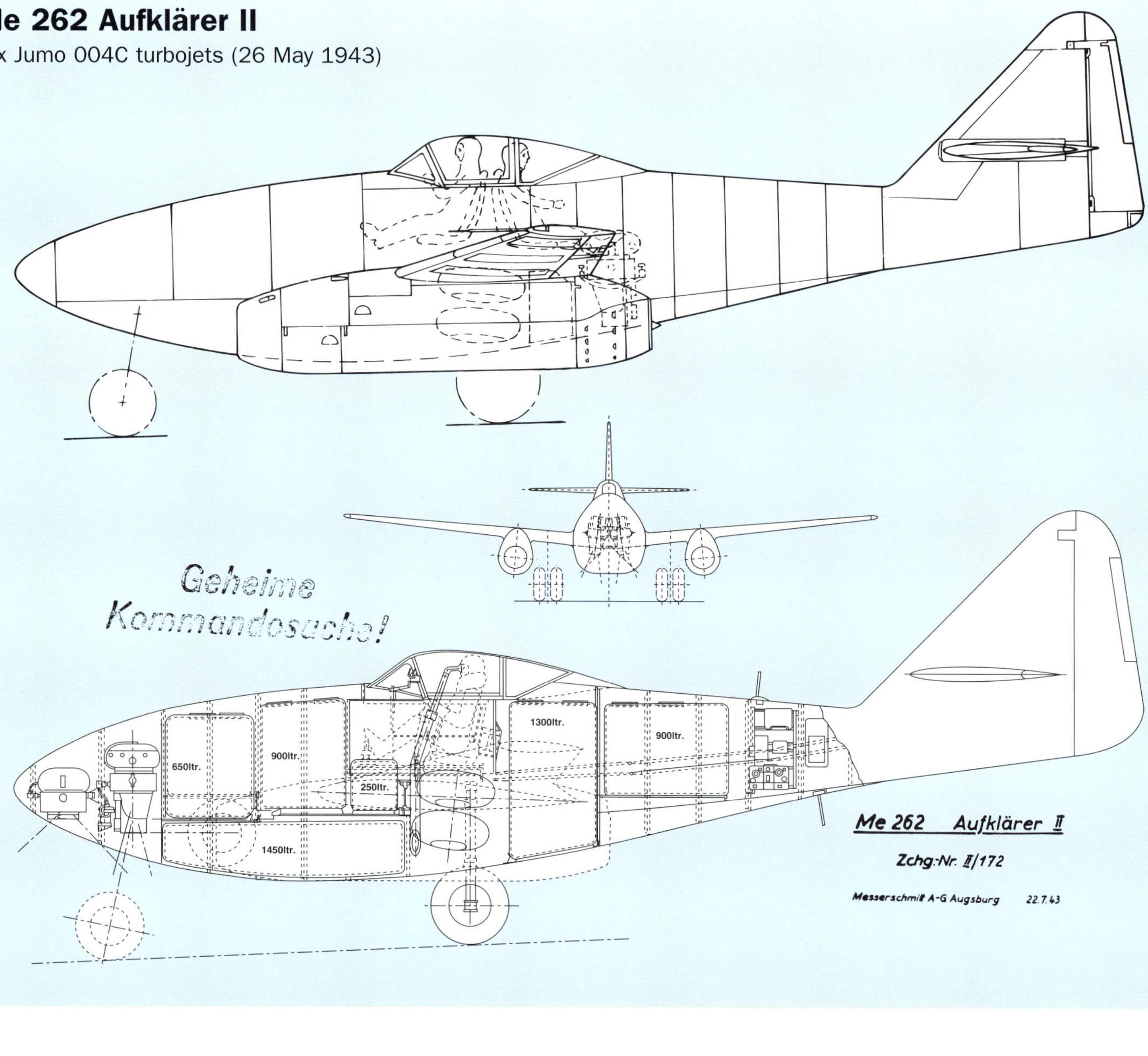

Endurance at: sea level	1.17 hrs	
6 km (19,700 ft)	2.06 hrs	
9 km (29,500 ft)	2.93 hrs	
Service ceiling	9,800 m	32,150 ft
Normal range at: sea level	980 km	609 miles
6 km (19,700 ft)	1,765 km	1,097 miles
9 km (29,500 ft)	2,360 km	1,466 miles
Landing speed	187 km/h	116 mph

Rb 20/30 camera

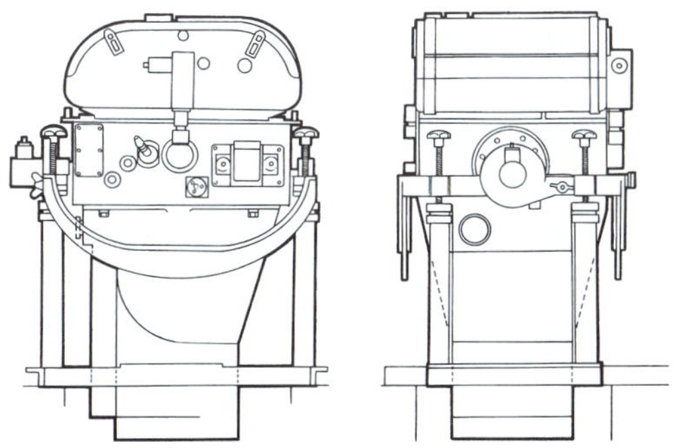

Rb 75/30 camera

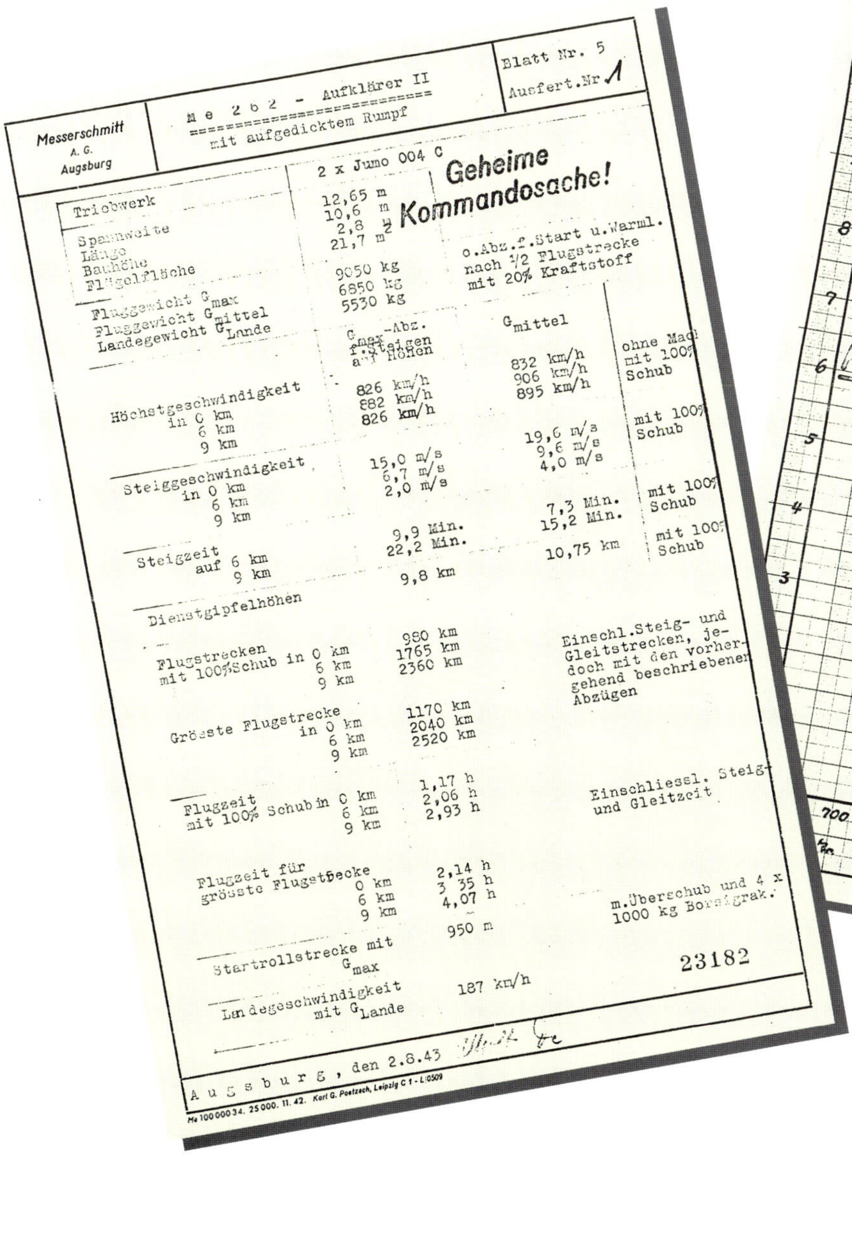

Messerschmitt A. G. Augsburg

Me 262 - Aufklärer II
mit aufgedicktem Rumpf

Blatt Nr. 5
Ausfert.Nr 1

Geheime Kommandosache!

Triebwerk	2 x Jumo 004 C		
Spannweite	12,65 m		
Länge	10,6 m		
Bauhöhe	2,8 m		
Flügelfläche	21,7 m²		
Fluggewicht G_{max}	9050 kg	o.Abz.f.Start u.Warml.	
Fluggewicht G_{mittel}	6850 kg	nach 1/2 Flugstrecke	
Landegewicht G_{Lande}	5530 kg	mit 20% Kraftstoff	
	G_{max}-Abz. f.Steigen auf Höhen	G_{mittel}	
Höchstgeschwindigkeit in 0 km	826 km/h	832 km/h	ohne Mach mit 100% Schub
6 km	882 km/h	906 km/h	
9 km	826 km/h	895 km/h	
Steiggeschwindigkeit in 0 km	15,0 m/s	19,6 m/s	mit 100% Schub
6 km	6,7 m/s	9,6 m/s	
9 km	2,0 m/s	4,0 m/s	
Steigzeit auf 6 km	9,9 Min.	7,3 Min.	mit 100% Schub
9 km	22,2 Min.	15,2 Min.	
Dienstgipfelhöhen	9,8 km	10,75 km	mit 100% Schub
Flugstrecken mit 100% Schub in 0 km	980 km	Einschl.Steig- und Gleitstrecken, jedoch mit den vorhergehend beschriebenen Abzügen	
6 km	1765 km		
9 km	2360 km		
Grösste Flugstrecke in 0 km	1170 km		
6 km	2040 km		
9 km	2520 km		
Flugzeit mit 100% Schub in 0 km	1,17 h	Einschliessl. Steig- und Gleitzeit	
6 km	2,06 h		
9 km	2,93 h		
Flugzeit für grösste Flugstrecke 0 km	2,14 h		
6 km	3 35 h		
9 km	4,07 h		
Startrollstrecke mit G_{max}	~ 950 m	m.Überschub und 4 x 1000 kg Borsigrak.	
Landegeschwindigkeit mit G_{Lande}	187 km/h		

23182

Augsburg, den 2.8.43

Me 100 000 34. 25 000. 11. 42. Karl G. Poetzsch, Leipzig C 1 - L:0509

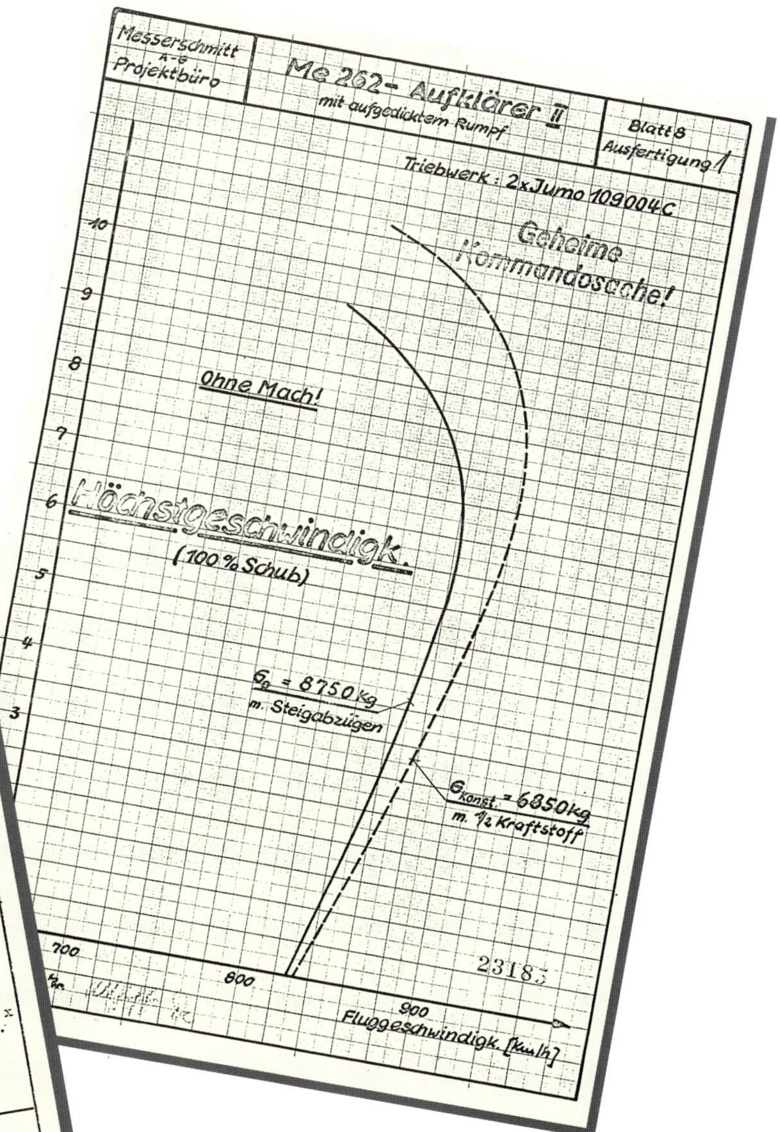

Perspective view of Aufklärer II in contemporary markings for 1943/44. The external appearance of the **Schnellbomber II** would have been similar.

Me 262 *INTERZEPTOR I*

The three interceptor projects were designed to boost take-off power so that the aircraft could reach its combat altitude as quickly as possible. To achieve this aim, each project was to use some form of rocket engine. The *Interzeptor I* had the twin Jumo 004 engines augmented by a 1,700 kg (3,750 lb) thrust Walter R II/211/3 (109-509 A-2) rocket engine mounted in the rear fuselage. Only the rear 900 ltr and lower 250 ltr tanks were used to house J-2 turbojet fuel, the forward 900 ltr tank containing *T-Stoff* rocket fuel. This was an 80 per cent hydrogen peroxide solution with a stabilizer. A new 625 ltr (135 Imp gal) tank was mounted in the rear fuselage to house *C-Stoff* (a 30 per cent solution of hydrazine hydrate in methanol), the other component of the rocket fuel. In addition a 395 ltr (90 Imp gal) tank of *T-Stoff* was mounted beneath the forward fuselage. All the interceptor projects were to carry an armament of six 30 mm MK 108 cannon and have additional 770 x 270 mm mainwheels designed to be jettisoned after take-off. Development of this project led to the Me 262 C-1 which will be described in a forthcoming volume of this work.

All-up weight	7,875 kg	17,360 lb
Landing weight	5,180 kg	11,420 lb
Flying speed with jet engines only at 12 km (39,400 ft)	800 km/h	497 mph
Time to climb to 12 km (39,400 ft) with jet and rocket engines firing (including take-off)	4.5 mins	
Endurance at 12 km (39,400 ft) with turbojets only	42 mins	
Endurance at 16 km (52,500 ft) with rocket engine	5.7 mins	
Normal range at:		
12 km (39,400 ft)	745 km	463 miles
16 km (52,500 ft)	495 km	308 miles
Landing speed	184 km/h	114 mph

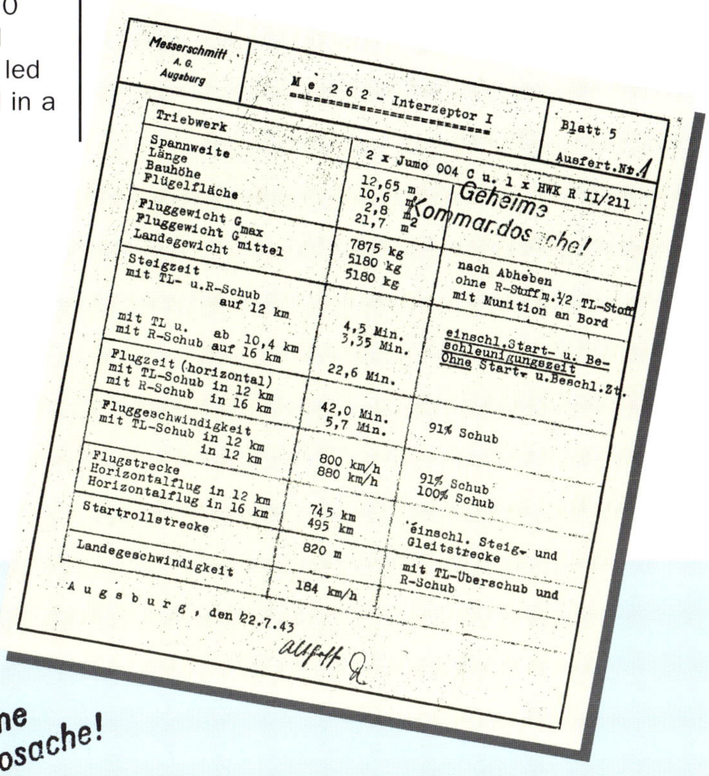

Messerschmitt A.G. Augsburg

Me 262 - Interzeptor I

Blatt 5

Ausfert.Nr. 1

Geheime Kommandosache!

Triebwerk	2 x Jumo 004 C u. 1 x HWK R II/211	
Spannweite Länge Bauhöhe Flügelfläche	12,65 m 10,6 m 2,8 m 21,7 m²	
Fluggewicht G_{max} Fluggewicht G_{mittel} Landegewicht	7875 kg 5180 kg 5180 kg	nach Abheben ohne R-Stoff m. 1/2 TL-Stoff mit Munition an Bord
Steigzeit mit TL- u.R-Schub auf 12 km mit TL u. mit R-Schub ab 10,4 km auf 16 km	4,5 Min. 3,35 Min.	einschl. Start- u. Beschleunigungszeit Ohne Start- u. Beschl.Zt.
Flugzeit (horizontal) mit TL-Schub in 12 km mit R-Schub in 16 km	22,6 Min. 42,0 Min. 5,7 Min.	91% Schub
Fluggeschwindigkeit mit TL-Schub in 12 km in 12 km	800 km/h 880 km/h	91% Schub 100% Schub
Flugstrecke Horizontalflug in 12 km Horizontalflug in 16 km	745 km 495 km	einschl. Steig- und Gleitstrecke
Startrollstrecke	820 m	mit TL-Überschub und R-Schub
Landegeschwindigkeit	184 km/h	

Augsburg, den 22.7.43

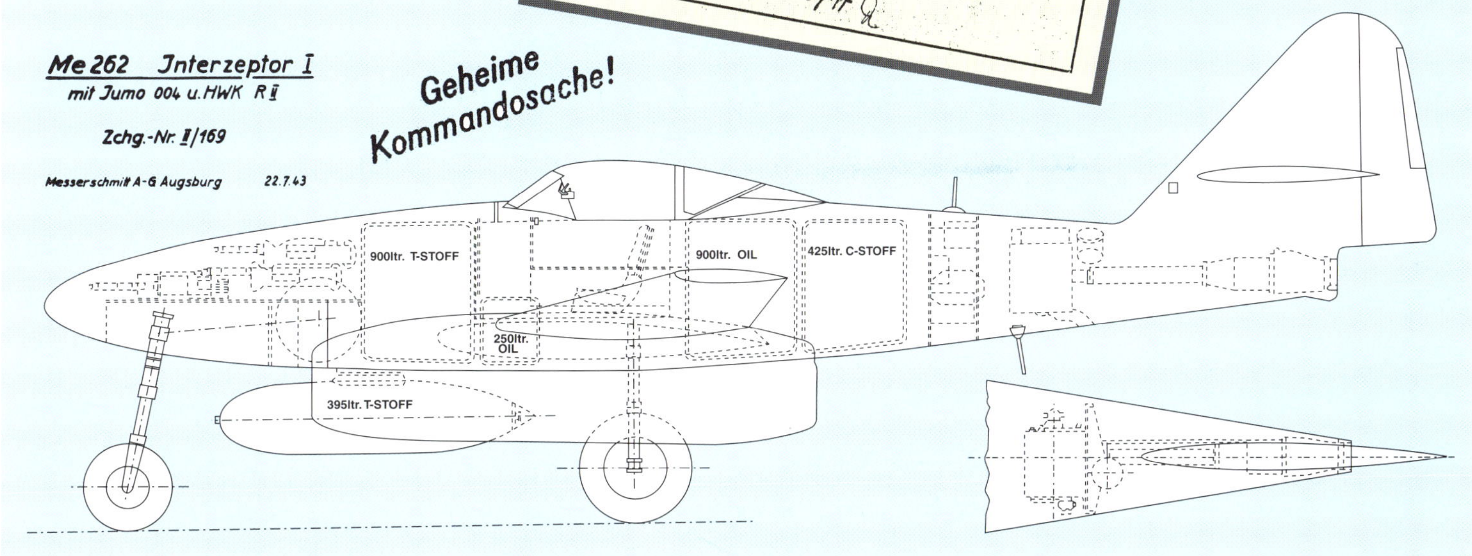

Me 262 *Interzeptor II*

This project was to be powered by a pair of BMW 003 R composite turbojet and rocket engines. This unit comprised a standard BMW 003 A turbojet to which was added the specially designed BMW P 3395 (109-718) rocket engine. This burned a mixture of *SV-Stoff* (concentrated nitric acid) and *R-Stoff* (Tonka self-igniting fuel) which gave the engine a thrust of 1,000 kg (2,200 lb) for three minutes. The propellant pumps for the rocket engines were electro-hydraulically coupled via a 125 hp extension shaft to the turbojets.

In the *Interzeptor II* the forward 900 ltr tank carried *SV-Stoff*, the rear, J-2 turbojet fuel. The 250 ltr (55 Imp gal) tank below the pilot's seat was also used to house jet fuel, with a 435 ltr (95 Imp gal) tank being provided in the rear fuselage for *R-Stoff*. A further 375 ltr (80 Imp gal) jettisonable tank was mounted below the forward fuselage for *SV-Stoff*. Like the earlier project, the variant was to have an armament of six MK 108 cannon and an additional pair of jettisonable mainwheels. The project was eventually built as the Me 262 D-1 (later redesignated C-2).

All-up weight	7,092 kg	15,640 lb
Landing weight	4,570 kg	10,470 lb
Flying speed with jet engines only at 12 km (39,400 ft)	740 km/h	460 mph
Time to climb to 12 km (39,400 ft) with jet and rocket engines firing (including take-off)	3.9 mins	
Endurance at 12 km (39,400 ft) with turbojets only	51 mins	
Endurance at 16 km (52,500 ft) with rocket engine	5.5 mins	
Normal range at:		
12 km (39,400 ft)	845 km	525 miles
16 km (52,500 ft)	588 km	365 miles
Landing speed	170 km/h	106 mph

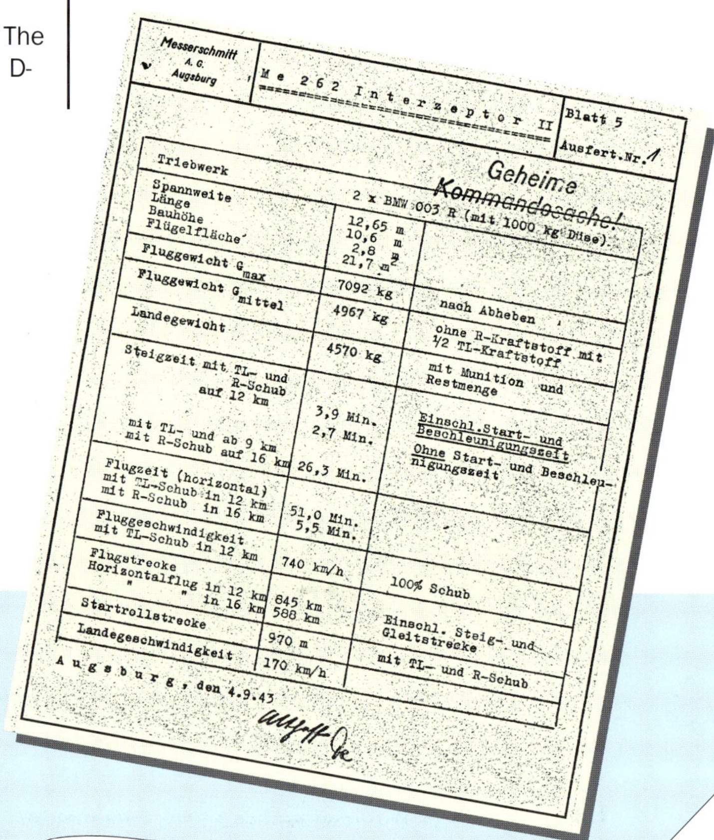

Messerschmitt A. G. Augsburg

Me 262 Interzeptor II

Blatt 5

Ausfert.Nr. 1

Geheime Kommandosache!

Triebwerk	2 x BMW 003 R (mit 1000 kg Düse)	
Spannweite Länge Bauhöhe Flügelfläche	12,65 m 10,6 m 2,8 m 21,7 m²	
Fluggewicht G_{max}	7092 kg	
Fluggewicht G_{mittel}	4967 kg	nach Abheben
Landegewicht	4570 kg	ohne R-Kraftstoff mit 1/2 TL-Kraftstoff
		mit Munition und Restmenge
Steigzeit mit TL- und R-Schub auf 12 km	3,9 Min. 2,7 Min.	Einschl. Start- und Beschleunigungszeit Ohne Start- und Beschleunigungszeit
mit TL- und ab 9 km mit R-Schub auf 16 km	26,3 Min.	
Flugzeit (horizontal) mit TL-Schub in 12 km mit R-Schub in 16 km	51,0 Min. 5,5 Min.	
Fluggeschwindigkeit mit TL-Schub in 12 km	740 km/h	100% Schub
Flugstrecke Horizontalflug in 12 km " " in 16 km	845 km 588 km	Einschl. Steig- und Gleitstrecke
Startrollstrecke	970 m	mit TL- und R-Schub
Landegeschwindigkeit	170 km/h	

Augsburg, den 4.9.43

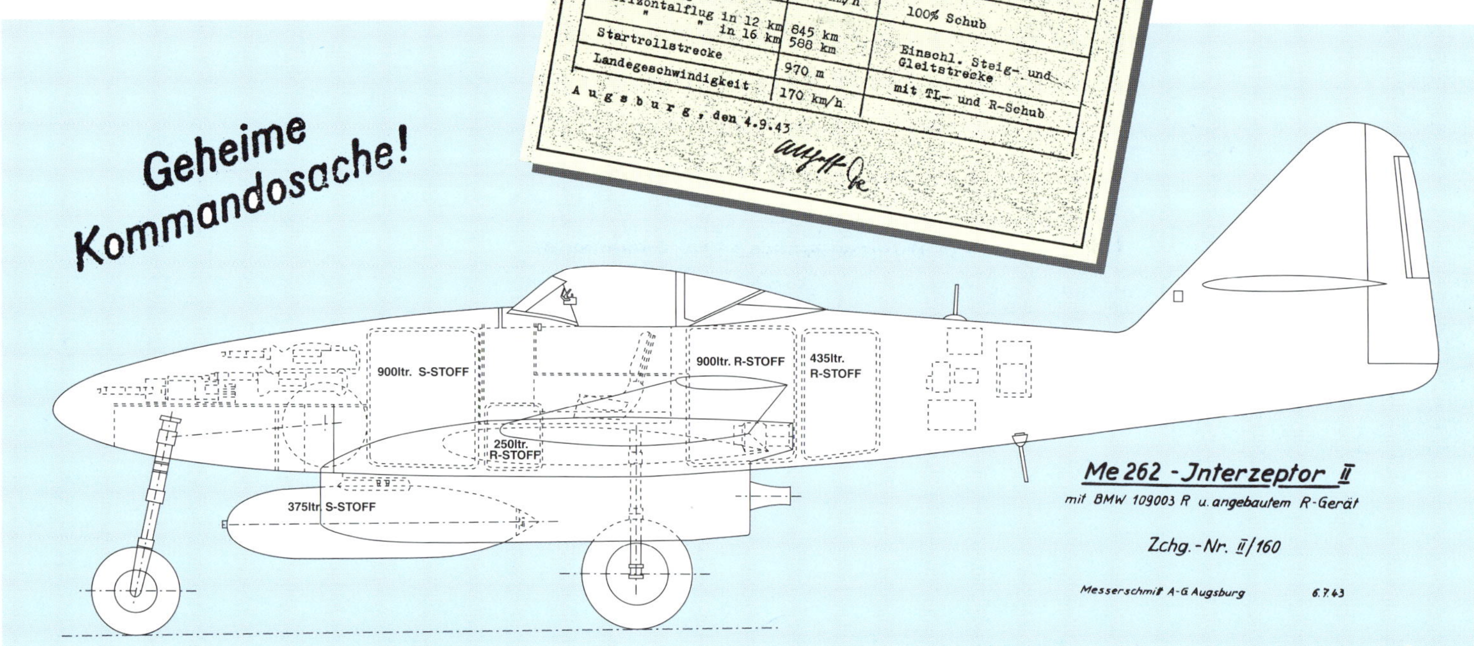

Above and to the rear of this BMW 003 TLR engine can be seen the BMW 718 rocket engine which burned a mixture of SV-Stoff (concentrated nitric acid) and R-Stoff (Tonka self-igniting fuel) and gave the engine a thrust of 1,000 kg (2,200 lb) for three minutes. The propellant pumps for the rocket engines were electro-hydraulically coupled via a 125 hp extension shaft to the turbojets.

Rear view of the BMW 003 TLR engine which was to power the Me 262 Interzeptor II project which eventually emerged as the Me 262 C-2b. The unit comprised a standard BMW 003 A turbojet to which was added the specially designed BMW 109-718 rocket engine.

The forward fuselage of a Me 163 rocket fighter with its wings and tail section removed. This shows the tail pipe of the Walter 109-509 rocket engine, a similar installation being mounted in the Me 262 Interzeptor I project which eventually became the Me 262 C-1a.

Me 262 *Interzeptor III*

The *Interzeptor III* was to be powered by two Walter HWK 509 rocket engines, one mounted beneath each wing. *T-Stoff* was carried in the two 900 ltr tanks with an additional 200 ltr (45 Imp gal) tank beneath the pilot's feet. The *C-Stoff* was carried in a 750 ltr (165 Imp gal) tank in the rear fuselage and a 220 ltr (50 Imp gal) drop tank. Because of the nature of the rocket fuels, all the tanks were to have a special protective lining. Again an armament of six MK 108s was to be carried but the *Interzeptor III* retained the standard mainwheels. Unlike the two earlier projects, it was not developed further.

All-up weight	6,964 kg	15,350 lb
Landing weight	3,720 kg	8,200 lb
Flying speed at 12 km (39,400 ft)	740 km/h	460 mph
Time to climb to 12 km (39,400 ft) including take-off	2.43 mins	
Climbing time to 16 km (52,500 ft) including take-off	3.07 mins	
Endurance at 12 km (39,400 ft)	7.6 mins	
Endurance at 16 km (52,500 ft)	4.2 mins	
Normal range at 12 km (39,400 ft)	292 km	181 miles
Normal range at 16 km (52,500 ft)	313 km	194 miles
Landing speed	154 km/h	96 mph

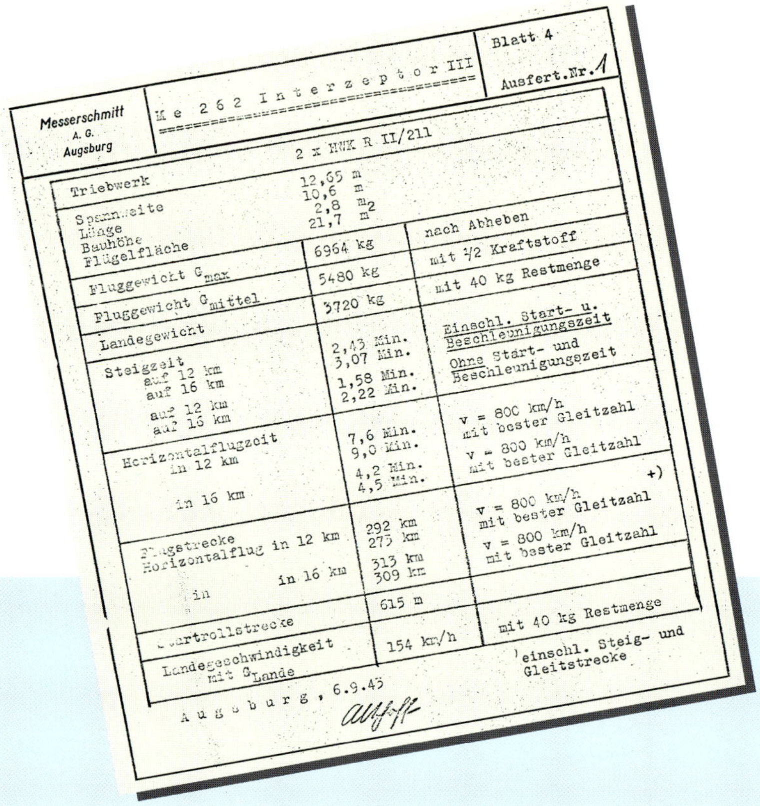

Messerschmitt A. G. Augsburg — Me 262 Interzeptor III — Blatt 4 — Ausfert.Nr. 1

2 x HWK R II/211

Triebwerk		
Spannweite Länge Bauhöhe Flügelfläche	12,65 m 10,6 m 2,8 m 21,7 m^2	
Fluggewicht G_{max}	6964 kg	nach Abheben
Fluggewicht G_{mittel}	5480 kg	mit 1/2 Kraftstoff
Landegewicht	3720 kg	mit 40 kg Restmenge
Steigzeit auf 12 km auf 16 km auf 12 km auf 16 km	2,43 Min. 3,07 Min. 1,58 Min. 2,22 Min.	Einschl. Start- u. Beschleunigungszeit Ohne Start- und Beschleunigungszeit
Horizontalflugzeit in 12 km in 16 km	7,6 Min. 9,0 Min. 4,2 Min. 4,5 Min.	v = 800 km/h mit bester Gleitzahl v = 800 km/h mit bester Gleitzahl +)
Flugstrecke Horizontalflug in 12 km in 16 km in	292 km 275 km 313 km 309 km	v = 800 km/h mit bester Gleitzahl v = 800 km/h mit bester Gleitzahl
Startrollstrecke	615 m	
Landegeschwindigkeit mit G_{Lande}	154 km/h	mit 40 kg Restmenge

+) einschl. Steig- und Gleitstrecke

Augsburg, 6.9.43

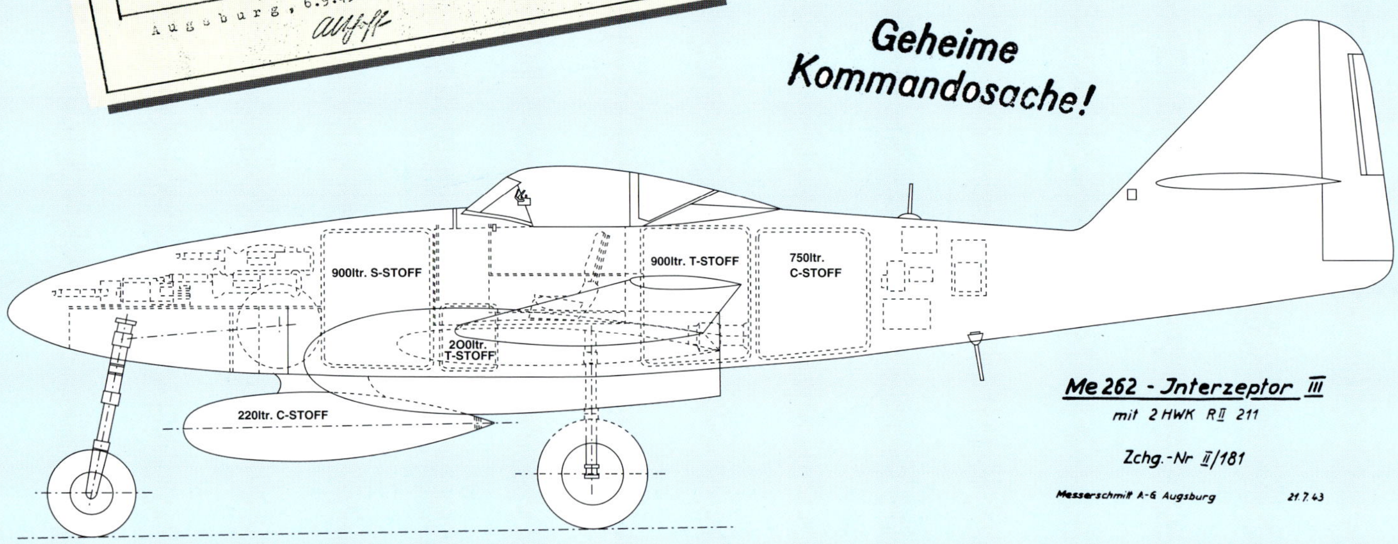

Me 262 *SCHULFLUGZEUG*

The *Schulflugzeug* was to have a lengthened crew compartment with room for an instructor to be seated behind the pupil pilot. Dual controls were to be provided, the cockpit being enclosed by a new Plexiglas canopy with blisters on either side to improve the instructor's forward view. The rear 900 ltr fuel tank was more than halved in size (containing only 400 ltrs or 90 Imp gals), but provision was made for two 300 ltr (65 Imp gal) drop tanks mounted on racks beneath the forward fuselage. The project could be powered by Jumo 004 B or C engines, all armament was to be removed and replaced by a 150 kg (330 lb) ballast weight and modified radio equipment was to be fitted. The variant was developed into the Me 262 B-1. The adjacent figures refer to the Jumo 004 B powered version.

All-up weight	5,240 kg	11,550 lb
Landing weight	4,800 kg	10,580 lb
Max. speed at: sea level	770 km/h	478 mph
6 km (19,700 ft)	840 km/h	522 mph
9 km (29,500 ft)	860 km/h	534 mph
Endurance at: sea level	1.07 hrs	
6 km (19,700 ft)	0.89 hrs	
9 km (29,500 ft)	1.10 hrs	
Normal range at: sea level	980 km	609 miles
6 km (19,700 ft)	1,765 km	1,097 miles
9 km (29,500 ft)	2,360 km	1,466 miles
Landing speed	175 km/h	109 mph

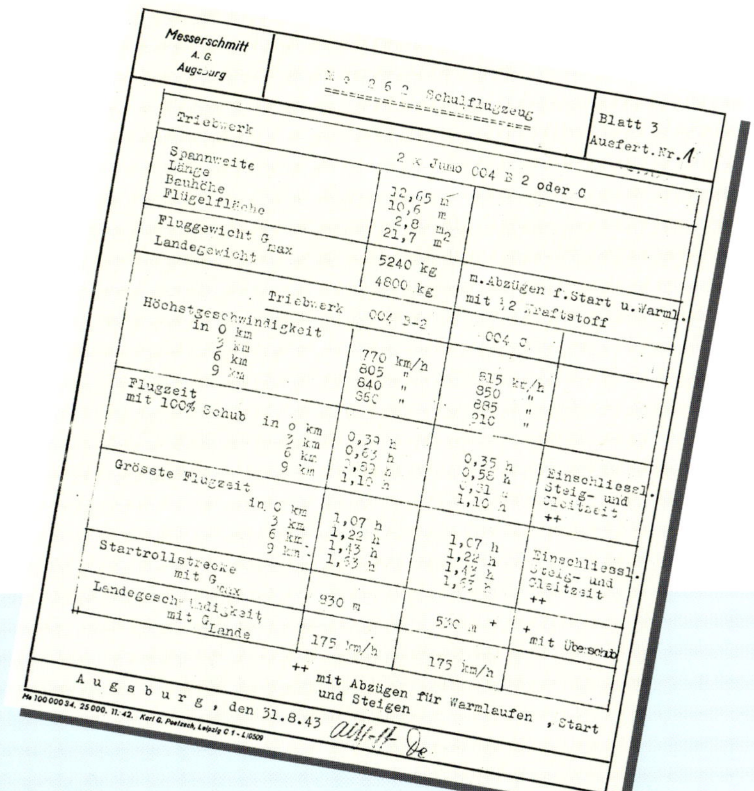

Messerschmitt A.G. Augsburg

Me 262 Schulflugzeug

Blatt 3
Ausfert.Nr. 1

Triebwerk	2 x Jumo 004 B 2 oder C		
Spannweite Länge Bauhöhe Flügelfläche	12,65 m 10,6 m 2,8 m 21,7 m^2		
Fluggewicht G_{max} Landegewicht	5240 kg 4800 kg	m.Abzügen f.Start u.Warml. mit 1/2 Kraftstoff	
Triebwerk	004 B-2	004 C	
Höchstgeschwindigkeit in 0 km 3 km 6 km 9 km	770 km/h 805 " 840 " 860 "	815 km/h 850 " 885 " 910 "	
Flugzeit mit 100% Schub in 0 km 3 km 6 km 9 km	0,39 h 0,63 h 0,89 h 1,10 h	0,35 h 0,58 h 0,81 h 1,10 h	Einschliessl. Steig- und Gleitzeit ++
Grösste Flugzeit in 0 km 3 km 6 km 9 km	1,07 h 1,22 h 1,43 h 1,63 h	1,07 h 1,22 h 1,43 h 1,63 h	Einschliessl. Steig- und Gleitzeit ++
Startrollstrecke mit G_{max}	930 m	530 m +	+ mit Überschub
Landegeschwindigkeit mit G_{Lande}	175 km/h	175 km/h	

++ mit Abzügen für Warmlaufen, Start und Steigen

Augsburg, den 31.8.43

Me 100 000 34. 25 000. 11. 42. Karl G. Poetzsch, Leipzig C 1 - L/0509

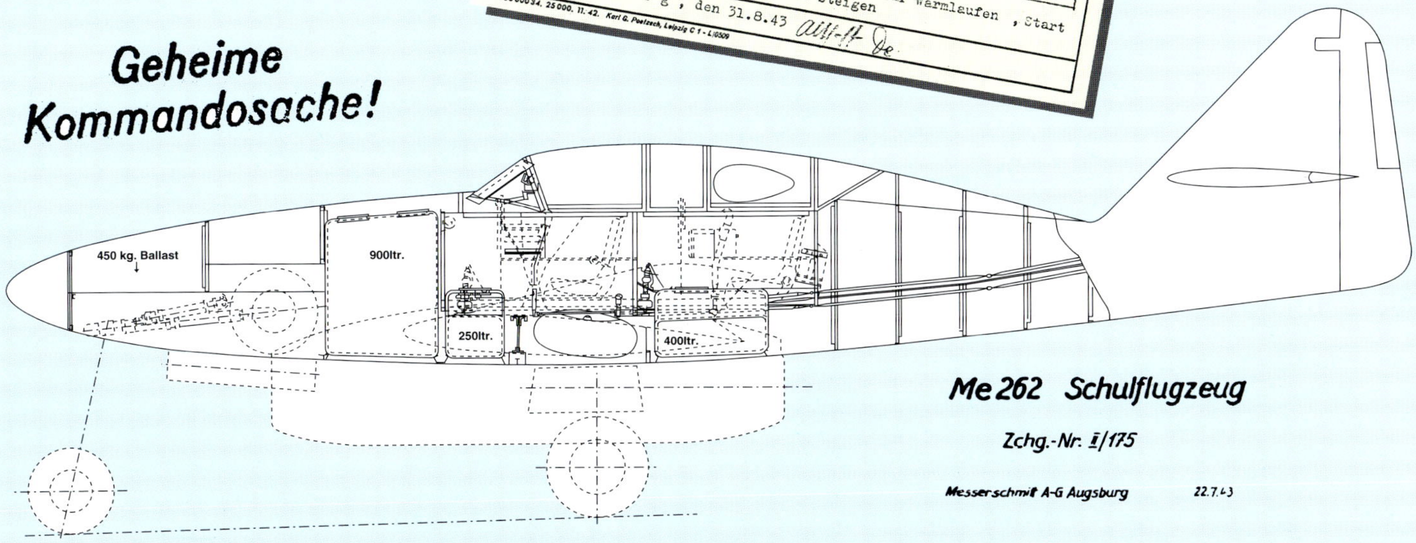

CHAPTER SIX

"I'M NOT INTERESTED IN THIS AIRCRAFT AS A FIGHTER"

On 19 July 1943, the Me 262 V1 which had been rebuilt to accommodate two Jumo 004 A-0 engines, joined the test programme. It was the first aircraft to have a pressurized cabin and carry armament, three forward-firing 20 mm MG 151/20 cannon being housed in the nose. One was positioned on each side of the nose and a third mounted centrally and above. A series of firing trials were carried out on the ground beginning on 10 July, the prototype making its first flight nine days later. Even at this stage it was realised that this armament was far from adequate to combat the US heavy bombers that were beginning to pound the German homeland.

A day after the V1 had flown, on 20 July, the Me 262 V5 was fitted with two 500 kg (1,100 lb) thrust Rheinmetall-Borsig 109-502 solid-fuel rocket-assisted take-off units. The initial trials were carried out by the Messerschmitt test pilot Karl Baur. During the first take-off, Baur ignited the rockets at about 160 km/h (100 mph). This immediately jerked the nosewheel off the ground, forcing him to push the stick fully forward to keep the aircraft from leaving the runway prematurely. He was forced to hold this position until the rockets burned themselves out, but still managed to get the aircraft off the ground before he reached the end of the runway. For subsequent tests, the rockets were realigned, which much improved matters, reducing the prototype's take-off run by some 250-300 m (820-980 ft). Assisted take-off rockets could be carried by all production aircraft but, in practice, were rarely used.

On 20 July, *Oberst* Petersen, the Me 262 *Kommisar*, was advised by Messerschmitt AG that it would cost, on average, 24,000 man-hours to produce the first 100 Me 262s, reducing to 3,500 hours in mass production, compared with the 4,200 man-hours for the Bf 109. In practice, the latter figure proved to be wildly optimistic, as a series-produced Me 262 airframe took around 6,400 man-hours to build.

Five days later, Gerd Lindner demonstrated the Me 262 V4 to Hermann Göring and Erhard Milch at Rechlin, this being the first time the two leaders had seen the aircraft fly. The return flight to Lechfeld on the following day involved an interim landing at Schkeuditz airfield near Leipzig. Despite previous lengthening of the runway at Schkeuditz, the Me 262 V4 failed to take off due to very hot weather conditions and crashed. Although Lindner escaped injury, the aircraft suffered 60% damage and was not repaired.[1] A little later, on 4 August, the Me 262 V5 was damaged when its nosewheel tyre burst on landing. This meant that the company now had only two aircraft available for testing, the V1 and V3.

To test the Me 262's tail flutter characteristics at high speed, without subjecting test pilots to undue risk, the complete fuselage and tail of a

The Me 262 V5 was the first prototype to be fitted with a tricycle undercarriage, the nosegear based on that of the experimental Me 309 piston-engined fighter. The undercarriage was not designed to retract but it did considerably improve the Me 262's take-off performance.

These photos show the Me 262 V5, which made its first flight on 6 June 1943, coming in to land. The prototype was fitted with a fixed, tricycle undercarriage which considerably improved the pilot's forward view and also prevented stones and other debris being flung up in the air by the jet efflux.

Me 262 was suspended beneath the wing of a Me 323 transport via a bomb shackle. The Me 262 fuselage was fitted with a 1,800 kg (3,970 lbs) ballast weight. To counterbalance this weight, two 1,000 kg (2,200 lb) concrete bombs were mounted beneath the other wing of the Me 323. The idea was that the entire test specimen should be released from altitude and measurements taken by a vibration recorder installed in the tail when sufficiently high speeds had been attained. Three movie cameras would also record the progress of the trials from the ground.

The first dropping trial of the rig, using the Me 323 S9 (W.Nr. 1109) took place on 23 October 1943, with the fuselage of the badly damaged Me 262 V4. The Me 323 was towed up to the required altitude by a five engined He 111 Z glider tug. On reaching 7,000 m (23,000 ft) the Me 262 fuselage was released and allowed to fall freely. After some 28 seconds, by which time the test specimen had reached about 870 km/h (541 mph) the ballast weight was jettisoned by explosive bolts and six braking rockets fired. When it had slowed sufficiently, three parachutes were released, but two failed to deploy causing the specimen to crash into the Bodensee (Lake Constance) at about 820 km/h (509 mph). It was destroyed, and no attempt was made to repeat the experiment.

Early in August 1943, production plans for the Me 262 received a setback when Hitler suddenly ordered that the Me 209 was not to be cancelled. (This order had resulted from Professor

On 20 July 1943 the Me 262 V5 was fitted with two 500 kg (1,100 lbs) thrust Rheinmetall-Borsig 109-502 solid-fuel rocket-assisted take-off units. Tests were carried out by Karl Baur, but severe problems manifested themselves until the rockets were re-aligned.

Cockpit view showing controls for RATO R-109-502.

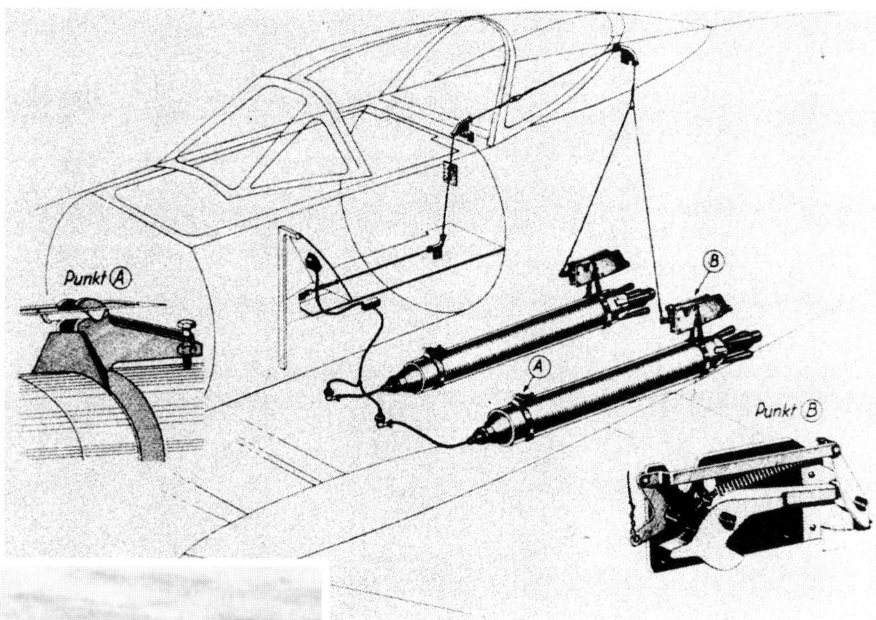

Installation of Rheinmetall-Borsig R-109-502 assisted take-off units (solid propellent)

The 500 kg (1,100 lbs) thrust rocket-assisted take-off units first fitted to the Me 262 V5. Although available, these engines were rarely fitted to operational aircraft.

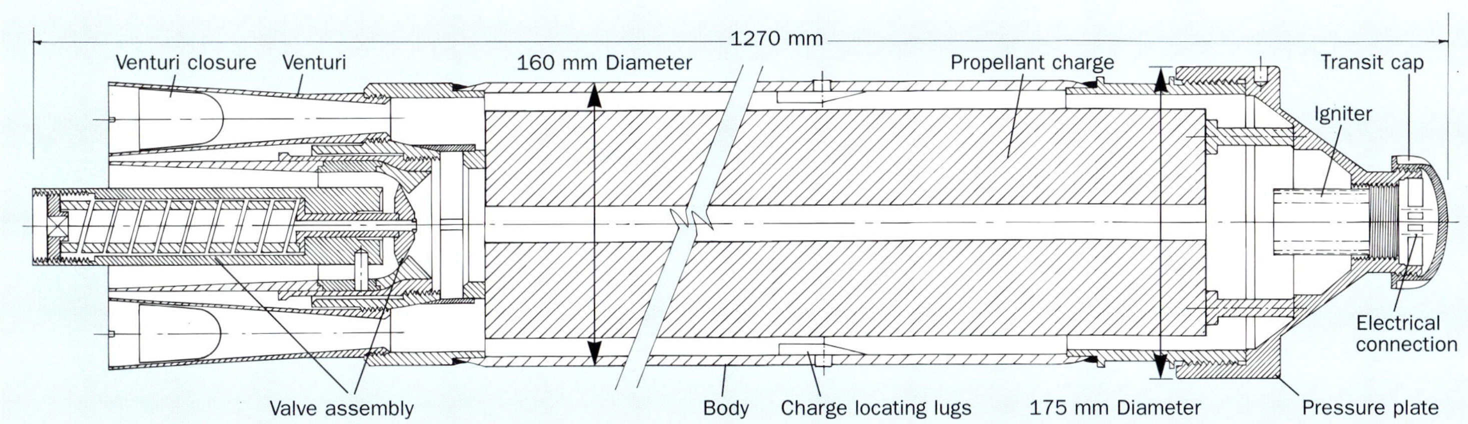

Rheinmetall-Borsig R 109-502

Solid fuel rocket assisted take-off (RATO) engine

Total all up weight	51.15 kg. (112.75 lb)
Peak thrust	771.12 kg. (1700 lb)
Time of burning	7.5 seconds

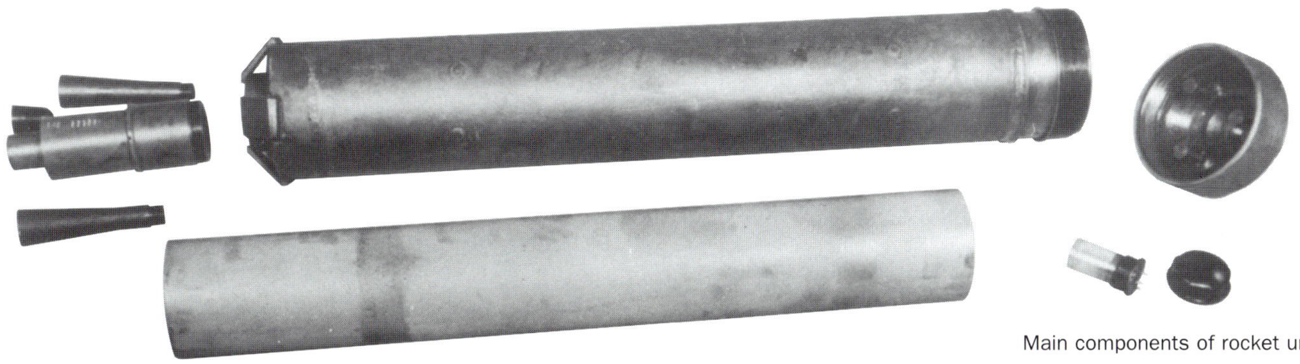

Main components of rocket unit.

Component parts of thrust regulator.

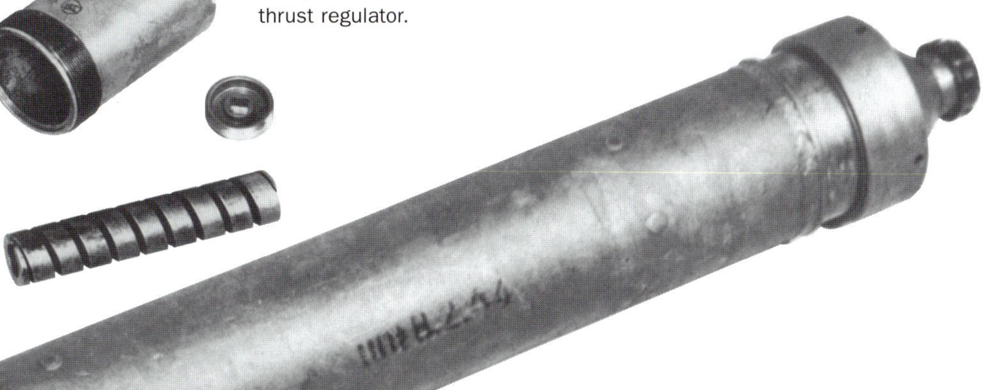

Complete assembly of rocket unit.

An Me 262 taking off with RATO engines firing.

Right and Below: To test the Me 262's tail flutter characteristics at high speed the fuselage of the Me 262 V4 was suspended beneath the wing of a Me 323 transport. The first dropping trial of the rig, using the Me 323 S9 (W.Nr. 1109) took place on October 23, 1943, using a five engined He 111 Z glider tug to assist the combination into the air.

Messerschmitt's visit to the *Berghof* on 27 June). At a GL conference held on 17 August when Milch announced a fighter production target of 4,000 machines per month in 1944, Galland demanded that 1,000 of these be jet fighters. Milch refused, however, explaining that he could not be expected to stop all other development projects just because of the Me 262. He explained his position: "The *Führer* feels that the risk is too great... I, personally, would go ahead and produce it, as we had planned, without all this business of discontinuing the Me 209. However, as a soldier, I have no choice but to obey orders. If the *Führer* orders caution, then we must be cautious". The *Führer's* intervention set back plans for mass production of the jet fighter; on 15 August a revised Programme 223 had been issued that proposed the following production schedules for the Me 262 and the DB 603 G-powered Me 209:

Month	Me 262 V	Me 262 A	Me 209
Jan 44	1	-	-
Feb 44	8	-	-
Mar 44	21	-	-
Apr 44	20	20	-
May 44	-	60	-
Jun 44	-	60	-
Jul 44	-	60	1
Aug 44	-	60	3
Sep 44	-	60	6
Oct 44	-	60	12
Nov 44	-	70	24
Dec 44	-	125	45
Jan 45	-	210	72
Feb 45	-	260	102
Mar 45	-	360	153
Apr 45	-	440	230
May 45	-	520	326
Jun 45	-	600	427
Jul 45	-	700	534
Aug 45	-	840	640
Sep 45	-	1000	746

Me 262 development received another blow when the US Eighth Air Force bombed the Messerschmitt plant at Regensburg on 17 August. In the chaos that followed, 400 people were killed and a large number of fuselage jigs and acceptance gauges for the Me 262 destroyed. Realizing that the entire development organisation at Augsburg was now at risk, the RLM made the decision to relocate key Messerschmitt departments to Oberammergau in the Bavarian Alps, but this only served to delay development of the aircraft still further. The move to Oberammergau began in the autumn of 1943, and included the *Projektbüro, Konstruktionsbüro* and *Statikbüro*, which were housed in former *Gebirgsjäger* (mountain troops) barracks on the eastern outskirts of the town. Located in an idyllic setting in an alpine valley, the barracks complex comprised about twenty buildings and was relatively safe from air attack because of the mountainous terrain. The transfer of the *Versuchsbau* (Experimental workshops for prototype construction) under *Meister* (Head Foreman) Moritz Asam followed in March 1944, and by October of that year some 2,230 Messerschmitt personnel were employed at Oberammergau. To protect the true identity of the Messerschmitt plant, the cover name of *Oberbayerische Forschungsanstalt* (Upper Bavarian Research Establishment) was adopted for the Oberammergau facility, and this alias appeared on all official correspondence.[2]

In July 1943, prior to the bombing of Regensburg, Professor Messerschmitt had opened negotiations for the purchase of a large,

After the death of Ostertag in the crash of the Me 262 V2, his place was taken by Gerd Lindner, here seen holding the propeller blade of a Me 210. Lindner was to become the most experienced Me 262 test pilot.

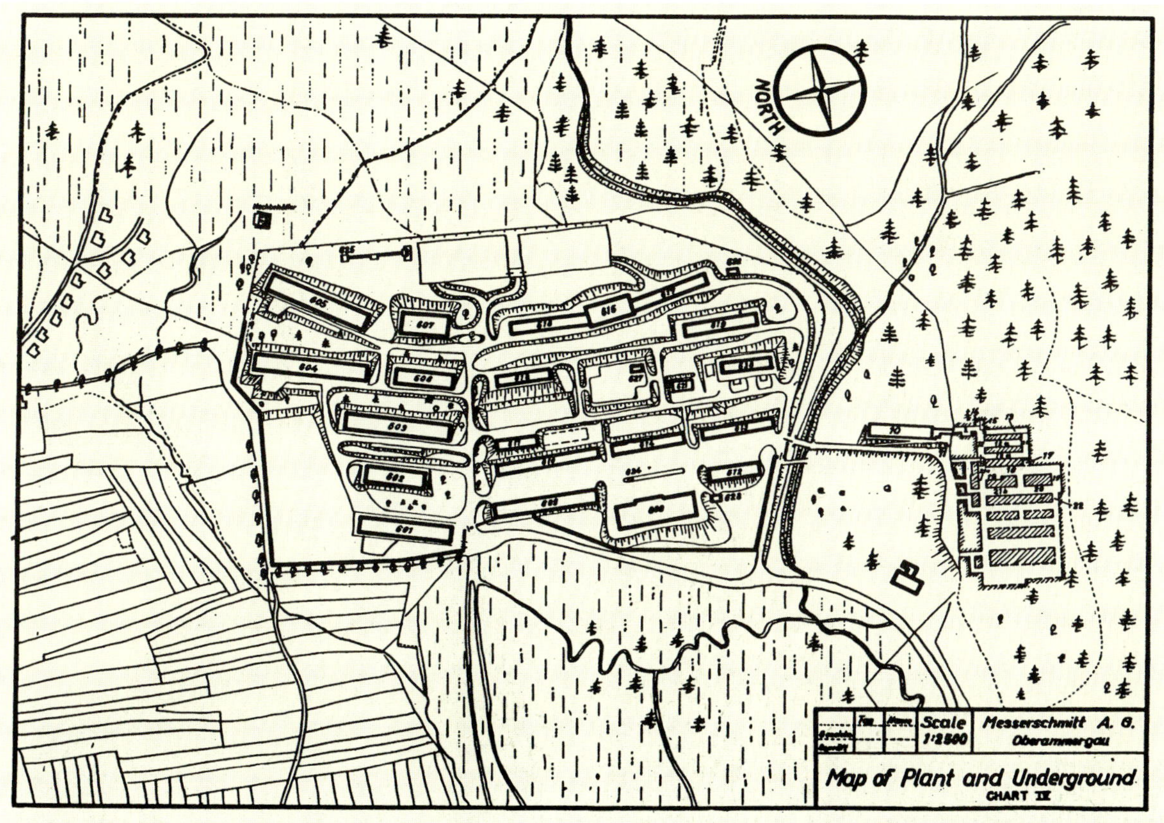

An Allied interpretation of the Messerschmitt A.G. Research Institute at Oberammergau based on a captured German map.

private house at Murnau, which, by a fortunate coincidence, was only 16 km (10 miles) to the east of Oberammergau. The purchase of the house, known as *Hochried* (High Marsh) - located on the outskirts of Murnau on the shores of the Staffelsee - was completed towards the end of 1943, and it became Willy Messerschmitt's main residence until the end of the war. Some of the Professor's closest colleagues at Oberammergau were temporarily housed at *Hochried*, and by January 1944, reception rooms for the board and management of Messerschmitt AG had been established there so that, in the event of a disaster elsewhere, the administration of the company could rapidly resume its normal functions at this remote location.

On 7 September 1943, Messerschmitt talked to Hitler at the *Führer's* headquarters, again emphasising the excellence of the Me 209.[3] He then spoke of using the Me 262 as a fast bomber which could attack the British Isles, a subject dear to the German leader's heart. "Its technical lead," he said, "is so great that this aircraft cannot come into service fast enough, otherwise we must expect the enemy to start coming over with similar aircraft before us, or simultaneously."

It has been said that this was the first time that the idea of using the Me 262 as a bomber had been put into Hitler's mind, but the minutes of *Protokoll Nr.9* of 4 March (over six months earlier) recorded that: " ... *as per the* Führer Befehl *(order), every fighter must henceforth be capable of performing in the fighter-bomber role. An installation capable of carrying 500 kg of bombs is foreseen for the Me 262, according to drawing Nr.II/141. A standard* Revi *sight is to be used. For fighter-bomber operations, the mainwheels are to be enlarged from 770 x 270 to 840 x 300.*" The *Führer's* order, which had been issued in February 1943 to cover all *Luftwaffe* fighters, may have been viewed with some scepticism, but a project for a fighter-bomber version of the Me 262 was produced as early as 26 March 1943.

Developments of this emerged, as has been described in Chapter 5, as the three *Schnellbomber* projects of summer 1943. Then, on 27 October, the *Führer* outlined his plan to combat the anticipated Allied invasion of France to Göring. "The jet fighter with bombs," pronounced Hitler, "will be vital, because at the given moment it will scream at top speed along the beaches and hurl its bombs into the massive build-up

Opposite top: On 17 August 1943, the US Eighth Air Force despatched a force of 146 B-17 Flying Fortresses of the 4th Bombardment Wing to attack the Messerschmitt plant at Regensburg. There was considerable destruction and loss of life, causing severe but temporary damage and interuption to Me 262 development. Here, B-17s of the 96th Bomb Group, one of the groups that participated in the raid, head out for a mission over the Reich. *Opposite below*: Aerial view of Messerschmitt A.G. Oberammergau showing Die Oberbayerische Forschungsanstalt (Upper Bavarian Research Establishment).

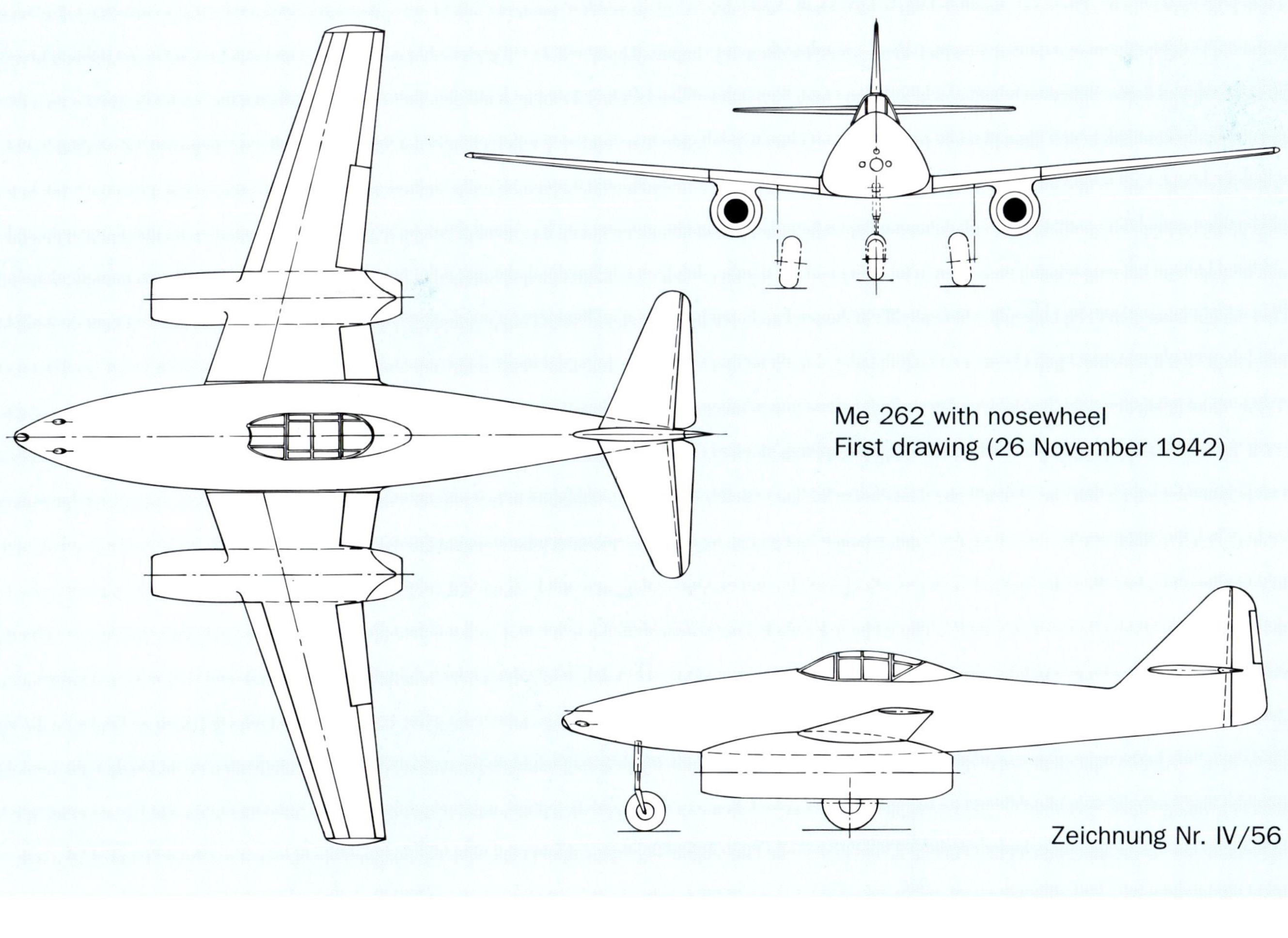

Me 262 with nosewheel
First drawing (26 November 1942)

Zeichnung Nr. IV/56

Me 262 V6 after the demonstration flight on 2 November 1943

Apart from being fitted to the Me 262 V6, the Jumo 004 B-0 engine was also fitted to the Ar 234 V2. This unit was very similar to the Jumo 004 A, but was much lighter, weighing 720 kg (1,590 lbs) as against 830 kg (1,830 lbs). This was achieved mainly by the use of non-strategic materials such as light alloy blades fitted to the rotor and first three stages of the stator.

that is bound to be there."

Ten days earlier, the Me 262 V6 had made its first flight. This was the first aircraft to be fitted with a fully retractable tricycle undercarriage. All three wheels were retracted hydraulically, but only the nosewheel had a means of extension, compressed air being used. The same system was used to lower the mainwheel doors, but the wheels themselves were extended by gravity, it being necessary to yaw the aircraft to lock them down. In addition to the new undercarriage, the Me 262 V6 was also fitted with three MG 151/20 cannon and, during November, it tested rocket assisted take-off units, these reducing the run from 715 to 450 m (2,350 to 1,480 ft).

As important as the tricycle undercarriage was the fact that the V6 was the first Me 262 to be powered by the new Jumo 004 B-0 engine. This unit was very similar in size and layout to the Jumo 004 A, but was much lighter, weighing 720 kg (1,590 lb) as against 830 kg (1,830 lb). This was achieved mainly by the use of non-strategic materials such as light alloy blades fitted to the rotor and the first three stages of the stator. In its

WILLY MESSERSCHMITT
PROF. DR. ING. E. H. DIREKTOR DER MESSERSCHMITT A.G.

Augsburg, den 17.11.43

NOV. 1943

Herrn
Professor Albert S p e e r
Reichsminister
für Rüstung und Kriegs-Produktion
B e r l i n
Pariser Platz 4

Sehr verehrter Herr Reichsminister!

Schon seit längerer Zeit wollte ich Sie bitten, nach Augsburg zu kommen und mir die Möglichkeit zu geben, Ihnen an Ort und Stelle unsere Neuentwicklungen an Flugzeugen zu zeigen und Sie über die Spezialprobleme unserer Fertigung ins Bild zu setzen.

Inzwischen haben der Führer und der Herr Reichsmarschall nach Vortrag über die Leistungen und taktischen Möglichkeiten des neuen Jägers, der Me 262, bezw. nach Vorführung der Musterflugzeuge den sofortigen Anlauf dieser Type in Großserie wegen ihrer kriegsentscheidenden Bedeutung befohlen. Bei dieser Sachlage und der Schlüsselstellung Ihres Ministeriums wäre ich Ihnen zu besonderem Dank verpflichtet, wenn Sie Ihren Besuch bei uns baldigst ermöglichen könnten, damit Sie einen persönlichen Eindruck von diesem Flugzeug und seiner Fertigung gewinnen.

Ich gebe mich der angenehmen Erwartung hin, Sie in Bälde in Augsburg begrüßen zu dürfen und verbleibe inzwischen, sehr verehrter Herr Reichsminister, mit besten Grüßen und

Heil Hitler

Ihr

WILLY MESSERSCHMITT
PROF.DR.ING.E.H. DIRECTOR OF MESSERSCHMITT AG

AUGSBURG, 17.11.43

Herrn
Professor Albert Speer
Reichsminister
for Armament and War Production

Berlin
Pariser Platz 4

Dear Herr Reichsminister,

For some time I have intended to ask you to come to Augsburg so I can have the opportunity to familiarize you with our latest aircraft developments and the special problems with production here.

Meanwhile, on presentation of a paper on the performance and technical features of the new fighter, Me 262, and following demonstration of the prototype, the Führer and the Herr Reichsmarschall have ordered the immediate start of large-scale production of the type due to its importance in the war. Under these circumstances and considering the key position of your ministry, I would be very much obliged if your visit could be made at the earliest possible time so that you may obtain a personal impression of the aircraft and its manufacture.

In the pleasant expectation to be able to receive you shortly in Augsburg, I remain, dear Herr Reichsminister, with best regards and

Heil Hitler

Your
very devoted Messerschmitt

Facsimile of a letter (and translation) from Professor Willy Messerschmitt to Reichsminister Albert Speer inviting the latter to the Augsburg plant in November 1943.

final production form the Jumo 004 B produced 900 kg (1,980 lb) thrust at a maximum speed of 8,700 rpm and a maximum operating temperature of 650° C (1,200° F). The first bench test of the Jumo 004 B V1 took place in February 1943, and the V5 was later flown beneath a Bf 110 carrier aircraft.

On 2 November, Göring and Milch visited the battered remains of the Messerschmitt factory at Regensburg. Later that day Göring and his entourage travelled on to Lechfeld where Gerd Lindner made a demonstration flight in the Me 262 V6. Göring then told Messerschmitt of Hitler's wish that the Me 262 be used as a bomber. "But *Herr Reichsmarschall,*" said the Professor, "we have always provided for two bomb racks in the aeroplane - to carry two 250 kg or one 500 kg bomb." When Göring asked how long this modification would take, Messerschmitt replied casually: "Oh, not very long - two weeks, perhaps. It isn't really much of a problem, just a matter of fairing the (bomb) racks."

The US Eighth Air Force daylight raids and the disastrous bombing of Hamburg by the RAF had resulted in Göring's credibility receiving a severe pounding. In an attempt to restore his declining prestige, Göring ordered Milch to organise a demonstration of the *Luftwaffe's* latest equipment for Hitler's benefit. This was held on 26 November at Insterburg airfield in East Prussia, not far from Hitler's 'Wolf's Lair' headquarters near Rastenburg. On show were two Me 262s, the V1 and V6,[4] the Ar 234 V3, an Me 163, the Hs 293 and Fritz X missiles, the Fi 103 flying bomb and various types of the latest radar equipment. As he approached the Me 262s, Hitler paused. "I'm not interested in this aircraft as a fighter," he said. "Can it carry bombs?" Eager to impress, Messerschmitt stepped forward and announced that it could carry one 1,000 kg or two 500 kg bombs, thus doubling his earlier figures. After thanking Messerschmitt, Hitler exclaimed: "At last, this is the aircraft I have been demanding for years! Here it is, but nobody recognised it!" Then the *Führer* clearly indicated his intentions when he stated: "I order this aircraft be built as a bomber!" At the time of the Insterburg display, however, the Me 262 was not capable of carrying a bomb load, but no-one in authority advised Hitler of this fact.[5]

Hitler's order was further emphasised in a telex sent by his *Luftwaffe* Adjutant, *Obstlt.* Nicolaus

Messerschmitt Me 262 V6 Nosewheel Detail

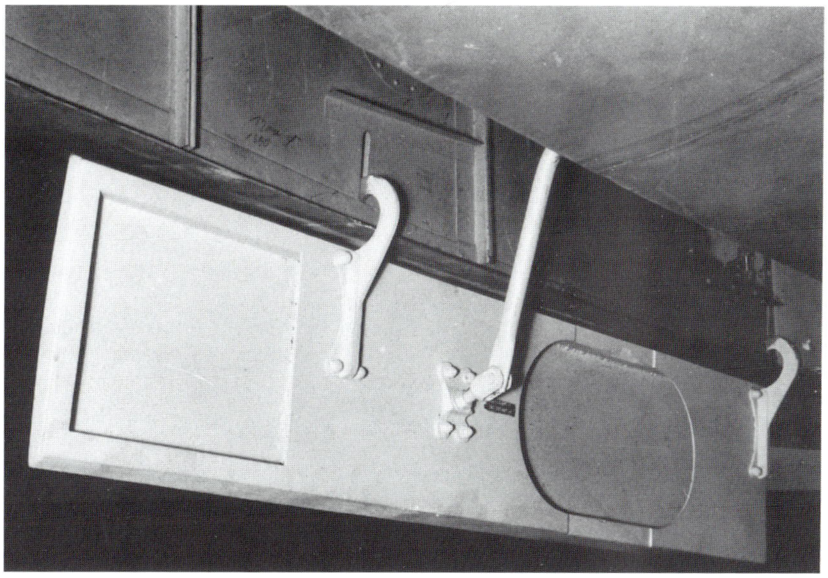

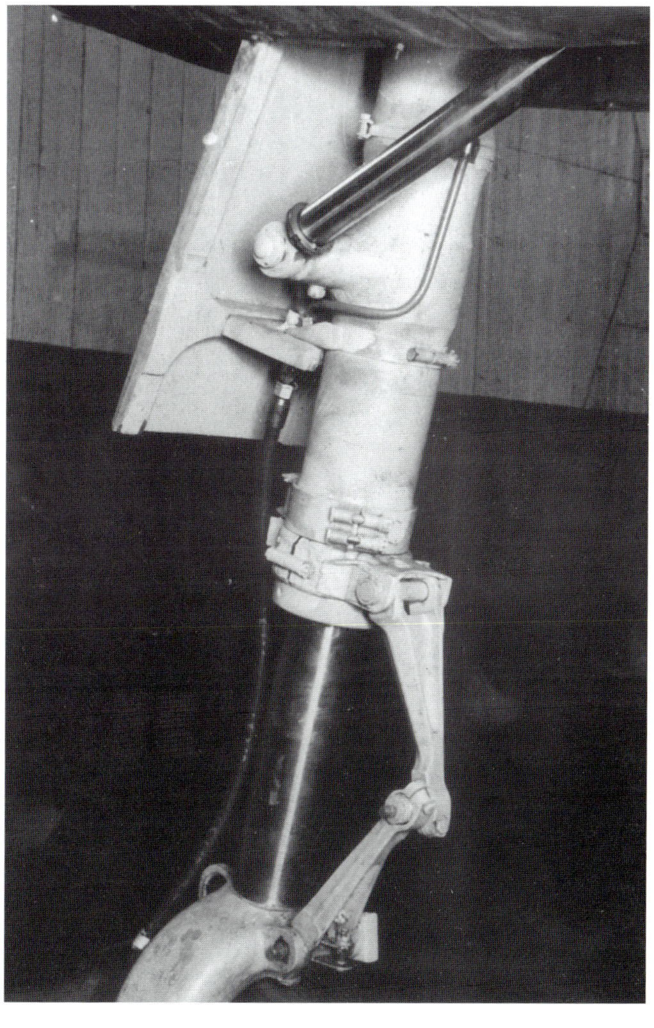

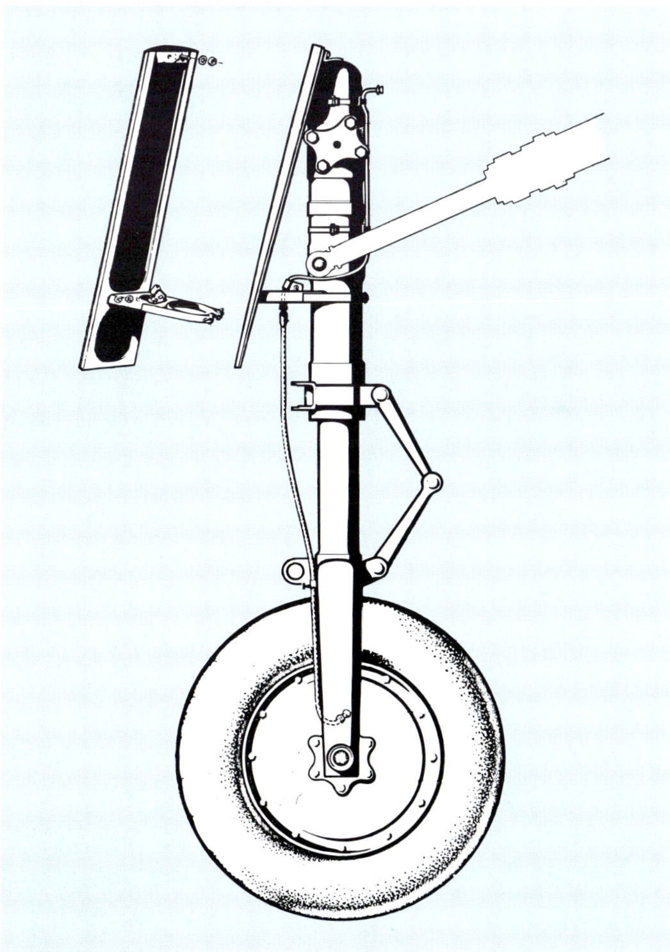

A series of photos showing details of the first retractable nosewheel installation on the Me 262 V6. The wheel measurements are 660 mm diameter x 160 mm width. Note the small towing eyelet which was removed on subsequent undercarriages as it was strictly forbidden to tow the aircraft by the nosewheel due to excessive stress on the structure. Note also the timber construction of the undercarriage door.

Messerschmitt Me 262 V6
Lechfeld, 2 November 1943
VI+AA W.Nr. 130 001

The Me 262 V6, which made its first flight on 17 October 1943, was fitted with Jumo 004 B-0 engines and a fully retractable tricycle undercarriage. All three wheels were retracted hydraulically, but only the nosewheel had a means of extension, compressed air being used. The same system was used to lower the mainwheel doors, but the wheels themselves were extended by gravity, it being necessary to yaw the aircraft to lock them down.
These photographs show the aircraft just prior to being demonstrated to Göring and Milch on 2 November 1943.

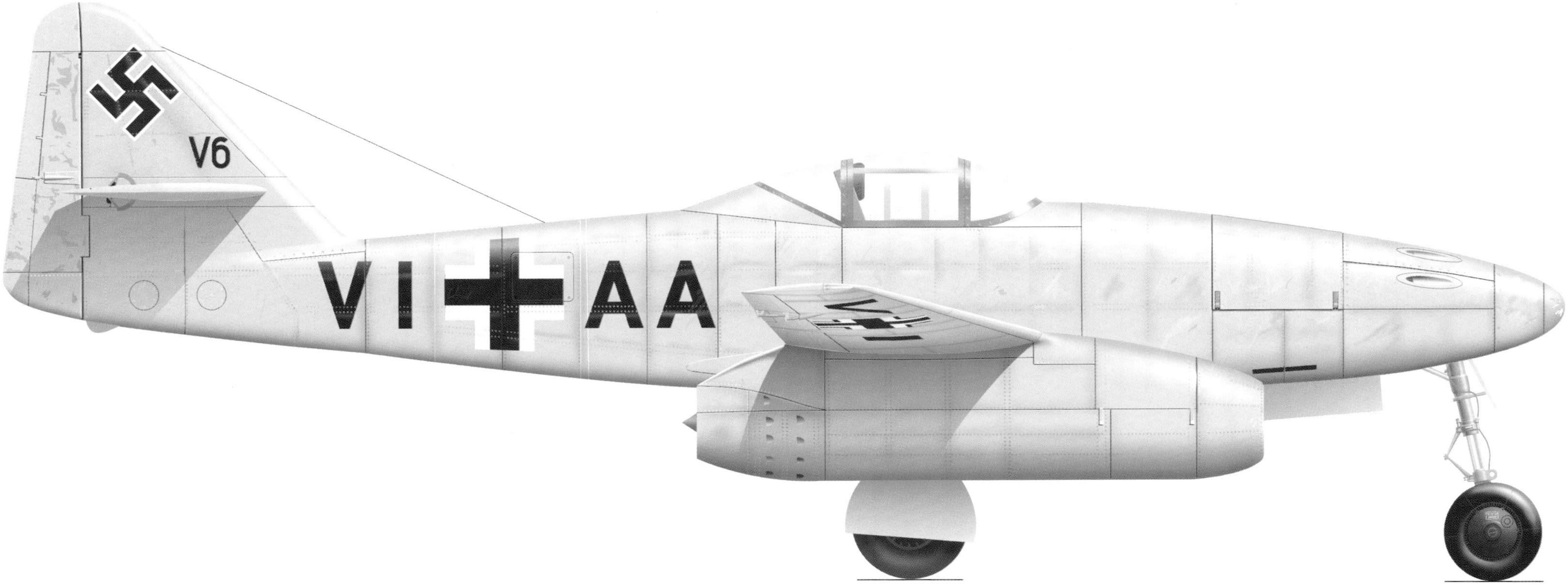

Me 262 V6 VI + AA W.Nr. 130001 with two Jumo 004B-0 engines

The V6 was the first aircraft to be fitted with a retractable tricycle undercarriage and powered by Jumo 004 B engines. It made its first flight on 17 October 1943 but crashed and was totally destroyed on its 28th flight on 9 March 1944. At this time it had accumulated 6 hours 31 minutes flying time. The finish was overall pale blue grey (76). Note the paint chipped from the rudder which was caused by severe vibration during its demonstration flight on 2 November 1943. The tail surfaces had counter balance horns moved to below its elevators. Note also the in-line empty cartridge case chutes which were later modified on the V8 and re-built V7.

Left and Below: Dr.-Ing. Anselm Franz (left), the designer of the Jumo 004 B-0 engines fitted to the Me 262 V6, talking to Göring and Willy Messerschmitt (right) at the demonstration flight on 2 November 1943 at Lechfeld.
Franz was born at Schladming in Austria in 1900, receiving his Diplom-Ingenieur from Graz University in 1924. After the war he worked at the USAAF Air Technical Service Command, Wright Field, Dayton, Ohio, and eventually became Vice President and Assistant General Manager of the AVCO-Lycoming Division in Stratford, Connecticut.

Messerschmitt Me 262 V6 Demonstration Flight Lechfeld, 2 November 1943

Left: Faces in the crowd: Karl Baur (second from left), General Karl Bodenschatz, Göring's "personal liaison officer" at the Führer headquarters (fifth from left), Adolf Galland (sixth from left), Göring, Anselm Franz (in hat with back to camera) and Messerschmitt inspect the Me 262 V6.

"But Herr Reichsmarschall," said Messerschmitt to Göring following the flight of the Me 262 V6 on 2 November 1943, "we have always provided for two bomb racks in the aeroplane - to carry two 250 kg or one 500 kg bomb." To the left of Göring in this photo is the pilot of the Me 262 V6, Gerd Lindner, Messerschmitt, and Fritz Wendel.

Göring (right) examining the Me 262 V6 at Lechfeld on 2 November 1943. To his right is Generalstabsing. Roluf Lucht, chief engineer with the RLM's Technical Department and at extreme left, Adolf Galland.

Opposite and below: The assembled entourage including Göring and Messerschmitt, walk forward to inspect the Me 262 V6 on 2 November 1943.

A group of personalities await the return of the Me 262 V6 following its demonstration flight on 2 November 1943. From left to right in the foreground are Fritz Wendel, Göring, Messerschmitt, Bernd von Brauschitsch, Göring's adjutant and Messerschmitt chief test pilot, Karl Baur.

The Me 262 V6 landing at Lechfeld on 2 November 1943 after its demonstration to Göring and Milch. The first aircraft to be fitted with a fully retractable tricycle undercarriage, the sixth prototype was destroyed on its 28th flight on 9 March 1944 after having accumulated 6 hours 31 minutes flying time.

Messerschmitt test pilot Gerd Lindner strides forward to shake Göring's hand after having landed in the Me 262 V6. After the war, Lindner assisted the Americans in testing the Me 262 at Lechfeld, but was killed in 1945 in an automobile accident.

Göring (centre) talking to Messerschmitt and Lindner after the latter's demonstration flight in the Me 262 V6.

Messerschmitt Me 262 V6 Demonstration Flight Lechfeld, 2 November 1943

On 2 November 1943, Gerd Lindner demonstrated the Me 262 V6 in front of Göring and Milch at Lechfeld. After the aircraft landed, it was noticed that paint had been stripped from the rudder as can be seen in this sequence of "walk-around" photographs.

Messerschmitt Me 262 V6

Believed to show the Me 262 V1 (PC+UA) after it was rebuilt with Jumo 004 engines. The aircraft was fitted with a production type canopy, but was destroyed on 7 June 1944. The large removable cowlings afforded easy access to the turbojets.

von Below, to Göring on 5 December. "The *Führer* has called our attention again," it read, "to the tremendous importance of the production of jet propelled aircraft for employment as fighter-bombers. It is imperative that the *Luftwaffe* have a number of jet fighter-bombers ready for front commitment by the spring of 1944. Any difficulties occasioned by labour and raw material shortages will be resolved by the exploitation of *Luftwaffe* resources, until existing shortages can be made up. The *Führer* feels that a delay in our jet aircraft programme would be tantamount to irresponsible negligence. The *Führer* has directed that bi-monthly written reports, the first due on 15 November 1943, be made to him concerning the progress of the Me 262 and the Ar 234."[6]

On 20 December 1943, the Me 262 V7 made its first flight. This was essentially similar to the V6, powered by Jumo 004 B-0 engines and having a fully retractable undercarriage. Its main difference was that it was fitted with an experimental rubber sealed pressurized cabin, a pressure differential of 1 : 2 being attained. In other words at 12,000 m (39,400 ft) a pressure equal to that at 6,000 m (19,700 ft) was maintained.

On the same day that the V7 flew, Hitler spoke at a war conference: "Every month that passes makes it more probable that we will get at least one squadron of jet aircraft - the most important thing is that they (the enemy) will get some bombs on top of them just as they try to invade. That will force them to take cover. And even if there is only one such aircraft in the air they will still have to take cover, and in this way they will waste hour after hour! But after half a day our reserves will already be on their way. So if we can pin them down on the beaches for just six to eight hours, you can see what that will mean to us..."

On 13 January 1944, the Me 209 was abandoned for the second and last time. This freed production capacity for the Me 262 but still there were not enough skilled workers available. During an Armament Ministry conference six days later, Speer's own trouble shooter, *Maj.Dr.* Krome, asked if workers could be released from the other special weapons projects. Milch replied: "*I cannot speak for the A4 (V2 rocket).*"

Krome then asked pointedly: "*Which do we need more, the A4 or the Me 262?*"

Milch rasped: "*We need the Me 262 more than*

Me 262 V9 (W.Nr.130004) which first flew on 19 January 1944. This was the first production model to fly with the new 'bubble' canopy intended for the production model and tested FuG 16Z and FuG 25a IFF radio equipment. After completing 176 flights by 1 October 1944, it was modified as the HG I prototype with swept horizontal tail surfaces and the Rennkabine or racing cabin.

anything else - more than submarines, more than tanks, because without this aircraft all armament production will become impossible...."

"That is what I said four weeks ago," replied Krome, *"but no-one drew the necessary conclusions."*

"Nor will they draw them in Germany!" exclaimed Milch. Turning to Karl-Otto Saur representing the Armaments Ministry, he appealed: *"Cannot the submarine and tank people realize that in four or six months time, Germany will not be able to manufacture one more tank or submarine? Saur, cannot you realize that something must be done?"*

Saur gave a non-committal reply.

Three days later, Speer and Milch were summoned to a conference with the *Führer* at which Hitler again emphasised that he was impatient to have as many Me 262s as could be made in the shortest possible time. "Since meanwhile," wrote Speer in his memoirs, "Hitler had let everything lapse, we could promise to deliver no more than sixty aircraft a month from July 1944 on. From January 1945 on, however, we could produce 210 aircraft a month.[7]

"During this conference Hitler showed that he planned to use this aircraft, which was to be a fighter, as a fast bomber. The air force specialists were dismayed, but imagined that their sensible arguments would prevail. What happened was just the opposite. Hitler obstinately ordered all on board weapons removed so that the aircraft could carry a greater weight of bombs. Jet aircraft did not have to defend themselves, he maintained, since with their superior speed they could not be attacked by enemy fighters. Deeply distrustful of this new invention, he wanted it employed primarily for straight flight at great heights to spare its wings and engines, and wanted the engineers to gear it to a somewhat reduced speed to lessen the strain on the still untried system.

"The effect of these tiny bombers, which could carry a load of little more than 500 kg of bombs and had only a primitive bombsight, was ridiculously insignificant. As fighter aircraft, on the other hand, each jet aircraft would have been able, because of its superior performance, to shoot down several of the four-engined American bombers that in raid after raid were dropping thousands of tons of explosive on German cities."

Just previously, on 19 January, the Me 262 V9 had made its first flight. This was the first prototype to fly with the new 'bubble' canopy intended for the production model. This aircraft was used initially to test radio and electrical equipment, a FuG 16Z transmitter/receiver and a FuG 25a IFF set being installed.

On 30 January, Allied reconnaissance aircraft photographed the Me 262 at Lechfeld for the first time. In common with standard practice, the aircraft was given the interim designation 'Lechfeld 42', indicating where it was first seen and its estimated wing span in feet. The

Gerd Lindner, who was to become the most experienced Me 262 test pilot. This photo shows him (second from the right) with the Me 262 V9 in the background.

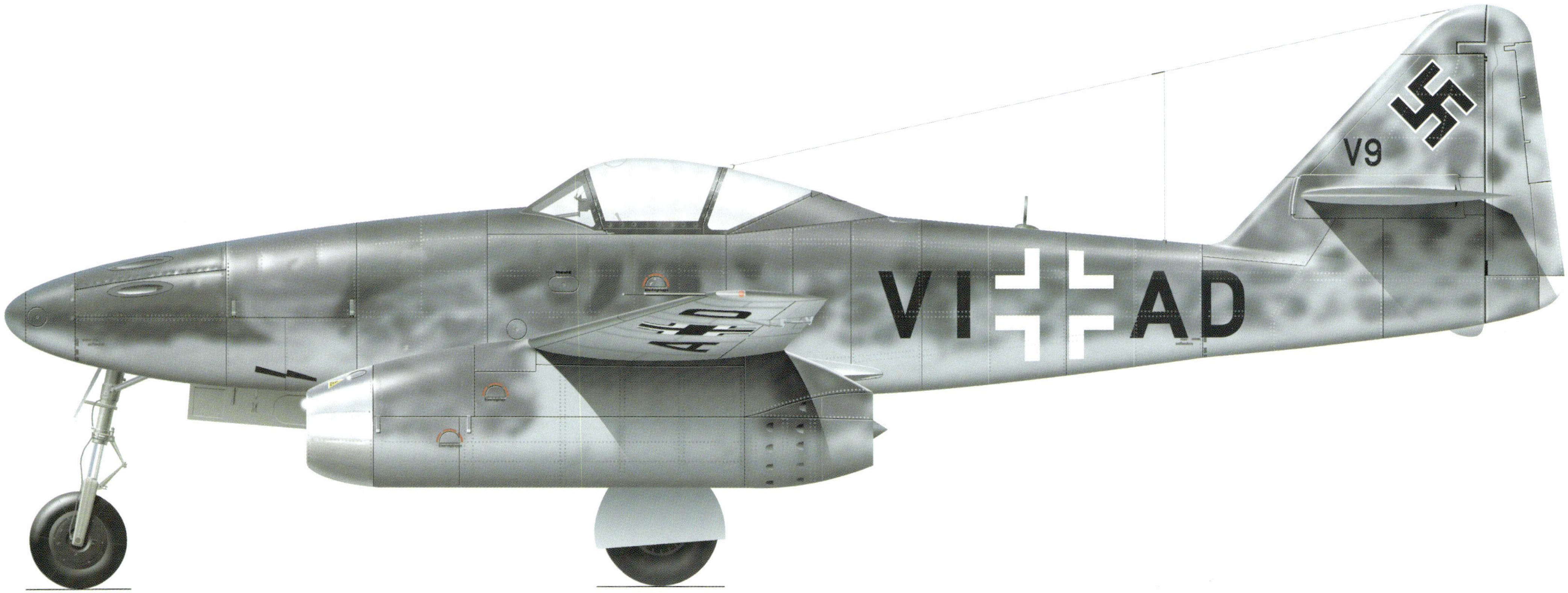

Me 262 V9 W.Nr. 130004 with two Jumo 004 B engines

The first prototype to be fitted with the new 'bubble' canopy intended for the production model. First flew on 19 January 1944, being used initially to test radio and electrical equipment, an FuG 16Z transmitter/receiver and an FuG 25a IFF set being installed. Completed 176 flights by 1 October 1944 totalling 41 hours 58 minutes. The aircraft was then modified as the HG I prototype with 40º swept back horizontal tail surfaces and the *Rennkabine* (racing cabin). By the end of March 1945 the V9 had completed 201 flights, accumulating 49 hours 22 minutes flying. Found at Lechfeld at the end of the war. Camouflage was pale blue grey (76) with dark grey (74) and medium grey (75) on the upper surfaces, and mottling of dark green (71) and RLM grey (02) on the fuselage sides.

accompanying intelligence report noted that it was possible that the aircraft was jet propelled. "The engine nacelles of the 'Lechfeld 42' are small and their separation corresponds with the separation between pairs of (scorch) marks, possibly caused by jet propulsion, which have been seen on Augsburg airfield."

By February 1944, consideration was being given to development of increased armour and additional equipment for the Me 262. *Protokoll Nr.24* dated 9 February discussed the installation of six MK 108 or two MK 103, two MK 108 and two MG 151/20 cannon, or even the provision of 50 or 55 mm calibre weapons. Other developments proposed included a pressurized cabin, a new two-seat fuselage and the installation of HeS 11 engines.

The Heinkel-Hirth HeS 11 was a rather complex engine featuring a diagonal flow impeller and a three stage axial flow compressor, designed to produce 1,300 kg (2,870 lb) thrust. Preliminary design studies for the engine were completed in September 1942, the decision being taken to construct five prototypes to establish a basic configuration. Problems immediately manifested themselves when the diagonal flow impeller failed after only an hour's bench testing with the HeS 11 V1. Many months of trial and error with the machining of the compressor followed, which were finally resolved with the aid of the Hans Voith company at Heidenheim. Early in 1944 work began on a series of definitive prototypes designated HeS 11 V6 to V25. One of these was test flown beneath a Ju 88 at Stuttgart before the end of the war, but no aircraft flew solely under jet power. By January 1945 four of the prototype engines had completed 184 hours bench running, although it was rare for thrust in excess of 1,100 kg (2,430 lb) to be achieved. Exact figures are lacking, but a total of about 20 prototype engines had been completed before Germany's collapse. It was intended that the 109-011 A engine should go into production by the end of 1945, but in April of that year difficulties caused by bombing attacks on transport and communications, combined with the evacuation of the Heinkel-Hirth works at Stuttgart, became so serious that development and preparations for series production were badly disrupted. For this reason, Heinkel-Hirth expressed some doubt in the possibility of starting series production by the end of 1945. Six 109-011 A-0 pre-production engines were assembled after the end of the war on the orders of the U.S. Navy.[8]

A minor problem occurred to the Me 262 programme on 21 February 1944, when *Feldwebel* Kurt Schmidt was forced to belly land the Me 262 V7 in snow due to a combination of bad weather and engine trouble. The prototype was repaired to fly again on 11 April. A much more serious event took place four days later when the US Eighth Air Force bombed Messerschmitt's Augsburg plant. The resulting fires gutted about 30% of the plant, which reduced production capacity by some 35%. It also damaged 30% of the machine tools and destroyed 70% of stored material. Fortunately for the Me 262 programme, transfer of the design office to Oberammergau had begun in October 1943 and final assembly had been moved to Leipheim and Schwäbisch Hall. Only the original ten prototypes and the first five production aircraft were built at Augsburg and, of these, both the V10 and S1 were damaged in the 25 February 1944 raid. In addition to Augsburg, Regensburg was also attacked again, this time by B-17s of the US Fifteenth Air Force.

The series of American raids on the German aircraft industry, which included that on

The Heinkel-Hirth HeS 011 engine was designed by Hans von Ohain to produce a static thrust of 1,300 kp (2,866 lbs). It was a rather complex design with a composite diagonal and axial flow compressor and because of this only nine A-0 pre-production engines were completed before the end of the war.

Feldwebel Kurt Schmidt examining the Me 262 V7 after it crashed into the snow following engine trouble in bad weather on 21 February 1944. The aircraft was painted pale blue-grey (RLM colour 76) overall with the radio callsign VI+AB in black.

Messerschmitt Me 262 V7
VI+AB W.Nr. 130 002

As can be seen, the canopy has been jettisoned on to the wing. After the aircraft was rebuilt, to fly again on 11 April, it was fitted with a production type bubble canopy.

Reichsminister Albert Speer (right), Hitler's ambitious and cerebral armaments minister and Hauptdienstleiter Karl-Otto Saur, (left), the energetic head of the Ministry's Technical Office.

Augsburg, was dubbed the 'Big Week' campaign. During February, 23 airframe and three aircraft engine factories were hit with a weight of bombs only slightly less than the whole previous bombing of aircraft plants. This meant that by the end of the month three-quarters of the airframe component and assembly plants had received structural damage assessed at up to 75% and damage to equipment and tools of up to 30%. The effects on production were to reduce the March output of all aircraft types to only 60% of schedule.

Besides the problems caused by Allied bombing, the RLM also considered aircraft production to be threatened by the introduction of a new tank production programme that had the personal backing of Hitler, and which encroached upon the sources from which the aircraft manufacturers drew their materials, semi-finished components and accessories. This problem affected more especially the aero engine plants that suffered from quite grave shortages of crankshafts, crankcases, sparking plugs, valves and, especially, injection pumps.

To improve conditions, especially regarding competition with other branches of the armaments industry, weekly meetings were arranged between Milch and Speer's staff. Although the two men had excellent personal relations, it was found that the latter's representatives were generally more inclined to favour the Army to the detriment of the needs of the *Luftwaffe*. Accordingly, it was decided, in view of the serious situation in the air, to create a special body known as the *Jägerstab* that would be responsible for maintaining and increasing fighter output.

To lead the *Jägerstab* or Fighter Staff, Milch rather shrewdly proposed *Hauptdienstleiter* (Chief Party Leader) Karl-Otto Saur, head of the Technical Office in the Armaments Ministry. Saur had hitherto been one of the most outspoken critics of the aircraft industry, and Milch considered that appointing him to head the new staff would change his views. Speer favoured his old friend, Karl Hanke, the *Gauleiter* of Lower Silesia, to fill the post. To Milch's relief, Hitler would not hear of this and Saur was appointed.

The *Jägerstab* was formally brought into being on 1 March 1944, under the direction of Speer and Milch with Saur as executive head controlling a staff of 25 officials. The new organisation was given responsibility for all single- and twin-engined fighter, fighter-bomber, ground attack and tactical reconnaissance aircraft production.

As mentioned, the primary function of the *Jägerstab* was to restore and increase aircraft production and to protect factories from air assault. The first measures introduced were to instigate a 72 hour week for the industry and keep a check on the efficiency of individual factories. A representative of the organisation was officially attached to each plant, Professor Overlach being attached to Messerschmitt at Augsburg for example. In addition each factory was also invited to send a representative to meetings of the *Jägerstab* in Berlin to discuss its particular problems.

A short term solution to the problem of an aircraft factory damaged by bombing was to send a 'flying squad' of five men of proven energy and

After being slightly damaged in the US raid on Augsburg on 25 February 1944, the Me 262 S1, W.Nr.130006, coded VI+AF, made its first flight on 19 April. The aircraft completed six flights before the wing and fuselage was damaged due to a tyre bursting on take-off on April 27.

power of decision to restore morale and assist in getting reconstruction underway. This team was made up of an architect, a machine-tool specialist, an electrical engineer, an expert in the provision of materials and an official to take charge of welfare arrangements.

To ease problems in the long term, a programme of dispersal was initiated, the 27 major aircraft factories being spread over 729 smaller works. By the end of August 1944 more than 300 of these dispersal sites had been put into production without any adverse effect on total production. The *Jägerstab* also drew up plans for providing over three million square metres (32.25 million square feet) of underground production space by the end of 1945.

At this time, the German aircraft industry was working to production Programme 225. According to this programme the following numbers of Me 262s were to be produced: 20 in April 1944, increasing to 60 in July, remaining at 60 from July through October, rising to 210 in January 1945, to 440 in April, to 670 in July and 800 in October 1945.

On 9 March 1944, the Me 262 V6 crashed and was destroyed, the pilot, *Feldwebel* Kurt Schmidt, being killed. Nine days later this prototype was replaced by the Me 262 V8 which, although similar to the V9, was fitted with what was to become the standard armament of four 30 mm MK 108 cannon.[9] These weapons were closely grouped in the fuselage nose, aimed to converge at between 450 and 500 m (1,480 and 1,640 ft), the upper two guns carrying 100 rounds each, the lower two 80. Some problems were experienced initially when the weapons were fired in a turn as this often resulted in centrifugal forces tearing the ammunition belts. This problem was later cured by a modification to the feed mechanism. The Me 262 V8 was to serve as the prototype for the A-series production model.

Apart from detail shots, this is the only known photograph of the Me 262 V8. This prototype made its first flight on 18 March 1944, and can be considered the production prototype, being fitted with four 30 mm MK 108 cannon.

1 *The fuselage of the Me 262 V4 was, as has been recorded earlier, used for dropping trials with the Me 323 S9.*

2 *This ploy proved successful, for Allied Intelligence remained unaware of the Oberammergau plant, and when US troops occupied the facility on 29 April 1945, they were astonished to find the entire Messerschmitt technical organisation still largely intact.*

3 *The purpose of Professor Messerschmitt's visits to the Führer's headquarters were frequently discussed at GL conferences. For instance, on 12 November 1943, Milch complained bitterly of Messerschmitt trying to circumvent his authority: "And then he scurries off with it to the Reichsmarschall or to the Führer, and lies until he is in the clear again".*

4 *The Me 262 V1 and V6 had been transported to Insterburg by rail, leaving on 21 November and returning on 3 December.*

5 *In the authors' opinion, this would seem to indicate that Milch, and possibly his senior advisers in the Technical Office, considered Hitler's intention to employ the Me 262 as a bomber as only a passing whim, which would be forgotten in the course of time. If this surmise is correct, it was to have far-reaching consequences for Milch some six months later.*

6 *See Monarch Series No.1 on the Ar 234 by J Richard Smith and Eddie J Creek published by Monogram Aviation Publications.*

7 *For detailed figures, see Programme 225 of 1 March quoted on page 167.*

8 *Some sources state that nine 109-011 A-0 engines were built for the U.S. Navy.*

9 *All German aircraft guns prefixed with the number "1" were developed by Rheinmetall-Borsig, with the number "2" by Mauser, with the number "3" by Krieghoff and with the number "4" by Krupp. It was therefore possible to conclude that the MK 214, for example, was built by the Mauser company.*

CHAPTER SEVEN

"WE NEED THE Me 262 MORE THAN ANYTHING ELSE"

On 8 May 1943, Voigt, Degel and Althoff had issued *Projektübergabe IV 'Me 262 Jäger und Jabo'* which detailed the first production models, the Me 262 A-1 fighter and A-2 fighter bomber. The A-1 was described in some detail in *Protokoll Nr. 19* dated 29 October 1943. It was to be an interceptor fighter powered by two 900 kg (1,980 lb) thrust Jumo 004 B-1 turbojets, carry an armament of four MK 108 cannon with a total of 360 rounds, 2,570 ltr (565 Imp gal) of J2 fuel and FuG 16Z and FuG 25a radio equipment.

On 23 March 1944, Messerschmitt proposed a heavily armoured version of the Me 262 to be known as the *Panzerflugzeug I*. This aircraft was to carry a total of 1,244 kg (2,740 lb) of additional armour, which would have increased normal loaded weight to 5,984 kg (13,190 lb). Estimated performance figures with a maximum loaded weight of 6,684 kg (14,740 lb) were:

Maximum speed	
803 km/h at sea level	499 mph at sea level
864 km/h at 6,000 m	537 mph at 19,700 ft
858 km/h at 9,000 m	533 mph at 29,500 ft
Climb	
18.2 m/sec at sea level	59.7 ft/sec at sea level
9.5 m/sec at 6,000 m	31.2 ft/sec at 19,700 ft
4.4 m/sec at 9,000 m	14.4 ft/sec at 29,500 ft
Service ceiling	
11,200 m	36,745 ft
Range	
288 km at sea level	179 miles at sea level
533 km at 6,000 m	331 miles at 19,700 ft
695 km at 9,000 m	432 miles at 29,500 ft
Landing speed	
185 km/h	109 mph

The re-built Me 262 V7 (VI+AB) taking off on a test flight.

Examination of the design studies for the *Panzerflugzeug* showed that the weight penalty of the additional armour, especially on the range of the aircraft, was far too great. Therefore, on 13 May a new study, known as the *Panzerflugzeug II*, was initiated. In this proposal, the weight of the additional armour was reduced to 580 kg (1,280 lb) which would have resulted in a normal loaded weight of 5,650 kg (12,460 lb). Estimated performance figures with a maximum loaded weight of 6,400 kg (14,110 lb) were:

Maximum speed	
805 km/h at sea level	500 mph at sea level
865 km/h at 6,000 m	538 mph at 19,700 ft
856 km/h at 9,000 m	532 mph at 29,500 ft
Climb	
18.4 m/sec at sea level	60.4 ft/sec at sea level
9.7 m/sec at 6,000 m	31.8 ft/sec at 19,700 ft
4.6 m/sec at 9,000 m	15.1 ft/sec at 29,500 ft
Range	
470 km at sea level	292 miles at sea level
690 km at 6,000 m	429 miles at 19,700 ft
920 km at 9,000 m	572 miles at 29,500 ft
Landing speed	
172 km/h	107 mph

As production of the Me 262 began to speed up, the second two production models, the S2 and S3 ('S' indicating *Serien* or Series) made their first flights on 28 March and 5 April 1944, respectively. The S1, as has been recorded in Chapter 6, was damaged in a USAAF bombing attack and did not fly until 19 April. Both the S2 and S3 were similar to the V8, all three being used initially for tests with the MK 108 cannon and the nose-mounted BSK 16 gun camera. On 11 April, the repaired V7, now fitted with the production type canopy, rejoined the test programme. Four days later the Me 262 V10 also flew again. Although this aircraft had made its first flight on 5 January 1944, it had been damaged in the attack on Leipheim on 25 February. At first the prototype was used to investigate the high stick forces that the aircraft was beginning to encounter in high speed turns. Several different aileron types were tested by the prototype but these failed to improve matters. Therefore a special geared control column was developed that enabled the pilot to exert much more pressure on the ailerons when he was manoeuvring the aircraft at high speed. This feature proved quite effective, but was not fitted to production aircraft.

On 24 April the US Eighth Air Force mounted

After the Me 262 V7 crashed due to bad weather on 21 February 1944, it was repaired and flew again on 11 April 1944. The aircraft was then fitted with a production type canopy as can be seen in this photo. The pilot standing on the wing is Oblt. Ernst Tesch, a Luftwaffe pilot attached to Messerschmitt's flight test division. The V7 was finally destroyed on 19 May 1944 killing pilot Uffz. Kurt Flachs.

a major bombing attack on one of the main Me 262 assembly plants at Leipheim, destroying nine aircraft which were under construction. Five aircraft were later identified on the airfield by Allied photographic interpreters. This attack was discussed at a *Jägerstab* meeting held the next day. "The attack on the tiny airfield at Leipheim," said Dr. Krome, "where the final assembly of the Me 262 is carried out, proves that the British are accurately informed. The question of getting Me 262 production underground becomes more urgent every day. Attacks will be made not only on the final stage of assembly but on the intermediary factories as well. However, no progress has yet been made on the intermediary stage. The matter must be pressed to the limit and the administration of the intermediary stage production must be compelled to make available the area that has been promised and demanded of it as quickly as possible. There should be no hesitation even in making a sharp cut. The *Feldmarschall* (Milch) is aware that I am referring to the possibility of A-4 (rocket) production being suspended completely."

Milch replied: "I think that it must be suspended, for it will not be produced this year."

The head of the RLM's Planning Office, *Oberst* Ulrich Diesing, commented: "I informed Korten of this and he wishes to raise the matter again at today's meeting with the *Führer*. He said that Saur must also state an opinion on this matter."

Dr. Krome concluded: "It is a choice between the A4 in a year or the Me 262 in three or four months."

It was not only production of the Me 262 airframe that was causing difficulties, there were also problems with the Jumo 004 engines. On 20 April, Messerschmitt wrote to Walter Cambeis, Production Director of the Junkers engine works at Dessau:

> *"You must have heard that, according to reports from our agents, the English and Americans intend to equip many units with jet aircraft in the autumn of the year. It is, therefore, a matter of life and death for us all to step up the numbers of Me 262s with your engines as rapidly as possible. I will try to accelerate the increase in the rate of airframe*

The Me 262 S1, unlike most production aircraft, featured a tail light which was smoothly faired into the bottom of the rudder.

production, but I can only do this successfully if I know that we are getting the corresponding numbers of engines.

"I would be grateful to you, therefore, if you could let me know, naturally without any guarantee, the expected numbers in the programme until the spring of next year. If you have bottlenecks where you might think I could be useful, I beg you to name them to me."

On 27 April 1944, the wing and fuselage of the Me 262 S1 were damaged due to a tyre bursting on take-off. By the end of the month, the five Augsburg built production aircraft had flown. The Me 262 S4 was similar to the previous aircraft, but the S5, which flew for the first time on 28 April, was later modified by Blohm und Voss as the tandem two-seat trainer prototype. The first Leipheim built aircraft were also beginning to make their appearance, approximately eight having been completed by the end of April. Of these, at least the S6 and S7 flew by the end of the month.

On 19 May 1944, the Me 262 V7 crashed on its 31st flight and was totally destroyed. The pilot, *Unteroffizier* Kurt Flachs, was killed. Four days after the loss of the V7, Hitler ordered Milch, Speer, Saur, Petersen and several aircraft production specialists to a conference at the *'Berghof'* to examine production targets. As Hitler gazed absently out of a large window at the magnificent alpine view, Milch began to read out the list of future aircraft production figures. When he came to the Me 262, listed under *fighters,* the *Führer* suddenly interrupted: "I thought the 262 was coming as a bomber!" The others exchanged uncomfortable glances. Milch replied that all aircraft had been completed as fighters. There was an awkward silence while Milch explained

The Me 262 S1 suffered damaged to its wing and fuselage when a tyre burst on take-off on 27 April 1944. It was later damaged again in a hard landing on 11 June.

These views (top photo looking towards nose, lower photo towards the cockpit) of the weapons compartment of the Me 262 S1 show the breeches of the four 30 mm MK 108 cannon. These weapons were closely grouped in the fuselage nose, aimed to converge at between 450 and 500 m (1,476 and 1,640 ft), the upper two guns carrying 100 rounds each, the lower two 80. Some problems were experienced initially when the weapons were fired in a turn as this often resulted in centrifugal forces tearing the ammunition belts. This problem was later cured by a modification to the feed mechanism.

The tail of the first series production Me 262 S1 (W.Nr.130006) which was coded VI+AF. This aircraft flew for the first time on 19 April 1944 and was damaged several times. The aircraft was painted pale blue-grey (76) overall with the code in black and the serial number in white. Unlike most production aircraft, the tail light (middle right) was smoothly faired into the bottom of the rudder. As can be seen from the photo on the previous page, the swastika was painted rather roughly in black edged in white, a not unusual circumstance.

Top right: Unlike the early Me 262 prototypes, the Me 262 S1 and subsequent production aircraft had a retaining wire to prevent the cockpit canopy from being over extended. Some earlier aircraft used a stay.

Messerschmitt Me 262 S3 VI+AH W.Nr. 130 008

On 16 June 1944 the Me 262 S3 (W.Nr.130008) coded VI+AH, was damaged in a crash landing at Lechfeld. The cause was attributed to excessive time taken to extend the nosegear because the pilot, Oberfeldwebel Becker, was late in switching air pressure to the undercarriage. The crash ripped off both engines and damaged the nose, wings and undercarriage. The aircraft had made its first flight on 5 April 1944 and was marked with a large red number "3".

Me 262 V7 VI + AB W.Nr. 130002 with two Jumo 004 B-0 engines

After crashing on 21 February 1944, the V7 was repaired and modified, being fitted with a production type canopy and new tailplane assembly, before flying again on 11 April. The profile shows the prototype in this modified form and shows the aircraft was painted overall (76) as before. It crashed again on its 31st flight on 19 May 1944 and was totally destroyed killing the pilot, *Uffz.* Kurt Flachs. The aircraft completed a total of 13 hours 36 minutes flying.

Me 262 V8 VI + AC W.Nr. 130003 with two Jumo 004 B-1 engines

The first prototype to be fitted with four 30 mm MK 108 cannon. As can be seen the cannon ports were edged in red. As far as is known, it was the only prototype from the original series to carry its *Versuchs* number in white on the nose. The prototype first flew on 18 March 1944, making 21 flights up to 8 April 1944. Damaged several times, but was finally written off in October 1944. The aircraft made at least 258 flights. Camouflage was similar to that of the V9.

The Me 262 S3 (W.Nr.130008) coded VI+AH, was damaged in a crash landing at Lechfeld on 16 June 1944.

that the aircraft could not become an effective bomber without extensive modifications.

The *Führer* lost his composure, realizing that the Allied invasion was due any day, and that the weapon on which he had placed many of his hopes for defeating it was nowhere near ready. "Never mind!" he shouted, "I only want it to carry a 250 kilogram bomb!" He then demanded precise figures as to the weight of the aircraft's guns and armour plate. "Who pays the slightest attention to my orders?" he continued. "I gave an unqualified directive that the aircraft is to be built as a bomber."

Saur then produced the figures and Hitler added them up. The total was more than 500 kilos. "There you are; you can take all the guns out. The plane is so fast it doesn't need guns." He turned to Petersen and asked if this was correct. Overawed, the Colonel replied that it could be done without difficulty. Galland attempted to protest, but was soon savaged into silence by the *Führer's* rhetoric. In desperation, Milch tried to urge Hitler to think again, but was subjected to a further torrent of abuse.

The Me 262 S4 (W.Nr.130009) coded VI+AI, which made its first flight early in May 1944, was totally destroyed on 19 July 1944 in an Allied air attack on Lechfeld. In this photograph the leading edge slats have been removed.

This was too much for the Field Marshall: "*Mein Führer*," he retorted before he could stop himself, "even the smallest child can see that this is a fighter, not a bomber!" This outburst led Hitler to turn his back on Milch and he completely ignored him during the remainder of the meeting. The officer sitting next to *Oberst* Petersen whispered: "Crashed in flames!", as if to signify the magnitude of Milch's indiscretion. This prophetic observation anticipated Milch's downfall from office.

Next day, Göring confronted his Chief of Staff, *General der Flieger* Günther Korten, his deputy *Generalleutnant* Karl Koller, the Chief of the Operations Staff, and Adolf Galland with the new situation. They all agreed glumly that modification of the aircraft as a bomber would cause major design problems. "You gentlemen seem deaf," said Göring, "I have kept repeating the *Führer's* perfectly clear order again and again. He doesn't give a hoot for the Me 262 as a fighter. He just wants it as a bomber, a *Jagdbomber*."

When Göring asked *Oberst* Petersen how long the modifications would take, he made a wild guess: "About three months.

Göring banged his fist on the table. "You

Me 262 S1 VI + AF W.Nr. 130006 with two Jumo 004 B-1 engines

The first series production aircraft, the S1 first flew on 19 April 1944. The aircraft completed six flights up to 25 April totalling 2 hours 49 minutes. The wings and fuselage were damaged due to a tyre bursting on take-off on April 27. After repair the starboard wing was damaged in a hard landing on 11 June 1944. The aircraft had its *Werk Nummer* painted in white below the tailplane and carried the series test number "1" in red on the nose.

Messerschmitt Me 262 S7 VI+AL W.Nr. 130 012

The Me 262 S7 (W.Nr.130012) coded VI+AL, which made its first flight in April 1944, crashed and was damaged on 1 June 1944 due to engine fire. This aircraft was the seventh series production aircraft, although the fuselage bears a large red number "6". These numbers indicate the Messerschmitt test number, the sixth production aircraft (W.Nr.130011) having being delivered to Hauptmann Werner Thierfelder, commander of Erprobungskommando 262.

Left: The two main problems plaguing the Me 262, were engine failure and nosewheel collapse. Amongst the most common faults with the undercarriage were hydraulic, mechanical and material failure. Here is a typical scene of a Me 262 being retrieved at Lechfeld in the Summer of 1944 after a nosewheel collapse. In attendance, from left, Meister Moritz Asam, in charge of prototype construction, Hptm. Werner Thierfelder (in uniform), the commander of Erprobungskommando 262, Gerhard Caroli (centre), in charge of flight testing and Gerd Lindner one of the main Me 262 test pilots. It is thought that the aircraft shown is the S6, the machine in which Thierfelder was lost on 18 July 1944.

gentlemen dare to do what no civilian would ever do – quite simply to disregard orders! The most ill-disciplined bunch in Germany, our armed forces, our officer corps!"

On 27 May 1944, Göring cabled his generals:

> *"The Führer has ordered that the Me 262 is to be operated purely as a high speed bomber. There is to be no mention of it as a fighter until further notice."*

On the same day Gerd Lindner made the first flight with the Me 262 V10 carrying a 250 kg bomb. Initially the ETC 503 rack was used, but this caused severe vibration which was only partially cured by the fitting of a special fairing. Therefore, the variant was later tested with the specially designed *Wikingerschiff* (Viking Ship) rack mounted below the fuselage immediately aft of the nosewheel well, offset to starboard. Using rocket assistance, the aircraft took off within 600 m (2,000 ft) and reached a speed of 740 km/h (460 mph). This first test proved successful, although Lindner did report a tendency for the aircraft to pull to the right. The ETC 503 was subsequently used by some operational Me 262s, but the *Wikingerschiff* was preferred.

Two days after this, on 29 May 1944, Göring called a conference of aircraft manufacturers and service chiefs to discuss the future of the Me 262. Besides Korten, Galland and Petersen, those present included Willy Messerschmitt, *Oberst* Walter Marienfeld, *General der Kampfflieger* (General commanding the bomber force), *Major* Otto Behrens, of the Rechlin Test Centre and *Hauptmann* Werner Thierfelder, commanding the Me 262 *Erprobungskommando* at Lechfeld. The *Reichsmarschall's* first action was to transfer the Me 262 to the jurisdiction of the General of the Bomber Force. "To avoid a misleading designation, I suggest that we call the new aircraft a 'super-speed' bomber rather than a 'fighter-bomber'. Accordingly, further development of this model will be entrusted to the *General der Kampfflieger*. The *Führer* will decide which of those experimental models equipped with armour will be developed further as fighter aircraft. It is not that the *Führer* wants the new model to be only a bomber – quite the contrary. He is well aware of its potentialities as a fighter. However, he does want all those presently in production to come out as super-speed bombers until further notice. It is his desire that we concentrate on the bomber question, and that problems of bomb-carrying capacity, bomb rack release design, bombsight development and bombardment tactics be given paramount consideration."

Göring then went on to explain how a super-speed bomber might be used in combating the coming invasion: "...on the English coast for

The first aircraft used for testing the new Wikingerschiff bomb carrier design, was the V 10. This front view clearly shows a much fatter carrier with concave sides. Note the original nose-wheel door (this was later replaced due to undercarriage damage) showing the aircraft prototype number and the inscription under reading 'Am Bugrad nicht schleppen' ('Do not tow on nose-wheel') set in a rectangular box. Both the box and writing are in red and this varies from the standard wording found on later Me 262 nosewheel doors.

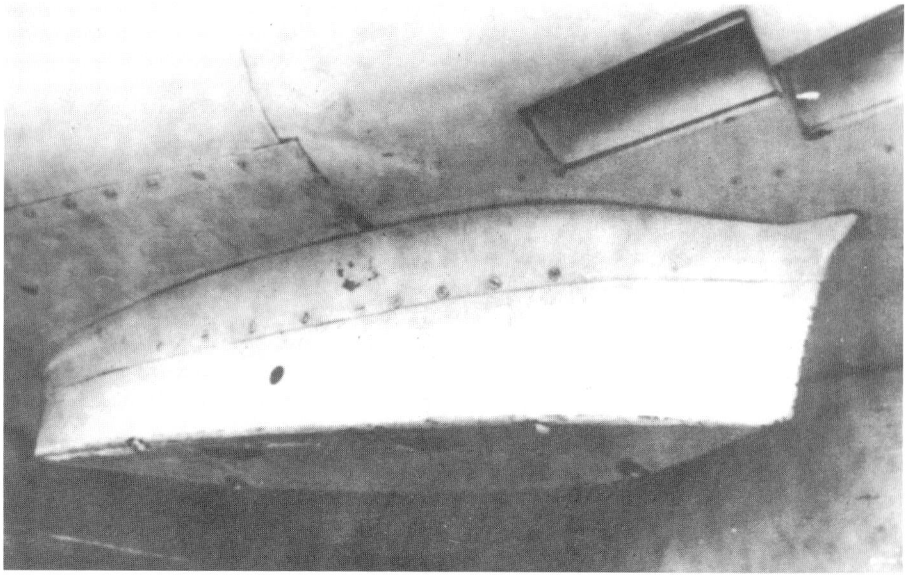

Left and Above: Two views looking from the front at the starboard side of a Wikingerschiff bomb carrier.

Below: After several frantic weeks, the Messerschmitt aerodynamics department finally came up with a new bomb rack design.
This was nick-named the Wikingerschiff (Viking Ship). The influence of the nick-name can be clearly seen from the final design which bears a marked resemblance to an ancient Viking Ship. The design was unique to the Me 262 and this view shows the top of the new carrier with clear details of the fuselage attachment lugs.

An underneath view looking towards the front of the Wikingerschiff bomb carrier showing the bomb attachment points.
The aim of the design was to allow easy attachment to – and removal from – any Me 262.

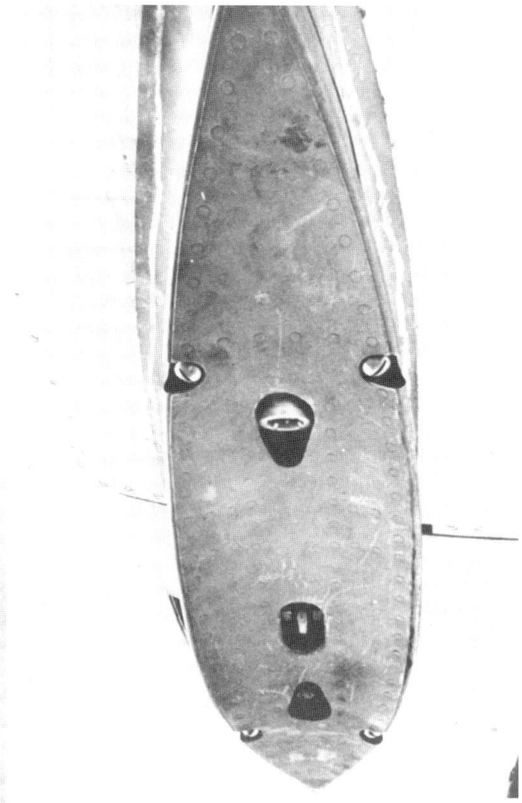

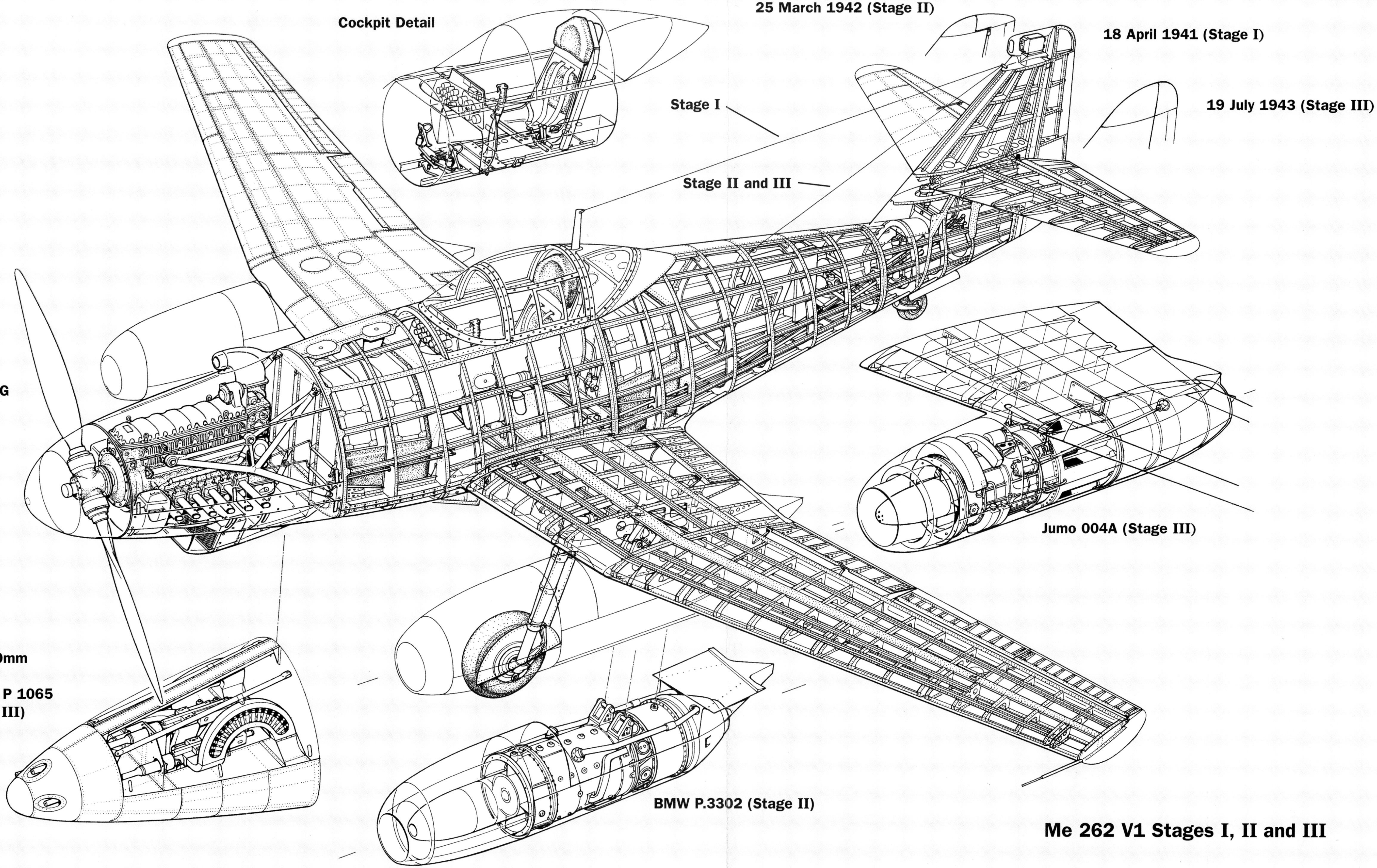

Me 262 V1 Stages I, II and III

Me 262 V1 PC + UA W.Nr. 262 000 0001 in its later form with Jumo 210G piston engine and two early BMW P.3302 (003) turbojets

Towards the end of 1941 the Me 262 V1 was fitted with two of the prototype series turbojet engines, the BMW P.3302 V2 & V10, although the Jumo 210 piston engine was also retained. The first attempted flight with these engines on 25 March 1942 failed due to both turbojets suffering compressor blade failures. This led the RLM to temporarily reduce its order for Me 262 production to five prototypes. The V1 was eventually rebuilt with two Jumo 004 A-0 engines with provision for cabin pressurisation and three MG 151 cannon. The first flight in this form took place on 19 July 1943 but the aircaft crashed and was damaged on its 95th flight on 7 June 1944 with a total flying time of 33 hours 11 minutes and probably never flew again.

These two photos show an SC 500 (500 kg) bomb and Wikingerschiff fitted to a Me 262, which clearly indicate the improved aerodynamic design.

The '*Wikingerschiff*' bomb rack was designed by Messerschmitt AG to improve the aerodynamic qualities of the bomb carrying Me 262

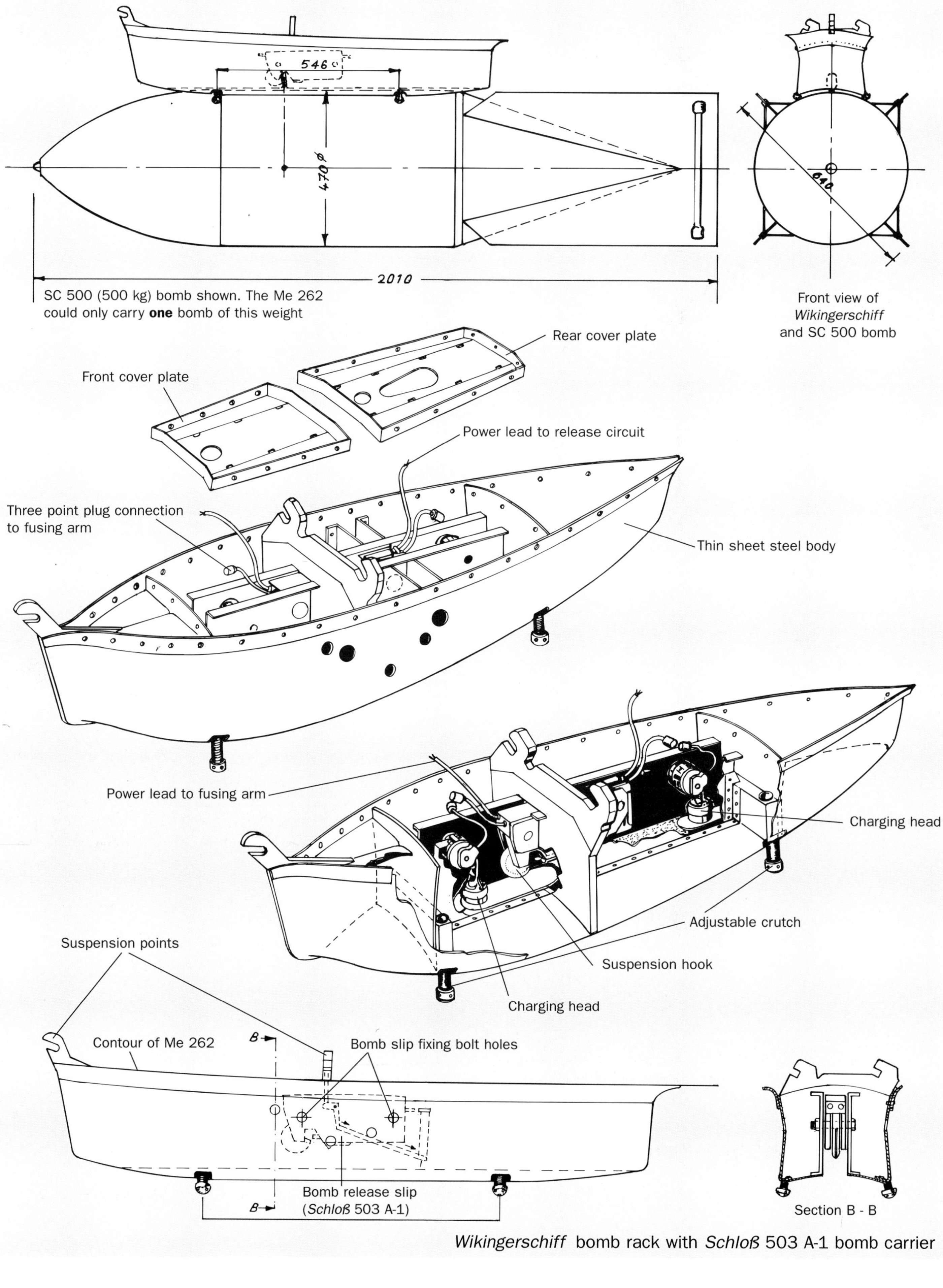

Wikingerschiff bomb rack with *Schloß* 503 A-1 bomb carrier

Standard ETC 503 bomb rack designed by Focke-Wulf for use on the Fw 190. This design was installed on the Me 262 but necessitated a modification of having a timber fairing fitted which was scribed to fit the underside of the fuselage.

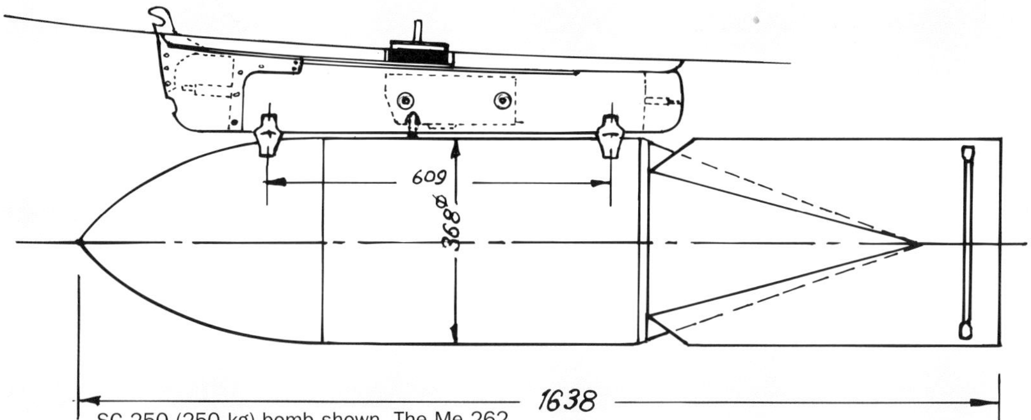

SC 250 (250 kg) bomb shown. The Me 262 could carry two bombs of this weight

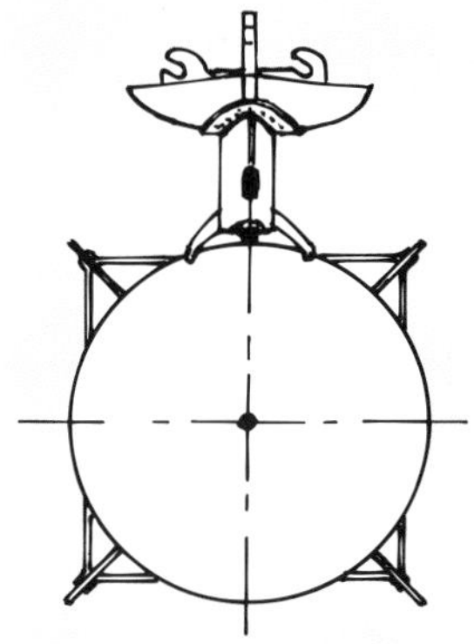

Front view of ETC 503 with SC 250 bomb

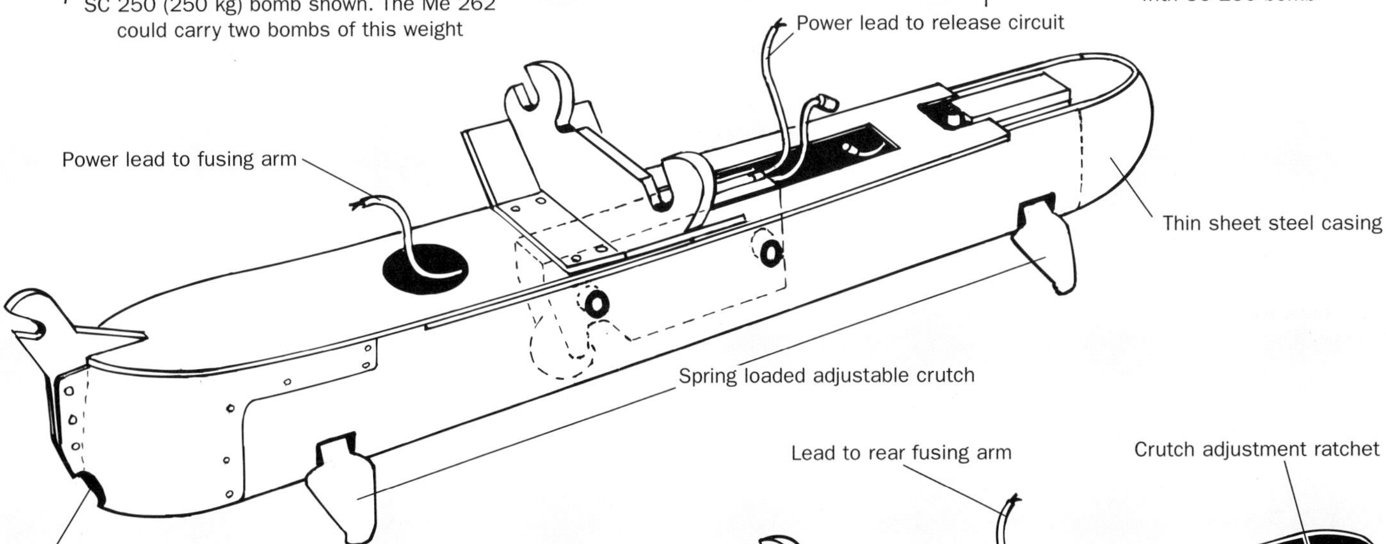

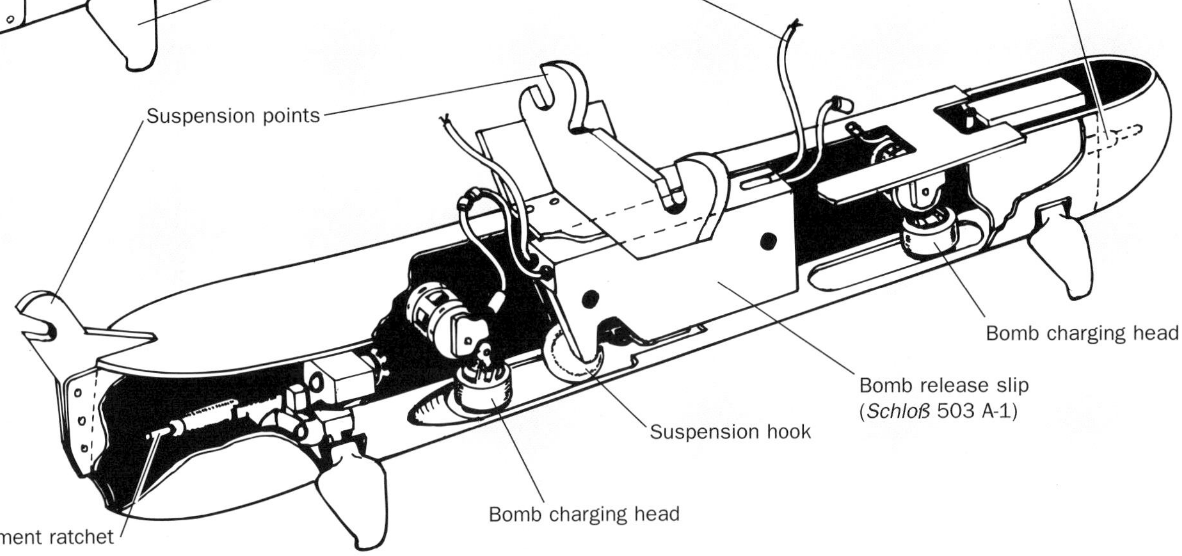

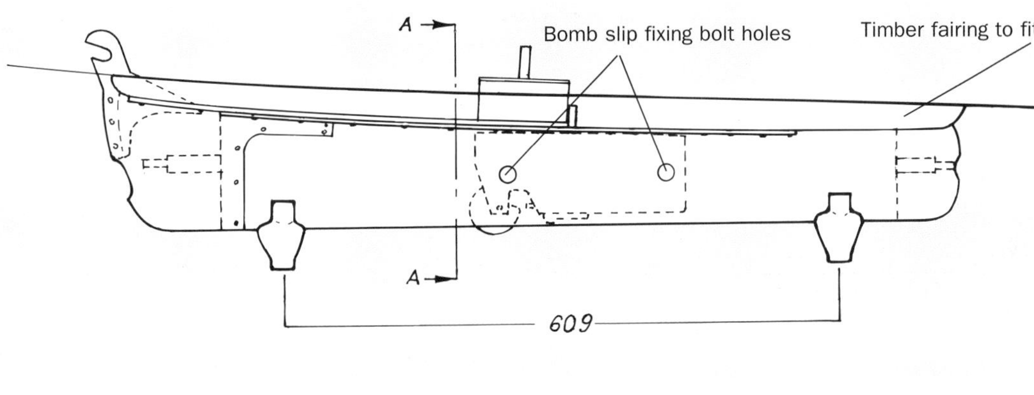

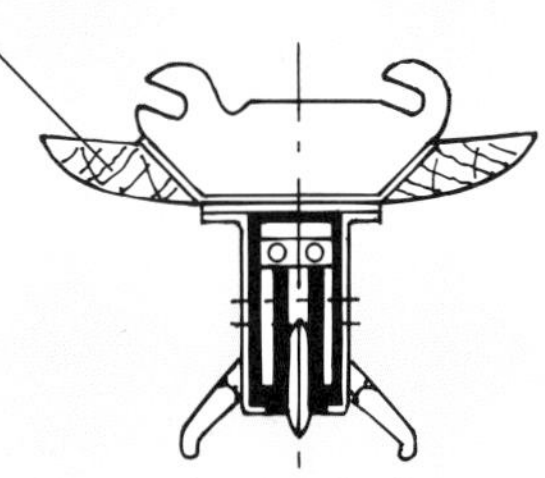

Section A - A

These photos show the Me 262 V10 fitted with a bomb rack of Focke-Wulf design, the ETC 503. The V10 was the first aircraft to be used in bomb trials during which it was discovered that the fitting of bomb racks under the Me 262 was not as straight forward as Willy Messerschmitt had led everyone to believe. During the flight trials there was severe vibration caused by air turbulence around the bomb carrying area which would have prevented the aircraft from attacking its targets at high speed. This major problem necessitated a complete re-appraisal of the bomb rack design.

Underside of ETC 503 showing cut-out for electrical cabling access to the bomb release mechanism.

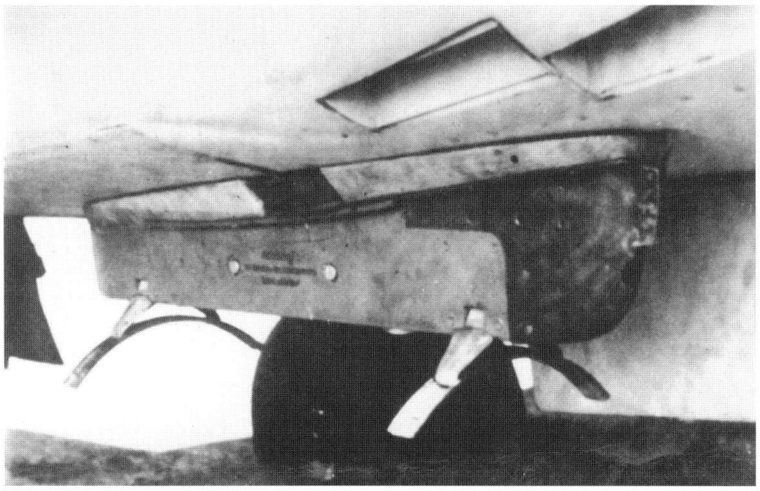

The ETC 503 was originally designed for carrying bombs under the wings of aircraft which, in view of the shallower curve of the Me 262 fuselage, necessitated the fitting of a timber fairing to match the fuselage contour. This starboard close up shows the bomb rack fitted with a provisional timber fairing which was intended to fair the carrier to the fuselage. Note the shell ejection chutes.

Port side of ETC 503 showing the poor fitting of timber fairing.

Even though the ETC 503 proved unsatisfactory, due to the lack of an alternative and the urgency of trying to placate Hitler, the bomb rack was installed on several Me 262s including some operated by Kommando Schenk and KG 51. Here a Kommando Schenk aircraft has been fitted with an ETC 503 where the timber fairing has been replaced with one of metal construction.

example, to bombard the beach while the invasion force was embarking and the boats and previously landed equipment during the unloading operations. As I see it, our aircraft could fly along the beach, dropping their bombs in the confusion below. This is the way in which the *Führer* envisages the deployment of the new model, and this is the way it will be!"

During subsequent discussion, when Messerschmitt inadvertently referred to the Me 262 as a fighter he was immediately interrupted by Göring who cautioned: "Will you please stop using that word *fighter*!" The *Reichsmarschall* almost begged those present to do nothing behind his back that would upset his plans. "The orders of the *Führer* must remain inviolable!"

On 1 June 1944, the Me 262 S7 crashed following an engine fire which caused damage to the nose, wings and both engines. It never flew again, being used for undercarriage tests. Six days later the Me 262 V1 crashed on its 95th flight while testing 'Baldrian' equipment. The left gear leg collapsed as pilot Heinz Herlitzius attempted to correct a swerve on landing and damage was so severe that the aircraft was written off. A more successful test was carried out by Herlitzius on 23 June 1944 when the Me 262 S2 attained 1,004 km/h (624 mph) in a 35 degree power dive from 7,000 m (22,970 ft).

On 6 June 1944, the event that the *Luftwaffe* High Command had long dreaded occurred when British and American forces began to land in Normandy. Allied air superiority was almost complete, their air forces flying 14,674 sorties in the 24 hours up to midnight on the first day. In contrast, the *Luftwaffe* was only able to mount about 100 sorties, none of these, of course, by the jet fighter-bombers. Even if these had been available, they could not have appeared in sufficient numbers to have more than a nuisance effect on the Allied troops below.

If Hitler's idea of using the Me 262 against the invasion had been a feasible one, once the Allies had gained a foothold in Europe, then surely efforts should have been redirected into producing the aircraft as a fighter to combat the ever increasing US daylight raids. In fact the Allied invasion did nothing to change the *Führer's* mind about the role of the Me 262. During a discussion between Hitler and Saur on 7 June Hitler confirmed that initial production of the Me 262 was to be limited to the bomber version, although he did not rule out testing the aircraft as a fighter. The only proviso was that: "...under no circumstances is bomber production to be delayed while waiting for the results of such tests. Not until these tests have been concluded and their result evaluated will fighter production be permitted to begin. Once this point has been reached, there is no reason why production capacity cannot be divided between the two versions."

Next day, on 8 June, Me 262 *Protokoll Nr.33* discussed various bomb sights for the fast bomber. These included the BZA 1C, TSA 2D and *Lotfe* 7H. The BZA 1C, a dive bombing computer which operated in conjunction with a periscopic sight, was never fitted to the Me 262.

The Zeiss TSA 2D *(Tiefwurf- und Schleuder-anlage* – low altitude bomb dropping and catapulting device) was an automatic bombsight fitted with a computer and a gyro. Used in conjunction with the *Revi* 16b gunsight, it permitted accurate bomb aiming even in bad visibility. The device computed speed, altitude and flight path inclination automatically, only the wind speed having to be entered manually. With the autopilot set to 'fast', the aircraft flew straight ahead for 20 seconds. This enabled a direct course to the target, which had been identified with the *Revi*, to be flown. After receiving a signal in his earphones, the pilot then pushed the bomb release button and pulled up immediately. The computer then released the bomb, but only after the calculated trajectory had been reached.

The *Lotfe* 7 was a tachometric bombsight. In this type of sight, the bomb aimer directed a sighting telescope at the target during his bombing run. The telescope was moved by a variable-speed electric motor and, having set the aircraft's ground speed and altitude into the sight, the bomb aimer moved the controls to hold the telescope's cross wires over the target. The platform supporting the telescope was gyro-stabilized and the act of holding the telescope on the target fed precise information on the aircraft's movement over the ground into the sighting computer. The computer generated course correction signals which, in the later versions, 'flew' the aircraft to the bomb release point via the automatic pilot. As the aircraft neared the target, the angle of the telescope approached the vertical and when it reached the release angle calculated by the sight's computer, a pair of electrical contacts closed to release the bombs automatically.

On 15 June 1944, *Oblt.* Tesch flew the Me 262 V10 for the first time with a 500 kg bomb and intensive trials followed with various loads. These established that a loss of speed of 40 km/h

Port side main undercarriage leg as fitted to the Me 262 V8, V9 and V10. The wheels (840 mm diameter x 300 mm) were the same as used on the Ju 87D which had a double braking system and fitted an axle of 60 mm diameter (this wheel was later also used on the He 219). On the Me 262 production series aircraft a new wheel to fit an 80 mm diameter axle was introduced.

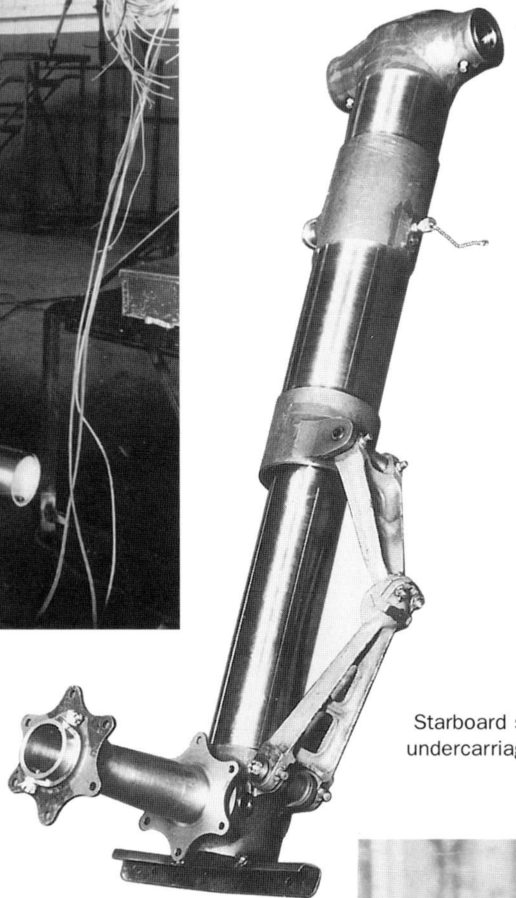

Starboard side main undercarriage leg.

Section through the first main-wheel (840 x 300 mm) showing the double brakes and 60 mm axle shaft.

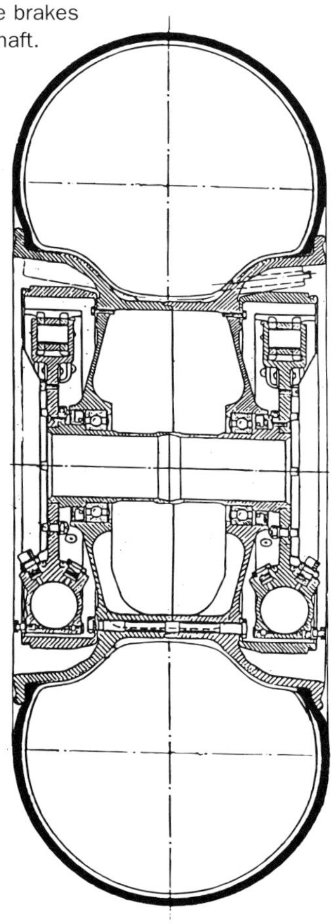

View of inner detail showing main-wheel undercarriage door and timber components.

Starboard view of main wheel showing detail of retraction gear.

(25 mph) was experienced with one 250 kg bomb, 75 km/h (47 mph) with two 250 kg bombs and 55 km/h (34 mph) with one 500 kg weapon. Although it was found that a maximum of two 500 kg bombs could be carried with the aid of rocket-assisted take-off equipment (tested by W.Nr.170303 on 4 January 1945), the normal operational load was two 250 kg bombs or weapon containers.

Seven days after the V10 flew with the 500 kg bomb, Saur addressed the *Jägerstab*, welcoming Galland, who he called the 'real father' of the Me 262, to the gathering. Yet again, he emphasised that the aircraft should be used as a bomber; only when the Ar 234 became available in sufficient numbers would the aircraft revert to a fighter. He went on to discuss the present confused production status. "It is now necessary to draw up a plan to get a clear picture of essentials, but we must not lose sight of existing circumstances so that we can master any difficulties that may arise. The *Führer* has been given the most varied accounts, which present a confused picture of the true state of affairs concerning this aircraft. I am thinking of the variations and of the story of the inspection, and there were miscalculations. I have heard from another source that there have been no miscalculations. Then there was the business about the undercarriage, which was suddenly supposed not to be strong enough. Then the nose – I was told recently that it would have to be changed after ten flights because it split near the gun ports and the aircraft could not fly for more than ten hours. Next the whole problem of the engine, the problem of 90% turbine blade failure. The recurring question is whether a proper supply of nickel will solve the problem or is it something more? Can the hollow blade be used freely, or is it limited, or is the sole purpose of the hollow blade to avoid using nickel and so on?

"There are so many different versions of the problems involved that I feel it is necessary to get the true facts and find out what the requirements are. It is for the engineers to find the answers to these matters. It is all dilettante speculation on our part that might lead us to draw false conclusions."

"I suggest the following plan. First a definite delivery schedule to be drawn up for the Me 262, a schedule based on the requirements of the front, which are undeniable. That is what I really want to talk about. Gentlemen, if we had the 262 to make raids on enemy targets beyond the range of other aircraft then, according to the statements of both the *Führer* and Göring, the situation on the invasion coast would have looked different from what it does now. And we are open to the most severe reproach, namely that we broke our promise in September and October of last year and substituted a Utopian dream for the facts. I refer to the idea that by January/February we should have enough aircraft to carry out proper tests, by March 30 to 40 aircraft, by May, 60, and then 75 and 80. Now it is June and we have not got a single aircraft. This is a reproach that must be levelled at us alone because we did not have the material to get on with the work at the necessary pace. In future I shall assume sole personal responsibility for these matters myself and I shall not rest until a change has been brought about..."

As the discussion continued, other points were brought out. *Herr* Heyne on the staff of the *Jägerstab* said: "As far as equipping the 262 fighter goes, everything is all right up to the end of June. There are no bottlenecks. I am worried, however, about one thing. I have tried, so far without success, to find out what equipment is required for the Me 262 as a high-speed bomber. As the first aircraft are being delivered as high-speed bombers, I should now be delivering the corresponding equipment."

Otto Behrens of the Rechlin test centre commented: "The *Reichsmarschall* has said that there is no change in the existing series. The whole series is now coming out as fighters and will then be used as high-speed bombers. The questions of equipment, instruments, etc. is now being considered at Messerschmitt but has yet to be approved by the *General der Kampfflieger*."

Saur replied: "Another question that is essentially of a technical nature. During the conference with the *Führer* and Göring, I was asked whether in view of the urgent need to place a sufficient number of these aircraft at the disposal of the *Luftwaffe* without further tests, the attendant dangers might not be obviated if one did not demand such a standard of speed. This must not, however, fall in any circumstances below 750 km/h (466 mph)."

Behrens replied that the figure was being lowered. "Because of poor construction," he continued, "the company's speed estimate for all aircraft has been reduced by some 40 to 50 km/h (25 to 31 mph). In fact we can do between 830 and 840 km/h (515 and 522 mph), but with the 250 kg bomb the speed is slowed by some 100 km/h (62 mph). If I deduct this it comes to 740 km/h (460 mph). The superiority that was formally ascribed to the 262 is no longer true of it as a bomber. I had heard Göring speak of 900

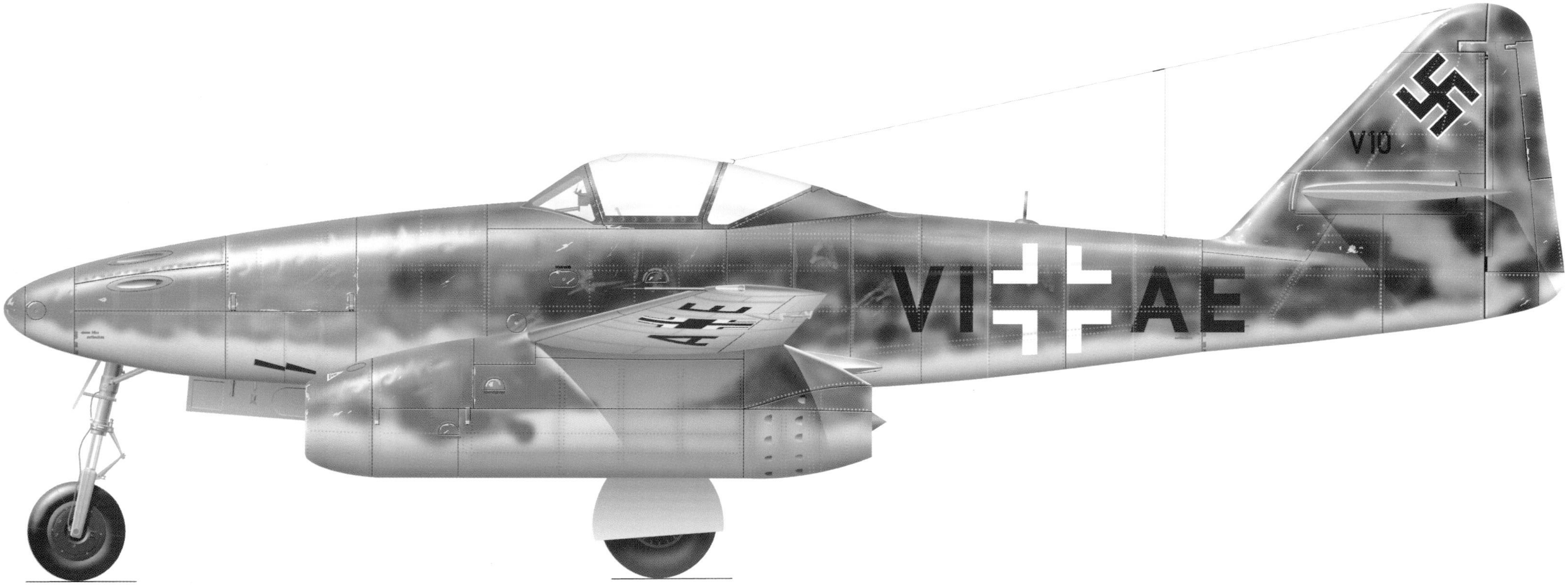

Me 262 V10   VI + AE W.Nr. 130005 two Jumo 004 B engines

The Me 262 V10 was damaged by bombing on 25 February 1944 and after repair, made its first flight on 15 April 1944. It was first used to investigate the heavy stick forces that the Me 262 was beginning to encounter in high-speed turns. It was tested with several different aileron designs and a specially geared control column. Later the prototype was widely used in bomb dropping trials. By the end of March 1945 it had completed 134 flights totalling 41 hours 5 minutes. The aircraft was found at Lechfeld at the end of the war. Camouflage was similar to the V9, but somewhat darker in overall tone.

km/h (559 mph). We have produced graphs to show that it was only 750 km/h (466 mph). That is something that should be pointed out. Everyone believes that they can fly at 800 km/h (497 mph) or more with the bomb."

Saur asked if the loss of speed was due to weight or air resistance. Behrens replied that the bomb and bomb rack affected the speed differently. At slower speeds there was poorer operating efficiency. With the 500 kg bomb there was a take-off loss of 70 km/h (44 mph).

Some indication of the problems being encountered by the Me 262, especially regarding production aircraft, can be gauged by the contents of a report detailing a comparison test carried out on 12 and 13 June 1944 between the Ar 234 V10 and an early production Me 262, possibly the S3, at Rechlin (this report is reproduced in translated form on pages 194-195).

The problems with the aircraft at this time are witnessed by the accidents that continued to be experienced during test flights. The starboard wing of the Me 262 S1 was damaged due to a hard landing on 11 June and five days later the fuselage nose, wings and both engines of the Me 262 S3 were damaged in a crash landing at Lechfeld. The cause was given as excessive time for extending the nosegear because the pilot, *Oberfeldwebel* Becker, was late in switching air pressure to the undercarriage.

By the middle of June 1944 several variants of the Me 262 A had been developed. As mentioned above, the Me 262 A-1 was the standard fighter, the *'Blitz'* bomber version being known as the A-2. Detailed in *Protokoll Nr.35* of 6 July, this variant was intended to be equipped with two ETC 503 A-1 racks beneath the forward fuselage, (but as mentioned, these never proved satisfactory), and have a *Revi* 16D sight but with armament reduced to two MK 108 cannon. The Me 262 A-3 was the original designation for a special variant to be fitted with an enlarged and partly glazed nose, the *'Bomberkanzel'*. This accommodated a second crew member lying prone who was provided with a *Lotfe 7H* bomb sight. A mock-up of this installation was examined on 28 June by *Oberst* Marienfeld, the *General der Kampfflieger*, and members of his staff, *Major* Schenk and *Hauptmann* Palliandi, together with *Major* Meister and *Oberleutnant* Bauer of KG 51. This bomber unit had been nominated as the first to receive the Me 262 and its operations will be examined in Volume Two of this work.

Me 262 V10 showing the Rheinmetall-Borsig R-109-502 rocket assisted take-off units (solid propellent). The electrical connection plug can be seen hanging from the unit. Note also the tail fins of an SC 500 bomb; particulary on short runways, such a bomb load needed RATO units.

The Ar 234 was the second jet aircraft to become operational with the Luftwaffe. Originally designed as a reconnaissance aircraft, it was later modified for use as a bomber, and more or less replaced the Me 262 in this role. This photo shows the Ar 234 V10 taxying along the runway at Alt-Lönnewitz. This was the aircraft used in comparison trials with the Me 262 at Rechlin in June 1944.

Obb.Forschungsanstalt Oberammergau	Besprechungsniederschrift	8/4039/44

Subject: Minutes of meeting concerning comparison flights between the Me 262 and Ar 234 at E-Stelle Rechlin

Present: H.Major Behrens, KdE
H.Caroli, FAH
H.Wendel,
H.Eisenmann, Probü
H.Braun, Probü

Following a discussion with Major Behrens, Herr Eisenmann reported on the results of comparison tests between the Me 262 and Ar 234 at E-Stelle Rechlin. Major Behrens reported as follows:

The test flight took place between a prototype Ar 234 and a standard production Me 262. The Ar 234 made an entirely more favourable impression than the Me 262.[1]

1. Workmanship
The workmanship carried out on the production Me 262 leaves much to be desired. Armament hatch covers, sheet steel cockpit, engine cowlings etc., were all poor as were those of most production machines. The surface finish is also coarse. Major Behrens wants a better surface paint to be used.

2. Take-off
The Ar 234 took off quicker than the Me 262. The take-off run was not measured. However, it should be borne in mind that the Ar 234 was not carrying its operational fuel load (1.7 tonnes instead of 2.8 tonnes) and no military equipment was fitted.

3. Horizontal speed
The Me 262 was approximately 80 km/h (50 mph) faster than the Ar 234. The speed achieved by the Me 262 was 800 km/h (497 mph) at 500 m (1,640 ft). It can be assumed that the aircraft would have achieved a greater speed if the airframe had been better finished.

4. Roll handling
The Ar 234 was more conducive to rolling than the Me 262. The forces acting on the ailerons were too high on the Me 262, therefore Major Behrens did not use full aileron deflection. Only in one instance, while executing a roll and applying full pressure, did full deflection occur. Because of the greater aileron angle, loss of power was again experienced.

5. Combat
Particularly unpleasant, and a bad reflection on the Me 262. Especially obvious was the much larger turning circle. Surface drag was probably larger with the Me 262, the reason to be found in the excessive elevator forces. Major Behrens could not pull up from maximum speed. The same was shown in gliding flight and straightening out. The Ar 234 could be straightened out considerably quicker.

6. Single engined flight
Single engined flight could not be correctly trimmed because the rudder tab was not responsive. With the V-machines it has been shown

that with clean handling of the rudder, single engined flight can be trimmed perfectly.

7. Major Behrens maintains that the bucket seat should be made more suitable for the parachute. At present the pilot is thrown about in the seat which is particularly annoying when the aircraft is performing aerobatics!

<u>Conclusions</u>

Power and power development in the production machine is considerably less favourable than in the V-models, especially the V6 and V7 that serve as examples.

The standard of workmanship observed on the V-models should be applied to the production aircraft. To establish tolerance levels, experimental work on turning circle measurements on V-models and on production models are being carried out at this time.

To come to a valid judgement on the flight characteristics of the standard production machines, the test pilots must be allowed to fly the V-machines and the pilots of FAV should fly the production models, and comparisons of individual cases made.

The intended measures concerning power reduction are to be carried out as a matter of great urgency.

a) <u>Adjustable control column</u>
Major Behrens suggested a test flight with the adjustable column at settings 0 and 4. During such a test, attention should be given to the behaviour of the ailerons.

b) <u>Modification of the wing trailing edge and fins</u>
Wind tunnel measurements have shown that by using the above mentioned methods the forces can be considerably reduced. The test flight confirmed this. The Project Office will give the size of the modified components in co-operation with the FAV.

c) <u>Aileron with improved nose & internally balanced elevator and rudder</u>
Experimental work has been conducted in the test building. Measures a) and b) can be incorporated in the present production series. Measure c) requires conversion work and will be initiated at a later stage.

<u>Distribution:</u>	H.Major Behrens, KdE	H.Wendel
	H.Prof.Messerschmitt	H.Helmschrott
	H.Dir.Schmidt	H.Degel
	H.Caroli	H.Eisenmann

Oberammergau 17.6.44 (signed)
Pr/Eis/Kß Eisenmann

1 *It should be remembered that the particular Ar 234 which was flown during these comparison tests was, in fact, a prototype aircraft, the V10. Being a prototype aircraft, the Ar 234 V10 was hand-built and thus displayed high-quality workmanship. If the Me 262 had been flown against an Ar 234 B-2 production model the comparison would not have been favourable for the Arado since the standard of workmanship on the B-2 model left something to be desired.*

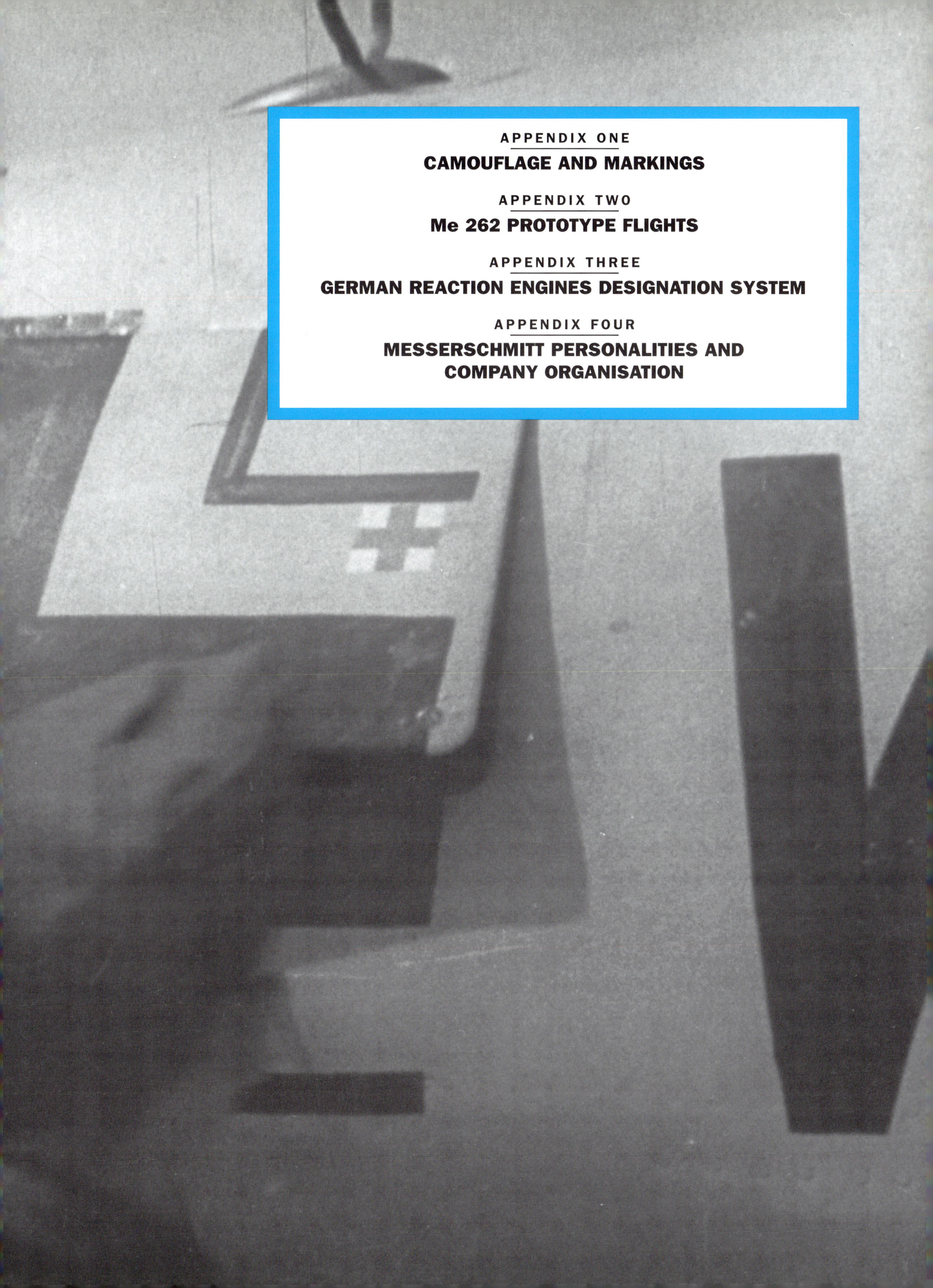

APPENDIX ONE

CAMOUFLAGE AND MARKINGS

APPENDIX TWO

Me 262 PROTOTYPE FLIGHTS

APPENDIX THREE

GERMAN REACTION ENGINES DESIGNATION SYSTEM

APPENDIX FOUR

MESSERSCHMITT PERSONALITIES AND COMPANY ORGANISATION

APPENDIX ONE

CAMOUFLAGE AND MARKINGS

By Kenneth A. Merrick

Camouflage Patterns and General Observations

The camouflage pattern used for the Me 262 prototypes was the revised one which had been introduced for the Bf 110 C series and which was also employed for the Me 262's contemporary, the Me 210. This revised pattern was to be retained by the Me 210, its successor the Me 410 and the Me 262 until the latter had its camouflage pattern again revised in 1944. However the tapered wing of the Me 210 and the even more pronounced sweepback of the Me 262 wing, produced a slight variation because the grid system of laying out camouflage areas allowed for a basic pattern large enough to accommodate a variety of wing shapes and sizes. The first Me 210 A-0 had been accepted from the production lines in April 1941 but which appeared first wearing the modified pattern, the Me 262 or Me 210, is not known, the production time for the first of both types being almost identical.

Prior to the introduction of all metal aircraft, a grid of equal-sized squares had been in use for laying out three tone camouflage splinter patterns. This was replaced by rectangles, the size of which were determined by dividing up the airframe as follows. Starting at the point where the fin met the fuselage on the side view, the length forward to the tip of the nose was divided into ten equal parts which included the spinner on single engined aircraft. The maximum vertical height of the fuselage was then divided into five equal parts as was the maximum width. This set the fuselage into a rectangular linear divided box as shown on the drawing opposite.

Above right: The newly introduced splinter pattern is clearly identified on this brand new Me 210, sporting the 74, 75 and 76 colours.

Right: Before the Me 262 V3 made its first flight at Leipheim, on 18 July 1942, the Jumo 004 A-0 engines were run up, churning great ruts in the muddy grass. As can be seen the camouflage pattern is practically the same as on the Me 210, using the same colours of 74, 75 and 76. The aircraft in the background is a Me 321 glider transport which were under construction at Leipheim during this time.

Standard splinter pattern layout for all Messerschmitt Aircraft from circa 1940

Note: For references to national markings please see
CLASSIC 1: *JV 44 The Galland Circus*, Page 324

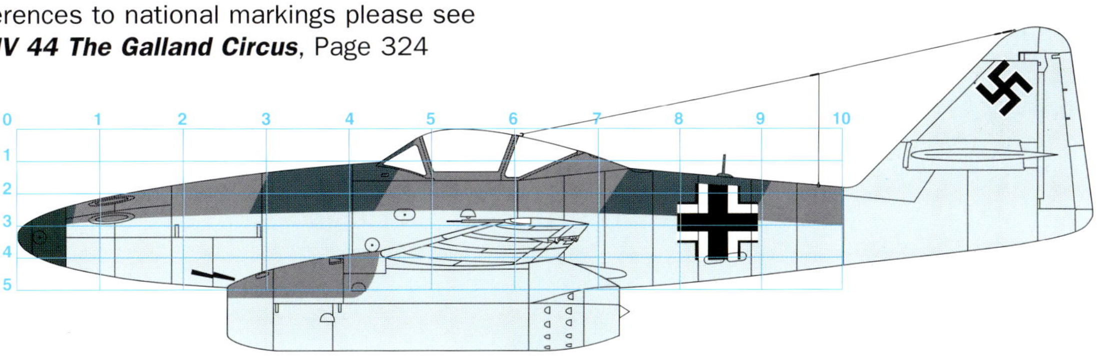

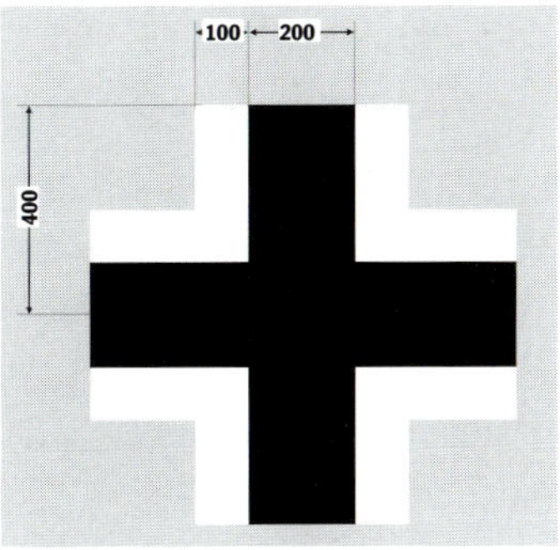

Under-wing Cross (B3)

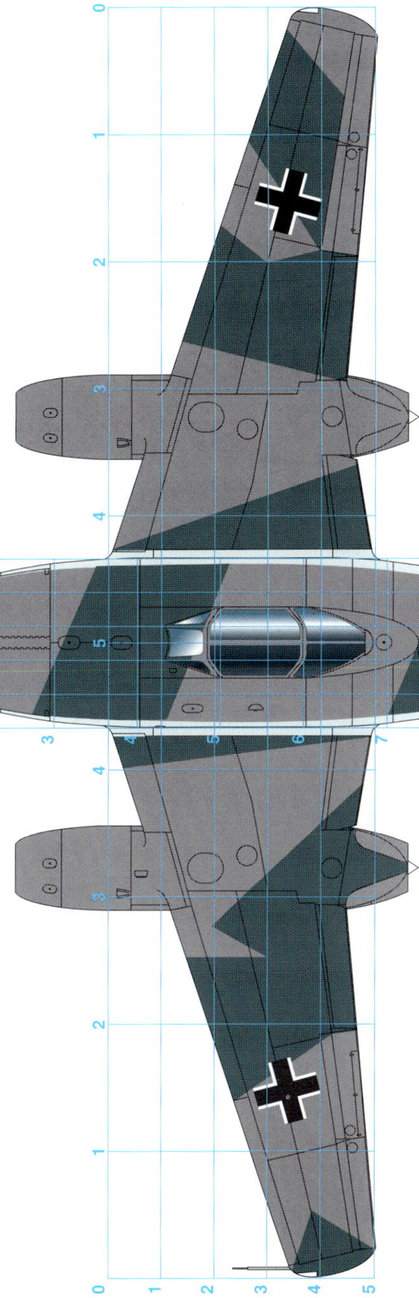

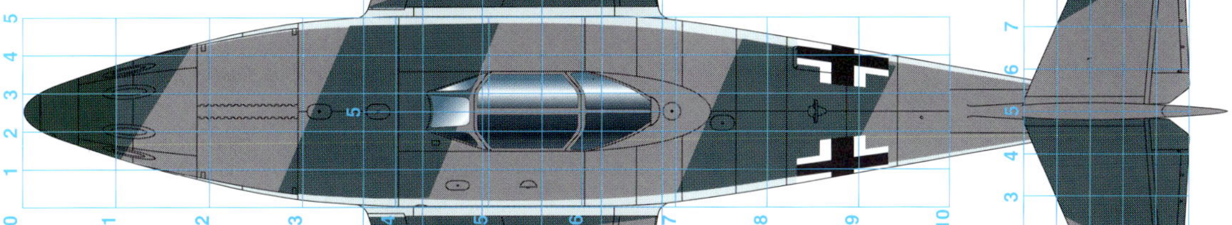

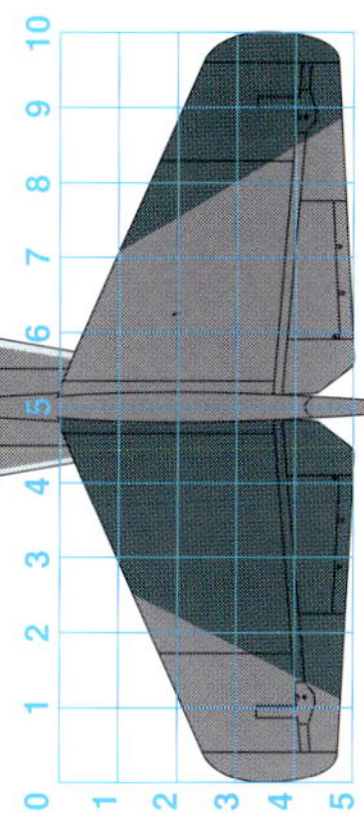

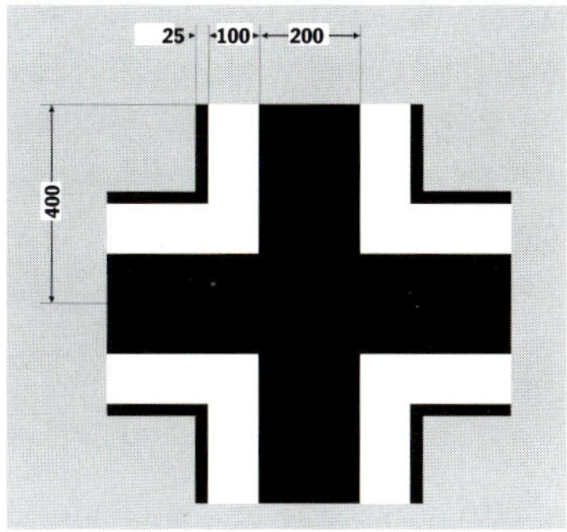

Fuselage Cross (B2)

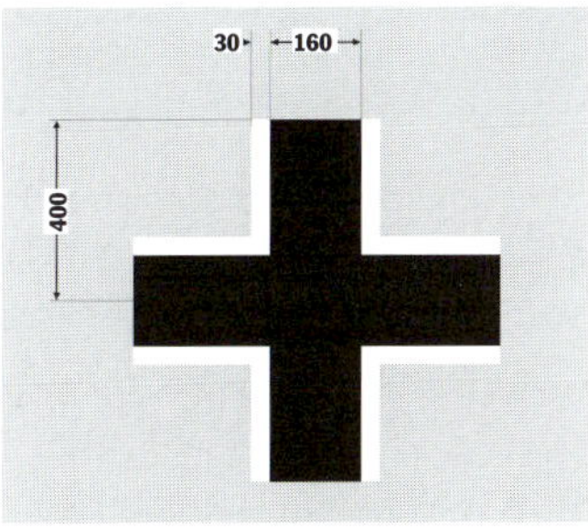

Upper wing Cross (B1a)

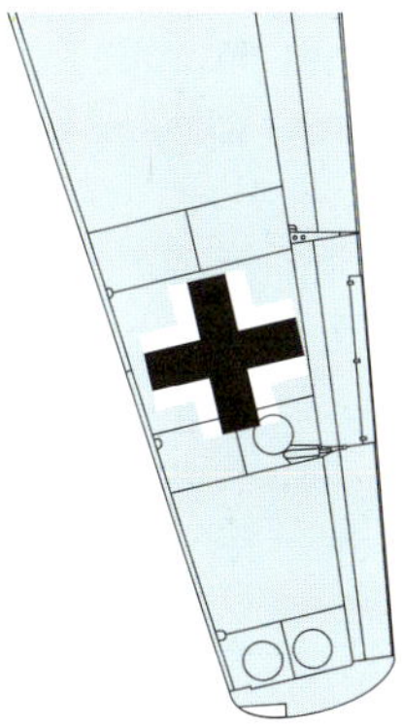

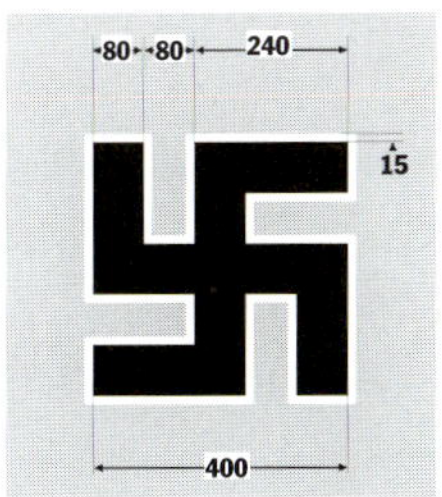

(H2a)

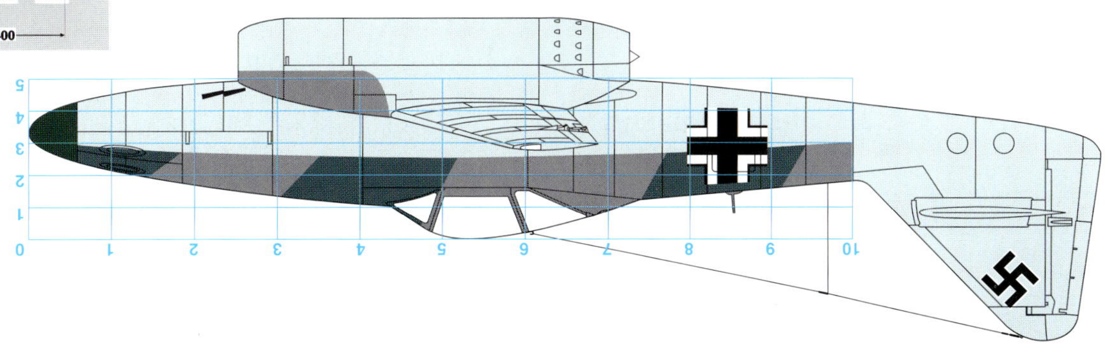

RLM 70

RLM 74

RLM 75

RLM 76

Two views of the Me 262 V6, including a close-up of the starboard side of the rudder after the demonstration flight on 2 November 1943 showing the paint chipped off due to excessive rudder vibration. The V6 at this time was painted overall in 76. Note the Hakenkreuz is outlined in white (H2a).

The vertical tail surfaces, including the rudder, were divided into five equal parts both vertically and horizontally. The wing planform, tip to tip, was divided into ten equal parts, five on each side of the aircraft centre line, while the wing chord was divided into five equal parts using the maximum width of the root chord as the base line. The upper surface of the horizontal tail surfaces was treated in the same manner as the wing.

Specific measurements could then be taken from a fixed grid reference point to produce any variation of pattern required. The upper and lower side surface colour demarcation line was set by projecting a line at 35 degrees from the horizontal, commencing at the lowest central point of the fuselage cross-section. Colour demarcation between upper and lower surfaces of wing and tailplane at the leading edge was again set on the datum line. The two upper surface colours were interchangeable. While a basic pattern existed, variations to suit individual aircraft designs were introduced as well as minor modifications. Occasionally the grid pattern was not shown on factory preparation drawings, only the camouflage pattern with dimensional markings from specific, clearly defined structural points being shown. Painting schedules for each type were issued, in abbreviated form, in a document entitled RLM-*Lackierungsformblatt (OS=Liste) mit Mustereintragungen*. The OS reference was an abbreviation for *Oberflächenschutz-Liste* (Surface protection list).

Camouflage Patterns and National Markings

In March 1940 when the P 1065 (*Projektbaubeschreibung* P 1065 Nr.3) was issued, the prevailing camouflage standard for fighter aircraft was two dark greens carrying the RLM designation 70 black-green and 71 dark green for upper surfaces with 65 blue-grey for lower surfaces. Interestingly, the style of *Balkenkreuz* marking shown was, in part, somewhat anachronistic, as markings for both fuselage and wing lower surface positions had been revised on 24 October 1939. That revision had called for the increase of the white angles to 1/8th of the overall width of the marking. The black outer edge was also increased in width to 1/32nd of the overall width. The retention of the red band and white disc background for the *Hakenkreuz* markings was also anomalous as they had been deleted on all front line military aircraft as of 1 January 1939. With the exception of the latter, this probably reflects, not an error of interpretation of the then current standards, but rather of the time when original concept work on the P 1065 had begun on 1 April 1939. See colour illustration of P 1065 Project drawing as taken directly from the *Projektbaubeschreibung* Nr.3 of March 1940.

The style of national markings that appeared on the Me 262 is a difficult subject to tie down as the same aircraft was often re-painted once it entered service or after damage. The photos of W.Nr.130167 shown in this appendix and in later volumes (in colour) give ample testimony of what went on. Furthermore, as the war drew to a close and Me 262 manufacture had become more dispersed, so the required standards became more and more eroded to the point where almost no standard was applied. It is even likely that the

Two interesting photos of SQ + WF showing mechanics gaining access to the main compass, oxygen bottle and radio compartment. Note also the first aid marking on the panel in the form of a red cross on a small white square. This marking was normally applied on a white circle. Another interesting feature is that the fuselage cross is devoid of any white paint. When this aircraft was later re-painted the cross featured only white angles.

One of the first production batch Me 262s (VI+??) still in colour 76 and showing a clear view of position and style of underwing cross and factory call sign.

Opposite page: Two interesting views of an Me 262 being assembled in the field. The aircraft is still in bare metal with the exception of the fuselage cross (B2) which is in black and white. The smoothed over joint filler paste is noticable as is the 111003,5a stencilled in black. This was the aircraft W.Nr. followed by the last section of the part number. This aircraft appears to have been finished to a reasonably high standard in full accordance with the preparatory instructions laid down by the RLM GL/C-E2 VII. However, in the late war period some aircraft did not have their finish completed beyond the state shown. *Right*: Attaching a complete nose section containing the four MK 108 cannon to the main fuselage. The fuselage is still in natural metal finish while the nose section has been painted in 76. The filler paste is still visible through the thin application of paint. This gives clear evidence that these parts were manufactured at different locations and brought together at an assembly point by what appear to be Luftwaffe personel.

indiviual assembly worker may have simply applied what he saw fit just to get the job done. It must be remembered that quality control at this late stage was extremely rudimentary. To illustrate this confusion there are many photos throughout these volumes that will demonstrate to the reader the variety of National Markings that were used. See LUFTWAFFE CLASSIC Number 1, *JV 44 The Galland Circus*, for illustrations of the various styles of National Markings.

The first prototype, the P 1065 V1 (redesignated Me 262 V1 after the official RLM designation 8-262), did not fly until 18 April 1941 powered by a Jumo 210 piston engine and was in bare metal finish. However, by that time fighter camouflage had undergone its first major transformation since 1937 when Bf 109s first appeared wearing the ground defensive camouflage of 70 black-green, 71 dark green and 65 blue-grey. (The RLM had introduced a system consisting of a four-figure code group which specified the *Flieglack* (aircraft lacquer) type, followed by a two figure code to identify the *Farbton* (colour) where one was included.) The new colour scheme consisted of the greys 74 and 75 for upper surfaces which were divided into alternate soft-edged blocks of the two. The overlap between the two upper surface colours was softly merged over an area 100 mm wide in which the two colours bled into each other whilst still maintaining a distinct line. The solid areas of colour were thus confined to the plan view. On the sides of the fuselage the two colours were used as a mottle to blend the upper camouflage with the side surface colouring of 76 blue-grey. The Me 262 V1, in its final form fitted with Jumo 004s, was eventually painted and flown in the 74, 75 and 76 colours.

The second prototype, the Me 262 V2, originally received only the primer coat of RLM green-grey 02 before being engined and subsequently the fuselage and engine cowlings received the same 74/75 mottling as the V3 which extended right down to the lowest 'edge' of the nose section. It also had the general area of the nose cone painted in 70 black-green, no doubt to confuse observers from a distance (whether domestically or by Allied photo-reconnaissance) into believing that the aircraft was powered by a conventional engine arrangement. Despite the general revision to fighter camouflage that had taken place, the spinner of piston powered aircraft remained specified as 70 black-green throughout the remainder of the war. This ruse was continued on the Me 262 V3 and V4 machines but with the change to a tricycle undercarriage on the V5 it was discontinued.

It is perhaps relevant to record here that the sequence of painting an aircraft varied between manufacturers and sometimes between plants of the same manufacturer. Messerschmitt employed a general rule of painting the entire airframe, internally and externally, with an undercoat of 7120.02 (RLM *grau*) green-grey, followed by a single coat of the lower surface colouring - in the case of the Me 262 this was 7120.76 blue-grey - which was also applied to the upper surfaces of both wings and tailplane, acting as an additional protective coat of lacquer. Upper and side surface camouflage was then added. However, when the Me 262 V6 emerged from the production line in October 1943, it retained only the overall 76 colouring, a practice continued only for a short period for some of the prototypes since the Me 262 V8, V9 and V 10 appeared in full camouflage. The first seven pre-production "S" series aircraft completed by April 1944, the S1 to S 7, and the second production batch up to W.Nr.130190, all, initially, had the overall scheme of 76.

Rules, Regulations, Principles and Practice.

All the aircraft mentioned so far were produced at the Messerschmitt Augsburg plant where, it appears, the practice of retaining only the base colouring was employed. The reason for adopting such a practice is not certain but savings in both weight and time (not only for application of the paint but also the drying period) may have been a consideration. The RLM standard thicknesses and dry weights that were set for each lacquer layer were; single coat 5/100 mm thick and 60 gm/square metre; two coats - 8/100 mm and 100 gm/square metre; three coats 1/10 mm and 150 gm/square metre. Specified numbers of coats of lacquer and appropriate drying times had to be strictly adhered to under the RLM system of control. Newly applied lacquered surfaces could only be exposed to weather after 48 hours from the time the last coat of lacquer was applied and at this stage of the development and production programme time was already at a premium due to the deteriorating war situation.

Some observations of the slipping production standards, which had begun to creep into parts of the German aircraft industry, can be gained from the report on the flight evaluation carried out early in June 1944 between the Me 262 and Ar 234 V10 by *Major* Behrens of the Rechlin Test Centre (see Chapter 7). In part, it criticised the declining quality control standards exhibited on the Me 262 tested and went on specifically to state: "The surface finish is also coarse. Major Behrens wants a better surface paint to be used."

The prevailing RLM standards were already quite strict; lacquer was to be applied only under specific conditions. There were to be no open fires or radiators present. Where spray applications were required, spray guns with apertures of 1.8 to 2.5 mm were to be used at a pressure of 3 to 4 atmospheres. Lacquer was to be applied first in one direction, then after allowing a short drying time, an application at right angles was to be made. Room and lacquer temperature was to be between 18 and 25 degrees Celsius, with relative humidity between 50 and 75%. Furthermore, room conditions were to be tested using a temperature and humidigraph.

The nose of Me 262 S3 showing the red numeral '3' and a 76 overall colour. The broad fabric strip used to cover the lower surface of the nose to fuselage joint can be seen. A similar strip was applied around the fuselage/empennage joint forward of the tailplane. These strips were not given the customary crimped edge cut.

Excess sealing material used on rivet lines was to be immediately removed; wet grinding or harsh grinding of joints was only to be done with the permission of RLM GL/C-E2 VII. Inaccessible areas were to be completely lacquered prior to assembly. On areas where, after assembly, adjoining areas were to be lacquered in full, the layers on top of each other were to be staggered to allow later joining of the lacquer sequences. Accidentally dirtied metal or wood surfaces could only be cleaned with 00 grade steel wool, care being taken not to blemish the metal or wood surface. Any lacquer removed by such action had to be replaced immediately. After ensuring that all traces of steel wool had been cleaned away any blemishes in lacquered surfaces were to be reported to the workshop chief. The finished lacquer application had to be as matt as possible, high gloss and gloss finishes on aircraft were allowed only with the consent of RLM GL/C-E2 VII. For touch-up of paintwork related to small repairs, room temperature and humidity conditions were not so strict but still required an enclosed area. Higher temperatures, to speed up drying times, could only be used after consultation with the RLM. Behrens' comments clearly reflect erosion of these strict standards.

Production markings.

Components used in manufacture of airframes were usually marked with a code number to identify the type of material. Perhaps the most common one was 3116.5, usually stencilled in black, found on the duraluminum sheeting used for the skin of most German aircraft. The marked surface was usually employed as the interior surface but declining manufacturing standards late in the war produced examples where the sheet skinning was fitted with the number on the

Me 262A-1a, SQ + WF W.Nr.130167 from the first production batch built at Schwäbisch Hall shows clearly the aircraft still in overall 76 colour. This aircraft first flew on 31 May 1944 and later became the V167, the second V5 but by then it carried full camouflage of 81, 83 and 76. See Volume 2 for colour photos.

Two mechanics inspect the MK 108 gun bay on SQ+WF W.Nr.130167. Note the detail of the hinged cover and stay to allow access to the guns. Interior surfaces of the door were painted in 02 as also was the diagonal adjustable torsion bar and the door locking bar. The rear face of the compartment was left in bare metal.

Fresh off the production line, a front view of SQ + WF. Note the lack of gun camera window on the tip of the nose. The nosewheel door carries the wording 'Am Bugrad nicht schleppen' set in a rectangle, both marked in red.

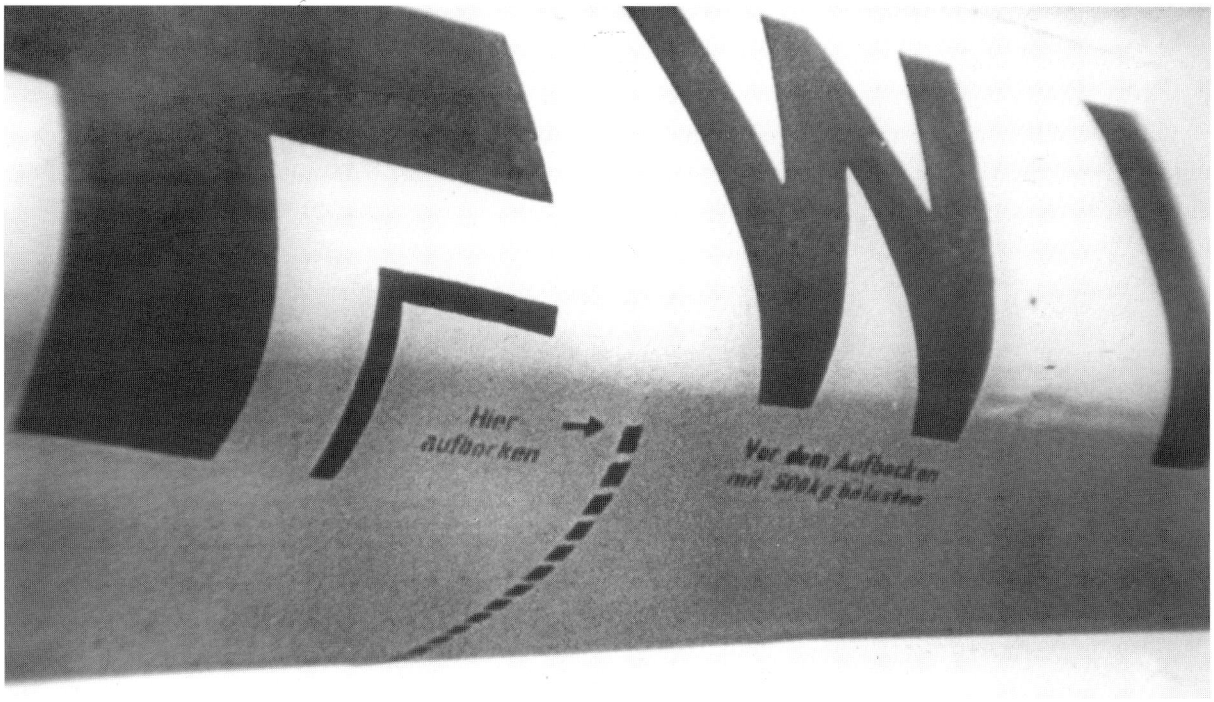

A view of SQ + WI showing clearly some of the black stencil markings. Note how far the black fuselage cross and lettering wrap around the underside of the fuselage. These details are dealt with more comprehensively in Volume 2.

Two views showing the underside of SQ + WI showing the main undercarriage and the 76 colouring which also appears to feature inside the nosewheel bay. It should be noted that generally all undercarriage legs and parts were painted RLM Grey (02).

exterior surface. This could sometimes be seen through the thin paint finish as dark marks.

Sub-assemblies were usually marked with the last three numerals of the *Werknummer* allocated to the complete airframe, aiding co-ordination of parts during assembly. This took several forms, sometimes by stencil in small black or large white numbers, but frequently hand painted. Most were lost under the final camouflage coat but with the increasing practice of using very thin single coat applications late in the war, larger ones, under certain lighting conditions, were sometimes visible as a discolouration of the outer painted surface.

IDENTIFICATION MARKINGS.

In keeping with normal practice, Me 262s were given at the point of manufacture, a regulation four letter *Stammkennzeichen*, (radio call sign). Although not always applied, especially during the last months of the war, these call signs featured a pair of letters which appeared in black on the fuselage each side of the individual *Balkenkreuz* marking. They should also have been repeated beneath the wing, one pair to each wing, spaced either side of the *Balkenkreuz* marking with the top of the letters nearest the leading edge. Early in the war, permanent lacquer was used for this purpose, requiring them to be painted out and the original camouflage restored. However, by the time that the Me 262 appeared, when applied, this was done using an artificial resin emulsion (possibly an alkyd resin emulsion) which could be removed by washing with benzine (petrol). Decals were also employed in some instances.

The airframe production number, the *Werknummer* (W.Nr.), was required to be applied to the vertical tail surface above the horizontal tail surfaces. This instruction was interpreted in several ways by different aircraft manufacturers. On the Bf 109, the Messerschmitt company had established the practice of painting the marking only on the port side of the fin, immediately above the fixed section of the tailplane. This was continued with the Me 210, with the occasional variation of marking it on both sides of the fin. The Me 262 was to continue this practice (on occasions using both sides of the fin) with its production aircraft but the prototypes displayed no such distinction.

The Me 262 V1 to V4 appear to have carried no marking, other than their *Stammkennzeichen*, to identify them. However when the re-built V3 appeared it did carry the marking in white at the bottom leading edge of the fin. The fully camouflaged Me 262 V5 utilised the simple designation V5 in white characters on both sides of the fin near to the leading edge. The Me 262 V6, which remained in 76 overall finish, carried its distinguishing V6 marking in the same places but in black. This practice then continued for the remaining *Versuchs* machines except for the V7 and V8 where it appeared in white.

The pre-production prototype, "S" series, were also distinguished by a lack of *Werknummer* marking other than for a hand painted 130006 in white below the tailplane of the Me 262 S1 when it still retained only its 76 overall finish. Identification of the S1 to S7 machines inclusive was made by means of a large numeral marked in red on each side of the nose section immediately aft of the gun bay access panel, except for the S6 coded VI + AK which carried no such number, but was handed to Werner Thierfelder for evaluation purposes during the establishment of *Erprobungskommando* 262. Thierfelder was later to lose his life in this machine. The red number 6 was applied on the S7 coded VI + AL.

Another Me 262 A-1a was from the first production batch built at Schwäbisch Hall. It was coded SQ + WI W.Nr.130170 and featured a new nose gear design. Again the aircraft was painted colour 76 overall. The wire engine protection cover seen here lying on the runway was painted red (RLM colour 23).

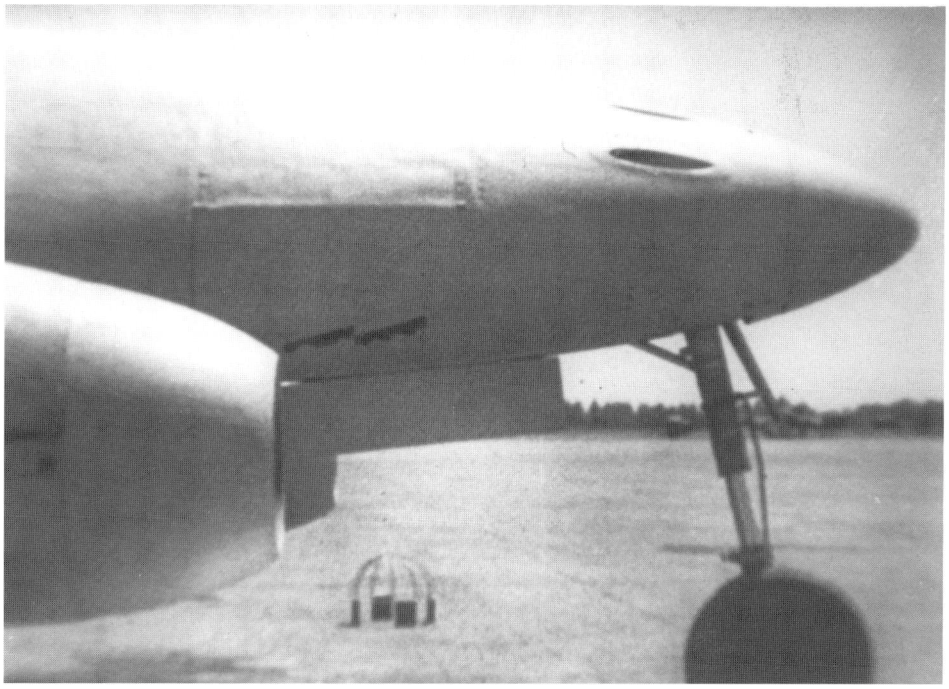

APPENDIX TWO

Me 262 FIRST SERIES PROTOTYPE FLIGHTS

	V1	V2	V3	V4	V5	V6	V7	V8	V9	V10
1942										
March	■									
April										
May										
June										
July			■							
August			■							
September										
October		■								
November		■								
December		■								
1943										
January		■								
February		■								
March		■	■							
April		■	■							
May			■	■						
June			■	■	■					
July	■		■	■	■					
August	■		■		■					
September	■		■							
October	■		■			■				
November	■		■			■				
December	■		■			■	■			
1944										
January	■		■		■	■	■		■	
February	■		■		■	■	■		■	
March	■		■			■		■	■	
April	■		■				■	■	■	■
May	■		■				■	■	■	■
June	■		■						■	■

■ *Indicates months when prototypes were flying.*

APPENDIX THREE

GERMAN REACTION ENGINES DESIGNATION SYSTEM

Early in the war, the Technical Office introduced a system of abbreviations for use when referring to reaction engines. The system included all types of engines under development or investigation.

TL = *Turbinen-Luftstrahl-Triebwerk* (Turbojet engine)

ZTL = *Zweikreis-Turbinen-Luftstrahltriebwerk* (Two-cycle turbojet engine, then commonly known as a ducted-fan engine, but known today as turbofan)

PTL = *Propeller-Turbinen-Luftstrahltriebwerk* (Turbo-prop engine)

ML = *Motor-Luftstrahltriebwerk* (Piston-engine driven ducted fan)

IL = *Intermittierendes-Luftstrahltriebwerk* (Pulse jet engine)

L = *Luftstrahltriebwerk* (Ramjet engine)

R = *Raketentriebwerk* (Rocket engine)

By 1943, various hybrid powerplants were also under consideration, some of which combined elements of two different reaction engine types. They included the following:

RL = *Raketen-Luftstrahltriebwerk* (Combined rocket and ramjet engine)

TLR = *Turbinen-Luftstrahltriebwerk mit Rakete* (Combined turbojet and rocket engine)

GTW = *Gasturbine mit Wärmetauscher* (Gas turbine with heat exchanger, ie. a turboprop for long-range flight)

PML = *Propeller-Motor-Luftstrahltriebwerk* (Piston engine driven ducted fan with propeller drive)

Hence, jet propulsion by turbojet was referred to as *TL-Antrieb*, and a turbojet engine as a *TL-Triebwerk* or *TL-Geräte*.

A six-digit code number was also introduced, the first three numbers (109) indicating turbojet, turboprop, pulsejet and rocket units as a distinct class from reciprocating engines (which, as described above, were identified by the prefix '9'). Numbers in the second group ranging from 001 to 499 were assigned to jet propulsion units, while numbers encompassing the range 500 to 999 were allocated to rocket engines (both liquid and solid propellent types). Thus a turbojet would be designated 109-001 and a rocket engine, 109-500.

Initially the second group of numbers were allocated at random to the first turbojet, turbofan and rocket engines which were awarded Technical Office development contracts. The numbers for turbojet and turbofan engines were as per the adjacent table.

Manufacturer	Technical Office Designation
Heinkel	109-001
BMW	109-002
BMW	109-003
Junkers	109-004
(not allocated at this time)	005
Heinkel	109-006
Daimler-Benz	109-007
(not allocated)	008
(not allocated)	009
Heinkel	109-010

In 1942, the Technical Office decided that the last digit of the second group of numbers should be used to identify the manufacturer, commencing with 109-011 for jet propulsion units. Thus all new Heinkel-Hirth designations ended in '1' (eg 109-011, 109-021), Junkers in '2' (eg 109-012, 109-022), Argus in '4' (eg 109-014, 109-044), Daimler-Benz in '6' (eg 109-016), and BMW in '8' (eg 109-018, 109-028). Towards the end of the war Porsche undertook design work on gas-turbine engines, and it is believed that they were assigned the number '5' (eg the 109-005 intended to power the FZG 76 B flying bomb).

A similar system was introduced for rocket engines. Thus, all WASAG designations ended in '2' (eg 109-512, 109-532), Schmidding in '3' (eg 109-513, 109-603), Rheinmetall-Borsig in '5' (eg 109-515, 109-545), BMW in '8' (eg 109-548, 109-718) and Walter in '9' (eg 109-509, 109-729).

APPENDIX FOUR

MESSERSCHMITT PERSONALITIES AND COMPANY ORGANISATION

Althoff, *Ing.* Karl Design engineer in the *Entwurfsburo*, responsible to Degel. In order to solve the problem of providing adequate space for the main undercarriage and fuel tanks with a low-wing layout, it was Althoff's idea to employ a triangular fuselage section in the P 1065. This was incorporated in the definitive configuration for the P 1065 which became the most distinctive feature of the resulting Me 262.

Arbogast, Josef In charge of tooling at Messerschmitt, Oberammergau.

Asam, *Meister* Moritz Leader of the Experimental Construction workshops (*Versuchsbau*). First at Augsburg and from March 1944 at Oberammergau.

Willy Messerschmitt and Hubert Bauer (right) discuss aircraft design in Messerschmitt's office.

Bauer, *Dir.* Hubert Born 1902, director responsible for production of prototypes, died 1986.

Baur, *Dipl.-Ing.* Karl *Flugkapitän*, born 13 November 1913, chief test pilot from 1940, went to the USA after the war, died in October 1963 in Arlington, Texas.

Bölkow, *Dipl.-Ing.* Ludwig Born 30 June 1912, joined Messerschmitt AG in 1939 as aerodynamicist, later became principle group leader of high speed aerodynamics (high subsonic speed) under Schomerus; 1942 head of project group responsible for single-engined fighters: 1943 took over Bf 109 development office in Vienna; 1944 returned to Oberammergau where he was assigned special duties and worked as aerodynamicist on Me 328 and P1101. Appointed liasion engineer to the *Entwicklungs Hauptkommission* in 1945. One of the founders of the post war Messerschmitt-Bölkow-Blohm (MBB) company.

Braun, Heinz Born 1910, aerodynamicist under Schomerus and Eisenmann, with Messerschmitt from 1935 to 1945, involved in Me 262 design, with MBB company after the war.

Bringewald, August *Typenbegleiter* for the Me 262, a civilian technician who was to direct manufacture of the Me 262 in Japan. Sent in U-234 which was forced into port in Norway for repairs. U-234 left Norway in March 1945, but surrendered in May 1945 in the Atlantic. Bringewald and the submarine's crew were interned in Canada.

Caspar, Viktor To be responsible for Me 262 production in Japan, also on U-234 (see Bringewald).

Caroli, *Dipl.-Ing.* Gerhard Born 1907, head of flight testing - Autobedarf Lechfeld, died 1981.

Theo Croneiss, Chairman of the board of Directors of Messerschmitt, in front of an M 23a sports aircraft during 1928.

MESSERSCHMITT PROJECT OFFICE ORGANISATION

Circa September 1940

Projektbüro
Project Office
Voigt, Woldemar
von Chlingensperg, Rolf

Preliminary design
Hornung, Hans
Althoff, Karl
Degel, Wolfgang
Seitz, Rudolf

Project development

Project engineer

Project design

Aerodynamics
Schomerus, Riclef
Bölkow, Ludwig
Eisenmann, Walter
Puffert, Hans-J.
Winter, Hans

Powerplant
Frey, Kurt
Geduldig, Wilhelm

Propellers

Armament
Schwarz, Friedrich

Equipment

Aircraft Systems

Mock-up

The offices of the Messerschmitt Projektbüro in Augsburg prior to transfer to Oberammergau.

Croneiss, Theo Born 28 December 1894 at Schweinfurt. Trained as a fighter pilot during the First World War, formed Sportflug GmbH, a sports flying club which trained many pilots who were to serve eventually in the *Luftwaffe*. Had close connections with the Nazi Party and attained the rank of SS *Brigadeführer*. Helped prevent the complete collapse of Messerschmitt company in 1932 and proposed the building of the factory at Regensburg. From 30 April 1942, Chairman of the board of Directors of Messerschmitt AG and Works Manager at Regensburg. Died in Munich on 7 November 1942 after a short illness.

von Chlingensperg, *Dipl.-Ing.* Rolf Deputy head of the Project Office from 1939 to January 1945. In 1945, together with Schomerus, was made responsible for licence production of the Me 163 and Me 262 by the Japanese. Disappeared en route to Japan in U-864, a Type IX D-2 U-boat, which was sunk on 9 February 1945 west of Bergen, by the Royal Navy submarine HMS *Venturer*.

Degel, *Dipl.-Ing.* Wolfgang Born 1910, project leader of the *Entwurfsbüro, Entwicklungsleiter* for the Me 262, Voigt's deputy after February 1945. Died 1995.

Dipl.-Ing Wolfgang Degel

Degenkolb, Gerhard A former director of the Demag engineering works, who in 1942 achieved great success as the Chairman of the Special Locomotives Committee, which directed an emergency locomotive construction programme. On 15 January 1943, Speer appointed Degenkolb head of the Special A4 Committee within the Armaments Ministry, with the task of finding the necessary component production capacity for the A4

Ludwig Hoffman photographed immediately after the war.

(V-2), and establishing assembly plants for the missile. His success in this role resulted in him being appointed, Commissioner for the Me 262 by the Armaments Ministry, on 1 February 1945.

Ebner, *Ing.* Georg Born 1899, engineer, stress office 1931-1945, died in 1982.

Eidinger, Head of the Patents Office.

Eisenmann, *Dipl.-Ing.* Walter Aerodynamicist, deputy head of the *Aerodynamik Abteilung*, involved with aircraft stability problems. Worked for the Ministry of Supply at Volkenrode. Helped to compile the AVA monographs.

Flachs, *Uffz.* Kurt, *Luftwaffe* pilot attached to Messerschmitt's flight test division, killed on 19 May 1944 in the crash of the Me 262 V7.

Frey, *Dr.* Kurt Performance engineer, calculated the performance of engines and propellers. Later department head in the *Probü* responsible for planning.

Helmschrott, Josef Me 262 production liason engineer with Messerschmitt at Oberammergau in 1945.

Herlitzius, *Fw.* Heinz, *Luftwaffe* pilot attached to Messerschmitt's flight test division.

Hoerner, *Dr-Ing.habil.* Sighard F. with DVL Berlin-Aldershof 1935-1936, with Fieseler 1937-1939, with Junkers 1940-41, to Messerschmitt between 1941-1945. Aerodynamicist involved with the Me 262 at late stage of its development. Worked at Oberammergau.

Hoffmann, Ludwig, Messerschmitt production aircraft test pilot, assisted General Watson in the transfer of several Me 262s to the USA.

Hornung, *Dipl.-Ing.* Hans Born 1910, head of the *Vorprojektbüro* from 1938 to 1945, died 1978.

Hügelschäffer, *Dipl.-Ing.* Fritz Project engineer, aircraft layout. Later involved with the main design of the P 1101 to P 1111 fighter projects, and also with special assignments and raw materials for the Me 262 in 1945.

Kokothaki, Peter Rakan Born 1902 in Munich, of Greek Cypriot descent, Kokothaki joined BFW in 1926. From 1932 was commercial director of BFW, later Messerschmitt AG. Purely a businessman, with no knowledge of the technical aspects of the company, he succeeded Croneiss in 1942 as *Betriebsführer* (General Manager) of the Augsburg works. Had close links with

Messerschmitt (right) discussing a document with Rakan Kokothaki, General Manager of the Augsburg works and Heinrich Hentzen, who had broken two world gliding records in 1922, and later became Works Manager (standing). Kokothaki, reported as a "rabid Nazi" in one Allied document, was appointed vice-president of Messerschmitt AG in January 1945.

MESSERSCHMITT PROJECT OFFICE ORGANISATION
Circa June 1944

- **Projektbüro / Project Office** — Voigt, Woldemar; von Chlingensperg, Rolf
  - **Preliminary Design**
    - **High-speed group** — Hornung, Hans; Büchler, Peter; Eberhart; Hügelschäffer, Fritz.; Thieme
    - **Project research** — Hubert, Josef
    - **Me 262 Variants** — Althoff, Karl
  - **Project development**
    - **Project engineer Me 262** — Degel, Wolfgang
    - **Project engineer Me 262 HG** — Seitz, Rudolf; Brutscher
      - **HG Committee** — Seitz, R; Asam, M; Behrbohm, H; Caroli, G; Ebner, G; Eisenmann, W; Helmschrott, J; Hubert, J; Winter, H
  - **Project design**
    - **Aerodynamics** — Schomerus, Riclef; Braun, Heinz; Puffert, Hans-J.
      - **Stability and Control** — Eisenmann, Walter
      - **Performance** — Wackerle; Begerow; Hoffmann, August
    - **Powerplant** — Frey, Kurt
      - **Propellers**
    - **Armament** — Schwarz, Friedrich
    - **Wind Tunnel** — Winter, Hans
    - **Equipment** — Forster
    - **Thermodynamics** — Geduldig, Wilhelm
    - **Aircraft Systems**
  - **Mock-up**

the Nazi Party, being a personal friend of the local *Gauleiter*. Appointed Vice-President of Messerschmitt AG in January 1945. Died 1975.

Knoll, Head of Messerschmitt's service engineering office.

Krauss, *Prof.* Julius Born 1894, formerly with the Udet Flugzeugbau, head of Messerschmitt's structures office, made a Professor in 1942, died in 1972.

Linder, Karl Director of Me 262 production.

Lindner, Gerd, Messerschmitt test pilot, replacement for Wilhelm Ostertag and probably the most experienced Me 262 test pilot by war's end. Assisted the Americans in the flight instruction of the Me 262 at Lechfeld, killed in 1945 (post-war) in an automobile accident.

Dipl.-Ing. Gerhard Caroli (far left) talks to Gerd Lindner. Centre with hat is Betriebsdirektor Fritz-Heinrich Hentzen. The identity of the other two individuals is not known.

Dipl.-Ing. Robert Lusser, head of the Messerschmitt Projektbüro

Lusser, *Dipl.-Ing.* Robert Born in 1899. A very accomplished sports pilot, Lusser won several notable flying events in the late 1920s/early 1930s. In 1925 he met Hans Klemm - known in Germany as "The Father of Light Aircraft" - whom he persuaded to teach him the art of aircraft design when Klemm was working for Daimler. In 1926, Klemm formed his own company and Lusser joined him at Klemm Flugzeugbau GmbH where he subsequently designed several very successful sporting aircraft including the L 25, Kl 31 and Kl 32. In 1932 he joined Heinkel as head of their sports aircraft design department where he designed the He 71 (a single-seat development of the He 64). Due to the dominating influence of the Günter brothers in aircraft design, Lusser left Heinkel and joined BFW on 1 November 1933 as head of the *Projektbüro*. Lusser's contribution to the preliminary design of such aircraft as the Bf 108, Bf 109 and Bf 110 has not been properly recognised and Willy Messerschmitt may not have achieved the measure of success which he did without the benefit of Lusser's outstanding talents. From February 1939 with Heinkel as their Technical Director; from November 1941 with Argus as a consultant, then from March 1942 with Fieseler where he directed work on the Fi 103 (V-1) flying bomb. In December 1944, appointed Chairman of the ESK-Flugzeuge, responsible for controlling the future development of all German rocket and ramjet-propelled aircraft. Worked as a consultant with the US Navy after the war, then with Messerschmitt from 1959 as Technical Director of *Entwicklungsring-Sud*. Died in 1969. One of the most brilliant and original German aircraft designers of his generation whose achievements have yet to be fully recognised.

Messerschmitt, Lilly Born into the Bavarian nobility in 1892 as Lilly *Freiin* (Baroness) von Michel-Raulino, she married Otto Stromeyer in 1919 from whom she was divorced in the late 1920s. One of the principal financial backers of BFW and an intimate friend of Willy Messerschmitt whom she married in 1952. By 1942, the largest single shareholder of Messerschmitt AG owning almost 30% of the stock. Died 25 December 1973.

Messerschmitt, *Prof.* Wilhelm Emil Born on 26 June 1898, for early history see Chapter 1. Awarded the *Ritterkreuz* with Swords of the War Service Cross on 25 March 1945. At the end of the war he was taken to London for interrogation, released in 1948, re-organised the Augsburg factory for the production of prefabricated houses and a "bubble" car. Established contacts with the Spanish Hispano aircraft company in 1951, signed a contract with the Egyptian government in November 1959, returned to Germany in August 1967. Formed and appointed chairman of the Messerschmitt-Bölkow-Blohm group in June 1969. Died on 15 September 1978.

Ostertag, Wilhelm, *Luftwaffe* pilot attached to Messerschmitt's flight test division, killed on 18 April 1943, in the crash of the Me 262 V2.

Ing. Walter Rethel (left) in discussion with Messerschmitt

MESSERSCHMITT DESIGN OFFICE ORGANISATION
1944

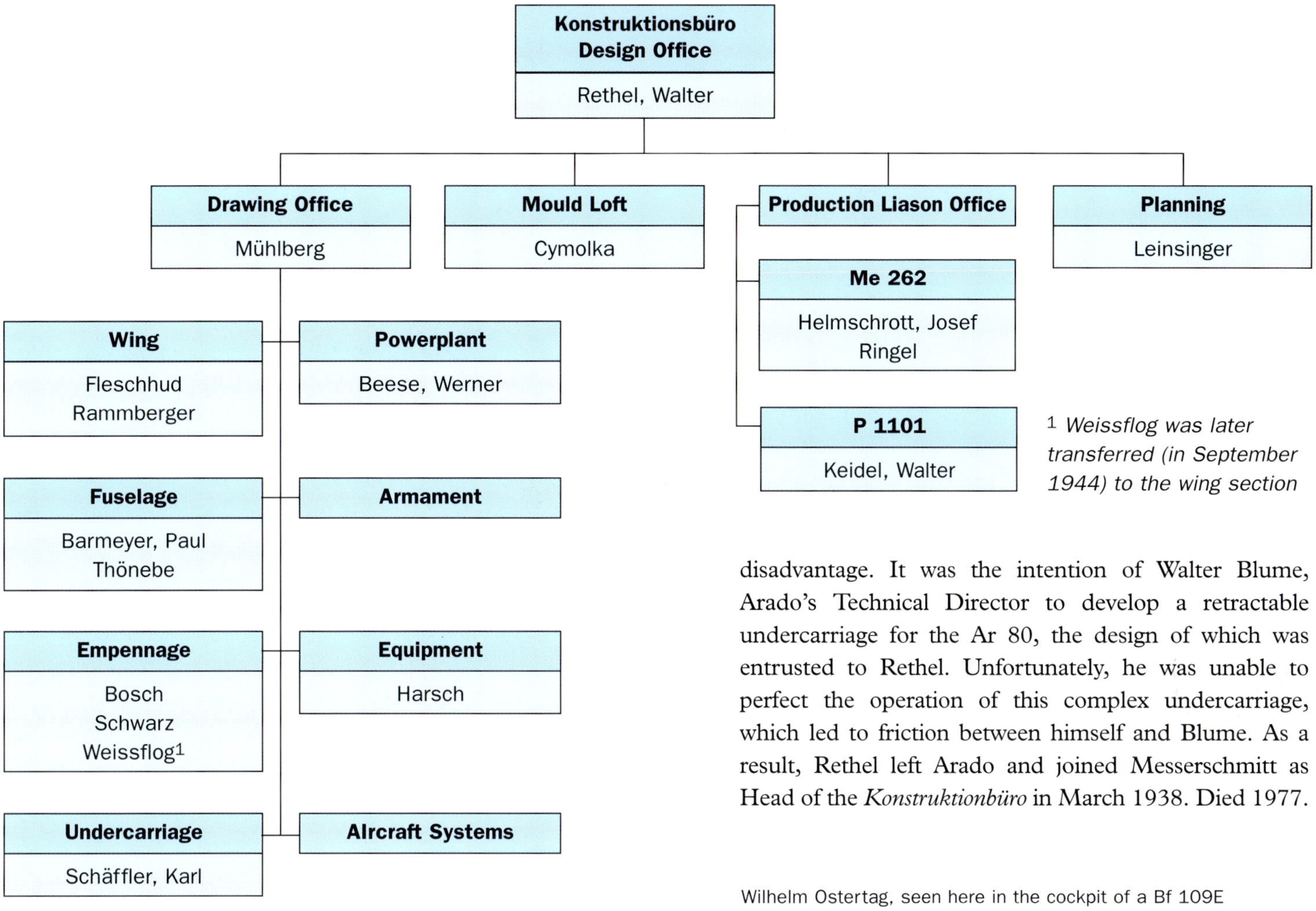

1 Weissflog was later transferred (in September 1944) to the wing section

Puffert, *Dipl.-Ing.* Hans Joachim Born 1912, at Messerschmitt between 1938 and 1945. Aerodynamicist in the Project Office, responsible for wind tunnel investigations and low speed aerodynamics. He took over Bolköw's position when the latter moved to Vienna. Died April 1997

Rethel, *Ing.* Walter Born 1892, chief designer for the Kondor Flugzeugwerke up until 1918. Later worked for Fokker in the Netherlands where his most notable design was the F.VII airliner which was further developed into the famous trimotor, built under licence in the USA. In 1926 he returned to Germany where he worked for the fledgling Arado company, being responsible for most of the company's early designs for training and fighter aircraft. The last type on which he worked for Arado was the Ar 80 monoplane fighter, initially with a fixed undercarriage. This aircraft was designed to compete against the Bf 109, but it's fixed undercarriage placed it at a serious disadvantage. It was the intention of Walter Blume, Arado's Technical Director to develop a retractable undercarriage for the Ar 80, the design of which was entrusted to Rethel. Unfortunately, he was unable to perfect the operation of this complex undercarriage, which led to friction between himself and Blume. As a result, Rethel left Arado and joined Messerschmitt as Head of the *Konstruktionbüro* in March 1938. Died 1977.

Wilhelm Ostertag, seen here in the cockpit of a Bf 109E

Schmidt, Kurt, born 1905, *Luftwaffe* pilot, joined Messerschmitt's flight test division in 1942, killed on 9 March 1944 in the crash of the Me 262 V6.

Schomerus, *Dipl.-Ing.* Riclef Born 1909, head of the aerodynamics department, killed in February 1945 during a voyage to Japan in a U-boat, (see entry for von Chlingensperg). He was delivering Me 262 information to Japan when the U-boat was sunk.

Schwarz, *Ing.* Friederich Born 1906, department head for armament and equipment, nicknamed "*Waffen-Schwarz*", died in 1982.

Seiler, Friedrich Wilhelm Replaced Croneiss as Chairman of the Board of Directors of Messerschmitt AG. Acted as mediator in dispute between Milch and Messerschmitt.

Seitz, *Dipl.-Ing.* Rudolf Project engineer in the *Entwurfsbüro*, involved with the early design of the Me 262, after early 1941 was responsible for the development of the P 1079 which later became the Me 328. Appointed head of the "High Speed Development Committee" in January 1944.

Senning, *Ing.* Fritz Project engineer, aircraft layout (structures), worked on fuel tank development in 1945.

Steigenberger, *Dr.-Ing.* Otto Moved from Henschel Flugmotorenbau GmbH, Kassel to Messerschmitt in 1939, made head of the power plant liaison group.

Tesch, Oblt. Ernst, *Luftwaffe* pilot attached to Messerschmitt's flight test division.

Voigt, *Dr.-Ing.* Herbert Head of dynamics department in Krauss' structures office.

Voigt, *Dipl.-Ing.* Woldemar Born 1907, joined BFW in 1932, deputy head of the Project Office from 1933 to 1939, then head from 1939 to 1945 (took over from Robert Lusser), to the USA after the war as part of 'Operation Paperclip', died in 1980. According to Seiler, Voigt possessed "an extremely versatile personality of a peculiarly creative scientific and technical mind."

Wackerle, *Dipl.-Ing.* Performance engineer, calculated the performance of aircraft.

Wendel, Fritz, *Flugkapitän*, born 1915, after pilot training and employment as a *Luftwaffe* flight instructor, joined Messerschmitt in 1936 as a production test pilot. On 26 April 1939, piloted the Me 209 V1 which set a new

Dipl.-Ing. Riclef Schomerus (centre). Also in this photograph is believed to be, second from left, Stabsing. Christensen and third from left, Wolfgang Degel.

Hitler congratulates Hermann Wurster following his accomplishment of the world landspeed record in the Bf 109 V13. Shown here from left to right: Messerschmitt, Hitler, possibly Julius Schaub (Hitler's SS adjutant), Willy Stör, Wurster and Wendel.

Seen watching a Me 262 trials flight at Lechfeld probably in 1943, Wolfgang Degel (far left), Adolf Galland (7th from left), Caroli (8th from left), Messerschmitt (4th from right) and Hentzen (3rd from right)

World Absolute Speed Record at 755 km/h. Later experimental test pilot for Me 262. Died in 1975.

Wurster, *Dr.-Ing.* Hermann Born 1907. After obtaining his doctorate in 1933, undertook test pilot training. From 1935-36 employed as a test pilot at Rechlin and Travemünde. From 1 January 1936 to 15 February 142, Chief Test Pilot of Messerschmitt AG. On 11 November 1937, piloted the Bf 109 V13 which set a new World Speed Record for landplanes at 611 km/h. Later worked in Lippisch's department on tailless aircraft designs. Directed development of "Enzian" anti-aircraft missile from 1943-45. Died in 1985.

In conversation following the first flight of the Me 262 V3 on 18 July 1942 are (left to right) Lilly Stromeyer, Willy Messerschmitt, Dipl.-Ing Wöckner, Fritz Wendel and Moritz Asam.

Flugkapitän Fritz Wendel.

Me 262 Infrastructure 25 April 1945

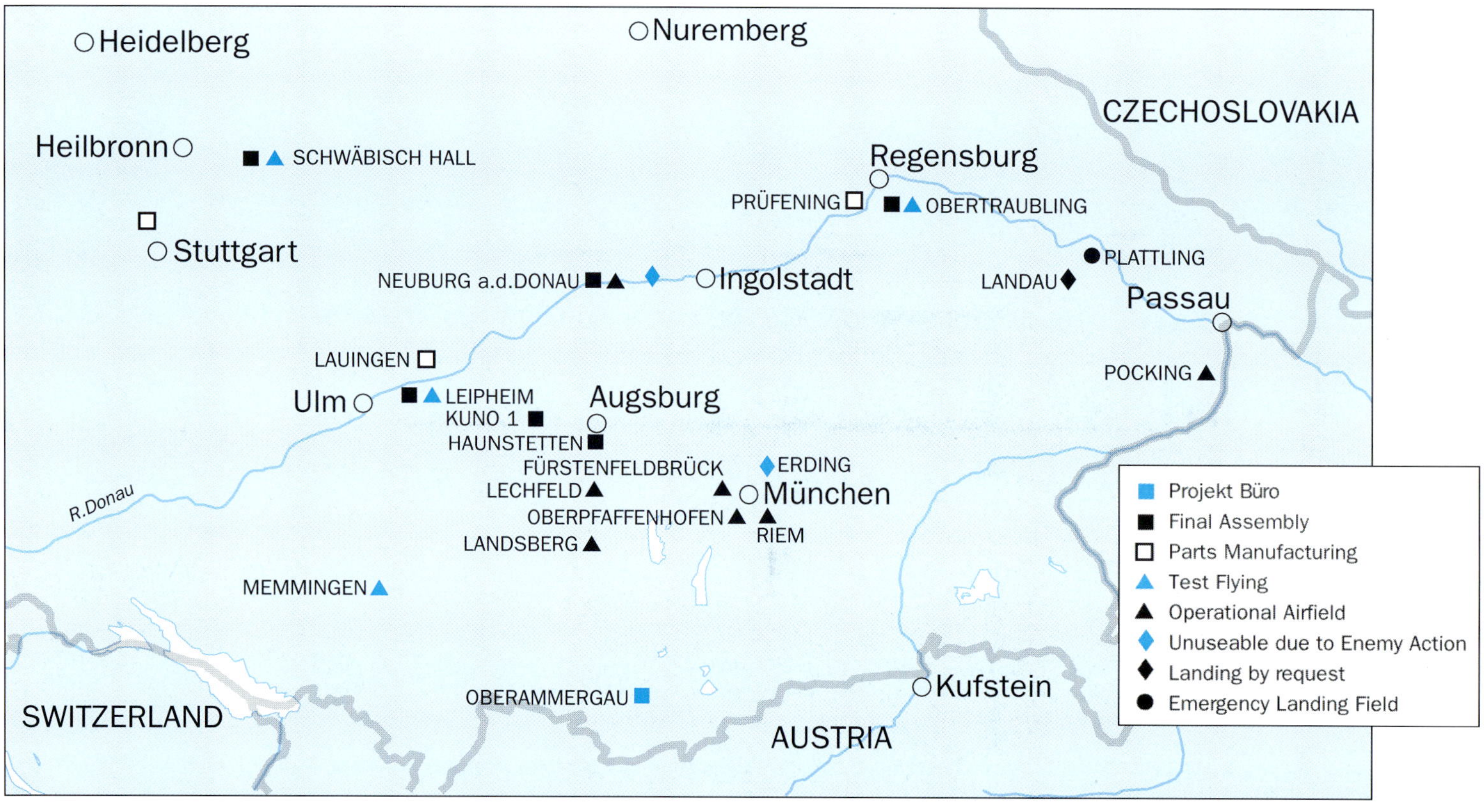

MESSERSCHMITT STRUCTURES OFFICE ORGANISATION
1944

- **Statikbüro Structures Office** — Krauss, Prof. Julius
  - **Stress Office** — Ebner, Georg
    - **Wing** — Krammerer, Wohack
    - **Powerplant** — Wieser
    - **Fuselage** — Fischer
    - **Equipment** — Baumann
    - **Empennage** — Bahr
    - **Control Systems** — Baukloh
    - **Undercarriage** — Ostertag
    - **Applied loads** — Behrbohm, Hermann
    - **Dynamics** — Voigt, Herbert; Nürnberg, F.

At the end of 1943/early 1944 the whole of the Project, Construction and Statistics Departments, were transferred from Augsburg to Oberammergau in Southern Bavaria where they took over the Gebirgsjäger Kaserne (Mountain Infantry Barracks). From here all of Messerschmitt's major research work continued undisturbed by the allies until the end of the war. By October 1944 some 2,231 employees were working in Oberammergau.

An aerial view of Lechfeld airfield taken by Allied reconnaissance aircraft. Me 262s were photographed here on three occasions between January and August 1944. The airfield was bombed on 18 July 1944. The view above shows the southern area of the airfield. Five Me 262s are visible as well as several Me 410s.

A selection of photographs showing the Me 262 V-8 through to V-10 in various stages of manufacture at the Messerschmitt works at Augsburg-Haunstetten.
Clockwise from top left: the nose section in skeletal form on its jig; a general view of the fuselage prior to the fitting of the fin, tail plane and nose section; an underview of a partially completed port-side wing; the nose section with cannon fitted to the main body; the nose section, complete with MK 108 cannon installed, resting on a cradle prior to assembly to the main body; a fuselage centre section; a close up of the wing-root.

Organisation Chart of *Messerschmitt A.G.* April 1945

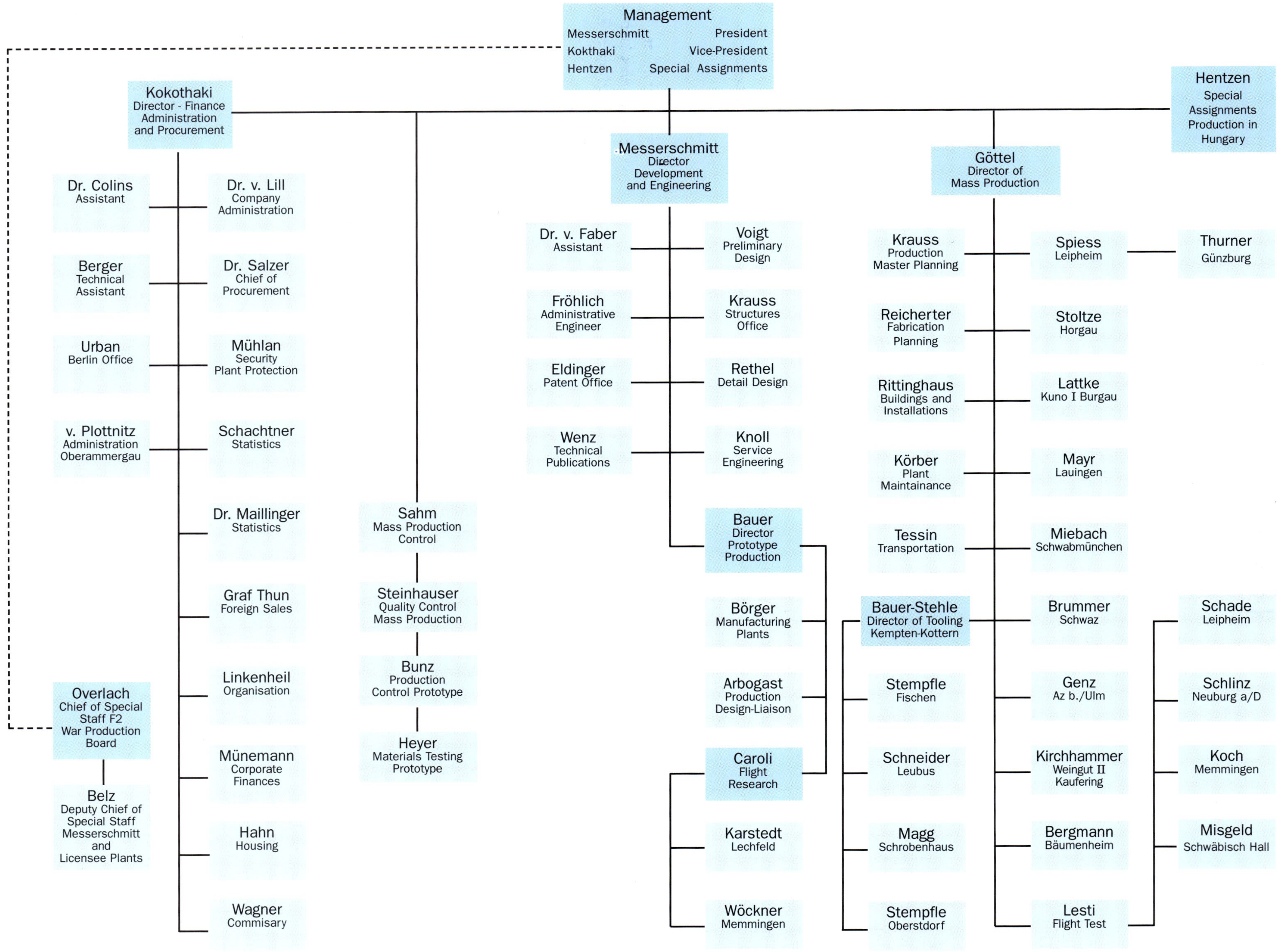

GLOSSARY

Abteilung	Battalion, department, section, detachment
Amtsprotokoll	Offical minutes of meeting or discussion
Aufklärer	Reconnaissance aircraft
Betriebsführer	Works Manager
Diplom-Ingenieur.	Academic degree in engineering subject
Entwicklungs-Hauptkommision	Main Development Committee
Entwicklungsleiter	Development Co-ordinator
Entwurfsbüro	Design office
Erprobungskommando	Test/experimental unit
Erprobungsstelle (E-stelle)	Test Centre
Flieger-Stabsingenieur	Flight Staff Engineer
Flugbaumeister	Master in Aircraft Engineering
Flugzeugbau	Aircraft Construction
Flugzeugwerke	Aircraft Works or Factory
Gauleiter	Regional Nazi Party administrator
General der Jagdflieger	General of the Fighter Arm
General der Kampfflieger	General of the Bomber Arm
Generalluftzeugmeister	Chief of Aircraft Procurement and Supply
Jabo	Jagd-bomber - fighter-bomber
Jagdgeschwader	Fighter wing
Jagdgruppen	Fighter group
Jäger	Fighter

Jägerstab	Fighter Staff
Kommissar	Commissioner or inspector
Konstruktionsbüro	Design Office
Interzeptor	Interceptor
Meister	Head Foreman
Nachtjagdverbände	Night-fighter units
Panzerflugzeug	Armoured aircraft
Pfeilflügel	Swept wing
Projektbaubeschreibung	Detailed Project description
Projektbüro	Project office
Projektübergabe	Project description
Protokoll	Record or report of meeting
Referent	Adviser with specialist knowledge
Reichsluftministerium (RLM)	Reich air ministry
Ritterkreuzträger	Holder of the Knight's Cross
Schnellbomber	Fast bomber
Schulflugzeug	School or training aircraft
Sondertriebwerk	Special powerplant
Staffel	Squadron
Staffelkapitän	Squadron commander
Statikbüro	Structures Office
Technisches Amt	Technical Office
Triebwerk	Powerplant
Typenbegleiter	Type co-ordinator/officer responsible for development of specific aircraft and operational trials
VTOL	Vertical Take Off and Landing
Zerstörergruppen	Destroyer Groups

INDEX

PERSONALITIES

Adenstadt, Dr. Heinrich 47
Althoff, Karl 57, 59, 170, 210
Alpers, Obst.Ing. 117
Antz, Dipl.-Ing. Hans Martin 56
Asam, Meister Moritz 147, 210
Bader, Paul 83
Baeumker, Dr. Adolf 42
Bauer, Oblt 193
Baur, Karl 97, 142, 210
Beauvais, Heinrich Dipl.-Ing. 83, 88, 89, 117
Beck, Dr. Ernst 51
Becker, Ofw. 193
Behrens, Hptm. Otto 108, 117, 183, 191, 193
Blume, Walter 13, 57
Bölkow, Ludwig 57, 62, 72, 210
Bruckmann, Dipl.-Ing. Bruno 49, 50
Cambeis, Walter 171
Caroli, Gerhard 117, 211
Croneiss, Theo 16, 20, 34, 211
Degel, Wolfgang 57, 59, 117, 171, 210, 211
Diesing, Obst. Ulrich 171
Eisenlohr, Hpt.St.Ing. Wolfram 43
Eisenmann, Walter 57, 212
Encke, Dipl.-Ing. Walter 44, 47
Faber du Fauer, Dr. Carl 117
Flachs, Uffz. Kurt 172, 212
Francke, Dipl.-Ing. Carl 30
Franz, Dipl.-Ing. Anselm 46, 47, 49, 62, 68
Friedrich, Dipl.-Ing Rudolf 40
Galland, Gen.Maj. Adolf 101, 108, 146, 178, 183, 191
Georgii, Walter 13
Göring, Hermann 24, 31, 34, 108, 113, 120, 142, 149, 151, 161, 178, 183, 189
Gundermann, Dipl.-Ing. Wilhelm 39
Hagen, Dipl.-Ing. Hermann 49
Hahn, Max 38, 39
Harth, Friedrich 10,11,13, 14
Heinkel, Dr. Ernst 24, 30, 38, 45, 120
Helmschrott, Josef 117, 212
Hentzen, Heinrich 13
Herlitzius, Heinz 189, 212
Hermann, Hans 14, 15
Hess, Rudolf 24, 26
Hirth, Wolf 13
Heyne, Herr 191
Hitler, Adolf 120, 121, 143, 146, 149, 151, 161, 162, 166, 172, 178, 183, 189, 191
Hornung, Hans 57, 212
Klemperer, Wolfgang 13
Kokothaki, Rakan 15, 24, 113, 117, 212
Koller, Gen.Lt. Karl 178
Koppenberg, Dr. Heinrich 40, 41
Korten, Gen.der.Fl. Günther 178, 183
Kraft, Prof. 47
Krome, Maj.Dr. 161, 162, 171
Leist, Prof. Karl 44
Lindner, Gerd 103, 142, 151, 183, 213
Löhner, Dr. Kurt 49
Lorin, René 38
Lucht, Gen.St.Ing. Roluf 34
Lusser, Dipl.-Ing. Robert 22, 23, 30, 56, 57, 214
Lysholm, A.J. 38
Madelung, Prof. Georg 44
Mader, Prof. Otto 40, 43, 45, 46
Marienfeld, Obst. Walter 183
Mauch, Dipl.-Ing. Hans 43, 46
Meister, Maj. 193
Messerschmitt, Prof. Wilhelm 56, 73, 97-100, 108, 113, 117, 120, 121, 146, 147, 149, 151, 166, 171, 183, 189, 214
  Awards 26, 30
  Early life 10 et passim,
Milch, GFM Erhard 24, 34, 83, 89, 96, 97, 103, 108, 113, 142, 146, 161, 171, 172, 178
  Poor relationship with Messerschmitt 22, 26, 34, 97, 117, 121
Müller, Dipl.-Ing. Max Adolf 40, 45, 46
Nallinger, Dipl.-Ing. Fritz 43
Oestrich, Dr.-Ing. Hermann 49, 68
Ohain, Hans-Joachim Pabst von 38, 39, 41, 45
Ostertag, Ofw. Wilhelm 101, 214
Palliandi, Hptm. 193
Pasewaldt, Obstlt. Georg 97, 98
Peppler, Wilhelm 40
Petersen, Obst. Edgar 108, 113, 142, 172, 178, 183
Pfister Fl.St.Ing. Heinz 117
Pohl, Heinz 14
Pohl, Robert 38
Puffert, Hans-Joachim 57, 215
Reitsch, Hanna 49
Restemeier, Hptm. 30
Rethel, Walter 57, 215
Sachse, Helmuth 43
Saur, Hpt.Dst.Leit. Karl-Otto 162, 166, 172, 178, 189, 191, 193
Schäfer, Fritz 99
Schelp, Dipl.-Ing. Helmut 42, 43, 46, 49, 51, 56
Schenk, Maj. 193
Scheuermann, Erich 15
Schleif, Oblt. 30
Schmidt, Fw. Kurt 164, 167, 216
Schomerus, Riclef 57, 216
Schruffer, Dr. Alexander 15
Schwenke, Obst.Ing. Dietrich 117
Seidemann, Maj. 30
Seiler, Fritz 34, 216
Seitz, Rudolf 57, 216
Späte, Hpt. Wolfgang 100, 101, 103, 117
Speer, Albert 161, 162, 166, 172
Stör, Willy 24
Student, Kurt 20
Tank, Kurt 32, 120
Tesch, Oblt. 189, 216
Theiss, Karl 15
Thierfelder, Hptm. Werner 117, 183
Trautloft, Oblt. Hannes 30
Udet, Ernst 14, 21, 27, 30, 33, 34, 44, 83
Ursinus, Oskar 13, 14
Voigt, Dipl.-Ing. Woldemar 22, 23, 57-59, 62, 68, 117, 171, 216
Vorwald, Obst. Wolfgang 98, 117
Wagner, Prof. Dr.-Ing. Herbert 40, 41, 45, 46
Warsitz, Erich 40
Weinrich, Ing. Helmut 50
Wendel, Fritz 32, 34, 72, 86, 88, 89, 97, 103, 216
Whittle, Frank 38, 45
Wimmer, Obslt. Wilhelm 24, 26
Wright, Orville 13
Wurster, Dr. Hermann 32, 33, 218

ENGINES

Argus As 014 83, 97
Argus As 044 83,
BMW 003 97, 137
BMW 018 97
BMW P.3301 49,
BMW/Bramo P.3302 50, 51, 62, 68, 83, 86,
BMW P.3304 50, 62,
BMW P.3395 136
BMW TL 58, 68,
HeS 1 39
HeS 3b 39, 40
HeS 8 40
HeS 8A 72,
HeS 11 97, 164
HeS 30 46,
Jumo 004 46, 47, 49, 62, 83, 86, 88, 89, 97, 99, 113, 126, 128-132, 135, 139, 142, 150, 151, 161, 170, 171,
Jumo 210 27, 30, 68, 72, 86,
Walter 509 83, 138
Walter R II/211 135,

ARMAMENT

MG 17 machine-gun 56, 63
MG 131 machine-gun 99,
MG 151/20 cannon 56, 63, 89, 98, 99, 113, 142, 150, 164
MK 103 cannon 98, 99, 164,
MK 108 cannon 89, 99, 113, 124, 125, 128, 131, 135-137, 164, 170

EQUIPMENT

BSK 16 gun camera 170,
BZA 1C bomb sight 189
ETC 503 bomb rack 183, 193
FuG VII radio transmitter/receiver 56, 63
FuG 16 ZY radio transmitter/receiver 89, 99, 113, 162, 170
FuG 25 IFF 68, 89, 99, 113, 162, 170
Lofte 7H bomb sight 189
Rb 20/30 cameras 130, 132,
Rb 50/30 cameras 83,
Rb 75/30 cameras 130-132
Revi 16B gunsight 113, 149, 189
TSA 2D (Zeiss) bomb sight 189
Wikingerschiff bomb rack 183,